W9-CCV-969

DISCARDED
JENKS LRC
GORDON COLLEGE

The Trouble with Computers

"Sorry, folks—it's not what you ordered, but everyone is getting fettuccine until we fix the computer."

Drawing by Handelsman; © 1993 The New Yorker Magazine, Inc.

The Trouble with Computers

Usefulness, Usability, and Productivity

Thomas K. Landauer

A Bradford Book
The MIT Press
Cambridge, Massachusetts
London, England

JENKS L.R.C.
GORDON COLLEGE
255 GRAPEVINE RD.
WENHAM. MA 01984-1895

© 1995 Massachusetts Institute of Technology
All rights reserved. No part of this book may be reproduced in any form by any
electronic or mechanical means (including photocopying, recording, or information storage and retrieval) without permission in writing from the publisher.

This book was set in Sabon by the Maple-Vail Book Manufacturing Group and
was printed and bound in the United States of America.

Library of Congress Cataloging-in-Publication Data

Landauer, Thomas K.
  The trouble with computers : usefulness, usability, and
productivity / Thomas K. Landauer.
    p.   cm.
  "A Bradford book.
  Includes bibliographical references and index.
  ISBN 0-262-12186-7 (hc : alk. paper)
  1. Computers. 2. Technological innovations. I. Title.
QA76.5.L3226   1995
659'.0285—dc20

QA
76.5
.L3226
1995

94-48745
CIP

For Libby

Contents

Preface

We see computers everywhere but in the productivity statistics.
Attributed to Robert Solow

I started doing research and prototype development with computers about fifteen years ago at Bell Laboratories. Before that, I'd done psychological research on human learning, memory, and thinking. I belonged to a department called Human Information Processing Research. Along with many others, I was captivated by the idea that computers offered a technology that could finally underwrite the kinds of power tools for human minds that motors have provided for our hands. It seemed but a matter of doing it to turn the extraordinary advances in computer hardware and software into devices that would help people think, remember, plan, communicate, express themselves.

Although I'm still at it, two things led me to a rather different view of the venture and to this book. First, my colleagues and I found it much harder to make computer aids that were significantly helpful than we had anticipated. For example, when we tested our first invention, a computerized reference manual that was obviously marvelous, we found that students did better with the original paper book. Second, a talk by sociologist Paul Attewell of NYU alerted me to the disappointing news that economists were having trouble showing that information technology contributed positively to productivity.

It seemed these two things might be related.

Around the same time, the late 1980s, I was a member of the Committee on Human Factors of the National Research Council and of a working group that was looking into the contributions that human factors research might make to labor productivity. But we got bogged down in trying to decide what productivity is and whether we wanted to take a frankly economic perspective or concern ourselves with social issues and the quality of work life. When my term on the committee expired, we were still debating. By then I had become intrigued with the relation between the way computers were being designed and developed and effects they were—or were not—having on the efficiency of their users. So, with the generous support of my employer, Bellcore (the descendant of AT&T Bell Labs whose custody was kept by the local telephone companies), and encouragement from my department head, Mike Lesk, I spent a great deal of time in the library and on email, followed by a great deal of time fighting with my personal computer. This book is the result.

Interestingly, the National Research Council will have just issued a report from the aforementioned subcommittee when this book appears. It contains an introductory chapter on the productivity paradox by Paul Attewell, and its content and conclusions, not surprisingly, are quite similar to my part I. Attewell and I read almost the same things it would appear, although it was Paul who put me up to it rather than the other way around. (I think his writing is delightful, and he does the job in fewer pages.) My first heartfelt acknowledgment goes to Paul Attewell. But after similar beginnings, my story and that of the committee take a different, complementary, turn. The committee explains how effective technology can fail to help organizations produce more, focusing on ways in which gains can get lost, wasted, frittered away. I, by contrast, find evidence that information technology doesn't help much in the first place, analyze why, and propose remedies. The remedies involve user-centered design, a telling idea and phrase ably pioneered and popularized by Don Norman, to whom I extend my second major thanks.

This book is based on the following four apparent facts; you will see the evidence and be the jury.

1. Computers have not contributed nearly as much to labor productivity as we had hoped, were promised, believed—or, by rights, they should.
2. For the jobs most people do in service enterprises, most computer applications make work only a little more efficient.
3. The efficiency effects of computer applications designed in traditional ways are improving very slowly, if at all.

4. Efficiency effects of applications designed with the new, user-centered methods improve very rapidly.

I discovered these facts by a lot of reading and analysis of published data. I couldn't have done it without the searching searches of my research assistant, Bob Nicholich, who also spent ten hours manually setting right the mess the automatic bibliographic system made of the references. Two able reference librarians at Bellcore were also involved: Don Sunday and Dan Patricia, who make online databases do the tricks they ought. My wife, Lynn Streeter, a computer researcher, developer, and manager, has lovingly tolerated my apostasy and gently set me straight on lots of things. Our splendid housekeeper-nanny, Marie Lamysere, made the hours possible and reasonably guilt free.

I owe a lot, as do the best parts of the book, in my estimation, to the wonderfully bright, creative, rigorous, congenial members of my research group at Bell Labs and Bellcore: David Ackley, Susan Dumais, Dennis Egan, Louis Gomez, George Furnas, Dan Ketchum, Carol Lochbaum, Jakob Nielsen, Joel Remde, and Scott Stornetta, and to the other splendid colleagues in that splendid environment. And to Libby, who interrupted my work early mornings by coming to sit on my lap and take over the computer that I hope will serve her better when she really needs it.

Prologue: The Trouble with Computers

What Trouble?

I went into a department store to buy a cheap watch. The man ahead of me said to the sales clerk, "I really like this one."

Clerk: *"I can't find its stock number; I can't enter the sale."*

The clerk went off to a back room where I heard her consulting one person, then another. A loudspeaker paged the manager. Eventually the clerk returned, apologizing, "It isn't in the book, and I can't find the manager."

Customer: *"There's one right here. Can't I just pay for it?"*

Clerk: *"I'm terribly sorry, I can't sell it without the number. Do you like this one? I have the number for it."*

Customer: *"I like the first one better."*

Clerk: *"Well, let's wait for the manager. Gosh, I'm sorry."*

Customer: *"I don't have much time. Can't I just give you the money?"*

Clerk: *"I'm really sorry. The manager should be along any minute."*

After five minutes of fidgeting and apologies, the manager appeared. She said, "Did you look for the number on the box?"

Clerk: *"Yes, but I didn't find it. And I asked the others. They didn't know either."*

Manager: *"I'll go look."*

Off she went. Five minutes later the PA system spoke: "I can't find the number either, would the customer like a different watch?"

Customer: *"No."*

What's going on here? Computers are wonderful. Maybe, if you're like me a few years back, the very title of this book would have puzzled you or made you mad. Trouble? Trouble indeed! Computers are fantastic, awesome. You love them; I love them. They're selling like hotcakes: maybe a little slower than they used to, but still they're the biggest bright spot in modern industry. Everyone wants one. Everyone uses them, one way or another. They're here, they're everywhere. Every accountant, author, secretary, scientist, businessperson, engineer has to have one. They're making new millionaires—no, billionaires—all over the place. Trouble? What trouble?

So finally it was my turn. By now I'd had plenty of time to select a watch and a couple of backups, just in case. No problem. My first pick had a number. So I gave the clerk my credit card. She put it in the machine for verification. The machine didn't take my card. She tried again, sliding the card faster. Again, slower. Again really fast. No go. Four more tries. Then she called across to the sales clerk at a nearby register. "What do I do when it won't accept the card?"

Answer: "Enter it with the keys."
Clerk: "I tried." Dutifully, she tried again. Once. Twice. Three times. Then she called across: "Do you put in the first three numbers?"
"Yes."
"Six, three, eight?"
"No, four, seven, two for that machine."
"Oh, thanks."
The rest of the transaction went smoothly.

This sad but true example is not an isolated case. I suspect that almost everyone in America has run into computerized check-out machines that slow transactions and frustrate operators and customers alike. Many companies have had sorely disappointing experiences with the introduction of information technology, failing to realize the economies that they were expecting, often promised. Indeed, everywhere you look, some computer system is gobbling dollars while doing silly things and making life hard for its masters and servants alike. Millions of "micros" bought for homes end up in closets. Millions of PCs bought for white-collar workers gather dust. And it gets worse—wait and see.

Then my wife found me, bearing a six-pack of Coke to which she had become attached during her long wait. I blithely took it and stepped into a check-out line with only one person bearing one item ahead. Oops. The item was a piece of loose glassware naked of stock number. Now ensued a repetition of the previous dialog, this time transmitted by a PA system and messenger but without the option of an exchange for an inferior alternative. Five minutes into the running back and forth, I asked if my six-pack of Coke could be checked out while we waited for the investigation to reach its conclusion.

"No," said the check-out clerk. "Once a sale is started, I can't take any other customers, and there's no way for me to cancel until its paid."

I occupied myself a while speculating why this would be so. Then I began counting customers in the line behind me. Seven, eight. One asked the clerk if she couldn't just enter the sale without a number. The others scowled knowingly, anticipating the clerk's polite answer that the machine would refuse.

Finally the manager arrived, this time with the proper number. Entry, payment, I sighed with relief—a mite too soon. As the glassware buyer disappeared into the parking lot, the clerk took a sheet of paper from the desk and logged the number, price, date, and time. Then she turned to me with a smile that said, "Business as usual."

What's going on here? Computers should make life easier and better. Computers are truly marvelous machines and getting more marvelous every year. Every day they get programmed to do astonishing new things. We're told over and over that we are in a computer revolution, that computers are leading us into a wonderful new information age. The computer and information revolution is widely predicted to be as consequential as the industrial revolution of the previous two centuries—throw in the printing press and agriculture as well. The money being invested in computers is probably comparable to the earlier investment in power-driven machines. "Muscle and movement" machines brought enormous increases in labor productivity. Solid evidence that the computer revolution has brought increased productivity, however, is very hard to find.

The Internal Revenue Service invested over $50 million in PCs for its agents. The systems were supposed to help agents enter and look up data and make calculations more quickly and accurately. But the number of cases processed by each agent in a week went down *by 40 percent.*

What's going on here? I believe that computers are in deep trouble. Certainly they have had and continue to have amazing triumphs; they've helped put humans on the moon, totally revised warfare, finally made it possible to solve centuries-old mathematics problems, led bursts of new scientific knowledge, taken over our bookkeeping and our telephone switches. Their raw power for calculation and storage continues to double every few years. But the promise that they would contribute to economics, to a vast improvement in standard of living, has not been kept. The nations, industries, and people who have invested in them heavily have not prospered proportionally (except those who sell computers). There is some sign that some corporations, usually very large ones, have had major successes with computers in the last few years, but it is not clear yet whether these successes were due to the computers themselves or to dramatic business revamping bred of recession pressures. We expected computers to bring across-the-board productivity help, work efficiency improvements for small and large alike. This they have not delivered.

A major insurance underwriter spent $30 million on a computer system to streamline the operation of its dental insurance claims department. Within a year, the number of claims processed each day by its sixty-five employees increased by over 30 percent. And the total cost of each claims transaction went up *from $3.50 to $5.00 (Zuboff 1988).*

Don't get me wrong. I'm a devoted software designer and a user and fan of computer systems. I'm using one to compose this book. I love the outline processor, a scheme that lets me enter bits and pieces, sudden thoughts and nifty paragraphs as they occur and reorganize it all later with a few keystrokes. I'm an electronic mail devotee. It saves me hours of telephone tag, lets me keep work communications short and to the point and personal interactions tactful, and allows me and my correspondents to do our communicating when it's most convenient, not just when we're both available. But I'm a very critical fan. Like several others we will hear from, I have a love-hate relationship with the computer. The outline processor lets me lose whole chapters at a stroke. It took it on itself to remove the indents and spaces from the customer-clerk dialogue I'd carefully formatted above, making a dense, indecipherable mass, and then it obstinately refused to let me change it back until I'd spent half an hour rereading the 800-page manual. I get twenty to fifty electronic mail messages each day—not instead of paper mail and telephone calls but *in addition,* and not all useful or entertaining.

My personal experience more or less captures the overall situation with computers: they do a lot of great things that could make us more efficient, and they do a lot of stupid or unintended things that get in our way, and they're not cheap. The bottom line is pretty smudgy. Not only are the economic data equivocal on the productivity effects of computing, but most direct evaluations of their effects on work efficiency are pretty disappointing—much, much inferior to the hope and hype attached to them in the popular press and mind.

Why? Poor Usefulness and Usability Due to Poor Evaluation, That's Why

So what's going on here? How did computer systems get this way? How come they aren't better than they are? Here's my overview of what has happened.

Since first leaving the research laboratories in the 1950s, computers as practical devices have been through two partly overlapping phases of evolution corresponding to two major realms of application. In the first phase, computers have been used for automation, to replace humans in the performance of tasks, either doing tasks that humans could do with no human help or doing tasks no human would be capable of. All of these tasks involve the manipulation of numbers. The amazing feats that computers perform in mathematics and science all depend on doing well-known mathematical calculations that in principle could be done by humans with a pencil and paper. The difference, of course, is that computers do calculations millions of times as fast as people and with many fewer errors.

Computers can do anything that can be reduced to numerical or logical operations, and that includes a vast array of chores. Almost any process that science, engineering, and statistics have captured in their theories can be carried out by a properly instructed (programmed) computer. This has also meant that we could invent things like radar-directed gunfire, where data arrive in such volume and have to be acted upon so quickly that humans couldn't do the necessary additions and multiplications. It has made it possible to invent CAT scan x-ray and MRI machines that allow doctors to see our insides in glorious three-dimensional detail. Each picture takes billions of calculations. They have allowed us to build much bigger, faster, cheaper electronic means for connecting telephones to each other, replacing the switchboards and electromechanical devices of the not-so-distant past. Without these new computer-based switches, we'd need 2 million more telephone operators than we had in 1950 and get much worse service at much higher prices. Computers have allowed us to build robots and electronically controlled lathes and milling machines and automatic process controllers for chemical plants and production lines. On the commercial front, their most important contribution has been the relief of bookkeepers. The endless, tedious copying, adding and subtracting, entering and retrieving of numbers on which banks and other businesses depend has almost all been handed over to computers.

Phase one is now running out of steam. Most jobs that could be simply taken over by numerical processors have already been taken over. It's getting hard to think of useful new jobs to do by arithmetic. Certainly the excitement is not over; many more marvelous computer-based inventions will come our way. But the pace of gain from automation will be much slower. The easily reached fruits have been picked.

Phase two of computer application is augmentation, encompassing that wide range of things that people do that cannot be taken over completely by a numerical machine. Most of the things people do—talk, understand speech and language, write, read, create art and science, persuade, negotiate, decide, organize, administer, entertain, socialize—

fall into this category. None of these things has yet been, or is likely soon to be, captured in a quantitative theory that can be executed as well by a computer as by a person. Although researchers are working busily, we're not nearly ready to replace humans with machines—even if we wanted to. Instead, computer systems have been designed and built to act as assistants, aids, and "power tools." It is here, in the design of these kinds of computer systems, that we have failed. Impressed with the successes of the automation machines, we have been eager to employ their offspring, the augmentation machines. And we have been paying good money for their services. But so far, they're just not working out. The evidence, which will be presented in detail, is that phase two helpers are not helpful enough to be worth their wages. Thus, the trouble with computers is that in their most recent applications—the jobs for which we now want them—they are not doing enough. Partly the problem is that they are still too hard to operate. Partly the problem is that they get misused, applied badly, and to the wrong jobs. Mostly the problem is that they don't yet do a sufficient number of sufficiently useful things.

What This Book Will Say

This book pieces together a picture of the situation, of how and where computers and related information technologies have failed to fulfill their promise to be helpful. Actually, this book is not about just computers but about the whole range of electronic technologies used in business. Many examples and data we will look at concern IT, or information technology—a grab-bag category of computers, telecommunications equipment, factory automation gadgets, and office gear. In dollars, computers are a very big part of this category, and many of the other things in it that don't have screens and flashing lights either contain hidden computers (copiers and cash registers) or rely on close friendships with computers (telephones and MRIs). It's this mix of stuff—computer-reliant or computer-associated information technology—that seems to be doing poorly. I'll offer an analysis and diagnosis of why computers and friends are not doing better than they are and suggest a set of remedies. Finally, I will speculate a bit on what the world will be like when computer power is finally properly harnessed.

The first chapter sets out some facts that pose the puzzle of computers and productivity—that tussle with the question of whether computers have contributed their share to productivity. Although large economic gains are not found, there are benefits, both obvious and hidden, and there are tantalizing exceptions. The real puzzle is not why gains do not exist but why they are so few and small. Next, I'll proceed to try to understand the puzzle. First I'll deal with some arguments that there really is nothing to worry about (I call these excuses). Then I'll examine a number of reasons that have been or might be offered for the problem. I settle on failure to design well for usefulness and usability as the main root cause, although I believe there are others, both derivative and independent. In turn, I will argue that the design failure is itself the result of a peculiar difficulty and resistance to evaluation of the real effectiveness of computer systems, a lack of feedback that cripples the normal processes of technical improvement. The following three chapters go into more detail, first on what's wrong with phase two computer systems as we know them, and how it is that such bad products get produced, sold, and even loved. Then I will offer some solutions that all have to do with how to direct and apply innovation to real human needs, rather than solving just traditional technical problems. They all hinge on methods for evaluative feedback. By name, the proposed solutions are UCD, UCD, and UCD, standing for user-centered design, user-centered development, and user-centered deployment. They don't need separate acronyms because at base they're all the same: techniques for getting and using empirical evidence on how systems help and hinder people in their work. There's already compelling evidence that these methods will work wonders. Unfortunately, there are also indications that getting them employed will be an uphill battle. I'll give you one or two chapters on each of the UCDs. At the end are two chapters on what I think would happen if the world followed my advice. These two short chapters are the most speculative, touching on what we might hope to get if the UCDs and computer phase two succeed, exciting new power tools for the human mind, and on what the world of work, education, and leisure may be like when they have succeeded.

I

The Productivity Puzzle

*"The biggest technological revolution men have known, far more inti-
mately affecting daily lives . . . than either the agricultural revolution in
Neolithic times or the early industrial revolution" (Snow 1966).*

*Productivity growth in the United States and other developmentally ad-
vanced nations went into a long, hard-to-explain slide from the early
1970s on, coinciding with the period of large-scale deployment of business computing.*

*Having spent several trillion dollars, the United States greatly outpaces
all other nations in buying computers. In most U.S. industry, information
technology is second only to real estate as capital investment. But the
United States trails almost all other major industrial nations in productivity growth.*

*For over three decades, banks, brokerages, and insurance companies led
the charge with vast investments in computers and related technologies,
yet overall productivity for this sector of the economy remained virtually
flat.*

*A 1992 report on French government ministries found that computeriza-
tion was cost-effective in only three of sixteen operations studied (Gillain
1992).*

*Paul Strassmann, a management consulting guru and erstwhile Xerox
corporate computing executive, studied the relation of computer spending by U.S. firms to their return on investment dollars. He found no consistent effect.*

*IBM's John Gould, a leader in computer human factors research, studied
the effectiveness of word processors. Ten professionals each composed
four letters with a computer and four in the old manner of handwriting
passed to a typist. There were no differences in judged quality of the
letters or in total work time.*

*The growth of sales of computers has diminished greatly in recent years.
The market is softening. Information systems budget increases in the
1990s are down substantially from levels in the last half of the 1980s
(Moad 1991).*

1

The Evidence

For over five years a debate has been in progress about how much—or even whether—computers contribute to improved productivity. Economists, work sociologists, computer scientists, and other relevant experts have offered a variety of facts, analyses, and opinions. Many, including Michael Dertouzos, head of the computer science department at MIT, Stephen Roach, a senior economist with the investment firm of Morgan Stanley, Martin Neil Baily, productivity economist at the Brookings Institute, Paul Attewell, a work sociologist at New York University and a member of the National Research Council Committee on Human Factors, and Paul Strassmann, a former chief of computing at Xerox, have concluded that computers have had very little positive effect on productivity. The bottom line, it has been variously asserted, is that while there are exceptions, most business investments in computers have yielded significantly lower returns than investments in bonds at market interest rates. Two analysts dissent from this view. Stanford University economist Timothy Bresnehan thinks there must be huge gains somewhere because there has been tremendous increase in the ratio of performance to price of computers themselves. Eric Brynjolfsson of MIT weighs in with a minority analysis purporting to show excellent results for heavy hardware investors among the Fortune 500 in recent years. Others have examined the possibility of errors in the measurement of productivity or proposed alternative explanations for the facts.

What seems most striking about this debate is that it has occurred at all. Given the marvelous powers of modern computing, its reputation in the public mind, and the vast amounts of money spent on its application, its economic benefits should be manifest. The fact that many serious and competent scholars can conclude that there has been little net productivity gain attributable to this technology seems enough proof that something is wrong.

History

In the United States, computers first entered commercial use in a big way in the early 1960s. In 1950 the decennial census counted fewer than 900 computer operators in the entire United States. In 1960 there were still only 2,000. However, by 1970 there were 125,000 and by 1985 close to half a million (or, for comparison, about twice the number of telephone operators) (Hunt and Hunt 1986). By 1985 computer and related information technology equipment purchases accounted for about 16 percent of total capital stock in the service sector, some $424 billion, up from 6 percent fifteen years earlier (Roach 1987). By 1991, the annual equipment outlay was running over $100 billion (Roach 1992b). And initial equipment costs are only the tip of the iceberg; the serious spending, which starts after the boxes arrive, at least triples the total. Operating and maintaining hardware costs as much as buying it. Software purchase or development adds another approximately equal share; most of the major applications of computers have required new software customized for the business or firm. Finally, computer use eats a comparable large slice. Expensive specialized labor is needed to debug, repair, or modify software. Because systems are so complicated and hard to use, end users (those whom the computer is intended to serve, as opposed to those who serve the computer) not only need extensive training but usually cannot use the computer fully by themselves; they need the assistance of systems analysts, consultants, trainers, or other intermediaries. Moreover, all of this needs supervision, organization, and management—whole electronic data processing and management information systems departments, not to mention the floor space and air-conditioning that they and their machines consume. Most of this outlay should be considered capital expense. It is all intended to make available a tool that is supposed to make other functions of production more efficient. Almost none of it is directly productive; almost none can be considered an input to production in the sense that raw material, energy, or most labor is.

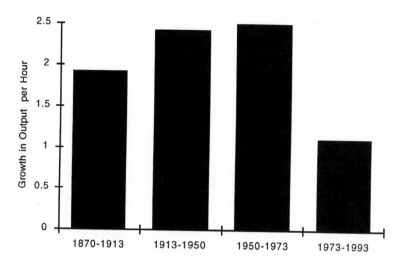

Figure 1.1.
Labor productivity growth in the United States, 1870–1993, measured as GNP per hour worked. (Maddison 1991; with newer data added (Bureau of Labor Statistics 1993; Nasar 1993; Thor 1994.))

Adding it all up, since 1960, something over $4 trillion (much more than an average year's GNP during that period) has been spent on computing, and total current expenditures for the United States amount to around 10 percent of GNP.[1] Although there was significant computerization, primarily of the phase one variety—complete automation in which the machine replaces a human—in the sixties, the overwhelming amount of phase two computer investment—in which computers are used as aids in the mentally demanding jobs of information workers—occurred from the early seventies onward, at a time when the United States experienced much slower growth in productivity (figure 1.1) than in any previous period for which comparable data are available (McKinsey Global Institute 1992).[2]

Quantitative estimates of productivity are usually calculated as the amount of value added for each person-hour employed—so-called labor productivity—or as the number of dollars worth of output for each dollar spent on labor and capital combined—so-called multifactor productivity. Between 1948 and 1965, overall growth in productivity ranged between 2 percent and 7 percent for industrialized nations. From the end of World War II through the sixties, the GNP, productivity, and standard of living of industrial nations grew steadily (Baily and Chakrabarti 1988; Denison 1989; Kendrick 1982). Annual labor productivity gains were in the range of 2 percent (for the United States) to 7 percent (for Japan). From about 1970–1975 onward productivity gains have been much smaller, ranging from 0 to 1 percent for the United States, up to 2⅔ percent for Japan. Gains in productivity since 1948 have always been largest in farming and manufacturing, but before 1970, they were nearly as good in other industries as well. Since the early seventies, productivity in the nonfarm, nonmanufacturing sphere has been essentially flat, even declining in some years. During this same period, of course, manufacturing and farming have become smaller portions of the overall economy, so the slow growth of productivity in other areas has affected the overall picture even more strongly.

Phase one computer application had considerable impact on manufacturing. Outright automation, mostly in the form of numerically controlled metal shaping machines and electronic controls for chemical and other production processes, were believed to have reduced the labor and capital required to produce a variety of goods, although there is conflicting evidence about the role of computers as such. Meanwhile, manufacturing has shrunk to around 25 percent of U.S. GDP (gross domestic product), and its direct labor costs to an even smaller part of the total (Baily and Chakrabarti 1988). Thus, it is not too much of a surprise that computers have not rescued overall labor productivity through their application to manufacturing.

There were major early phase one computer applications in some nonmanufacturing, nonfarming segments as well, notably in banking, finance, and insurance, where computers were first used to automate record keeping, accounting, report generation, and billing. Some analysts have found healthy productivity growth for some periods in some segments of these businesses and for particular functions within them. For example, the insurance industry maintained normal labor productivity growth while its extensive bookkeeping, contract preparation, and arithmetic for figuring premiums were automated (Baran 1987). As a group, however, these closely related industries have registered declines in productivity growth since widespread adoption of electronic information processing beginning in the late fifties, despite a six-to-one increase in real (inflation-adjusted) investment per employee—largely in computers and other information technology. The number of bookkeepers and billing clerks even continued to grow briskly in U.S. industry as a whole as computers ostensibly took over all the record copying and arithmetic. The number of file clerks multiplied by two and a half between 1960 and 1970 as computers were reputedly replacing them. And although their increase was very modest in later years, file clerk jobs were still not on the endangered species list (Feldberg and Glenn 1987; Hunt and Hunt 1986).

With the important exception of telecommunications, to which we will return, the remaining nonfarm, nonmanufacturing industries, such as transportation, public utilities, trade, and services, have shown nearly flat productivity over the last two decades. These industries should be, and have been, the primary candidates for phase two computer applications. It is for them that word processors, PCs, laptops, spreadsheets, office automation machinery in general, electronic cash registers, inventory management, and management information systems have been designed.

While it would be rash to conclude solely from the recent stagnation of productivity that computers have no positive net effects on work efficiency, the historical trends in productivity certainly give no evidence of large improvements during the period when phase two computer use has been rapidly expanding.

Country Comparisons

The situation when comparing countries is less clear, but what is visible is not much more encouraging. For the first two decades after World War II, the United States had by far the highest productivity in the world and relatively high annual growth in productivity as well. Its position is no surprise; all other major industrial nations had been devastated by the war, the United States had a commanding lead in science and technology, as well as in installed base of capital equipment, and, not least, a vast domestic market for industry to tap. But in the last two decades the other

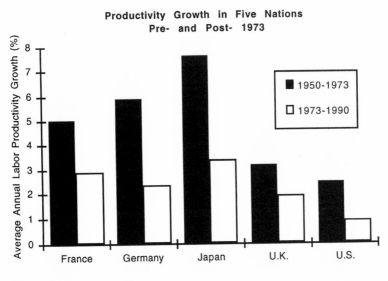

Figure 1.2.
Productivity growth before and after 1973 for five major industrial nations. (Author's summary estimates based on data from Maddison 1991; McKinsey Global Institute 1992; Thor 1994.)

industrialized nations have been rapidly gaining on the United States; their rates of increase in productivity, though also down, have been much greater. Figure 1.2 shows growth rates in output per hour worked.

The United States is still well ahead of most other countries in absolute productivity, but the margin is narrower. In terms of GDP per hour worked (with currencies adjusted to equal consumer purchasing power) France has caught up (figure 1.3).[3]

The relative performance of nations would be plausible if one could assume some limit to labor productivity—that it can't go on improving at the same rate forever. If everything were totally automated and there was no labor cost at all, the end would be reached, and all countries would be the same. Perhaps as we get closer to this unreachable goal, marginal gains in labor productivity will be harder to achieve and thus decline. As the other industrial nations catch up with the United States, their rate of gain in productivity might be expected to decline as well. This situation seems most likely to exist for manufacturing, since labor costs for this sector are only a small part of an economy as developed as

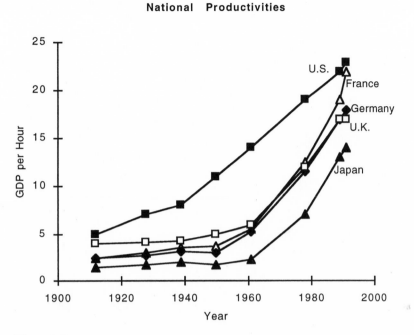

Figure 1.3.
Productivities of five major industrial nations in the twentieth century. This graph gives a longer-range view of productivity trends. The post–World War II catch-up of other nations and the even slower relative growth in the United States after 1973 are apparent. Data from Maddison 1991; Thor 1994.

that of the United States, and thus productivity gains in them cannot be a large contributor. In short, the relatively large gains in productivity in Japan and Europe have come primarily from catching up to America's lead in manufacturing. Meanwhile, it is primarily in services—white collar or "information work"—that productivity has suffered the most pronounced stagnation. U.S. and Japanese spending on services far outstrips that of the other major industrial countries (figure 1.4).

Perhaps Japan's relatively low absolute productivity despite very rapid gains and many triumphs in manufacturing are a result of its large expenditures on services. Perhaps productivity growth in other nations will also slow as they exhaust the opportunities in manufacturing and agriculture and begin to devote larger shares of their economic energy to services.[4]

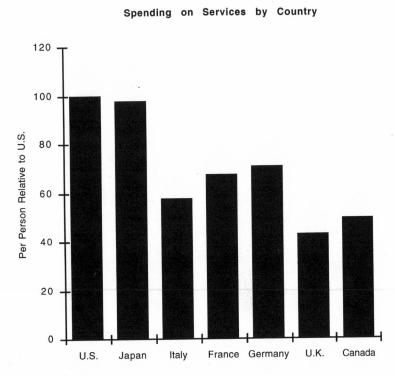

Spending on Services by Country

Figure 1.4.
Relative spending on services in the late eighties in the Group of Seven industrial democracies. Data from Roach 1991.

Be this as it may, productivity growth in nonmanufacturing and non-farming industries appears to have been no worse in the last two decades in other countries than in America despite the fact that America has been investing much more heavily in phase two computer applications. Word processing, PCs for managers, and the rest of the armamentarium of information technology originated in the United States and became wide-spread there sooner than elsewhere (although France may offer a recent important exception, having invested more heavily than the United States in its public information handling infrastructure, notably its Minitel national data communications network). Greater U.S. computerization appears true even in the computer industry itself; programmers in the United States have had their own terminals or workstations, while in Japan several programmers have usually shared a terminal.

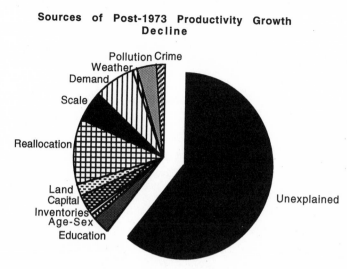

Sources of Post-1973 Productivity Growth Decline

Figure 1.5.
Denison's estimates of contributions to the post-1973 slowdown in productivity growth in the United States. Data from Baily and Chakrabarti 1988, p. 32.

Thus early, prolonged, and heavy investment in computers and information technology, of phase one applications in manufacturing and financial services and, especially, phase two applications in the rest of business, failed either to prevent a virtual collapse of productivity growth in the United States or to maintain its relative productivity advantage over other industrialized countries.

Econometric Analyses of the Productivity Slowdown

Several economists have estimated the contributions of various factors to the post-1973 slowdown in productivity growth. Econometric analyses try to find equations in which the sum of several different economic measurements (e.g., capital investments and labor hours), each multiplied by the right constant, equals another measurement that is especially interesting (e.g., total output). (These methods are often called computer models, not just to give them cachet but because the calculations are so complicated that computers are needed.) Figure 1.5 shows the results of an econometric analysis by Edward Denison, a leading productivity expert, of the factors in the post-1973 U.S. downward productivity growth trends (Baily and Chakrabarti 1988, p. 32). The estimates are based entirely on quantitative data. According to this analysis all the measurable influences on productivity known to economics account for only 40 percent of the slowdown.

Michael Mohr, in a similar analysis, added informed judgments about the uncertainty of the numbers and about certain qualitative factors (Baily and Chakrabarti 1988). He concludes that 50 to 80 percent of the changes might be explained. Still another economist, Angus Maddison, finds he can account for 51 percent of the slowdown (Maddison 1991). For earlier periods—before 1973—the variables considered in these analyses could account for almost all trends in productivity over time. That is, equations with measurements of all of them gave close predictions of productivity changes. In contrast, in all analyses of changes from before 1973 to after, known influences on productivity leave much unexplained. Baily and Chakrabarti, who reviewed and revised these analyses, conclude that the lowest estimates may be a bit conservative in the amount of influence assigned to known variables, and the highest too enthusiastic in crediting questionable factors. For example, estimates of capital quality—how wisely investment was spread over more or less productive uses—may beg the question of why more productive uses were not available. Baily and Chakrabarti conclude that about half, 1.0 to 1.25 percent, remains unexplained out of a total 2.0 to 2.5 percent decline in the growth rate. All of these authorities guess that the unexplained part is due to a failure of innovation or "technological progress" to make as big a contribution to productivity growth in later as in earlier years.

Comparisons between Industries

Let's now look at the differences in particular sectors of business in the United States. For a broad view, we can compare the change in productivity from the largely precomputer era before the early seventies, to more modern times for a whole range of industries. Figure 1.6 shows comparisons based on U.S. government industrial classifications and productivity data.

Productivity in farming continued to rise at a strong pace, much as it has over the last hundred years or so, getting even stronger after 1973.

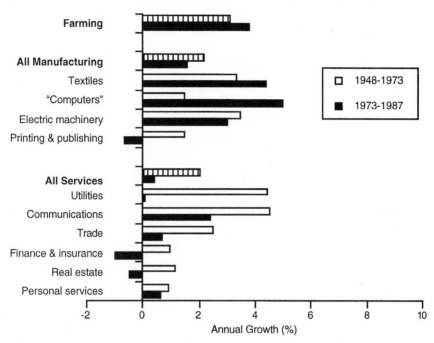

Figure 1.6.
Total factor productivity growth rates before and after 1973 for some major industrial groups. Data from Thor 1990.

Productivity in manufacturing also continued to rise at a rate that, although down by about a quarter, was not far off the historical trends that have led to enormous improvements in standards of living. However, there was considerable variation among different manufacturing industries. Indeed, the picture for manufacturing as a whole would not be nearly as rosy if we excluded the manufacture of computers themselves (shown as "computers," the quotation marks to indicate the inclusion of some similar industries in the government classification), which we would want to do to look for their effects as tools rather than as products.[5] Baily (1986b) and Kendrick (1982) estimate that the overall productivity gains in manufacturing would have been a whole percentage point, or 33 percent lower without the manufacture of computers as an industry itself. In the non-goods-producing industries labor productivity growth slid from an annual average of 2.5 percent between 1948 and 1973 to only 0.7 percent from 1973 to 1987, at the same time that this sector became the dominant user of both capital and labor.[6] It appears that these expanding industries, which were moving heavily into phase two computing, suffered productivity stagnation to a much greater extent than their more conservative siblings.

We should also try to look at who was winning after the game had gone on a while, so that the effects of computerization would have had time to be felt. Figure 1.7 shows the relation between total net stocks of IT and productivity in 1987 for nine major sectors (Baily and Chakrabarti 1988). Each point is for one industry, showing its productivity relative to the others as a function of how much IT capital it was using in 1987. The two points in the upper left of the graph, where productivity was relatively high and IT investment very low, are for mining and utilities. The two points in the lower left, where both productivity and IT investment were low, are for transportation and construction. The points in the left-middle with moderate IT stocks and relatively low productivity include manufacturing, trade, financial services, and other "services." The point in the upper right, the only segment with both high IT stocks and high productivity, is communications.[7]

Figure 1.8 shows the rate of growth in productivity after 1973 as a function of the proportion of capital of the various industrial sectors devoted to IT. Here there is some evidence of a positive effect of IT investment, but again only the communications industry appears to have exploited the technology to significant advantage.

This last point is an important one. The only major subclassification within nonfarm, nonmanufacturing that had nontrivial productivity gains between 1973 and 1987 was communications. Communications is composed primarily of television, radio, and telecommunications; the telephone companies are the biggest component, with total revenues over $100 billion a year. From more detailed data, it appears that the telephone business accounts for the superior productivity record of this category.

From 1973 to 1983, telephone company productivity increased by over 6 percent annually. During the same period, there were productivity increases of just 1.5 percent in air transport, under 1 percent in retail

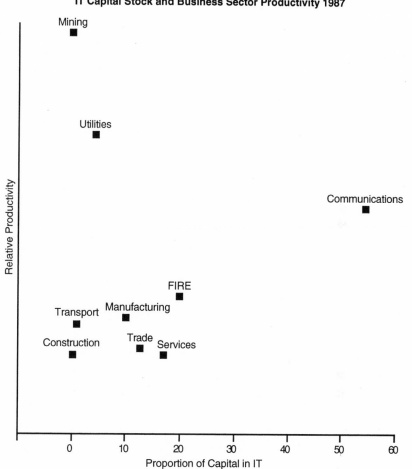

Figure 1.7.
Relative productivities of nine business sectors in the United States, in 1987, as related to capital accumulations in computers and communications equipment. Services are direct business and personal services (to be distinguished from alternate uses of the term *services* to refer to all non-goods-producing industries or to white-collar occupations). The correlation is essentially zero. Data from Baily 1988. (FIRE = finance, insurance, and real estate.)

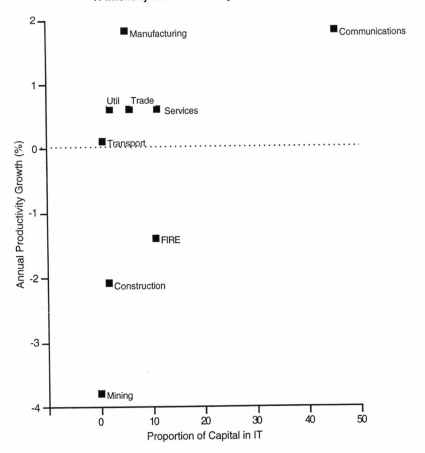

Figure 1.8.
IT investment intensity and productivity growth rates, 1973–1985. Data from Baily 1988. The IT figures are for proportion of capital in computers and related equipment and are my estimates, based on interpolations, of the typical intensity of such investment during the 1973–1985 period. Note: More precisely, the narrow definition of services includes lodging places, business and personal services, repair and maintenance services, movies, recreation services, health care, legal services, education and social services.

food stores, and absolute declines in restaurants. All of these, like the telephone business, are non–goods producing but have easily countable output. They are also industries that were using computers and in which one might have imagined computerization to be effective (U.S. Department of Labor 1983). However, telephone companies were the leading and largest users of both phase one and phase two computing, and they did well. We will examine this dramatically countercurrent industry in detail later.

Most other service industries have also invested heavily in computers but have not done well at all. Probably the second largest investors in phase two computing, as well of phase one application for record keeping, have been the brokerage, banking, and insurance businesses. Although there was apparently significant variation among subsectors, these businesses as a whole have shown a strong net decline in both labor and multifactor productivity since 1973.

Let's take one more look, from a slightly different angle. By 1980, service industries had had almost a decade of experience with IT. How did their investments in IT pay off in the following years? Figure 1.9 shows data for seven large service industries selected for close study by a National Research Council committee investigating the impact of information technology. The graph shows by what percentage each industry's IT capital increased between 1981 and 1989 and the percentage by which its labor productivity increased, measured by the amount of value added by each hour of work. There is no sign that industries that expanded their IT most rapidly improved their productivity the most; if anything, the opposite appears to be true.[8]

Two agencies of the U.S. government collect and analyze economic data in enormous detail: the Bureau of Economic Analysis (BEA) and the Bureau of Labor Statistics (BLS). Most of the numbers cited so far, including most of the productivity figures, originated with them. However, these agencies do not always aggregate the data in the most revealing way for a particular purpose or make all the adjustments that might be desired to be confident in particular conclusions. Such is the case here. We have seen presumptive evidence that the major lag in productivity growth has been in service industries, broadly defined. But the government agencies do not publish data on an entirely appropriate category

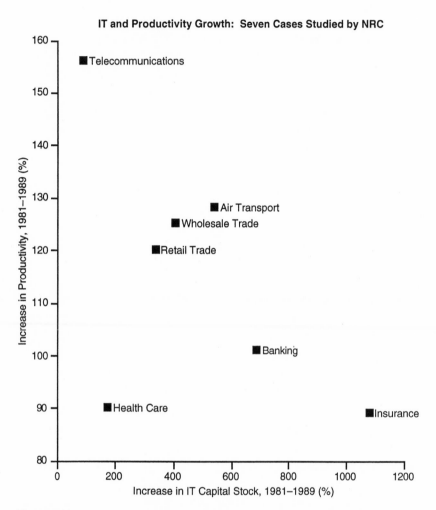

Figure 1.9.
IT and productivity growth. In the eighties, service companies expanded their use
of IT. Across seven major service industry segments, those that increased IT the
most were not those that improved productivity the most. Productivity here is
value-added per hour of labor, 1981=100%. (National Research Council 1994a.)

of business, those with major concentrations of information work, where phase two computerization is most relevant and most prominent. The closest one is the nonmanufacturing, nonfarm sector, but it includes mining and construction. In addition, the measurement of productivity is more difficult in services than in manufacturing industries, and in some cases the government agencies either finesse the issue entirely or do not do as good a job as many economists would like. Fortunately, both of these deficiencies have been vigorously addressed by first-rank economists.

Stephen Roach, senior economist at the New York investment house of Morgan Stanley, has done a number of careful reanalyses of the government productivity data to separate service information work from other activities. It was these analyses that led him to be among the first to announce the existence of a "computer productivity paradox."[9] Figure 1.10 shows Roach's figures for productivity per information worker and per production worker separately over time. The analysis is for workers in non-goods-producing sectors. Roach did the same analysis for the part of industry that produces goods and obtained very similar results (Roach 1985). Even in goods-producing industries, which have shown better productivity growth, output per information worker hour did not improve during this era of increasing computer use.[10]

Let us now follow Roach's comparisons of the broad service sector (services, communications, wholesale and retail trade, finance and insurance) with the goods sector (manufacturing, mining, and construction). Roach calculates that during the eighties, service sector productivity rose only 0.7 percent per year—less than one-fifth the rate in the manufacturing sector (Roach 1992a, 1992b). On the other hand, he estimates that over 80 percent of the investment in information technology hardware (computers, telecommunications—itself highly computerized—and other high-tech office equipment, with computer hardware and software the most expensive items) has been in the service sector. For 1991, he counted service's IT investment share at 88 percent, much greater than the sector's 57 percent share of GDP, and well over $100 billion. Thus, dividing the economy into manufacturing versus services shows the

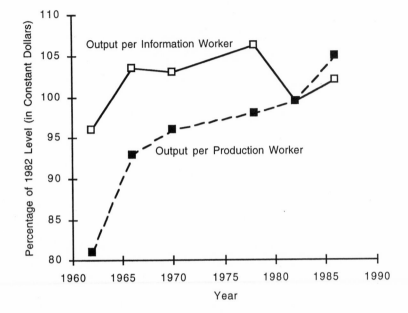

Figure 1.10.
Comparison of output per information (or white-collar) worker and per production worker over time. Note that both curves are relative to their own standard of 1982 productivity levels; that is, they depict relative changes, not absolute differences in productivity between the two classes of workers. Data from Roach 1987.

part with the greater IT investment growing slow in productivity. The situation is even more lopsided than these figures suggest. Roach is counting only hardware purchase prices. About half of these were computers in the eighties. But computers carry with them relatively large downstream costs for software, operation, and hand holding by nonproduction personnel. Moreover, services started from a lower productivity base from which more rapid improvement might have been expected. Roach also provides a more detailed analysis of the correlation over time between IT investment and productivity in service industries (figure 1.11).

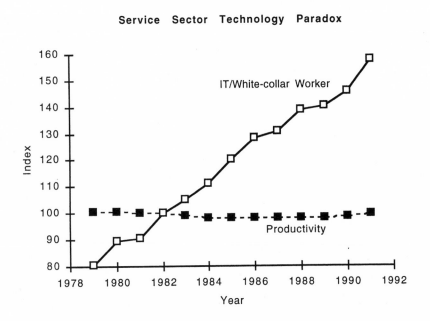

Figure 1.11.
IT capital and productivity in the service sector (non-goods-producing industries). While IT investment went up rapidly, productivity growth slowed. Data from Roach 1992c.

Comparisons between Firms and over Time

We can narrow in on a closer look at computerization effects by examining differences between firms and to particular firms over time. Two sorts of studies have been done: econometric analyses of the statistics of companies as they use capital and labor to produce outputs and the relative success of companies that follow different IT investment strategies.

"If the customer walks in with a magnetic-strip-reader card and identifies herself as customer X, we can track every single thing she buys and do all kinds of wonderful things with that information. . . . We can have frequent purchaser programs and so on." Senior vice president of a major supermarket chain (National Research Council 1994a).

Before embarking on this course, however, heed a special warning. If firm X spends more on computers and does better than firm Y, the conclusion is not necessarily that computers improved productivity. X may use its computers to increase work or processes efficiency, but it may also use them to capture market share. Airline reservation systems automate booking, but they also allow their owners to aim marketing campaigns at their competitors' best customers. The success of a single firm depends strongly on its competition with other firms in the same market. Output per labor hour may be better in winner firms because they are winning rather than vice versa.[11] On the other hand, if we find that IT use does not correlate with output or business success, it is unlikely that it is bringing major increases in efficiency.

Econometric Analyses of the Productivity Effects of Information Technology

Several econometricians have analyzed correlations between output and computer investments. Of the half-dozen such studies of which I know, only one has found a positive effect. I'll review three of them—two of the negatives and the sole positive.

Gary Loveman, in a study done at MIT's Sloan School of Management as part of its Management in the 1990s research program, worked with data from sixty manufacturing units of twenty firms located in the United States or Western Europe (Loveman 1986, 1990). His model equations sought to account for differences in productivity growth between different units and different years between 1978 and 1983. The analyses revealed consistently small, usually slightly negative, effects of investment in information technology. That is, the more money firms invested in information technology, the less—very slightly—their productivity grew from one year to the next. He looked for delayed effects and for effects of IT indirectly through better utilization of labor or better management. Nothing. There was a hint of better IT results in firms that produced tangible, as compared to intangible, goods, but even here it was not significant. These results contrasted sharply with differences in non-IT capital inputs, things like buildings and machinery, which, he found, had strong effects on productivity growth. These negative results for IT are perhaps especially noteworthy because they concern manufacturing.

Manufacturing has experienced better productivity gains than the rest of the economy, and it has been tempting to take this as evidence that computers have been a positive influence in this sector. However, as Loveman notes, most computerization in the period of his analyses, 1978–1983, was aimed at information work rather than production automation, even in manufacturing industries.

In interpreting his results, Loveman speculated that IT may have had much more favorable effects in the nonmanufacturing segments for which they were better suited and in which they were more heavily used, especially in banking and insurance. Richard Franke, a professor of management at Loyola College, Baltimore, analyzed data from the U.S. financial industry (Franke 1987). His analysis of IT effectiveness offers little such comfort. The financial industry—banking, insurance, and brokerage—was the first major sector of the U.S. economy (excepting telephony) to employ electronic data processing widely. Magnetic ink character recognition (MICR) was introduced in 1958. By 1980, 97 percent of banks had computers, which accounted for half of their capital expenditures other than buildings. But productivity stagnated in the 1970s, while clerical employment in the industry continued to climb at least as rapidly as before. Gross output increased by 4.7 percent per year from 1948 to 1958 but by only 3.6 percent per year from 1958 to 1983, a period of intense computerization. Meanwhile capital investment soared; from under 3 percent growth per year before 1958, it rose to almost 10 percent per year in the early eighties. Capital productivity rose strongly between 1948 and 1957, perhaps reflecting a positive influence of phase one computer applications. However, much accelerated computer investment thereafter was accompanied by a plunge in returns to one-fifth their 1957 peak by 1983. These trends are displayed in figure 1.12., which shows labor and capital productivity measures along with the amount of capital per employee.[12]

Service industries, like finance, have traditionally provided very little capital equipment to their employees. The greater productivity of manufacturing has been taken to be a result of finding ways to use machines to multiply the efficiency of human labor. Managers hoped that computers and other IT would do the same for services. To estimate the relative quantitative effects on productivity growth of capital and other input

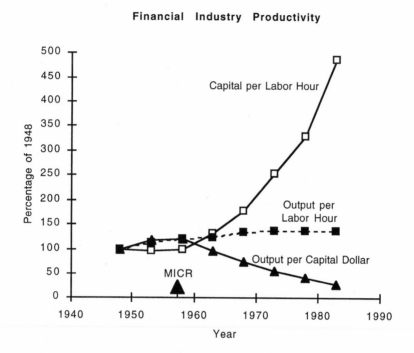

Figure 1.12.
Capital and productivity in U.S. banking and insurance, 1948–1983. Computers were introduced for bookkeeping in these industries in the early 1950s. Magnetic ink character recognition devices (MICRs) were introduced in 1957. Data from Franke 1987. Note: Output was computed as the inflation-adjusted value-added of the industry, based on deposit turnover, new insurance written, and sales of securities (Franke 1987).

variables, Franke carried out a detailed analysis of the year-to-year changes. The output measure of capital productivity he used was the inflation-adjusted value-added of deposit turnover, new insurance policies written, and sales of stocks and bonds, relative to the total accumulated real value of buildings, land, equipment, and inventories. In the equations that he derives from the data, capital per employee has a highly significant positive influence on output growth before 1958 and a strongly *negative* effect for the later period as a whole. The trend for the last decade of his analysis, 1973–1983, is more encouraging; the function improves almost to the point of a neutral effect for capital investment. Reasonably, he attributes the upturn to better performance for price of more modern computer equipment. Has this trend continued, turning IT investment beneficial in the decade since Franke's study? New studies are needed, but overall recent performance in the financial industry doesn't seem to reflect a leap forward.

The positive finding comes from a recent analysis by MIT economists Erik Brynjolfsson and Lorin Hitt (1993). They used a much larger and more recent sample of firms, ranging from 135 to 293 large companies, all Fortune 500 firms in the top half of their industries, for each of the years 1987 to 1991. The solution of their modeling equations yielded estimates of a 58 percent return on investments in computer hardware in manufacturing and a whopping 81 percent when service industries were included. Their results certainly paint a rosier picture and led to a number of announcements in the press that the "computer paradox" has been vanquished.

Unfortunately, the study has some serious problems. For a start, it uses a very steep and suspect deflator for computer prices, one based on the rapidly falling cost of mips and bytes. Thus, it assumes that computer capital for the earlier years of the study was really worth less than half what was actually paid for it, and so forth. For the purposes of estimating the relative value of computer capital, this method isn't cricket. Since we're trying to determine whether computers are valuable at all, we can't assume that their economic value is directly proportional to their computational power, a naive notion in the first place. For comparative purposes, the price adjustment for computers should be in terms of what firms would have had to pay for the things they could have bought if they hadn't bought computers. Substituting such a price correction suggests that Brynjolfsson and Hitt's estimates of computer hardware expenses were low by at least 50 percent.

Second, Brynjolfsson and Hitt counted only hardware costs, and as they and many others have observed, hardware is only a fraction of the cost of using computers. The real cost is about three times as much (some accountants and economists place the ratio at only two to one, but they count only software and operation, not hardware and software maintenance, user training, and so forth). All told, then, the costs appear to be low by a factor of four or five, and thus the real returns must have been much lower than estimated.[13]

There are still more problems with this study. One is that the results say that more successful firms invested more heavily in computers. Did computers cause success, or did success permit lavish computer spending? Another caution is that the sample consisted of the biggest, most successful organizations to be found. Are these firms successful with computers because computers are wonderful or because these firms are wonderful? Brynjolfsson and Hitt found that the apparent effects of computer capital were stronger if measured two years after the spending than if measured immediately. This favors the computers-bring-money over money-brings-computers explanation. However, their equations predicted output, that is, sales. Return on investment benefit was inferred from the greater sales of companies that spent more on IT. It is likely that much of the sales success of heavy users was due to strategic applications, that is, market share maneuvers, rather than lower prices from greater production efficiency. This is what many industry experts describe as the major benefit of computers.

Nevertheless, these results may in part reflect positive productivity gains. Brynjolfsson and Hitt speculate that the big high-return firms they studied have been using computers a long time, have revised their applications repeatedly, and have lately redesigned business processes to use them better. I'm inclined to give partial credit to their conclusion. There have been many opportunities for using computers to reduce duplicate work and improve coordination. Surely someone somewhere should have begun doing it.

The most significant fact about the Brynjolfsson and Hitt study is that the relation between computer investments and output was positive where it has not been before. Regardless of all the caveats and the difficulties in interpreting the size and cause of the effect,[14] this is a good omen. However, while it certainly offers reason to hope, joyful victory celebrations such as *Business Week*'s June 1993 article, "The Information Technology Payoff," stimulated by this study, are seriously premature.   •

No macroeconomic analysis is above suspicion. They are all at bottom efforts to determine causes from correlation. The investigator has to make many assumptions in deciding what to include in the model and how to measure it. The procedure is plagued by obscure statistical disorders such as colinearity. Econometric models also include assumptions about how one factor, for example, demand, influences another, say, price, that are taken from established economic theory. Anyone who follows published predictions of economic growth knows how unreliable all this machinery can be. One criticism that can be aimed at all the analyses is that they do not include a direct measurement of gains passed on to the consumer in better quality and convenience. What most of the analyses have shown is that computer investments didn't correlate with output from the firm's perspective. But perhaps computer investments helped not the firms but only their customers. However, all these analyses find that other capital investments boost productivity. Why wouldn't the benefits of money spent on new stores and better materials, for example, also be passed on to consumers? Similar analyses have found strong effects of research and development expenditures on the productivity of firms. Why does R&D help firms, but computers do not? Thus, we find computer investments in a peculiar position.

Computers and Business Success

In addition to studying the relation between computer investment and output or productivity measures as such, we can look at its overall effects on business success. In a competitive capitalist economy, a technology is not likely to contribute to economic well-being if it does not tend to improve the profitability of businesses that adopt it.

Paul Strassmann is a careful analyst and sensible advice giver in this arena. Before becoming a business computing consultant, lecturer, and author, he spent over thirty years bringing modern computing to both the internal management and product lines of several major companies, retiring as a vice president of Xerox's Information Products Group. He has written two excellent books on the business uses and value of computers. The first, *Information Payoff* (1985), was devoted mostly to advice on deploying and measuring the effectiveness of information technology. In it he reported having been able to find only one methodologically acceptable study that compared the success of comparable firms that spent smaller or larger amounts on computing. This was a study by Cron and Sobel (1983) of data from some 138 small to medium-sized medical supply wholesalers. They were divided into four groups:

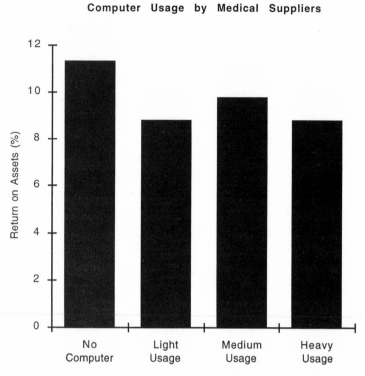

Figure 1.13.
Return on assets for wholesale medical equipment suppliers compared to their usage of computers. Data from Cron and Sobel 1983.

those that had no computers, those that made light or moderate use of them, and those that were heavy users. Return on total assets was greatest—11.3 percent—in those *without* computers and least—8.8 percent—in those that used them most (figure 1.13). The spread in success was greatest in the heavy-use group; although 43 percent of them were in the lowest quartile on returns—many of them relatively small firms—some heavy users did quite well. Perhaps we have another hint here that while computerization does not help on average, some firms can use it well (or succeed despite it?). We will see more evidence of that later.

In his later book, *The Business Value of Computers,* (1990) Strassmann reported a large number of studies of his own of this kind—comparisons across many different firms categorized in various ways, with

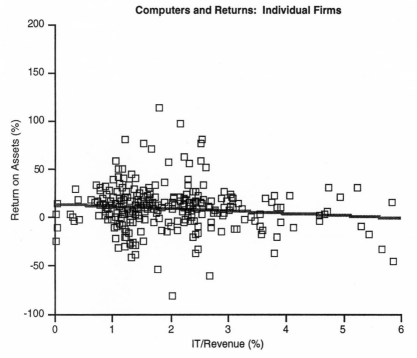

Figure 1.14.
Relations of business success to IT investment, here measured as return on assets (net income over total worth of company) as a function of the proportion of gross income spent on computers and other information technology. Data from Strassmann 1990.

both business success and degree of computerization measured in several ways. He was unable to find any conclusive evidence of positive value of computer use. A sample of some of his graphs is shown.

The first (figure 1.14) shows an overall plot of investment in computers for 254 firms versus their return on assets. Here the measure of computerization is investment as a ratio of revenues—what portion of the dollars taken in was spent on information systems. An interesting feature of this plot is that it is the only one in the book for which statistical analysis indicates that the data could not likely have been produced by splattering dots randomly on the graph.[15] It shows a negative, although very slight, relation: firms that spent a larger portion of their income on computers

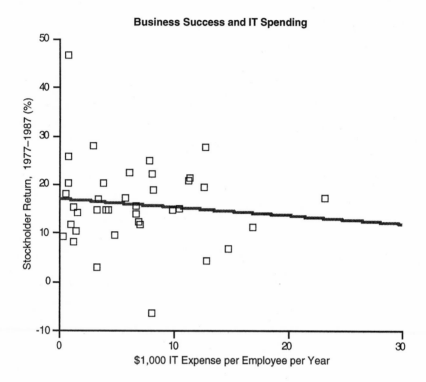

Figure 1.15.
Return to stockholders compared to money spent by individual firms for information systems on a per employee annual basis. Data from Strassmann 1990.

tended to do just a little worse than those that spent less![16] However, it is not clear that the usefulness of computers should always increase proportionally as a company spends a larger part of its revenue on them. Maybe doubling computer investment will make revenues triple, so that companies that are using them well will have low ratios of IS to revenues.

For a smaller number of firms, Strassmann was able to make a similar plot in which the measure of computerization was the amount of spending on information systems per employee per year. This seems like a more direct measure of how much the company is exploiting computer power. The results are about the same for this measure (figure 1.15). There is a slight tendency for companies that spent more to do worse, although again the relation could easily be just chance.[17] The next Strassmann

Business Success and IT in Service Industries

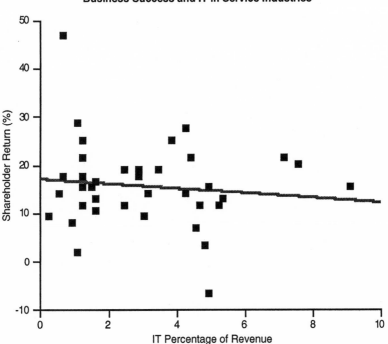

Figure 1.16.
Returns to stockholders of thirty-seven service industry companies compared to IT expenditures as a percentage of revenue. Data from Strassmann 1990.

graph (figure 1.16) shows data for service companies only, with computerization again measured as spending as a percentage of revenue. No significant relation was observed.[18]

Figure 1.17 looks even closer, at fourteen large banks—banks being among the heaviest computer investors and those with the longest experience and greatest dependence on the technology. This graph uses IT expenditures as a ratio of deposits, a bank's traditional source of earnings, as the indicator of degree of computerization. Figure 1.18 again shows shareholder results for large banks, but this time the computerization measure is computer systems costs per employee. The positive trend when computerization is measured this way is more encouraging. Statistically, however, it is still far from significant; that is, the two- or three-

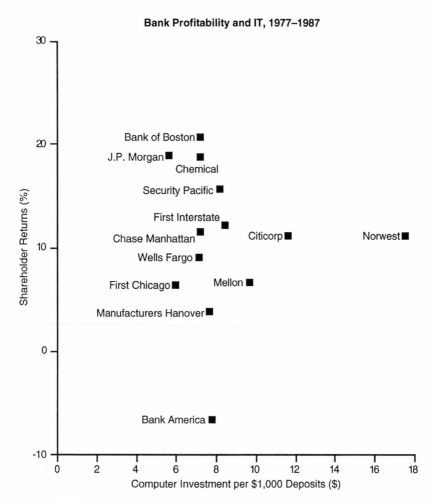

Figure 1.17.
Business success for large banks related to the amount spent on computers. The measures are IT expenditures as a ratio of deposits and shareholder returns. Data from Strassmann 1990.

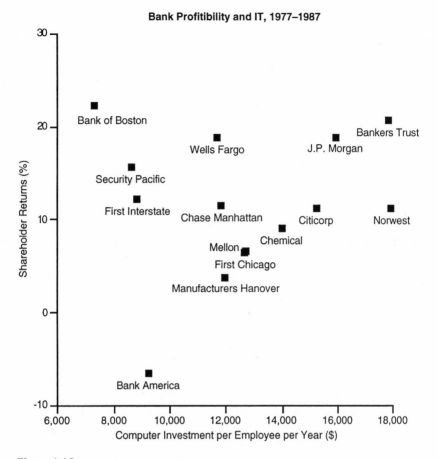

Figure 1.18.
Business success for large banks related to the amount spent on computers. The measures are IT expenditures per employee per year and shareholder returns. Data from Strassmann 1990.

point average difference between the smallest and largest IT users could easily be just chance.[19]

Many of these figures use shareholder returns as the measure of success. The issue of whether superior efficiency or effectiveness from computerization could be showing itself in other ways is difficult to resolve definitively. Strassmann reports getting similar negative results with return on assets, return on shareholder equity, earnings per share, and earnings-per-share growth as the dependent measure. It is still possible that real productivity growth was devoted to other purposes, for example, higher wages, better working conditions, unreimbursed customer services, or better products at the same price. However, it is worth noting that the period in which these data were collected, the late seventies to late eighties, was not notable for the altruism of management to labor. Across the board, real wages declined. Nor did most management appear reluctant to retain profits for stockholders rather than selflessly plowing them back into advantages for their customers.

Strassmann himself approached the success measurement problem by defining a quantity he called "management value-added." First he calculates value-added by summing the prices received for all outputs of a firm and subtracting the costs of capital and directly producing labor. Then he divides by all the rest of the costs of running a business. These latter, management costs he takes to be the prime target of computers; the lower they were relative to value-added, the higher would be his measure. He was apparently unable to show a clear positive effect of computerization by this measure either; at least he does not report any finding of this kind in either of his books. He does report analyses suggesting that "overachiever" firms tend to spend more than "underachievers" but a little less than "average achievers" on IT for management, although spending more on IT for operations doesn't seem to be beneficial.[20]

Putting Two and Two Together: Could Computer Failure Be the Missing Piece in the Productivity Puzzle?

How much of the post-1960s slowdown in productivity growth could be due to the failure of computer investments to pay off? (To simplify the arithmetic I will use round numbers.) We saw that as much as a 1.5

percent per year portion of the deficit in the growth of productivity in the decade following 1973 could not be blamed on the usual suspects. This would mean that total output was 1.5 percent below model predictions each year. GNP averaged roughly $2 trillion during this period (Johnson 1989). Thus up to $30 billion per year in expected output had gone missing and unaccounted. The total value of IT capital equipment at work in America averaged roughly $225 billion during this period. If IT capital yielded an average of 13.3 percent less than other forms of investment, it would have generated $30 billion less output than the normal equations predicted, and thus the shift of investment to IT would account for the missing money.[21] Is it reasonable to suppose that computers had this poor a relative return? Franke's estimate for the financial industry during the same decade is that a dollar of capital, which was primarily IT in that period, produced just a dollar of output, a nil return on investment. Loveman estimated the contribution of computer investments to productivity growth during the latter part of this period as slightly negative for manufacturing. Strassmann's statistical analyses show close to zero returns on investment from computer spending over a wide variety of industries. Strassmann's data also provide an estimate of the usual size of returns on assets without computers. It was around 13.3 percent. The deficiency in IT returns by these calculations was thus 13.3 percent of $225 billion, for an average annual deficit of $30 billion.[22] The numbers fit quite well: up to $30 billion missing new GNP per year, about $30 billion per year worse return on new investments. Indeed the lower yield of IT capital accounts for a residual growth failure at the high end of the range of econometric estimates.[23]

The low return from investments in computers, and IT generally, appears to be the missing piece in the productivity slowdown puzzle. It has the right economic size and shape. It has an appropriately gray background, and it looks like part of a cloud. Does it fit into a detailed picture of specific economic causes and effects of which it is a part? Let us look.

2

What Computers Do

So far, we've treated computers and information technology as merely a general kind of investment, like gold stocks or mutual funds, and asked how well it performs financially. But computers are supposed to do particular jobs and to have more specific, concrete effects.

We are interested in how computers affect productivity and how they affect workers. These related issues have two aspects: how computers influence employment and what they do to wages, morale, and the quality of work life. These issues are critically important in their own right, and they form essential parts of the bridge between technology and its economic consequences.

Employment

Total white-collar employment rose strongly through the 1970s and 1980s; between 1972 and 1982, the number of clerks increased by almost 30 percent and the number of managers by over 40 percent. Blue-collar employment grew over the same period by less than 10 percent (Hunt and Hunt 1986).[1] These data could mean that computers fueled a great expansion of activity in the service sector, that they failed to reduce the labor needed, or both. Osterman (1986) tried to partial out the effects by econometric modeling of changes in deployment of computers and employment of labor. The analysis compared earlier and later years that were at comparable points in the business cycle between 1970 and 1978. Overall, he concluded that greater computerization was associated with less growth in clerical and management employment for the average of a variety of manufacturing and nonmanufacturing industries. On the other hand, he found evidence that computers tended to reduce employment in these categories for the first two years after their introduction and then to increase it for the next two years. He says, "The displacement effect seems to be concentrated in the period immediately following the expansion of computing power. Within a reasonably short time, employment expands, presumably in response to the coordinating or bureaucracy effect. The evidence of this pattern is stronger for managers than for clerks, as should be expected since managers are more likely to benefit from the added bureaucracy effect."[2]

When it comes to employment quality, the situation is even less clear. Real wages have not improved as much in recent decades as in earlier eras, a reflection of labor productivity trends as well as forces that have led to upward redistribution of income. Effects of computers on the wages of their users are mixed. Some computerization, such as bank bookkeeping and utility company billing systems, is intended to allow the same work to be done by workers with less skill and lower pay. However, the overall impact of this strategy is hard to assess. In the insurance business, fewer employees did low-paid routine filing and data entry, and more carried out previously difficult functions like deciding who was a good risk (Baran 1987). In many businesses, the typist of yore has been recast as a word processing clerk with greater training requirements and a higher salary.

There is a host of articles and books on the effects of technology, and of computers in particular, on the quality of work life. Two leading authorities sum it up thus: "Research literature on the impact of new information technologies on job content and job satisfaction provide a mass of contradictory findings" (Attewell and Rule 1984). Apparently phase two computerization can improve work, or degrade it; enrich it, or demean it; make it more challenging, interesting, and comfortable, or duller, more repetitive, and stressful. It figures. Computers are infinitely flexible, powerful devices; they can be used in many ways to make work richer or poorer, better or worse, to bring workers either sickness or health.

One careful study of the effects of a narrowly aimed computerization found both good and bad effects. Kraut, Dumais, and Koch (1989) surveyed and observed several hundred service representatives of a large telephone company before and after a new computer-based billing system replaced the old paper and microfiche records. They found that self-reports of work challenge and overall job satisfaction went down, while indicators of mental health and stress—like headaches—improved. The difficulty of the job decreased for the service representatives but increased for supervisors. In addition, the size of all these effects differed dramatically by office. (We will recount more such facts from this methodologically elegant study in chapter 14.)

Individual Firm Experience

What happens in individual firms as they computerize? Unfortunately, private companies are generally reticent with detailed financial data of this kind, especially if they might reveal mistaken business decisions. There are many anecdotal reports and strong opinions in the popular press and the academic management literature as well, many lauding computers strongly, some critical, but almost none with trustworthy quantitative data. Nevertheless, there are a few useful reports.

Franke's study (1987) of the finance industry included a detailed analysis for one large northeastern bank that shared historical data. The econometric equations for this firm showed the same overall pattern as the industry as a whole, with capital returns somewhat more negative than for the average. An interesting detail from this analysis was the finding that capital was even less effective during the years after the bank began installing automatic teller machines (ATMs).

On the positive side of the bank ledger is a report in *The Office* for February 1976, entitled, "We Increased Typing Productivity 340%" (O'Neal 1976). It recounts the experience of Illinois National Bank of Springfield in moving correspondence typing to a word processing center using telephone-accessed dictating machines and electric typewriters with magnetic card storage. With just six people, according to the author, the new center was able to do work previously done by twelve full-time secretaries and twenty half-time clerk-typists, while cutting turnaround time for letters by 70 percent and increasing typing accuracy and letter image quality tremendously.[3] Among other positive reports is a 1979 survey of insurance companies whose respondents reported average typing output gains per operator of 70 to 85 percent (Baran 1987). Examination of the survey questionnaire suggests, however, that the output gains were estimates based on how much typing was done before word processing was introduced and what proportion was boilerplate and re-typed sections of documents. The authors apparently assumed that word processing would save all that time and took no account of any of its negative effects.

A report of another extensive and possibly more pertinent questionnaire study came out of Quebec in the mid-1980s (Benoit, Cossette, and Cardillo 1984). One hundred twelve organizations, most of them private service businesses, answered detailed questions about technology and employment changes and gave estimates of how many manual typists would be needed to replace the ones that had been equipped with word processors. The subjective estimates agreed closely with the insurance company answers—an average output increase of 80 percent. Actual figures on the number of secretarial employees before and after introducing the machines were not as impressive: a total *increase* of 19 percent. At the same time, the businesses reported that work flows had gone up an average of 58 percent. Dividing one by the other gives a net efficiency gain of 33 percent. Unfortunately, we're not told the source of the greater work flow—for example, whether it represented more business product, new uses of documents, or merely additional drafts.[4]

These reports seem more in line with the kind of effect we've hoped and supposed IT to have. The stampede of American business to word processing centers would suggest that similar experiences were widespread (although many firms subsequently abandoned them because of undesirable organizational side effects). Considerable caution is needed in interpreting the early reports. As we will see shortly, word processing tends to multiply the number of drafts of each document. If the efficiency gains that people claimed were based on pages of output per operator, a common measurement in typing work, the effects could be an illusion. I suspect that the absence of any more recent, more objective studies reflects dawning industry awareness that overall output gains are much less than promoters had claimed. Still, suppose we take these reports at face value. How much help for white-collar productivity would they imply?

A very small proportion of labor time is actually devoted to typing, and typing jobs are relatively low paid, so efficiency gains of this magnitude, especially when offset by expenses, might not even show up in overall white-collar productivity measures. Roughly 5 percent of nonfarm–nonmanufacturing workers are typists or secretaries (Hunt and Hunt 1986). They spend perhaps 60 percent of their time actually typing. If we add in the typing time of people like me whose hunt and pecking is not in their job descriptions, we still can't get more than 5 percent of white-collar hours at the word processor keyboard. Even if the efficiency of this work had increased for everyone by 80 percent, it would be a once-only productivity gain of only 3.2 percent. Amortized over the twenty years since its introduction, its contribution would have slowed the decline by less than 0.1 percent per year.

If there were real gains of 80 percent across all white-collar tasks, it would be a different matter. Then we would be looking at a compounded productivity growth of 3 percent per year. Unfortunately, it appears that effective phase two applications so far exist for very few tasks, and even the best—realistically including word processing—have rather small impact.

To determine what size of efficiency gain *would be* impressive for an individual application, we can look at the effects of technology in industries that have experienced major productivity gains. One of many late-nineteenth-century advances in cotton thread production resulted in three times as much—a 200 percent increase—in the number of yards produced per worker per hour. Cumulative inventions over a fifty-year period reduced required labor hours per yard by a factor of over 150, for a 37,000 percent improvement (Mokyr 1990). Even during the productivity doldrums of the 1970s and 1980s—the very age of the word processor—inventions for thread spinning and weaving brought 400 percent efficiency gains [Baily and Chakrabarti 1988].) Such technological efficiency enhancers are the main driving force of productivity growth.[5] How do such huge improvements in particular processes translate into overall industry productivity? Not directly, of course, and not nearly on a one-to-one basis. The local component of production that is speeded up has to be imbedded and managed in an overall process that may hedge in and limit its impact. Thus, the textile industry exploited its amazing new technologies for a healthy but "mere" 4.2 percent annual multifactor productivity growth from 1973 to 1985. If IT is to fuel major productivity growth, it will probably need to find hundreds of applications with at least tenfold effects, and the improvements will have to be repeated over and over in succeeding decades or less.

Individual Worker Efficiency

Finally we can ask what happens to individual worker efficiency when phase two computer aids are introduced. The most informative data are results of controlled experiments comparing the efficiency and desirability of computer-assisted work to the same work done without a computer. We would like such evidence for all major applications of phase two computer work aids: text editors, spreadsheets, information storage and retrieval systems, order entry and billing systems, inventory management systems, meeting support software, message systems, desktop publishing programs, graphics drawing programs, computer aids for design, automatic teller machines, point-of-sale devices and so on. Unfortunately, very few such programs have been tested against preexisting work methods.

Before loosing drugs on the public, pharmaceutical companies do extensive controlled tests of efficacy in both the laboratory and carefully monitored clinical trials. But software is not usually perceived as a health threat, so most "testing" of its efficacy is left to the uncertain vagaries of the marketplace, where snake oil sometimes triumphs. Nevertheless, there has been a sufficient number of well-controlled studies of several types of systems to provide an instructive, if not conclusive, sample. The results of such studies are of special interest.

Let's start with one of the most encouraging—a case study of telephone service representatives and their new billing records system (Kraut, Dumais, and Koch 1989). The researchers did not have access to company productivity records but did get reports of the number of tasks completed per day from the reps themselves, who keep track of their performance as part of their job. With the new system, they reported processing approximately 50 percent more customer interactions each day. The time saving came mostly from being able to pull up records instantly on the screen rather than engaging in the clerk's three Fs, fishing, ficheing, and fetching. We don't know whether they were more effective in making collections or satisfying customers (and there's some reason to believe these aspects could have suffered), but at least we have here a likely case of significant labor efficiency improvement. An important aspect of this finding is that the system studied is only one of a large number of similar systems introduced by telephone companies over the last twenty years, and we will shortly see circumstantial evidence that its achievements were not unusual.

Next to put in evidence are some controlled experiments on the effectiveness of text editing (table 2.1). Gould (1981) enlisted ten office professionals from his organization, IBM research, as subjects. They were all accustomed to writing letters in the traditional way—penciling a draft and passing it to a typist—but were also familiar with a computer-based text editing program. Each wrote four business letters the old way and four with the text editor. The four letters were of different types, ranging from dull sales information transmittals to unpleasant late-payment negotiations. Letters produced with word processing were modified an average of forty-one times, handwritten ones only eight. Other office professionals found no discernible differences in quality. Handwritten letters took an average of twenty-one minutes of the professionals' time for composition and proofreading, plus fourteen minutes of secretaries' time, for a total of thirty-five minutes labor. Text editor letters took an average of only thirty minutes, but all by the professional. If, for the sake of illustration, we assume the professionals' time to be worth $20 per hour and the typists' $10 per hour, the text editor–produced letters cost $9.83 apiece in direct labor costs, handwritten ones $9.44.

Stuart Card of Xerox's Palo Alto Research Center, a laboratory that nurtured many widely acclaimed advances in user-friendly computing, found it difficult to accept Gould's results. Gould, he said, had used an early model of word processor, a so-called line editor, one in which the user has to tell the machine where to make a correction by typing arbitrary "commands" (for example, "7s/hte/the" to correct a misspelled word in the seventh line). Card knew that newer full screen or display editors, in which the user simply positions a mark on the screen to indicate the text that needs changing, were easier to use (Egan and Gomez

Table 2.1
Two experiments on text editors versus handwriting

	Number	Time (min.)	Pay rate	Cost
Gould (1981)				
By hand and typist:				
Composing		19.2	$20/hr.	$6.40
Typing		13.9	$10/hr.	$2.31
Modifications	8.5			
Proofreading		2.2	$20/hr.	$0.73
Total		35.3		**$9.44**
With a computer text editor:				
Composing		29.5	$20/hr.	$9.83
Typing				
Modifications	41.3			
Proofreading				
Total		29.5		**$9.83**
Card, Robert, and Keenan (1984)				
By hand and typist:				
Composing		21.7	$20/hr.	$7.23
Typing		13.9	$10/hr.	$2.31
Modifications	5.0			
Proofreading		2.2	$20/hr.	$0.73
Total		37.8		**$10.27**
With a computer text editor:				
Composing		22.8	$20/hr.	$7.60
Typing				
Modifications	23.5			
Proofreading				
Total		22.8		**$7.60**

1985; Gomez et al. 1983; Roberts and Moran 1983). However, such editors had not, like the one Gould tested, been compared to precomputer technology for the same tasks, so Card performed an experiment of much the same kind as Gould's, using a better, more up-to-date text editing program (Card, Robert, and Keenan 1984). Appropriately to the changing times, participants were habitual and proficient users of text editors. Except for the text editor, the Xerox group copied Gould's experiment in most respects: the same paired sets of four business letters, half by handwriting, half by text editor, and so forth. An expert on English composition did the blind quality ratings.[6]

The new results were barely more encouraging than the old. Again, authors made about five times as many revisions with the text editor, and again there was no appreciable difference in quality. In time spent, there was less disadvantage to the text editor method for Card's authors than for Gould's; they took twenty-three minutes to compose a letter with the computer, hardly any longer than the twenty-two minutes they spent handwriting one. Card did not report transcription times for the handwritten letters. However, since the instructions were the same and the letters were of almost identical length, it seems appropriate to use Gould's transcription times to calculate total costs. This has been done in table 2.1. As shown, if the author's time is worth twice a typist's time, the estimated total labor cost of a letter is now about 26 percent less using the text editor, an encouraging but not impressive difference, especially if the additional labor costs for learning and maintaining the technology are taken into account.[7]

The results from these text editor experiments are particularly distressing for two reasons. First, they are controlled experiments, not subjective reports of managers who have committed themselves to the technology. Second, the investigators in these experiments were exceptionally competent and worked for companies with a vested interest in computerized office technology, so it's unlikely that the results were biased against computers.[8]

There are probably better uses for text editors than having professionals use them to produce their own business letters. The survey results from the insurance industry and from Quebec businesses suggest that typing pools equipped with word processors are 33 percent to 100 percent more productive than typists with typewriters, although we need to worry whether the respondents were counting drafts or finished output. Presumably the use of text editors for legal documents such as contracts, which often need a large number of revisions and final drafts that are letter perfect, would show even bigger benefits. I know of no good data for such specialized applications, although they may have formed part of the work behind the insurance company reports. Of course, there may also be applications of word processing that are less productive than the ones studied in the experiments. For example, many professional scholars, university professors, and industry and government scientists have been migrated away from the use of secretarial help toward the typing of their own manuscripts on computers. Here, since the salary of the person to whom the job has been moved is usually very much higher than that of the people whose job it used to be—perhaps three to five times as high—and the scholar or professional's skill at typing relatively lower, it seems likely that the true economics are positively terrible. One survey (Sassone 1992) confirms this expectation.

The other day I was printing out this section for local distribution. Table 2.1 got automatically separated onto two different pages, with a long footnote in between. At one point there were three expert users in my office for fifteen minutes trying (fruitlessly) to figure out how to fix it.

The area of phase two computer application for which the most extensive comparison data are available is computer-aided instruction (CAI). Instruction was the domain of some of the earliest attempts to use computers to help people better use their time and brains. Emerging in the mid-1960s, CAI even predated the popularization of text editing programs. Probably because the early versions of CAI were largely the work of academic educational researchers, for whom the testing of novel teaching methods against standard approaches is a professional obligation, the relative effectiveness of these systems was evaluated in literally hundreds of experiments.[9] Not all of the results were positive, but most were. Applications to the teaching of well-defined technical topics were most successful, and their use in industrial and military training was the most extensive. Researchers reported that such applications, when done well, reduced learning time by around 30 percent (Clark 1985; Eberts and Brock 1988; Kulik, Kulik, and Shwalb 1986; Kulik, Kulik, and Cohen 1980; Orlansky and String 1979).[10] Because industrial training is a big expense, and getting bigger with the information revolution, improvements of such magnitude, if repeated in following generations, could make a significant contribution.

Unfortunately, some caveats are needed. First, most of the gain from "computerizing" instruction apparently comes from careful analysis and pruning of the content, followed by detailed planning of the order in which core facts and skills should be introduced, and especially from individualized instruction. Individualized instruction allows students to progress at their own rates, rather than all moving at the rate that most members of a class can handle. Thus, if ten students each learn at their own speed, the average completion time is the average of ten individual learning times. If the same ten students learn in a standard classroom, the teacher will probably go at a speed that keeps the eight best students on board—likely to be about two-thirds as fast.[11]

Although good analysis and individualization is essential, or at least obviously desirable, for computer-based instruction, it is often employed without computers. Indeed, it has been institutionalized under the title of "instructional technology" (Clark 1985; Eberts and Brock 1988; Gagne 1974, 1987; Kulik, Kulik, and Schwalb 1986; Kulik, Kulik, and Cohen 1980; Orlansky and String 1979), which customarily uses only lectures, standard audiovisual aids, and printed materials. Even when administered with only traditional media, individualized instruction produces large improvements in learning efficiency (Block and Bums 1978; Bloom 1984). Thus, the role of the computer as such in CAI gains is not obvious.[12] Of course, if putting a lesson on a computer encourages better teaching, or if it makes the process cheaper, replacing all or part of a teacher's time without adding compensating expenses, there would still be good reason to adopt CAI.

After almost thirty years, however, CAI has made only small inroads into education and training. The main reason is probably not lack of effectiveness, although CAI is easier to apply effectively to some kinds of material than others. Desirability is probably an important factor; many people want personal interaction between students and teacher. Cost may be the biggest hurdle. The cost of writing good materials and programs for computer-based lessons can run two to many hundred times that for preparing traditional classroom lessons (Avner 1979). Add outlays for hardware, maintenance, operation, space, and administration, and CAI may not compete well with its paper-based instructional counterparts. Thus, the promise of 30 percent efficiency gains, which also, apparently, did not multiply with succeeding generations, did not succeed in greatly reducing human labor in instruction.[13]

Another phase two computer application that has been compared with noncomputerized benchmarks is the retrieval and presentation of textual information. These systems have seen widespread use in bibliographical searching—that is, finding not the actual article or book that the searcher wants to read but a reference to where to look for it in paper or microfilm. Usually the electronic reference is identified by title, author, publisher, date, a few subject category nouns, and, sometimes, a short abstract of its contents. There is a large literature of theory and tests concerning how well such systems succeed in returning all and only those references that a user wants (we will discuss some of this research later.) Unfortunately, few compare how well the highly evolved prior technologies of card catalogs and paper indexes serve the same purposes. Generally the proponents of electronic information retrieval have been pleased if people using the systems do as well with them as with so-called manual methods using printed sources (Cleverdon 1979). The two techniques usually produce rather different qualitative results; online methods search more potential titles, but manual methods detect relevance more intelligently. One doleful conclusion is that "an on-line search cannot substitute for a manual search and vice-versa: the two methods complement each other" (Murphy 1985, 178). If libraries do *both* kinds of searches for a request, there will be no cost savings.

A handful of rather limited studies have sought to compare search times and overall costs (East 1980; Murphy 1985; Roose 1985), but the cost accounting and evaluation methods in these studies leave much to be desired; for example, they do not always involve the same search topics, or there are no exhaustive search data available with which to compare, or the cost of equipment or training, on the one hand, or of printed source material, on the other, are omitted. Nevertheless, the results are encouraging. Librarian work times range from around two-thirds as long for online as for manual searches down to as low as one-seventh. That is, labor productivity for reference librarians in this aspect of their job improved by factors of 70 percent to 600 percent. Labor costs for provision of the online service were not broken out but are included implicitly in the service provider's charges. Overall the total cost of manual and online searches appears to be roughly the same. However, the most recent of these studies is now eight years old (a noteworthy and discouraging fact itself). It is likely that computer and communications costs have come down considerably, although other components, such as average royalty payments, probably have increased.

An interesting aspect of this case is the way IT has been used. For manual searches, each library maintains its own extensive and expensive set of reference books and indexes. Online computerized systems use a single centralized set of databases to serve a large number of libraries. If the systems allowed libraries to dispense with their own reference-work collections, the efficiency advantage could be significant. Individual libraries should reap large savings in book purchases and storage space, as well as library staff time. But experience so far has been duplication rather than replacement of resources. I have been unable to find any documentation of such "cooperative operations" savings, or of any remarkable decrease in relevant library staff employment.[14] Indeed, a whole new employment category of library personnel has evolved: information specialists, who know how to use the various computer systems and the myriad databases, each with its own method of operation, to which the systems are connected.

Often such systems allow the searcher—or the searcher's trained intermediary—to locate materials in many far-off places: libraries throughout the California university system, for example, or legal abstracts stored on a single immense, centrally located, commercial database. Such a facility can be a powerful tool for scholars, lawyers, physicians, business analysts, and other intensive knowledge workers. The commercial success of the remote database industry, represented by such firms as Dialog, Mead Data, and Dow-Jones, implies that these new computer-based services add significant real value to the economy. Yet their net productivity, as compared to other methods for doing the same work, is hard to assess. The same intensive culling, indexing, and abstracting by subject matter experts is required, and insofar as similar compendia have been provided in paper books (for example, *Index Medicus* or *Chemical Abstracts*), the principal advantages of the computerized versions are speed and economy of delivery and updating—that is, telephone line access instead of printing and physical shipping—plus the savings in shelf and office space. Each lawyer, chemist, or stock analyst needs only a terminal instead of a multivolume paper document. Obviously, if these economies result in more useful knowledge for more people, there is another significant gain. But how the dollar value of all these advantages stacks up against their added computer, communication, and specialist costs is not known.

A recent addition to the area of computer applications is hypertext. Hypertext uses computers to deliver and display the full content of written information rather than just references to it; the information is supplemented by links between segments of text, and between text and figures, data, references, and notes, all of which can be brought to the screen with a click of the mouse. I have found nine studies comparing hypertext with old-fashioned paper book technology as a means for people to find and absorb information. In only two of these studies was the computer-based method superior, and this particular system is quite different from almost all the many hypertext systems on the market. In most cases, hypertext actually *decreased* user efficiency relative to paper and ink. In one especially telling case, both objective performance and user satisfaction were significantly worse with hypertext, despite the fact that the text was explicitly designed for a popular hypertext program. We will go into the matter of hypertext, and the design of SuperBook, an exceptional case, in detail later.

There are several other phase two applications for which strong claims have been accompanied by reports of study "data." Although some of these results are tantalizing, none is convincing. For example, it has been claimed that "groupware"—computer systems to help run meetings—reduces meeting time needed to plan and manage projects by half. Such an effect could have significant productivity implications because a large portion of the time of highly paid managers and professionals is spent in meetings. But the "controls" in these studies are merely estimates by either the authors or the participants of how much time would have been needed without the computer system. Such estimates are much too vulnerable to bias to be taken seriously. By contrast, a survey of all published controlled behavioral experiments (McLeod 1992) found that although they improve decision quality slightly, such systems usually significantly *increased* the time groups spent making decisions.

There are also phase two systems for which no objective comparison data are available but which are so widely used with such apparent success and strong testimonial acclaim that it is hard to doubt their effectiveness. The prime example is computer-aided design (CAD). These systems help designers of integrated circuit chips, airplane wings, or buildings get all the parts in all the right places. Circuit design is probably the most important use of this technology. Very large-scale integrated (VLSI) circuits can have millions of components that have to be connected by millions of wirelike conducting paths. The components have to be arranged so that they can dissipate heat without destroying each other. All the paths have to go to and from the right places. To be efficient, and sometimes even to work at all, all or most of the paths have to be as short as possible. And the whole design has to be verifiable by inspection of some sort. All this poses a daunting, probably impossible, task for an unaided human. But the task is not yet fully automated; a highly skilled human who can see and think the whole layout is still needed. The computer system helps by making it easy to copy, multiply, and move components, by suggesting component placements and path arrangements based on computationally intensive algorithms, and by doing much of the checking. It is said that the use of such systems reduces the time to design complex circuits by large factors.

The productivity effects of these tools has been felt most directly in the computer industry itself, which has shown extraordinary growth. The effect in other industries has apparently been less, probably because design is not so difficult without computers and because design work is not as large a contributor to costs or effectiveness. The fraction of labor time spent in design is limited. CAD systems take months to learn, sometimes years to master. No one can make a computer chip without CAD, but for other products, their value is often marginal. An architect may prefer to sharpen her pencil. Much of the popularity of CAD is not attributable to actual salary savings for designers but to belief that CAD will reduce the cycle time to get a high-tech product to market. This may be a critical consideration for a competitive company, but the productivity effect is negligible.[15] Since the real payoff for CAD is in the new or improved products they make possible, we would have to turn to indirect economic and business success data for evidence, discouraging evidence that we have already reviewed.

Let us take one last well-known, and disappointing, example. ATMs, automatic teller machines for banking, are almost always thrown up as a counterexample when I give talks on this material. Members of my usual audiences—primarily computer scientists, human factors professionals, R&D managers, high-tech business types—are near-unanimous fans of ATMs. Yet banks have experienced neither overall productivity gains nor reduction in clerical staffs as a result of their introduction. Nor have they generally offered higher interest, lower transaction fees, or other incentives for the use of ATMs. Indeed, many banks make additional charges for ATM use. What's up? A fascinating study of a large western bank chain tells the tale (Haynes 1990). Of all customers with debit cards for the company's wide network of machines, only a third ever used an ATM, and among those who did, the average use was once per month. Overall, only about 5 percent of all customer banking transactions were completed with ATMs. Most of the planned economies from the machines were based on expectations of much higher use, of many more labor-saving transactions to offset the costs of hardware, servicing, and real estate for their location. Haynes quotes estimates that ATMs as used reduced a bank's cost for a transaction by roughly half as compared to a teller transaction. Over the whole country this would represent a multimillion dollar cost saving. However, the small proportion of business costs involved, especially in relation to the rather large capital and management expenditures, does not add up to a significant influence on bank productivity. We will have more to say later about why those who love ATMs love them, why the transaction rate is so low, and why banks have chosen to deploy them so aggressively.

What about all the myriad other uses of computers? Sadly, for both the analysis and for progress, I have about exhausted the available direct data on productivity and efficiency effects (table 2.2). For some applications there is indirect evidence from which we can draw tentative infer-

Table 2.2
Summary of work efficiency effects of phase two computer applications

Application	Evidence	Improvement with computer
Word processing	Experimental studies	Worse to +25%
	Survey reports*	+33 to 100%
Computer-aided instruction	Meta-analyses*	**+30%**
Information retrieval	Studies of users	**None** to +500%
	Estimates for librarians*	+70 to 600%
Electronic document delivery	Studies of users	**Worse** to +100%
Meeting support systems	Experimental studies	**None**
ATMs	Usage analysis, $ benefit	Almost nil

Note: Estimates with asterisks require cautious interpretation for reasons given in the text. Estimates in boldface type are based on several to many studies, those in regular type on only one.

ences. For example, consider all the applications of PCs for use in the home. The productivity effects of home computers, and services and software to go with them, are quite difficult to assess. The government does not try to measure the productivity of domestic households, and none of the economists interested in the productivity crises has either. We have already reviewed evidence on several kinds of programs that such machines often support: text editors, information retrieval systems, and instructional software. But home computers are also usable for many other purposes for which we lack similar data. It appears from various surveys that a high proportion are not used at all, and that among those that are, the primary use is for playing games. The extent and time-efficiency effects of home computers for tasks like budgeting, bill paying, and tax return preparation have not been properly evaluated, to my knowledge. Because home computers are used only occasionally by a small number of people, they must have a minor effect on total private time utilization. (Compare their time-saving effects, price, and learning time with washing machines, vacuum cleaners, and clothes dryers.)

There have been several attempts to apply home computers to facilitate other services, for example, information services supplied over telephone lines. In the United States, Canada, Japan, and most of Europe these have gone through several cycles of failure. Although fairly large numbers of network memberships have been sold, such services have not been financially successful. The nearest to successful is the French Minitel system, which, begun in 1980, will break even on the enormous investment of the French government in 1993, 1995, or 1998, depending on which of three audits you believe (Pinsky 1991). The secret of French success, in addition to the large social investment (France Telecom initially distributed half a million free terminals and will have spent $7 billion by break-even), appears to have been a comparatively simple, easy-to-use interface and the market evolution of many thousands of different services that can be accessed through the network. Recent evidence suggests that the French data network has reduced transaction costs for the businesses that use it but that their overall return on investment has yet to show an effect.[16]

Because there are so many uncontrolled factors, inferences about productivity from facts about market success and usage are not very compelling and will not be pursued further in this chapter. Similarly, there have been many reports of good and bad user experiences with various computer applications, but it is impossible to add them together for an estimate of net productivity. These kinds of evidence will be important in later chapters, where we consider how to make things better.

Silver Linings

In this long stream of dismal productivity trends, comparisons, and individual efficiency studies, a few fish swim against the tide. These successes are particularly important to examine because they may offer clues about what is wrong (in the data or in the effort) in the other cases, and they may point a better way. We will consider the source of exceptions at the individual efficiency level—where we have just seen a number of modest successes—in later chapters. Here we concentrate on the only major service industry that has maintained strong productivity growth into the information age: the telephone business.

Despite all the negative results to date, the promise of computers for productivity is tremendous. But given the length of time they have been around, one would think that if they really have great potential, some-

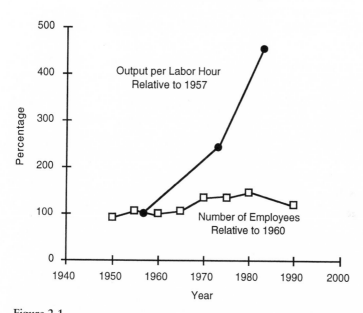

Bell System Labor Productivity

Figure 2.1.
Bell Company (plus AT&T after 1984) employment and labor productivity. Data from FCC and Baily 1986.

where someone should have pulled off a major, lasting productivity success with them. There is such an example: the telephone industry.[17] We saw evidence of this before in the relatively healthy overall productivity gains of communications as a whole in the critical phase two computerization years following 1973. We also saw that the telecommunications sector is the only major service industry with top-ranking productivity results. According to the Bureau of Labor Statistics, dollar output per labor hour grew by 6.1 percent per year from 1957 to 1973 and by 6.7 percent from 1973 to 1983 (figure 2.1). There was no post-1973 slowdown but, rather, a modest acceleration in labor productivity growth.

There is even more direct and impressive evidence. Between 1950 and 1990 the number of access lines (essentially lines with separate telephone numbers) increased fourfold, while the number of employees needed to install, operate, and maintain them grew by less than 40 percent. Measuring productivity as customer lines per full-time employee, the companies averaged 2.7 percent gains each year from 1950 to 1970 and 3.6 percent from 1970 to 1990. Employees per line is a rather interesting pure labor productivity measure but somewhat conservative.

Later lines were much more useful; they connected to many more destinations and did so faster and with better sound quality.[18] At the same time real (after inflation) wages of telephone employees increased, work hours per employee decreased, the cost of telephone service went down, revenues grew steadily, and shareholders earned respectable returns and appreciation. Some of the data are shown in figures 2.2 and 2.3.

Thus in telephony there was obvious and substantial improvement over the time period in which phase two computing was integrated into the business. (Note that we can't measure telephone business productivity meaningfully in terms of return on investment because the public utility commissions set a fixed rate.) The telephone business was able to continue America's traditional double-time march of progress: the industry cut costs, improved its product, lowered prices, and generated ever increasing demand whose supply created ever more jobs at ever higher wages.[19]

There were other credible contributions to these gains besides the effects of computerization: lower unit costs of transmission facilities, lower per line cost of switching equipment, and increased labor efficiency due to more reliable and easy-to-handle hardware. Probably the rapid expansion of the total telephone service market as more people were connected more easily to more people, and consequently made more calls, played an important role. However, a large part of the productivity improvement also has to be attributed to what telephone people call mechanization. The biggest and earliest, and continuing, mechanization was of the job of connecting a calling line with a receiving line. The switches that do that work in response to rotary dial pulses or keypad tones are, and always have been, computers. The first ones, introduced in the 1920s (initially by independents, then by Bell System companies), were fairly crude electromechanical devices (although some operating on the same principles are still in service). Nevertheless they perform the same function as their modern digital, VLSI-based replacements. They "compute" and establish a path between two points. They were, of course, special-purpose computers but computers nonetheless.

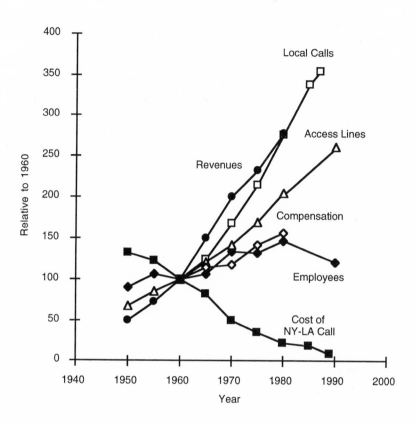

Figure 2.2.
Productivity in the Bell System before divestiture and the regional telephone companies plus AT&T thereafter. Data from FCC and BLS in constant dollars relative to 1960.

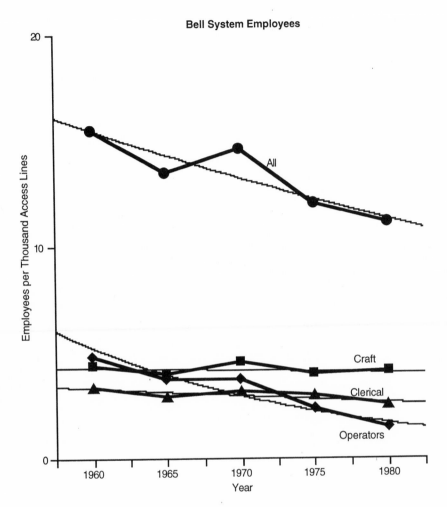

Figure 2.3.
Change in ratio of employees to customer lines in Bell System companies, 1960–1980. Data from FCC and Bellcore.

Switching machines are the purest of pure automation computers. Each succeeding generation of switching computer has enabled telephone companies to connect more lines, faster, and at lower capital and operation labor cost per line. (If we were still doing it entirely by hand we would need over 3 million telephone operators to handle today's calls, if we could.) However, their effect in reducing the total number of employees needed was slowing rapidly long before the last manual switchboard was melted down. As the number of lines and the volume of traffic grew, there was a continuing potential increase in labor requirements because each line entailed a telephone number, an order to process, a monthly bill, and an opportunity for repair, and each call presented the possibility of a request for assistance in finding a number or collecting a toll. After about 1960, we might have expected at least a linear increase in labor costs as the network expanded. Each new customer or call added increased demand for employee services. Actually, the number of employees needed to provide the services would grow even faster than the number of new customers because the complexity of some of the individual jobs depends on how many total customers and calls there are. When a caller asks for a telephone number, the directory assistance operator takes longer to find it if there are a hundred thousand listings than if there are only twenty thousand. It also takes a billing clerk longer to find a record, a cable splicer longer to find a particular wire pair, and so forth the more of them there are. Some such tasks may tend to require labor in proportion to the square of the number of lines rather than just in proportion to the number.

To keep costs down as the customer and traffic base grew, starting in the mid-1960s, the telephone companies began to develop phase two computer applications to ease and speed the work of employees; deployment on a large scale got underway in the 1970s. These operations support systems have been primarily databases used to keep track of all the wires, cables, repeaters, plug-in circuits, trucks, addresses, telephone numbers, bills, and payments and to help in the planning, designing, and administering of the network. Most of these functions still require human intelligence; only certain record-keeping, calculation, and printing or display aspects of the jobs are performed by the computers, and usually in close collaboration with workers. Although the development and deployment paths of these systems have often been rough and their net effects on labor productivity not always immediately favorable, in the aggregate long term they have made a major contribution to keeping costs down. The number of employees per line continued to fall even after full automation of switching and even as the size and complexity of the network expanded rapidly; from 1965 to 1990, the number of lines more than doubled—and the traffic and complexity grew much more—but employment rose by only 14 percent.

Prior to the break-up of AT&T, the Federal Communications Commission collected detailed information on the number of telephone employees and their jobs (figure 2.3). In terms of number of workers for each thousand customer lines, the biggest gains from 1960 to 1980 were in operators, representing a continuation of automation of connection, especially long distance, plus augmentation of directory assistance and specially billed calls. There were also significant gains in efficiency for clerical jobs. The craft jobs of installation, maintenance, and repair continued to demand almost the same effort on a per line basis despite improvements in equipment but also despite the growing size and complexity of the system.

How did the telephone companies succeed where, it seems, most others failed? Part of the reason probably lies in the kinds of tasks supported by computing. The telephone companies had huge numbers of employees doing a number of well-subdivided, highly routinized tasks. Many of these jobs were well understood and had already been reduced to simple "if this, do that" operations that were relatively easy to automate or aid. For example, many jobs involved entering, correcting, or retrieving information from paper records, or creating tabulations, reports, or work orders on the basis of information received from a customer or employee or displayed by a switching machine. Often the computer could be an effective aid merely by putting all needed information in one convenient place so that employees did not have to search physically separated file drawers and make copies and transcriptions by hand. But the most important factor in the success of telephone operation mechanizations was the way in which they were designed and evolved. In particular, AT&T and the Bell System companies had a long tradition—to some extent mandated by their regulated status and in some ways directly assisted by statisticians at the Federal Communications Commissions and other public utility commissions—of careful, objective, quantitative monitoring of the efficiency of office and business operations. Moreover, meaningful quantitative measurements of labor efficiency were relatively easy to obtain: time to handle collect and directory assistance calls, number of equipment troubles and the time to fix them, and so forth. In addition, because of the crucial importance of reliability in the telephone system, telephone companies always test new computer systems extensively with real operators handling real work loads before they replace old procedures or systems. (It is surprising how rare such testing is in other business applications.) All this provided the kind of feedback that I will argue is the most critical need for progress in phase two computing. We will return to more detailed description of this aspect of the case later.[20]

"If you look back a few years, our personal lines operation, for example, had 80 to 100 field offices. And all of the policies . . . were in tub files and desks in those offices. So if you wanted to see all the policies you would have to go to 90 offices and read through 2 million policies in tubs and desks. Then all of a sudden a person could just issue a few commands to the computer and we'd zip through it for him. That's a huge change." Larry Bacon, senior vice president of information systems, Travelers Companies (National Research Council 1994a)

"During the three year period from 1989 through 1991, we reduced our annual output of computer-generated print from 1.3 billion to about 400 million pages . . . downloading print files electronically to client desktops and providing the ability to view information directly from computer screens." Howard Sorgen, senior vice president and chief technology officer, Merrill Lynch & Company (National Research Council 1994a)

No other segment of the service economy nearly as important as telephony has a good record with computers, but there are individual firms and activities within firms that have posted notable successes. A well-known company success story is the case of Federal Express. Through a combination of bar codes, hand-held devices, and a widespread computer network that enables it to track and manage each package, it was able to implement guaranteed next-day delivery service, a new and profitable form of business.

Within companies, the process of handling complex orders has given rise to most of the dramatic reports of efficiency gains from computers. Most of these gains are in turnaround time, but often labor is also greatly reduced by making records more accessible and reducing hand-offs, checking, and error correction. Retailers such as Wal-Mart and Kmart have plugged their stores into computer networks that collect statistics on what sizes of clothing are needed and what CDs are selling, thus reducing waste, stocking labor, and accounting.

We will see more of these tantalizing examples later when we analyze why there have been so few and how we can get more.

3

The Productivity Paradox

The subject of this book is computers—their problems and how to make them better—but the analysis has taken us deep into the broader puzzle of stunted productivity growth. Before going on about computers in particular, let us see if what we've learned suggests an explanation of the overall productivity problem.

The Productivity Slowdown: A Hypothesis

The United States, with the rest of the industrial nations lined up a few steps behind, has learned to automate its factories and agriculture so that little human labor is needed. About a third of the population produces almost everything people used to want—food, clothes, cars, trinkets, houses. It turns out, though, that the rest of us aren't ready to retire. So as a society, we've had to invent new work to do for each other and pay each other for doing—a new set of exchanges. We cook meals for each other, take in each other's dry cleaning, entertain each other, govern each other, write books and produce movies for each other, take each other on long trips, care for each other when sick, and organize gambling games—finance and insurance, lawsuits, lately banking. These activities are not entirely new, but they are being greatly expanded as a proportion of production and consumption. They are called, loosely, "services." Most of the work is "information work."

Trouble is, this kind of work, doesn't have as good a ratio of labor hours to dollars paid for the output as do the highly automated means of production for food and other tangibles. Service labor productivity is generally lower than that for goods-producing industries (Maddison 1991). It's not entirely clear why. Maybe services are not inherently as valuable as food, shelter, defense, and things. Maybe there's something unfathomable in the way money and services get related to each other; perhaps the market economy simply makes an hour's worth of someone's service labor worth the same amount to the buyer as to the seller (as some government measures of productivity do). I don't believe these two theories. Once adequately fed, housed, and bored, a person ought to be willing to give up a twentieth pair of shoes for a good meal or massage. A simple amplifier turns one hour of a musician's time into a hundred hours of listeners' enjoyment; a television broadcast raises the productivity ratio much more.

A better explanation is that most services, unlike telephony, don't know how to use capital productively. It is an economic truism that productivity gains come from the substitution of capital for labor. Before computers, service industries were stingy in putting capital to work for workers. Services didn't use many machines and were not much automated because most of the work is mental, and, before the computer, machines to help mental work were few and far behind.

The service industries have expanded. In the United States they employed 54 percent of the work force in 1950 and 63 percent in 1987, while their productivity grew at less than 1 percent per year. In Germany, the comparable numbers were 35 percent and 55 percent, with 2 percent annual productivity growth (McKinsey Global Institute 1992). Thus a large number of workers have migrated from industries with high output per worker to ones with lower output and slower growth. Although the workers may be doing similar tasks, the service industry is turning out less added value because it does not exploit capital as well. The reason is that sufficient high-quality capital, in the form of effective augmentation technology, is not to be had.[1]

How has the service sector managed to expand so strongly? I think the exhaustion of opportunities in manufacturing is the push and information technology is the wagon. New jobs were needed, so new services were invented. Many new or expanded services depended on computers: a plethora of investment instruments—complex new mutual funds and trading schemes, a deluge of new insurance policy types and options, a myriad of debit and credit cards, dozens of new kinds of bank accounts and novel banking services offered from widely dispersed branches and machines, multitudes of new medical diagnosis techniques and therapies, fast food restaurants, fast copy stores, fully filled planes with frequent flyer plans, mom and pop mail order firms, direct marketing, PC maintenance, and so forth.

"Aetna Insurance Company once analyzed the impact of IT on expense-revenue ratios over a 15 year period. Although the study concluded that IT had had little impact on these ratios, it also noted that the company could never have increased its handling of health insurance claims from 250,000 per week to 1.3 million per week without using IT." (National Research Council 1994a, 101).

Computers made these expansions possible but didn't make them any more productive. Indeed, productivity growth in services, always slower than in other sectors but nevertheless measurable, virtually ground to a halt after 1973 (McKinsey Global Institute 1992). Service sector managers bought most of the computers made in this era. They needed computers to keep up with exploding work loads in traditional jobs—many more checks cashed, many more rental cars reserved. They needed computers to support new lines of business—index funds, automated blood tests.

Service managers thought that buying computers would set straight the imbalance in capital support for work—that computers would do for service productivity what the assembly line and fertilizer had done for tangibles. They were misled. IT made it possible to do more work but not to do work more productively. Usually each added dollar's worth of IT capital produced just a dollar's worth of output before it was retired. The new workers produced about the same amount of added value each day as did the old. The total new output from services just about equaled the total new input in IT equipment and the labor hours it required.[2]

The proposed explanation of the productivity slowdown thus goes like this. IT was used primarily to expand the service sector. It created more output, thus supporting more jobs—many of them supporting the IT itself—and allowed the absolute size of the economy to grow along with the working population, despite shrinking opportunities in manufacturing and farming. However, the newly created work was not significantly more productive than the old.

This view of the productivity story casts the computer in an odd role: both the hero, the rescuer of work life, and the villain, the slacker that flattens our standard of living. This view nevertheless resolves the paradox in our perception of computers. We see them as wonderful engines of the modern economy and are perplexed that productivity has stagnated since their arrival. But there is no contradiction. Both as product, where they've shored up average manufacturing productivity, and as tools, where they have enabled expansion of the service sector, they have performed impressively. Success, however, did not require that they increase productivity, *only* that they made possible more work at the same productivity level. Service expansion depended on computers. The new products, processes, and conveniences are just affordable with computers; they would have been impossible or prohibitively expensive without them.

We are now left not so much with a paradox or puzzle about computers as merely with a problem. We can be proud of them for keeping us going but would like them to help us go faster. So we have come back toward our main track: Why are computers not better productivity tools, and what can we do about it? Before joining these issues directly, we have a few untied strands to deal with—objections to the computer productivity conclusions—and will take these up in the next chapter. Meanwhile, let us review the bidding.

Summary of the Evidence against Computers

Beginning around 1985, a few economists began to sing the blues about a disappointing love affair between American business and computers. Since then, the refrain of these soloists has turned into a chorus. I have replayed here all the major themes: the downturn of productivity growth over time coincident with widespread computerization, the concentration of growth failure in industries most heavily involved, the failure of labor productivity in services to respond positively to lavish information technology, the long-term lack of correlation of business success with investment in this new technology. And we have looked closely, wherever a view was to be had, at the direct effects of computers as they try to lend a hand to people at work. Almost everything points to the conclusion that computers have failed to work wonders for productivity. Yet there are exceptions to raise hope at each level of the story: some apparently successful countries, industries, programs. Our next endeavor will be to understand why the majority of the picture looks so grim. Both negative and positive cases should help us find an explanation, which should lead to a response.

II

Solutions to the Puzzle

I have presented the material covered this far many times to audiences of computer professionals. At this point hands wave all over the audience. People are eager to refute the apparent implications of all these facts. Many of the refutations consist only of declarations of love for the computer or recount some special program or function that he or she "could not do without." Another form of refutation is to point to known success stories, like computer-aided design or bank bookkeeping or to note the large number of sales, and penetration in numbers of, for example, PCs, spreadsheet programs, and ATMs. If these products have sold so well they must be good, the reasoning runs. Certainly this is all true in a sense. But if these uses of computers have not increased productivity—and it seems they have not—then we need to find some other explanation of their popularity.

Clearly the introduction of computers has not had the dramatic effects on measurable productivity and living standards that other comparable technological revolutions have. We must understand why this is or appears to be true and also, if possible, why computers have nevertheless become so popular, before we can move on to well-founded discussion of where the trouble lies—if trouble there is—and what to do about it.

The objective evidence seems quite at odds with the widespread perception and advertisement of computers as effective productivity tools. So on what are the enthusiastic opinions based? I believe they come partly from commercial promotion and media hype, but primarily from word-of-mouth testimonials by users. However testimonials, no matter how earnest, are poor evidence; they can be found to support all sorts of magical cures for cancer, ways to beat the stock market, or lose weight.

The Card (1984) word processing study is an especially telling example. Card, a leading expert in human-computer interface research and design, as well as a regular computer user, initiated the research because he shared the popular conviction that word processing greatly improved productivity in document preparation. He was sure that Gould's earlier negative results must have been a fluke or due to the use of a no-good primitive text editor. He was confident that a well-done experiment using the "vastly" better newer style of full-screen text editing would show major advantages. He was wrong. The new style of text editing was only marginally better than the old and did not provide a substantial productivity benefit.

The point is this: If such expert judgment can be so overoptimistic, how much should we trust the testimonials of ordinary users? Still, it seems that the conclusion that computers are failing us is against intuition and common sense. In such a situation it is prudent to examine the evidence very carefully, to see whether there is something wrong with the data or inferences, whether there is not some more palatable explanation of the facts. If we cannot outright explain away all the unwelcome evidence, then we ought to consider all plausible reasons for the phenomenon before looking for ways to deal with it. In the next two chapters, we take these two routes in turn. Telegraphing my conclusion in the matter, the first route, criticizing the evidence, is covered under the heading "excuses"; while the second route, chasing down the possible real causes, is treated under "reasons."

4

Excuses

Given that the computer business has become a major industry, employing in one way or another well over a million people and causing hundreds of billions of dollars a year to change hands, it's hard to accept the implication that these machines bring no net improvement in economic efficiency. Certainly they must be delivering something of value to the millions of people plunking down hard cash for them. Since computers seem to have been designed and intended as productivity tools, to help work get done more efficiently, productivity would seem to be the first place to look. Thus it is tempting to try to find a way to deny appearances. Here is a bunch of good tries.[1]

Counterarguments

Perhaps the easiest way out is to deny the conclusion and to assert that despite the data, computers do or must contribute substantially to productivity, or at least to net well-being. Three forms of this argument are heard most often; one relies on the undeniable fact of computer power, the second on the undeniable fact of computer popularity, the last on proponents' undeniable personal enthusiasm.

The Productivity of Computer Manufacture
In its simplest form, this argument states the obvious: computers are wonderful machines that can do marvelous things; therefore, they must improve tasks to which they are seriously and vigorously applied, including productivity. Q.E.D.

The most sophisticated form of this argument was put forward by Stanford economist Timothy Bresnehan (1986). He says that when some popular product starts out expensive and later becomes cheap, there is a social welfare spillover; consumers reap the benefits. If because of technical or manufacturing improvements people now pay $1 for something for which someone used to pay $11, the world must have gained $10 in value received for each additional unit purchased at the new price. If we multiply by ten the increased number of purchases at the $1 price, we can calculate a welfare gain from productivity. Applying this reasoning to computers, Bresnehan totes up how much the prices per million calculations per second (CPU power in megaflops, or MIPs) and per million stored data items (memory size in megabytes) decreased between 1958 and 1972, using low and high estimates of 19 percent and 34 percent per year price improvements. Bresnehan used purchase data from the financial services sector from 1958 to 1972, a period when regulatory and business conditions in the industry were relatively stable, as was the basic computer technology and its modes of application. Financial services, the heaviest users of computers in those years, used computers operated by service bureaus to do bookkeeping and record keeping. He multiplies the number of new megaflops and megabytes of computer power delivered to the industry each year by their price declines and comes up with an enormous productivity improvement contributed to the overall economy. By these calculations, the value added by computers was over five times their cost. By extrapolation he concludes that "in current (1986) terms, the downstream benefits of technical progress in mainframe computers since 1958 are conservatively estimated at 1.5 to 2 orders of magnitude [thirty-two to one hundred times] larger than expenditures.

What should we make of this extraordinary conclusion? It certainly paints a different picture from the superficial productivity and business data and from the other econometric analyses as well. It finesses the use of suspect measures that underestimate productivity in financial service industries. However, the analysis has some glaring defects. First, consider overall plausibility. If we update Bresnehan's figures to 1995 and extend to all computer uses, and there is nothing in his logic to discourage us from so doing, we get astronomical numbers. Total cumulative CPU and memory purchases have mounted to well over $1 trillion, and their unit price has declined by another factor of ten or fifteen. Following Bresnehan's reasoning, the accumulated welfare benefit of computers in the United States comes to at least $300 trillion, their current beneficence to some $40 trillion a year, or over six times GNP. The average person's real standard of living is seven times what it was in 1958 because of the added pleasures and convenience of life supplied gratis by computers!

Bresnehan's method seems silly. Here is an only slightly facetious example of where it could lead. In the late 1950s, all-aluminum skis came on the market. They sold for approximately the same price as the best wooden skis. Sales figures and race results showed that they were not quite as good, and they eventually disappeared, but for a while they sold quite briskly. A purchaser of aluminum skis would have fallen heir to one of history's most remarkable productivity improvements. One hundred and fifty years earlier, the aluminum of which they were made would have cost about $35,000 instead of $3. By Bresnehan's logic, this saving in the manufacturer's potential cost was passed on as a welfare benefit to each buyer. How I regret having bought wooden skis.

Let us apply this analysis more seriously to computers. Suppose my new workstation were actually worth $50,000 in extra output from me over its lifetime, and it cost my employer $10,000 to purchase and $10,000 to support, for a net gain of $30,000. Fifteen years ago I could have bought a maxi-mini and terminal with comparable capacity and almost as good functions for, say, $200,000 purchase and $100,000 support, for a loss of $250,000 relative to my $50,000 increase in output. Obviously a wise employer would have rejected my purchase request in 1980 but granted it with smiles this year. How much benefit has come from the reduction in hardware costs? By Bresnehan's method, the answer is the difference in price, $200,000 − $10,000 = $190,000. But it seems much more sensible to credit the machine with only the $50,000 − $20,000 = $30,000 net increase in output it is responsible for. What happened to that big price decrease Bresnehan wanted to count as a present to society? It never existed. My employer wouldn't have bought me a computer at the higher price; it had negative utility. The "savings" is totally fictional. It's a lot like the $100 my mother-in-law "saves" when she pays $100 for a dress she would never have dreamed of buying at the asserted "suggested retail" of $200.

The same story applies to historical computer purchases in the financial service industries. In 1958, only the largest firms with the greatest volumes and highest manual processing costs would have seen a gain in buying computers (if such there was, as it turned out). Their net utility for the purchase would be the cost savings from doing transactions with their help. It might have been estimated at, say, 10 percent (we don't really know; this is for illustration). For other firms, the net utility, given the total costs of hardware, software, and fixed support expense, was negative, and they sat on their hands. As hardware prices dropped, more firms saw the same 10 percent positive margin and jumped in, so we get the same gradual saturation of the market as the hardware component of prices drops, and processing by computer gets cheaper than processing by hand, but nowhere does the full difference between the old and new price appear in anyone's pocket.

The flaw in Bresnehan's calculation is not its underlying logic. Indeed, applied to food or cotton thread, where the true value to the consumer of the output is more obvious, and—at least in the short run—increases in proportion to the amount of the goods a person can get her hands on, I have no quarrel with it. The problem is in taking megaflops as the index of utility. This is not what purchasers were buying. They were buying computers to help with their businesses. By assuming a direct relation between megaflops and "utility to someone" Bresnehan is able to compute that "someone" must have gained a lot by the decrease in price and increase in demand for megaflops. In a sense, this reasoning is circular. Only if computation measured in megaflops is assumed to be directly valuable to the world will Bresnehan's method tell us how valuable it was.[2]

Holding my five-year-old daughter, I presented our two coach tickets for the cross-country flight. The agent asked, "Are you two traveling together?" Me: "Yes." He: "You've been booked into rows 13 and 37. Would you prefer to sit together?" Me: "Yes indeed; I wonder how we got separate seats?" He: "Face it, computers don't have much compassion."

Despite what advertisements claim, the proper measure of utility of a computer is not its numbers of calculations and stored bytes but the speed, convenience, and effectiveness with which it can serve some useful purpose for the buyer. Flops and bytes are not even a computer's intermediate product—information—much less its economically meaningful product—what can be done with the information. Most of the new capacity of PCs has been devoted to graphics and user interface improvements, and these do improve their usefulness and usability somewhat. The comparison between Gould's early and Card's later text editors, for example, showed an increase in work efficiency of about 25 percent (but none in letter quality) during a period in which byte and flop capacity improved by at least 600 percent. Similar comparisons are sometimes better but never by an enormous margin. Often poor or ill-aimed software uses much more capacity to deliver the same information processing functionality. For example, the search algorithms in most commercial word processors need one hundred times the hardware capacity to deliver the same retrieval speeds as the algorithms used by Bellcore's SuperBook text browser. In addition, new information processing functions provided with new capacity are not necessarily of great value. Many programs use the tremendous capacity lately available to offer computationally expensive, but for the user merely pleasant, graphic decorations, or hundreds of features that are rarely used by anyone. Most computers are never used at full capacity and are idle or lightly used most of the time. Bresnehan's theory implies that computation itself was a valuable end product, and that getting it cheaper was necessarily a boon. Not so. Calculating the utility for price of computers that way is like valuing an automobile by its engine's peak rpm—not even its horsepower—rather than by its utility as a means of transportation and enjoyment.

Popularity and Sales

Computers have sold like few other technologies and have found their way into important functions of almost all of modern society's activities. All the largest economic entities—governments, armies, huge industries—rely on them utterly. They must be good.

Let's take first our main successful example, the telecommunications industry. The nation's telephone companies were among the first to install massive record-keeping computer machinery. It was probably a matter of survival, at least if they were to fulfill their mission of universal service; the growth in customers and business was so phenomenal that it would probably have been impossible to keep track of all the things that needed to be kept track of without computers (although an awfully good job of it was done for an awfully long time). The same is probably true of the large systems used by many other organizations whose information work load has expanded enormously in recent years: banks, insurance companies, airlines, stock and commodity markets, the IRS and the Social Security Administration, for example. Certainly computers must be just as critically useful and productive for them. But there is a danger here of drawing a doubtful, circular conclusion. As Joseph Weizenbaum observed in his influential 1976 book, *Computer Power and Human Reason*, what such facts tell us is merely that these organizations could not function the way they do today without computers—not that they could not have found some other, perhaps equally satisfactory way to perform equally valuable functions.[3] Who is to say that the particular functions firms have evolved based on heavy use of computers are better than others that might have evolved in their absence? As we have seen, the overall economic impact of the chosen course offers no stunning proof of its superiority, so the mere fact that the large, complex organizations and processes that exist today are dependent on computers does not prove that the computers are productive. The huge pyramid building enterprises of ancient Egypt were as utterly dependent on enormous quantities of slave labor as our own enterprises are on computers, yet few would argue that slave labor must have been especially productive or that it improved the lot of humankind.[4]

The argument from sales is equally seductive—and similarly fallacious. It goes thus: Surely large, successful businesses would not have invested billions, and continued to invest billions, if the technology was not a boon to them. The argument begs the question, assumes its own answer. By this line of reasoning, no business decisions, at least no consensual decisions of the whole business community, can ever be wrong, and no industry or national economy can suffer productivity stagnation or major competitive losses.

More pointedly, there are documented cases of widespread adoption of technology that turned out to be unproductive. For example, in the early 1980s (Baily and Chakrabarti 1988) the U.S. electric power industry, for a few years a rival of telecommunications as an exception to the productivity crisis, invested huge sums in two promising new kinds of generating plants, supercritical steam turbines and nuclear. Both turned out to be no more productive than their predecessors—the first because they never operated reliably at predicted capacity and were unexpectedly hard to maintain, the second because unanticipated technical and political problems ballooned their construction and maintenance costs. We cannot assume that a large investment is proof of its own economic wisdom.

Individual Testimonials

Many people are certain that computers are productive. Among them are people who sell computers, ones who buy and use them, and many who do computer research and development. It's probably best to ignore the sales promoters, who may tend to exaggerate. (Following news of the productivity paradox, software companies began advertising their wares as "productivity tools.") The opinions of buyers and users are more interesting, if fairly predictable. Those of professionals responsible for the quality of computers should be the most objective and well articulated.

Insider Testimonials

Early on in this endeavor, I found myself doubting my own pessimistic conclusions. All the negative results on computer productivity did not convince me in the face of their obvious popularity, so I tried to calibrate my attitude against those of colleagues in the computer business. My area within computer science, human-computer interaction, is the fastest growing subspecialty and arguably the one most closely involved with issues of what computers are designed to accomplish, how well they can be used, and with their design and evaluation from the user's point of view. I tested my views on this community in two ways. One was by giving talks on the theme of this book to audiences—numbering by now several thousand researchers and practitioners in the field—at various conferences and meetings. Perhaps more interesting is a second effort. In late 1990, I began an electronic discussion with two special subsets of people in the field: an informal organization whose participants come from about a dozen research laboratories, about half at universities and half in industry, that are among the leaders in this field, and the group of officers and volunteers who run an international professional organization for this field—the Computer-Human Interaction Special Interest Group of the Association for Computing Machinery—and its annual meeting. Participants in both sets keep in touch by electronic mail. I sent out a broadcast message briefly outlining the lack of evidence for productivity gains from computers and raising the issue of what they thought of this—its validity and the reasons for it if true. In follow-up messages I asked for any evidence of major productivity gains from applications of computers.

The lively electronic mail discussion that ensued grew to include many knowledgeable people around the world to whom the query was forwarded. A certain number of my colleagues did not like my attitude; they thought that computers are of such obvious and huge value that my questions must be either frivolous or mischievous. Others took my question in a different sense than I had intended, and described how decisions about computer purchase and support are actually made in large organizations (virtually never on evidence of productivity or profitability enhancement), how to market computer systems and what causes them to be bought, or how to convince upper management in computer or software firms that the added value of usability was worth the expenditure to support people like us. Many offered examples of computer applications that they thought were superb and that they were sure must be great productivity enhancers, although they admitted that they were unable to marshal any hard data to support this opinion. (My own candidate in this genre is electronic mail. The ability to have this wide discussion with experts of all kinds from all over the world in a matter of days, to do it all with little effort, and to have the results in a form that I can easily search and edit seems utterly magical to me. It must be an enormous boon to my productivity, although I have no evidence to prove it.) Another common theme of my respondents was that the compulsion to find quantitative proof of productivity gains was misplaced. The values of computers are to be assessed some other way, they urged. Academic colleagues stressed esthetic and scientific values and left me feeling rather crass and commercial; business colleagues stressed competitive advantages and left me feeling hopelessly idealistic.

A few people raised examples of cases with apparently irrefutable economic value. In every instance, however, these cases had to be chalked up as victories in automation or use of computers to do work that humans couldn't. No one proffered solid cases with supporting data for augmentation tools, though these are the kinds of computer programs on which my correspondents and their organizations all work and which are currently needed for large productivity gains.

The flavor of the debate is captured in some samples, somewhat paraphrased and interpreted by me, of this correspondence:

Donald Norman, former chair of the Cognitive Science Program, University of California at San Diego, now Apple Fellow, is the author or editor of several books on computer design. After citing an article in *Macweek* (March 13, 1990) that Peat Marwick, an accounting firm, believes its heavy use of computers is worthwhile but cannot document it, Norman goes on to say, "We live in a society obsessed with quantification, but we forget that in order to quantify one must extract the problem and do some measure that can be counted . . . and quite often in doing so, we have thereby lost the important aspect of the behavior. To quantify the savings from computers is also to ignore the changes in morale, in style, in kinds of [things] being performed that otherwise could have not been done." Norman declares that he is not against quantification and assessment; quite the contrary, he thinks they are very important. However, he believes that good things are done that are hard to quantify and that it is important to appreciate and promote qualitative values in the absence of quantitative measures.

I agree. I do not wish my case to be narrowly interpreted as a request for proof only by dollars and cents returns. On the other hand, I do not want to adopt technological solutions solely because proponents claim them to be good. There are plenty of other kinds of objective evidence besides accounting cost savings or profits. There are good ways to find out if the quality of life is improved by the addition of a computer system.

We saw a modestly positive example in the study of telephone company mechanization by Kraut and Dumais. The field needs a whole range of good means to tell whether it is accomplishing its objectives.

Jonathan Grudin, a prolific author of papers on usability engineering and a trenchant critic of systems that don't deliver, has worked at MCC (the Microelectronics and Computer Consortium in San Antonio), Wang research, and the Computer Science Department, University of California at Irvine: "I have never used a secretary. I produce a lot more now. Just typing up a reference section used to be painful enough to make me stop reading anything. A lot of professional writers use word processors, too, probably not just to be chic. Cheer up. It's not all for naught. . . . Another real productivity booster, perhaps, is this ability to transfer documents, with formatting, graphics, scanned-figures, etc. . . . I find it far easier . . . but more important it appears to be more motivating for the recipient to receive a wonderful looking document."

He makes a good point. But how clear is it that he couldn't have gotten equally good results with a typewriter, copy machine, overnight mail service (although these probably owe their existence to some computer technology), and a part-time assistant a little greater cost than his computer facilities and heavily subsidized network?

Ruven Brooks is a usability engineer who works for Schlumberger Laboratory for Computer Science: "Almost all off-shore oil fields are a result of computer processing. These fields have all been developed in the '60's or later, after Texas Instruments pioneered digital recording of seismic data. It is probably possible to track down actual dollar estimates for many of these off-shore fields." A nice score for the "doing something you couldn't without computers" box. The analysis of seismic data is similar in spirit to medical imaging and requires enormous numbers of calculations that couldn't be done by humans. It is indeed the kind of application that has had positive productivity consequences. But note that it was introduced over twenty years ago.

Industry Leader Testimonials

"Everybody's secretary must have a 486 chip in his or her PC because it's much faster. And the question becomes, So what? The metrics for

*measuring this kind of productivity are not very good" Martin Stein, vice
chairman, BankAmerica (National Research Council 1994a)*

A committee of the National Research Council, the government and public advising arm of the National Academy of Science, was commissioned
to "study the impact of information technology on the performance of
service activities." For a major portion of their evidence, the committee
conducted a survey of eighty high-placed executives from forty-six companies in seven major service industries. The companies were chosen for
size, rate of growth, profitability, innovation, and heavy, reputedly effective use of IT. Just under half of the interviewed executives were chiefs
of computing divisions; most of the rest were CEOs. Their advice and
example on how to deploy IT is valuable. Unsurprisingly, only a few said
they had wasted their company's money on IT. A strong majority claimed
their returns were at least comparable to other investments.[5] Here is a
sample of their comments—some positive, some not.

J. Raymond Caron, president of CIGNA Systems, told the committee,
"When it comes to PC platforms . . . we find it very difficult to develop a
useful cost-benefit measure. We've taken the position that we shouldn't
waste time trying to do it."

By contrast, James Stewart, executive vice president and chief financial
officer of CIGNA Corporation, said, "I'm not yet convinced that dis-
persal and utilization of PC-based technology have proven to be efficient.
. . . I see increasing expenditures for what I perceive occasionally as 'toys
in the business world' which don't add up to measurable output or improve our results."

Richard Liebhaber, executive vice president and chief information officer for MCI, said: "It [a system that allows customer service agents to
pull up all correspondence on bills] is an opportunity to improve the
image, the feel, the touch of MCI. Intuitively, I would tell you it's going
to provide market share, customer satisfaction, bottom line. I can't prove
it. I'm not going to waste my time trying."

And Robert Elmore, partner and worldwide director of the Business
Systems Consulting Group at Arthur Anderson, was quoted thus: "Strategic use of information is often dealing with a 100-to-1 return or at
least a 10-to-1 return, and in these cases returns should be obvious. For

example our electronic bulletin board was installed about four years ago, and there is no question among our practitioners that it gives us a competitive advantage and that it has made a direct contribution to sales growth."

What to Make of the Opinions
The more enthusiastic of the comments resemble the content of large numbers of articles in computer and business magazines, as well as in a plethora of advice books for managers. Most assert that computers are of terrific value, and many appealing examples are offered, supported by the author's experience and reasoned enthusiasm. I by no means deny the truth of these claims. However, the well-known psychological phenomenon of dissonance reduction—when people have invested heavily in a decision, they are reluctant to judge it a failure—must be reckoned with. So must the many failure stories and negative opinions, which offset the hopeful words and examples. The real problem is separating the wheat from the chaff. If we judge on the basis of the overall economic results of computers, the weighted sum of the effects of all systems put together is near zero, so probably many are good, many are bad, and many are neutral. In all likelihood the proportion of good ideas among those testified to by experts is better than the average of ideas peddled. But, especially in computer technology where hyperbole, fad, and unfulfilled predictions are as dense as pollen in September, there are too many examples of highly touted and widely admired schemes that have turned out to be losers to rest the case on expert testimonials.

"Salomon Brothers expects that employees trained under this new arrangement will complete transactions more quickly" (Gabor 1992).

My survey of case studies of business uses of computers in the popular press, trade magazines, and academic business journals has yielded the following rule: headlines and titles announcing large productivity gains are almost always followed by an article about the gain a firm "expects" or "projects." Those announcing disappointing results are all based on retrospective information about actual performance. Even in the paper telling of "340 percent" productivity gains from centralizing typing, the bottom line was in the future tense: "Holding the staff steady will more than compensate for the cost of word processing equipment and cost savings will increase in the future" (O'Neal 1976). Of course, few firms install systems without thinking positively, so stories of rosy prospects are not surprising. However, the dearth of rosy histories is somewhat shocking.

We need more and better evidence. It would be unwise to ignore the judgment of so many buyers, so many experienced business people, clever technologists, and wise scholars. There must be a pony in there somewhere. Perhaps all we need is better ways to get better information, better knowledge of what works, what doesn't, and what to do.

Measurement Problems

Another appealing way to make the problem vanish is to reject the validity or importance of measured productivity. The recent National Research Council reports rely heavily on this excuse to dismiss the productivity paradox and turn to other questions. In essence they say, "the productivity statistics are not entirely accurate, so we will discount the hard-to-believe story they tell."

Economists readily admit that productivity measures are sometimes crude, indirect, and insensitive. One criticism points to the way that government agencies collect and analyze the data. The recent decrease in productivity growth is primarily in service industries, and output in services is especially hard to measure because the product does not stay the same over time. Twenty years ago most banks were highly regulated, ultraconservative holders of large savings accounts and reluctant lenders to well-scrubbed borrowers. Now they are purveyors of vast quantities of consumer, business, and real estate credit to the masses and managers of huge pension funds. Are their earnings on deposits and loans paying for the same services as they were of yore? How do you value the output of insurance companies equivalently when they begin selling many more different kinds of policies or of investment brokers when they move into instruments like mutual funds? There are indeed great difficulties, sufficient to cause one of the agencies that puts together these indexes, the Bureau of Labor Statistics, to throw up its hands in measuring some industries, in particular financial services, for which it just equates output with labor input. To pose the matter even more simply, what is the relative value of a cash withdrawal transaction with an ATM and with a traditional teller? Suppose you're one of those who think that the ATM provides more convenience or less waiting time. If a thousand ATM money withdrawal transactions cost half as much in labor time and capital as a thousand teller money withdrawals, is "productivity" only double? Suppose you prefer a human teller. Is the new service worth just half the old?

What, exactly, is the product? The assessment of comparable output is usually easier, more intuitively obvious, in goods manufacturing or construction. The statisticians can count the "constant dollar" production of 200-horsepower four-door passenger automobiles or 2000-square-foot single-family houses. Of course, even that's not completely straightforward. Automobiles added seat belts and fuel injection; houses added double-glazed windows and central air-conditioning. Still, measurement is obviously more slippery in services. Establishing the correct constant dollar—that is, deflating the value of goods and services—is difficult as well. There is no guarantee that the same deflator (e.g., the Labor Department's market basket measure) stays the same relative to different products as the mix of products consumed by the public changes, or that it is equally applicable to goods and services. In some studies, different deflators are used for different industries; the opportunity for error is all too apparent.

Maybe productivity has been improving in services as computers have been brought in to help but hasn't been measured. Economists who have studied and modeled service productivity have taken the matter seriously, and most believe that there could be real unmeasured benefits of IT in services, especially in financial services. However, most also agree that mismeasurement cannot be the principal villain. John Kendrick, professor of economics at George Washington University, says, "Even after allowances for understatement, however, it seems clear that productivity growth in most services groups, other than communications and trade, has been significantly below the U.S. business sector average" (Kendrick 1988). Edward Denison, senior fellow of the Brookings Institution agrees: "I consider it unlikely that such [measurement] errors were large relative to the observed change" (Denison 1989). The fact is that there has always been a certain amount of slop and underestimate in measuring services, but they used to show healthy productivity growth anyway. As Roach (1988) says, "It seems an extremely remote possibility that the service sector's productivity disappointments of the 1980s would disappear if the numbers could, in fact, be corrected for statistical problems that date back into the 1950s." The measurement problems don't appear to be much different since the advent of computers.

Mr. K needed to know how to get a brochure about his company benefits and had an hour in which to get the answer. He called the human resources office and was transferred to the voice mail of a counselor, for whom he left a call-back message. After twenty minutes he called again and talked to a different recorded voice. And a third. After an hour, he gave up.

Baily and Robert Gordon, of Northwestern University, who examined the mismeasurement issue in detail (Baily and Gordon 1988), found fault with many aspects of the standard measures of productivity, and with the way constant dollars are sometimes computed as part of the process.[6] For example, they note that BLS usually measures output in financial services as equal to labor input; thus there can be no productivity gains. To get a realistic but limited appraisal for this industry, Baily and Gordon studied the number of shares traded, and their total market value, per worker in the security industry. Productivity measured in shares traded grew strongly from 1965 to 1979; while measured in market value, it declined. From 1979 to 1987 both measures showed very strong growth—over 11 percent per year. They also looked closely at insurance and banking and noted that government inflation adjustments probably make insurance productivity figures look worse than they really are, and that factors such as BEA's not counting credit card transactions in the measure of checks handled cheated the banks a bit. They also found problems with the accounting for airline transportation. However, most of these measurement deficiencies existed before 1973, so they don't help much to explain the post-1973 slowdown. (Indeed, for parts of the economy, productivity was more optimistically estimated after 1973 because of changes in government statistical methods.) Putting all the evidence together and adding a dollop of considered judgment, they conclude that errors in measuring output did not contribute more than 0.2 percent to the total growth slowdown.[7]

My wife ordered fifteen items from a mail order clothing company. They arrived in fifteen different shipments spread over two months.

One view of the measurement problem has been a particular favorite of computer professionals: perhaps new ways of doing business create value in the form of greater quality, convenience, or pleasure for consumers without anyone's paying for it or BEA noticing. This conjecture was also prominent in the National Research Council reports that dismissed the productivity problem. Before examining the evidence more closely, let us note what this hypothesis needs to explain. By 1995, the cumulative shortfall in output—the total amount by which measured annual GNP in the United States would have been larger if productivity growth had continued at precomputer rates—is, conservatively, about $1 trillion per year.[8] That's roughly $4,000 per year for each man, woman, and child, about half the average family's disposable income. Whether the increased convenience and variety of products and services attributable to IT is worth that much to the average person is a matter of opinion, but an opinion that might be measured. We could roughly allocate the cost to different products—banking, insurance, airline service—and ask those old enough to remember whether the changes are worth their imputed values. No one has done this. Instead reports like those of the NRC committees are sprinkled with anecdotes and testimonials by the people who supply the services, and they tend heavily to cite quick loan approvals and ignore the demise of price labels and telephone receptionists. The most frequently cited examples of new service applications are airline reservation systems and complex mutual funds. Unquestionably the reservation systems have underwritten vast increases in air traffic. Dynamically changing discount fare "yield management" systems keep planes more fully occupied and total revenues higher. But I doubt that the cattle car crowding, skimpy meals, crap-game fares, complex restrictions, and multi-hop routes that have become part of the unmeasured quality of the product are viewed by travelers as positive contributions to their pleasure and ease. Unquestionably the number of shares and shareholders in mutual funds has increased enormously. Many people enjoy the opportunity to choose among several hundred different funds, even if their performance is not reliably different from any other or as good as the market average. But I have to wonder whether the touted competitive advantages and increased pace of business and finance also attributed to computers—things like mergers and leveraged takeovers—have not contributed to the decreased stability of the blue-chip companies, the AT&Ts and IBMs, that used to be havens for small investors.

Now let's look more directly at the evidence as to how much IT has actually accelerated changes in service quality. The main changes claimed by the defense are greater variety and convenience. For example, if concentrating everything anyone ever wanted in one giant supermarket, or installing electronic checkouts, on average saves customers time, it might be fair to count that time at some rate of pay. If customized insurance policies are more valuable to buyers but no more expensive, it might be fair to count the extra value as output. Still, this line of reasoning presents several problems. First, almost all the trends that might be counted in this column, such as self-service outlets, a greater variety of items under one roof, and redesigned payment methods, were growing about as rapidly before 1973 as after (Baily and Chakrabarti 1988). For example, the average number of items carried by supermarkets rose from 9,000 in 1972 to 17,500 in 1985, a compounded yearly increase of 5.2 percent; the number had risen an average 6.6 percent per year over the previous twenty-two years.[9] Figure 4.1 shows the data in more detail. There has been exponential growth in supermarket variety ever since World War II but no sign of a change in the *rate* of growth since the computer age. Part of the supermarket variety increases is due to improved preservation and transportation that give us raspberries in the dead of winter and from competitive strategies that proffer almost 200 varieties of breakfast cereal, among them at least a dozen nearly indistinguishable brands of corn flakes, at prices that include only about 10 percent for ingredients.[10] Information technology presumably contributed by making it easier for stores to keep track of it all, thus helping the trend to continue. However, even if we accept greater variety as equivalent to greater quality, the

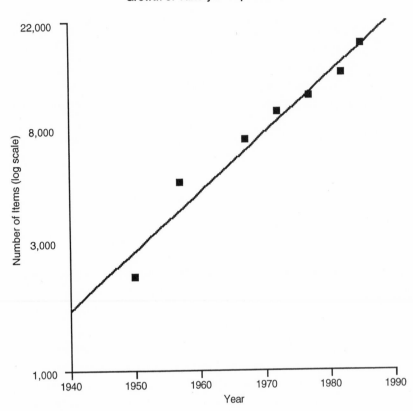

Figure 4.1.
Growth of product variety is frequently cited as an unmeasured quality gain facilitated by computers. A common example is the increased number of items on supermarket shelves (National Research Council 1994). However, as this plot shows, supermarket item variety has been increasing for a long time. The overall average yearly growth of 5.4 percent per year is shown as a solid line. If anything, growth in this quality measure has been slightly slower since computers became widespread.

claim that supermarket quality has grown faster since computers still has no basis.

Second, there is a logical problem for basic economic theory in assuming that businesses would choose to lower their productivity by giving away all the fruits of technology. Indeed, a theoretical modeling effort by Baily and Chakrabarti suggests that the apparent stagnation in services cannot be accounted for by assuming that IT's benefit has all been passed on gratis to consumers. The models indicate that the observed effects could not result if IT was really reducing the labor needed to perform work. I don't trust such disembodied economic theorizing very much, but I also feel queasy about crediting the economy with large unmeasured "convenience" values on the basis of informal impressions. While there are ATMs and car reservation systems that offer improved consumer convenience through computing, there are also those touchtone menu telephone answering systems (if you want information on opening times, touch 1; if you want to listen to Musak forever, touch 2; to enter 3, touch 5 . . .), and impersonal bill payment accounting systems (Dear BigCompany: I've written explaining your error twice. Why is it still on the bill?).

Before explaining away the economic and profitability shortfall with unmeasured customer service improvements, we should at least *try* to measure them. For example, what is to prevent the BEA from asking people how much they like the new financial services they are getting and how much they would be willing to pay to get them back if they were rescinded?[11] The fact that banks and brokers usually supply these conveniences "free," as marketing gimmicks rather than products with a price tag, suggests that the answers would not always be overwhelmingly positive. In any event, the world, if not the producers of these systems, should want service enhancements that increase real revenues or decrease costs rather than just moving constant-value market share around.

It's Too Early to Tell

Significant effects on productivity can take a long time to wend their way through the crooked corridors of business practice, labor resistance, accounting credit, market growth, acceptance, adaptation, diffusion, and perfection. Thus, some large benefits of computerization, may not have become visible yet.

Whether IT, and the computer in particular, has had time to show its stuff is open to debate. Some economists, for example, the Nobelist Leontief (Leontief and Duchin 1986), have compared the computer revolution to the industrial revolution, the building of national rail networks, or the arrival of industrial assembly lines, all of which took many decades to produce dramatic improvements in productivity. According to Franke, fifty years passed after the introduction of Watt's steam engine in 1775 before substantial improvements in productivity, and he quotes Leontief and Duchin's conclusion that "the introduction of mechanical power continued to transform western economies and society over a period of some 200 years. The computer revolution became visible only a few years ago, and by the year 2000 it will be no more advanced than the mechanization of European economies had advanced by, let us say, the year 1820" (Leontief and Duchin 1986) [12]

A more recent precedent, the exploitation of electricity, is described by Stanford economist Paul David (1990, 1991). Dating the industrial use of electricity from the first dynamo installed by Edison in New York in 1881, he reports that demonstrable effects on productivity did not appear for over forty years, until the 1920s. But when they finally appeared, they were substantial, contributing, he estimates, almost 2.5 percent per year to a spurt in national productivity growth. What caused the delay was slow diffusion due to ineffective early application and reluctance to replace old plants and machines. He believes that productivity gains are hard to see until about half the potential users have adopted a technology and that this didn't happen with electric motors in manufacturing until around 1920. Counting the beginning of computers from the first VLSI devices about 1970, David likens our current perspective to that of an observer of industry in 1900, and reckons that we shouldn't get impatient with them for another twenty years.

David's time comparison with IT is way off the mark. VLSI processors and memory chips were a major step forward for computers but hardly marked the beginning of their commercial use. Recall that by VLSI-time, 1970, there were already 125,000 computer operators and well over $100 billion worth of IT in the United States. Even the electronic computing machines used by scientists, bomb builders, bankers, brokers, and insurance companies in 1950 were further along the technological learning curve than Edison's primitive direct-current dynamos and employed some 900 operators.[13] By 1980, every bank with more than one vice president had a computer; David estimates that only 5 percent of manufacturers were using electric motors in 1900. A random sample of U.S. firms found 100 percent using computers in 1992 (Kraut and Streeter in press). David's divide of half adoption was well crossed by the mid-1970s in the mass of companies large enough to have payroll or accounting departments, and word processing had nearly reached that level as well. A more realistic comparison would expect IT to have started raising productivity statistics by 1975 if it had followed the electric motor's career path.[14]

But this is quibbling. Different technologies take different amounts of time to mature. There is no reason that computers should take exactly the same time as electric motors. David's main point is merely that superior technologies do not increase productivity immediately, so the lack of an effect now does not prove that there won't be one sometime.

The effects of a superior technology on productivity growth are strongest during the diffusion period, as more and more firms start using it (Kraut and Streeter in press). David's model puts the maximum growth effects somewhere near the 70 percent adoption point. Since computers have long since been almost universally adopted in commerce, the inescapable conclusion is that they are not yet superior.[15] The question before us is when, if ever, will they become so? How long should we wait for business as usual to make computer dreams come true?

None of the historical analogies, even electric motors, is very helpful here because we live in a different world. The rate of change in technology, industry, and patterns of consumption is much faster now than during the historical revolutions of the nineteenth century or the pre–World War II era of the twentieth. We have much greater capital, labor, baseline productivity, and market resources; a more widely educated population (both workers and consumers); much improved means of communication; much cheaper and faster transportation; and dramatically better scientific infrastructure and engineering methods with which to perfect and bring technology to bear. In addition, we have different attitudes: widespread expectation of miracles from technology have replaced nineteenth-century skepticism and turn-of-the century investment caution.

Thus the pace of refinement, adoption, and utilization of new technology is much more rapid than was possible in earlier times. Witness the rapid introduction of jet aircraft and the extraordinary growth rates of television and other consumer electronics. The earlier technologies appealed to in this excuse—railroads, steam engines, assembly lines, electric motors—took much longer to achieve full deployment. Moreover, the investment this time out looks enormously larger. Tens of trillions of (1990) dollars were not pumped into any earlier technology before it paid off, as Leontief's and David's projections would have us tolerate. I doubt that 10 percent of England's GNP was being spent on not-yet productively superior steam engines, or of the United State's on not-yet superior electric motors and their operation, forty-five years after their first commercialization, as was the case with computers.

Perhaps the size of the total investment in energy machines of all kinds, canals and water-powered looms as well as railroads and steam engines, during the first industrial revolution matched the current outlay for information machines. Plausibly this is a better analogy and raises some interesting issues. If we viewed the totality of the first industrial revolution as equivalent to what is happening now, we would want to ask how we are doing now relative to, say, forty or fifty years after the start of the earlier boom. But when did that start? With the invention of the steam engine? The automobile? The birth of commercial computers seems easier to place. However, it is a mistake to view the computer as a single technology. More appropriately, each major application is a new technology harnessing information processing capability, much as the electric motor, the locomotive, and the jet plane all harnessed energy-transforming capability.[16] Suppose we consider all the advances of the energy evolution as one prolonged development. Would any forty or fifty years after introduction of its major technological innovations, say from 1765 to 1810 (steam engine), 1865 to 1910 (steel, railroads, textiles), 1880 to 1925 (electricity generators), 1900 to 1945 automobiles, assembly lines), or 1935 to 1980 (airplanes, everything else), show the near-zero productivity growth in their primary sectors of application, let alone the total economy, that has occurred with information machines and the sum of all their uses to date?

Yes, it is too early to tell. It is too early to conclude that computers will never bring improvements in work productivity, but it is too late to be complacent. No logic compels every innovation, or every immense investment, to improve productivity. Surely computer use is still in a learning stage, still improving. Industry leaders are optimistic and believe that businesses are beginning to use IT effectively. They point to examples of major local gains from coordination and waste reduction. Crude estimates suggest that the efficiency effects of text editing could be improving about two-thirds as fast as the very long-term averages for, say, textiles.[17] But these tantalizing hints and expressions of faith are not enough. We have few repeated winners, few phase two applications with as strong a claim as text editing. And surely we'd rather not wait fifty years to see each application mature—if it does. We don't want to wait as long as from the steam engine to the jet—200 years—for information machines to complete their conquest. Our challenge is to foster faster growth and learning, to make the technology pay off in our young programmers' lifetimes.

Coincidence

Another way to escape the conclusion is to assert that the evidence we have considered is simply an accident or, rather, an elaborate set of accidents. Perhaps there are genuine and large effects on work efficiency, but they are masked by other factors that happen to have reduced productivity in just the same times and places that computers have increased it. For example, the worldwide recession of the mid-1970s was very pronounced in the United States at just the time when productivity growth took a downswing. Recessions cause productivity decline by softening markets, leading to unused but still expensive production capacity. But they also lead to labor force reductions, removing fat in payrolls, thus increasing productivity, a proposition marshaled by Roach (1992b) to sound a note of optimism for the 1990s.

One part of the slowdown period corresponded with the oil crisis. Remarkably, productivity in some transportation industries increased during this period. Banks and some other financial institutions have experienced unusual woes in the last decade as a result of deregulation, oil crises, and unlucky real estate deals. U.S. industry has suffered from the gradual accretion of mountainous government reporting requirements regarding employment, safety, pollution, pensions, and taxes, all of them piling nonpaying loads on management information systems. Indeed, the finger of blame for low output figures has been pointed in many different directions: labor recalcitrance, educational crises, management greed, inflation, taxes, short-term business focus, the takeover craze, service industry complacency, the low personal savings rate, the oil crisis, unfair competition from the Japanese. Perhaps we could explain away each and every time period, industry, and individual firm where computers have disappointed, an exercise that would leave as the only evidence that computers haven't helped a handful of laboratory and field studies showing limp efficiency effects of specific uses. This would be a slender reed to stand against strong winds of favorable opinion. In the late 1970s, some economists gave serious consideration to the multiple-causes explanation of productivity growth slowdowns, which the *Los Angeles Times* labeled "the revised Murphy's Law—Everything that can go wrong will go wrong at the same time." However, the doldrum has persisted for another decade, and this mode of denial now requires so many coincidences as to stretch credulity. As just one example, all the negative factors would have had to be relevant to service industries (except telecommunications) [18] but not to manufacturing, and it doesn't ring true; strikes, environmental impact statements, oil prices, foreign competition, and almost all the others have been at least as burdensome for manufacturing. [19]

More telling, perhaps, are the quantitative analyses, which left a large part, between 20 and 60 percent of recent productivity slowdowns unexplained. After a well-worth-reading examination of all the other factors they consider credible candidates, Baily and Chakrabarti choose as their prime suspect insufficient innovation of productive technology. Even Denison (1983) conjectures that "slow . . . advance in knowledge itself, and . . . the incorporation of knowledge into production" is a primary cause. Since there was, in fact, enormous investment in information technology during this period, and relatively little in other innovation, especially in the service sector, it is nearly impossible to avoid the conclusion that investment in information technology hasn't paid off in productivity. Moreover, to explain away the studies that correlated investment in IT with low productivity growth or return on investment in individual firms, one would have to find some reason why highly computerized firms were buffeted more strongly by other factors than were their more conservative counterparts, and that in itself would be damning.

Competitive Success

The next two excuses come from well-documented commercial accomplishments of computers. Several applications of computers have yielded dramatic competitive advantages for the people who pioneered them. ATMs provide a good example. They were introduced in large numbers by CitiBank in New York, which as a result increased its market share from 4 percent to 13 percent within a very short period of time. A direct order entry system introduced by Blue Bell, manufacturers of Wrangler jeans, by which their retail outlets could instantly respond to fluctuating consumer style demands, resulted in a large increase in business, amounting to some 13 percent of their total revenues. When Merrill Lynch was the first to introduce a cash management account for its customers, a very elaborate computerized system that required 100 programmer years to construct, it attracted large numbers of accounts from other brokerage houses.

In all of these examples, the other major players in the same markets fairly soon followed suit, and some or all of the initial market advantage dissipated. However, that's not the real issue here. The issue is whether the use of computers as instruments of strategy for gaining market share, that is, shifting sales from one company to another increases productivity. In the case of ATMs, there seem to be contradictory data and opinion as to whether they have brought about any net improvement in productivity for banks. At least for small banks early on, the cost of installing and maintaining these devices was more than the labor saving that they provided (Brand and Duke 1982). When installed beyond bank lobbies, they can entail substantial real estate costs and require expensive support by relatively high-paid technical personnel not needed for human tellers. It is obvious that ATMs have provided something that some customers wanted—some mix of convenience, longer banking hours, and novelty. People apparently make more frequent but smaller withdrawals from ATMs than from tellers (Brand and Duke 1982). My wife chooses the ATM in the bank lobby over the human teller, even when there's a line for the ATM but not for the teller. She says ATMs are more fun than writing checks.

Support of successful competitive strategy alone does not necessarily constitute evidence of productivity. It is possible that ATMs could have increased the productivity of users, if not of the banks. For example, if ATMs free people's time for more productive work, total GNP might have reflected it, but possibly in such a small way as to be invisible. Perhaps ATMs are generating a pure welfare benefit, as economists call it, in which the investment is good for the world but not necessarily for the company or the economy as measured by paid-for output. An example of a welfare investment is industrial air pollution abatement (although this presumably has some long-term payoff in reduced medical bills, lower agricultural costs, and other human benefits). We could postulate that computers and information technology are in large part simply making life better without making it more productive. When a government invests extra money in the routing of a superhighway to make it more scenic, the goal is not higher GNP but greater satisfaction of the citizenry. ATMs may be a similar product. The increased convenience and availability of cash, and the fun of operating a simple device that hands over money, might well be expected to make ATMs popular even if they had no productivity consequences at all—that is, provided that they did not cost banks enough money that a competitive advantage could be gained by doing away with them and reimbursing customers for the loss with higher interest rates or lower fees.

Consider this: There is no reason that ATMs and similar service products that are good, not because they reduce business costs but just because people like them, should not show up as productivity gains. If people like them enough, they should be willing to pay for their use; the service feature should become a new product. If the new product is being produced at low cost relative to what people will pay—for example, in the fees that some banks charge for ATM transactions or in lower interest rates that customers will tolerate—then the industry's ledger sheet should show a productivity gain.

On the other hand, services like this could attract customers from one provider to another with no effect on productivity at all. Advertising is generally considered to be largely such a service. Imagine a hypothetical computer system that produces better decisions on plays for a football team. The team might win more games as a result, but overall productivity in the football industry (the gross per player salary megabuck) will not depend on which football team is the most frequent winner. In a similar manner, leveraged takeovers of companies, by focusing on short-term financial gains for stockholders, can be construed as winning for someone, but they may have negative effects on long-term productivity. Perhaps the game metaphor is more apt than might appear. As an economy gets closer and closer to having all the goods and services that people really need or want, more and more of peoples' proportional effort might come to be devoted to just playing competitively, either for the sheer joy of competition or to see who gets the greater share of the pie. Other countries than the United States may be improving their productivity relatively more by the use of technology, such an argument would go, because they are not as far along on the economic success curve and are thus still devoting more of their energies to greater efficiency and less to the market share game.

Another area of documentable success for computers is in inventory and resource management. Bookstores, for example, have made effective use of International Standard Book Numbers (ISBNs), bar codes, and computers to allow them to stock only popular books and keep on hand only enough of each title to meet day-to-day needs. Ignoring the fact that this use has made every chain book outlet a twin of every other and left customers with a greatly impoverished list of titles from which to choose—a decrease in public welfare presumably—the retail book trade has reputedly increased its productivity. Similar stories are told about manufacturing resource planning (MRP), in which the raw materials, piece parts, and flexibly assigned labor are all kept track of and marshaled in minimal numbers at just the right time so that capital is not unnecessarily tied up in unused resources. Borg-Warner is said to have increased productivity by 20 percent by such means. The consulting company Booz Allen has been quoted as saying that such techniques can yield up to 29 percent gains in profits for many manufacturing companies. Better management of capital should improve multifactor productivity, if not labor productivity directly. The mystery is why these effects are not more prominent. There have been healthy improvements in productivity in manufacturing in the last twenty years, possibly—despite Loveman's (1986) data to the contrary—due in some part to such computer-based methods. However, manufacturing has shrunk to a small part of overall economy, so these gains may not have greatly affected the overall measures at which we looked. Retail trade, however, has continued to experience productivity losses. Perhaps inventory control techniques such as those instituted by bookstores have been insufficiently adopted (although the ubiquity of bar codes and scanners suggests the opposite), have too small an effect on the average, or are being counterbalanced by other forces.

We've Come About as Far as We Can Go

Another possible out is to believe that productivity, at least in the United States, has topped out or come close. As in the case of direct labor costs for manufacturing, the total contribution to the economy has shrunk drastically, so little overall effect can be felt by improvements here. However, jobs in the service industries—financial services, marketing, design, advertising, engineering, maintenance, customer service occupations—which have grown apace as manufacturing has declined, are associated with relatively low productivity and slow productivity growth. Is it possible to believe that these too have topped out on productivity? Normally we'd expect a sector with low baseline productivity to provide much greater opportunity for improvement. But with some rather fanciful arguments, we can hypothesize the opposite in this case. Suppose that most of these service jobs are ones whose dollar value is defined directly as personal labor. For an example, consider babysitting. You hire a sitter by the hour to keep a watchful eye on one or more small children. Excepting some farfetched notions of robotics or telepresence, there is no way of improving the sitter's productivity; in an hour a sitter can do an hour of sitting; that's all the product there can be. Occupations in which the supplier's personal time and presence are the definitions of value may be growing—professional athletes, servers in elite restaurants, entertainers, personal trainers, masseuses, chiropractors, and nude dancers are other examples—but they are certainly not yet a major factor.

Complacency

Stephen Roach (1992a) offers another, rather imaginative, rationalization. He suggests that the vast computing resources acquired by business in the 1980s and 1990s were grossly underutilized because there was so much regulation, so little competition from abroad, and such easy success that managers just didn't care about productivity. Says he, "The technology paradox is traceable to the service sector's legacy of complacency and inefficiency." Although a great fan of Roach (he has done much to open eyes to the computer paradox), I find this one hard to swallow. Roach's main evidence is a reduction in "back office" white-collar job growth in the first part of 1992, which he attributes to mergers of large banks and subsequent consolidation of back-office processing capacity. One reason why I am so doubtful of his conclusion is that it seems highly unlikely that banks actually had large excess processing capacity. "Sizing" of computer systems for such operations is a fairly accurate engineering art, especially when the processing load grows gradually over time. In telephone office business support systems, for example, capacity is usually stretched to near its limit (Srinivasan, 1992); it is often impossible to add even a modest new software feature without first adding more computer power. That large and growing firms would have enough capacity to spare for consolidation to make a big difference in hardware requirements is not credible. Indeed, studies in the mid-1980s found no cost savings from bank mergers (Srinivasan 1992). As of this writing it is impossible to tell whether the 1992–1994 "restructuring" of the U.S. service business (economists' euphemism for permanent layoffs) will continue, will result in genuine and lasting productivity gains, especially ones that combine increased output with strong employment and high wages as in the past, or will turn out to be a temporary cost-cutting binge that will leave the economy weakened and well-being diminished. Only time will tell.

My second reason for doubting the "complacency" hypothesis is that I see no evidence or basis for the existence of complacency or its complicity in underuse of technology for productivity. Although regulation and weak foreign competition in some parts of the service industry may have had some local moderating effects on the pitch of activity, there has certainly been enough incentive to keep management in hot pursuit of productivity improvements. There has obviously been vigorous pursuit of market share, for example, even in banking; witness ATMs and overdraft accounts. And surely increased productivity—the sword the Germans and Japanese used to maim the American steel business—is in itself a highly effective competitive tool. Wouldn't domestic service firms have used it on each other if they could? Moreover, in the most tightly regulated, least competitive sector of the service industry, the telephone business, productivity improvements continued at a normal clip. Disincentive effects of regulation and weak competition won't do as explanations.

Summarizing the Excuses

We have now reviewed all the plausible ways to convince ourselves that there really is no computer productivity problem. Each is seriously wanting. And even if all of these objections and excuses were to be rather generously credited, they are not sufficient to undo the conclusion that something is wrong with computers. Surely there is plenty and more room for greater efficiency in the white-collar and service sectors of the economy. There must be many ways to make the provision of building maintenance, retail customer services, hospital care, hotels stays, car washes, restaurant meals, doctors' exams, lawyers' advice, and health club workouts more labor and capital efficient. But somehow these jobs seem not to be getting more productive very fast. Why haven't phase two computer applications done something to aid this majority part of our economy? Surely there is a great deal of profit and glory to be accrued by inventors and suppliers of technology to enhance productivity in these domains. For example, if word processing, spreadsheet, and database programs for PCs were as wonderful as their devotees would have us believe, if they increased the efficiency their users by factors of many hundreds as the inventions of the industrial revolution did, they would have been exploited in the businesses just named to more effect. There is enormous room for computer-aided gains in productivity. The fact that it hasn't happened must not be swept under the rug.

5

Reasons

I picked up a couple of bikes that had been repaired by a shop I've dealt with for many years. The proprietor and an assistant spent a good five minutes entering a record of the work and parts and presented me with an impressive two-page receipt and a ticker tape listing items like "067-deraileurred bike" and "214labor UPS." Gesturing at the sales computer, the proprietor—unsolicited—said, "Boy this thing produces paper; my whole house is full of paper. If I'd have had any idea what I was getting into, I wouldn't have bought the thing."

"Do you have more paperwork to do now, since you have the computer?" I asked.

"Oh, yes, lots more," she answered.

Buying computers and related technology appears to be about 13 percent less productive for business than average capital investments. Expenses for computing to date total up to over $4 trillion. Duly compounded, over $3 trillion seems to have been misplaced.

Where did all the money go? Was it just thrown away, the capital goods scrapped? To some extent, yes. Computer hardware and associated software depreciate quickly—many R&D organizations use a three-year depreciation for internal accounting purposes—partly because computers are somewhat fragile but mostly because of the astonishing rate at which the technology has advanced. Computer models can become obsolete in as little as three years. Rapid obsolescence brings not just the temptation to replace still-working machines with ones that are more powerful but often is required because the hardware is no longer supported by the manufacturer, desired new software won't run on the old hardware, or, dismayingly often, the manufacturer goes out of business. Similarly, the cost of operating computers, of making them useful, is very high. By the mid-1980s, almost 2 percent of the U.S. labor force was producing or repairing software, an activity most of which is not directly productive. Computerizing demands new expert labor to help users get information in and out of the whirring boxes and to retrain and coordinate all the users and helpers. Thus, there are many money leaks in the system. Another possibility is that sufficient revenue increases or cost savings were just never there. Excepting scientific applications, Nintendo, and a few other cases, computers usually don't produce anything of direct value. Their output is information, usually a strictly intermediate product, which becomes valuable only when used to reduce the costs or increase the value of some other product for which people are willing to pay. A computer is thus something like a lathe used to manufacture machine tools; its output is another tool. A computer's economic impact depends on the usefulness of the tools it produces. We have seen little evidence that such tools are markedly superior to their predecessors.

A very cautious conclusion for what has been said so far is that computer technology has failed to yield adequate labor productivity improvements, especially in the increasingly important nonmanufacturing portion of the economy, where investment in IT is dominant. Computers, as powerful information processing devices, would appear to be the right tools for achieving this goal. The need is apparent, and the economic rewards would be large. People in all parts of the computer business have hoped and intended to achieve this goal. So we must ask what has prevented success.

High Cost

Most phase two computer equipment is aimed at offices and office workers. Compared to the prices of the equipment of old—such things as typewriters and file cabinets—even discount PC clones can appear quite expensive. Since the mid-1970s, when dreams of automated, paperless offices were more fervid, the price of computerizing a position has come down considerably, while the computing power and facilities that are made available have skyrocketed. A mainframe or minicomputer serving a set of dumb terminals would have cost $10,000 to $20,000 per station (in 1990 dollars). A current high-end setup might have color graphics PCs or Macintoshes interconnected by Ethernet or equivalent local area network and supported by a file server machine with a few gigabytes of storage (about ten to twenty four-drawer paper files worth). It might cost $3,000 to $10,000 per station.[1] The initial outlay for equipment is compounded by substantial expenses for equipment maintenance, software purchase, customization and updating, operation, and, especially, user training and support. It's a rather interesting sidenote to this whole story that typists and secretaries who use word processors command higher salaries than those who use ordinary typewriters. It appears to take more training and skill to use this "aiding" technology than to do without.

Thus, if there are only modest productivity gains to be realized with computerized offices, their payoff is likely to be somewhat long term and uncertain. Business has been repeatedly faulted for failure to make long-term investments in productivity-enhancing technology. The authoritative summary issued by the MIT Commission on Industrial Productivity (Dertouzos, Lester, and Solow 1989) concurred with many before in blaming shortsighted investment policies for the flight of steel, semiconductor, and consumer electronics, among others, from America to Japan. American managers get their rewards primarily for good short-term performance—quarterly or annual—and have little motivation to make large commitments to methods that may take as long as ten years to pay off. Perhaps this factor has contributed to the problem. If many more industries had had even more computing technology more widely deployed over a longer period of time, there would have been even more opportunity for it to evolve, for effective uses to have been invented, sorted out, and amplified, and for less valuable ones to be discarded.

In Japanese business, reluctance to make long-term investments does not provide an adequate explanation for the failure of computerization to yield productivity gains. But the Japanese may have had insufficient time, since the problems of fitting PCs to their writing systems and work norms has inhibited the spread of information technology in offices, as well as the fact that they are still well behind America in exploiting the older and more proved techniques of productivity enhancement.

Slow Learning

The story with electric motors was that at first people substituted them for steam engines and waterwheels driving the shafts and pulleys that transmitted energy over factory floors. Electric motors weren't especially good at that—too low powered, too energy inefficient. Then engineers figured out that they could attach a small motor to each machine and use wires instead of cumbersome shafts and pulleys to distribute energy in the factory. They could even make machines that workers could lift, move, and hold. This learning took about twenty years (David 1990; Mokyr 1990), but the rate of learning for electric motors was seriously inhibited by slow adoption. By comparison, the learning of productive computer applications appears severely retarded.

Why so slow? We don't know. Are we now on a faster learning curve at last? It is impossible to tell. We simply don't have the data. Some crude, fragmentary evidence suggests some acceleration, but my impression is that overall progress remains sluggish. Yet even if we were learning at the speed of electric motors or steam engines, we'd be in trouble. This is the post-jet age.

Rapid Change and Incompatibility

The market for phase two computer equipment contains a bewildering array of machines, systems, and software, most of which require a great deal of scarce expertise to select and connect and which are often incompatible with most of the others. (In a Rand Corporation survey, 79 percent of computerized offices used equipment from more than one vendor, 32 percent from four or more.)

Putting together an office computing environment is not like assembling stereo equipment. You might decide to buy Apple personal computers because of their reputed ease of learning, but don't expect them to connect to your IBM mainframe where your data are stored. You might decide to buy a UNIX operating system on its reputation for software development, but don't expect it to run it on your PCs. Moreover, when you buy a computer from company X and the next year attempt to add extra memory, also from company X, you often discover that they cannot be used together; you'll have to buy a new computer as well. If you are foolish enough to buy two or more different kinds of desktop computers for your staff, say Macintoshes for some and IBM clones for others, the expensive software that you buy for one will not operate on the other. Rarely will this year's new program run with a six-year-old operating system (the basic software that reads, writes, and manipulates the bits) or a ten-year-old machine. A new program may not even operate on last year's model of the same machine. And yet every few years each software package will be "updated" to one with more features and different bugs. You hardly dare pass up the relatively inexpensive update package lest the next generation leaves yours obsolete, incompatible, and unsupported.

Many of the most promising uses of computers and communications gear lie in connecting workers to each other and to common repositories of data and information. However, because they can't afford the considerable expertise required, many smaller companies pass on the opportunities for local nets. The annoyance, expense, incomprehensibility, and inefficiency of this situation greatly inhibit the exploitation of information technology.

Unreliability

One day a few years back I arrived, weary and bedraggled, infant in arms, at a Mongo-Chain Hotel near London's Heathrow Airport. I had a reservation, but "the computer was down," so they couldn't give me a room. They knew they had plenty of rooms available, but they didn't know which ones. The man next to me was trying to pay his bill so he could get to an airplane—no luck. Eventually they sent us to a room that was unoccupied—temporarily. The man who had left the suitcases in it was at breakfast.

We've all had experiences of this kind. It's getting to be a common excuse when things go wrong in service establishments: "The computer is down." "It's not in the computer, Miss. I'm sorry." And the tone of voice with which these alibis are offered seems to imply that the situation is no one's fault, certainly not the clerk's or the establishment's; it's an "act of

God," like a fire or hurricane. I haven't located any hard data on whether the average hotel service from the customer's point of view is better or worse since computerization. Hotels used to keep a large ledger with each room and night having its own little box, which was either filled or not—virtually foolproof and lost only in real hurricanes or fires.

The fact is that computers as we mostly know them, the ones that are used as phase two productivity tools in business, are highly unreliable. The hardware is forever crashing unexpectedly; the software is full of bugs that cause errors, unexpected glitches, and complete shutdowns. (When a software malfunction causes the machine to completely stop responding, it is said to "hang". An appropriate fate, I sometimes think.) Unreliability isn't a necessary condition of computers. The computers used to switch telephone calls or to control highly critical and dangerous military applications have been built to have virtually errorless operation over years of service. But such reliable computers are extremely expensive. Ones that are practical as work tools have poor reliability compared to the methods that they have replaced.

Reluctant Labor

On some occasions in some industries, organized labor has resisted the institution of computer-based methods, or at least made their introduction more expensive than they might otherwise have been. Perhaps the earliest and best example is the printers' and compositors unions' in New York, which at first fought and then cooperated with the movement to replace manual typesetting machines with computer-based systems. The compromise solution was a guarantee that the improved productivity would be realized not through layoffs but only through natural attrition, an approach widely used in Scandinavian and other European countries.

The resistance of labor to labor-saving devices surely increases the difficulty and expense of introducing them. But this is not an insurmountable or permanent obstacle. New technology has always managed to make its way when its value is large and obvious. Record-high labor costs and work restrictions in West Germany, for example, do not prevent the textile industry there from being the third largest in the world as the result of imaginative use of technology and management innovations.

Indeed, it can be argued that the very contentment and cooperativeness of the highly unionized, highly protected, and highly paid labor force has been an integral and necessary part of Germany's productivity improvements. Labor and other groups in the United States have tried, and in some cases succeeded, in having laws passed that regulate and restrict the use of computers or the conditions of their use. Thus, although the proportion of American industry that is unionized has declined greatly, there is still a real, although small, inhibitory effect of labor resistance.

Computer Illiteracy

It is often asserted that one of the problems with computers is that too few people know how to use them. The population is accused of being computer illiterate. When calls are made for schools to provide better education in computers, it's not clear what is in mind. Almost all the uses that might improve productivity require operators to interact only with programs, not to write programs of their own. Should schools teach students to operate word processing systems or use spreadsheets? If so, which programs? (There are many of versions of each, each rather different from most others.) Fortunately evidence shows that learning one word processor makes it easier to learn another, no matter how different they appear (Singley and Anderson 1985). As long as the technology is not changed too fast and the important applications next year are not too different from this year's, training in high schools and colleges could certainly increase the utility of computers in business.

Businesses relied on high school typing classes to make typewriters useful; perhaps word processing will not be fully productive until all typing classes are word processing classes.

It's interesting to note, as an aside, the important role of typing in the use of computers. There is almost no serious computer application that does not require the user to type (the recent short-lived hoopla over pen-based computers notwithstanding). This is one reason why few gray-haired male executives have computers on their desks. Wizard computer programmers tend to be extremely fast typists—it has been said that professional Mac programmers typically type 75 to 125 words per minute (Tognazzini 1992). In all seriousness, then, I would recommend touch typing—with a word processing system, of course—as the fundamental required course for computer literacy.[2] It is more relevant than an introduction to how computers work or to the elements of programming—things that most future computer users will need to know about as much as telephone users need to know about photonics, switching machines, and cable splicing.

The Organization of Organizations

Management advisers such as Drucker (1991), Scott-Morton (1991), Strassmann (1990), and Dertouzos, Lester, and Solow (1990) agree that the effective use of information technology, and increased productivity in information age industries, will depend on major changes in the way businesses are organized. In particular, many call for a flattened hierarchy of authority. Rapidly changing technical content, tools, and skills will require a "more involved, less specialized, continuously learning work force" (Dertouzos, Lester, and Solow 1990). Such people will be highly valuable specialists who must be given adequate authority and access to the parts of the organization that depend on them. In turn, the increased flexibility and directness of the communication tools that information technology provides make obsolete the deep hierarchical command and control structures that originated in preelectronic military organizations.

In spite of much talk along these lines and spasmodic dumping of middle managers in times of economic crunch, no dramatic flattening in large industrial organizations seems to have occurred yet. For example, from the first quarter of 1992 to the first quarter of 1993, 400,000 new managerial jobs were created, while about the same number of clerical and administrative support jobs were lost (Mandel and Farrell 1993).

Some of the failure of computers may thus be attributable to inertia in changing organizations to exploit the new means of information passing, coordination, and decision making that they could underwrite.

Mismanagement

Some say that management has not been employing computers well and cite several ways in which computers are mismanaged.

Overuse

Many experts speculate that IT's failure is largely due to its use in generating ever greater amounts of expensive but insufficiently useful management information. Once a computer is in place and all of a company's inventory, sales, and expense data are available for electronic access and manipulation, the opportunities for analysis are dizzying. Managers can see where the money is coming from and going to; they needn't guess how much xerography is costing them even if its expense is dispersed in a hundred different departmental budgets. But, as often happens, true opportunities hatch false temptations. If the data needed for an analysis are there, why not do the analysis? If it seems that someone might be able to use it, go ahead. If a manager requests a figure, write the program to report it. Once the program has been written, why not report the result every month? Every manager now gets reports measured in stack-feet per month. Nobody can read it all or digest what they've read. My group once worked on a project to sort through a two-inch-thick daily printout to find and display the few lines that were useful to the manager to whom it was provided. According to one commentary, "It looks as if the administrative bureaucracies have swallowed a large share of total investment without making corresponding improvements" (Baily and Chakrabarti 1988).

If substantial programmer and MIS department time goes into excessive report production, even greater excesses probably happen in individual use of spreadsheet programs. Such facilities can be useful. The individual manager can now track results of her own operation without hassling with and waiting for the MIS department. She can see what would happen to the bottom line if she added 10 percent to every expense account as requested by the sales force. But she can also spend the afternoon on computer daydreams calculating her bonus if sales are at the minimum, maximum, or average of what each salesperson predicts. Undoubtedly, many times as many financial analyses are being conducted as before, many on different data—some worthwhile, many not, many repeating each other, few shared widely. The MIS department is redundant in much of what it does, except that reconciling, merging, and taking advantage of all those separate analyses is virtually impossible, so a central job for the whole company is still needed.

A particularly favored target of the useless information criticism is the reporting requirements of government. Once computers were in place, many government agencies decided that companies could easily produce detailed reports to demonstrate their conformance to tax laws, pension and benefit fund regulations, equal opportunity employment rules, environmental protection guidelines, and a zillion other things. Strassmann (1990) estimates that 3 percent of employee wages goes into tax reporting. A substantial fraction of this amount must be the result of opportunities for analysis and report made attractive by computers and accomplished with them.

It is a bitter irony. If reporting had been kept simple, computers might have made its labor costs nearly vanish. As it is, much of the increased computer capacity of many firms is occupied with these activities.[3] Many forests have given their lives to the cause. Just mailing the reports to Washington and Sacramento must cost enough to notice. I doubt if anyone reads them, but many are paid to file them.

Underuse

My favorite example of underuse comes from a speech by Michael Dertouzos to a group of industrial supporters of MIT's graduate programs in the spring of 1992. He pointed out that computer processing has greatly speeded the handling of checks by American banks through magnetic ink readers to identify the payer and the payer's bank, and speedier, lower-cost bookkeeping and transfer operations. However, there are still at least two points in each check's life when human labor is used: when the issuer, if an individual, writes the check and enters it in a checkbook and when someone transcribes the amount from the face of the check into a computer. Until these costly parts of the process are eliminated, doing business by check remains expensive. In France, far fewer transactions are done by check, many more by direct funds transfer, and the cost of money transactions is much lower (McKinsey Global Institute 1992).

The process of trying to get a whole business process to flow electronically into and out of common databases using common software and with minimum human work and "rework" is often called "enterprise integration." It's hard to do. Many companies that are heavily computerized got that way by jumping in early, when programs were available or built for this use and that, sometimes incompatibly, never at the same time for everything. Since then, each has accreted features and functions and gadgets and gizmos. Getting them to work together now is a nightmare of complexity. Starting over is ghastly difficult and expensive. Therefore, we are saddled with a maze of different computer systems that do only part of the job and periodically hand the work back to humans.

Misuse

I heard Malcolm Forbes Jr. interviewed on PBS about the future of the American economy. He waxed enthusiastic over the coming benefits of information technology using as his prime example Wal-Mart. Once, he said, it used IT to detect that a major competitor was out of stock on blankets and instantly raised its own prices.

The most serious complaint about computers, at least by those who are concerned with productivity, is that their primary role has been to support merely redistributive marketing and financial activities. Almost all the commentators cited up to now point fingers at this problem. We've looked at several examples already—for instance, the ATM case and the explosion of insurance policy and bank account varieties. The complex fare schedules for airlines are another example. Impossible without computers, these schemes, which can involve tens of thousands of different fares for one airline's various flights, have been credited with improving the competitiveness of many (some now failing since they all started doing it) airlines while offering great variety and savings (when you can get them) to customers. However, some airlines have switched back to simpler fare schedules, advertised as more convenient and less expensive. Computer-managed stock trading programs that try to capitalize on minute-by-minute changes in prices are another example of using expensive hardware and programmers to move money from one pocket to another without producing anything.

The Design of Software

This, as the perceptive reader may have already inferred from my subtle hints, is my candidate for the principal culprit. The shortfall in computer design has two aspects: usability and usefulness.

Usability

Computer equipment is hard to choose, install, maintain, and, especially, operate. The flexibility of digital computing equipment, the fact that it can be redesigned to be operated in just about any way anybody would wish, that it is not constrained by mechanical limitations, should make it infinitely easier to use than past technologies. Mysteriously, this opportunity has not been grasped. Computers are widely viewed as arcane, complex machines that only smart, technically oriented people are comfortable with. In principle, a computer attached to a typewriter should make it easier to learn to type and easier to produce letters and other documents. It is anomalous that typists need to go back to school to learn to use a word processor. Something has gone seriously off track. Since most of the rest of this book attacks this problem, I'll save the details for later.

Standardization

A part of the unusability of computer systems is lack of standardization. No two word processing or text editing systems, of the dozens available, no two database query languages of the scores available, no two spreadsheets work in the same way. The way to load a diskette or log on is not the same on one computer as the next. Because most people tend to work with the same computer frequently over a long period of time, they can usually adjust to superficial idiosyncrasies without enormous effort. More serious is that different programs, called "applications" (for "applications of the computer"), on the same machine use different terms, require different actions for the same results (k for "kill" or k for "keep"), have the options of their menus differently labeled, organized, and located. The same icon has different meanings (a circle might mean "draw a circle" or "grab everything in this circle"); different icons are used with similar meanings (the coffee cup, clock, or hour glass for "the computer is busy"). Incredibly, these "features" are sometimes patented—tantamount to patenting the words of English and expecting speakers to observe proprietary claims as well as correct grammar. The way a user finds a file, determines available storage space, moves or resizes a "window," and every other operation changes not only from one computer to another but from one program to another, even on computers with the best reputations for friendliness. When an office has several different machines and personnel with varying backgrounds, the situation gets ludicrous. Scores of different programs are needed. One person can't pass a document file to another without a special conversion program: a veritable tower of babel. The personnel department now asks clerks not if they can type but what word processor they know and hires only those intimate with the local species.

Complexity

Almost all software systems are arcane and complex. The user manuals accompanying even the smallest and simplest user-oriented systems are thick volumes. With a few of the very best brands, it is possible to unpack the machine from the box and do a few trivial, if pleasing, computer tricks (like typing something, filing it, and getting it back on the screen) within fifteen minutes. Nevertheless, anyone who wants to do serious work needs to devote significant amounts of time to learn how to use the machine. I've watched professional computer scientists come up to speed with new Macintosh computers—reputed to be the easiest, most transparent ones around. Only after days of concentrated effort can they do useful work, and months pass before the presumed advantages of their new toy are experienced as an advance over the system they used last. The excuse is that these systems are so rich, so powerful, have so many nifty features, that to master all of them, or even some of them in the context of all the others available, is necessarily difficult—but worth it. Fans also sometimes assert that knowing other systems rots one's mind, makes it harder, not easier to get good with a wonderful new one. But this is balderdash; such "negative transfer" has never been documented.

The real problem is simple enough: the systems are not simple enough. They are too complex, have far too many features, give the user far too many options. Almost all users use their computer for only a few operations. Nevertheless, their machines and minds are loaded up with a vast junk pile of options, commands, facilities, doodads, and buttons, most of them superfluous to the user and there just because somebody knew how to program it. Having this mountain of stuff available usually means that doing even the simplest operation can be extraordinarily difficult. It's like trying to turn on the intercom in a jumbo jet cockpit. If the intercom switch were the only one available, any child over two could do it. But finding it among the hundreds of switches and lights and dials in the cockpit is no easy matter.

Usefulness

Worse, much worse, than the sheer difficulty of operating today's computers is the minute number of truly useful things that they make possible. Computer designers and devotees will protest this assertion loudly, claiming, with some truth, that they use their computers for scads of things, and use them effectively. However, it remains to be shown in most cases that the things that they do with their computers are actually being done dramatically better or faster than they are being done by the computer deprived. More important is the fact that ordinary users of computers, people who have other jobs to do than use computers and really want tools, not computers, rarely use more than a very small handful of the hundreds of features and functions that have been designed and marketed. By and large, PC users use word processing programs, spreadsheet programs, or database programs. Many of them use only one of these functions; rather few use them all. Some 10 percent of PCs, those equipped with modems and communications software, are sometimes also used for sending and receiving electronic mail. Recently many managers and professionals have begun to use drawing programs to produce transparencies with some graphical content other than typescript. Leaving aside powerful but highly specialized uses by engineers (CAD-CAM) and scientists (e.g., Mathematica, numerical simulation), that is the sum and substance of the useful things now widely being done with personal computers. Add the accounting, record keeping, billing, and payroll calculations usually done with minis or mainframes, and you've about covered the waterfront. But you haven't even touched, much less provably helped, most of the work of most of the people in the service economy.

Often systems that are deployed do the wrong thing. There was an interesting article in the *New York Times* a few years ago about long lines at a state agency for issuing goods transfer licenses. The long lines were caused by the introduction of a computer system that was intended specifically to reduce the shorter lines that existed prior to its purchase. Apparently in the process of contracting and building the system, its original intent was lost track of. Certainly no effective method for finding out whether the system performed its desired function was in place.

I will not belabor this point much further since the rest of the book is devoted to it. However, let's look quickly at a function that keeps being reinvented. Almost every computer system has a program for keeping a personal calendar, and these have frequently been expanded to "joint scheduling calendars" that are intended to be shared by members of an organization. Computer-based calendars are imagined to be especially useful because they can record a full lifetime of events. They have no space limitation imposed by little boxes or pages and can be programmed to give automatic notifications of important events. In my highly computerized environment, almost nobody—except a few diehards who spend their whole day in front of their screens programming—uses the online calendars. Unless you dutifully print out the day or week's entry and fold it for your pocket, you're without your engagements when you walk away from your computer. In any case, you can't record directly into your engagement calendar unless you are at a terminal somewhere. When the machine is down, as it often is, you miss appointments. Even if you have a terminal with telecommunications at home, to find out what your first appointment is tomorrow morning, you need to turn the machine on, log in, enter a password, and go through a set of commands. People soon rediscover the superior ease and convenience of a small black book. Joint scheduling calendars are imagined to be useful because each person in the organization has recorded his or her busy times and others can work around them in scheduling appointments or dropping in for a visit. The problem is that for the joint calendar to be useful to others, each person must be honest and conscientious in filling it in. Unreliable data can be worse than none. Many managers, and managees as well, don't really want everybody to know exactly what they are doing all the time. They have good reason to want to block out periods of time in a flexible manner. They may want some people but not others to claim priority but don't want to advertise this fact. The complexity and nuisance of making all of these decisions ahead of time, even if it were possible, is overwhelming. I know many people who are required to use these gadgets; I know few who prefer them.

How We Got Here

What has happened is this. There has been a great shift of the role of technology in the world. Not so long ago many of the things that people wanted, and knew they wanted, were not to be had. They wanted brighter lights so they could read easily at night. They wished they could visit Aunt Beth hundreds of miles away often, or cities across the ocean ever. Whether they lived in Moline or Toulouse, they wished they could market their wares in Paris. They wanted materials and construction methods that would let ordinary citizens own comfortable houses. They wanted to dig big holes fast, pave wider highways, harvest bigger grain fields easily. They wanted to get messages to people in distant places quickly. What stood in the way of all of these desires was that there was no technical means to satisfy them. Technology advanced at a creep for thousands of years. And then, seemingly, it took off. Suddenly you could build machines that could dig a foundation hole or carry 400 people across an ocean in an afternoon. For about a century the challenge was to build such machines. Each new advance—each harvester, flying machine, automobile, electric light, or telephone—was a major technological triumph. People were so delighted to have some of these new devices that they were willing to spend years in learning to operate them. After all, the craft skills of the past on which production depended required such practice. So it was not alarming that steam shovel operators needed a seven-year apprenticeship, as do airline pilots still. Cars are such useful devices that no one minds spending hundreds of hours learning to drive.

In the last forty years something quite astonishing has happened in the world of technology. The underpinnings of science and engineering, and the vast accumulation of technical know-how, experience, and components have virtually turned the tables. Now a very large proportion of things that people would obviously want can be built with a reasonable amount of energy and money. It is even possible to send a few people to the moon. With the great power and flexibility of modern technology, with its almost unlimited talent to produce new things, more and more of the obviously desirable things have been done. The issue used to be: "Here is something we wish we could do, but, gosh, how can you do it?" Now, more often, it is: "Here is something we could do; would it be desirable?" Unfortunately, we have not gotten used to asking the second question often enough, nor have we developed sufficiently good methods to answer it. Instead we've gotten into the habit of saying, "Here is something I can do with my technology; I'll do it!" Thus, we have computerized appointment calendars that nobody uses; unnecessarily expensive computers, because of all of the unused features that have been programmed into them; home computers mildewing in closets because they are too hard to use for so few things that anyone wants to do. Home computers have tried to appeal by adding programs that let their users copy recipes into files on the computer, then later log into the computer to retrieve them, gooey fingers on the keyboard bringing tiny pages of green letters into view far from the stove; by providing budget programs with which users can enter all their budgetary items and goals and later log in to receive help in adding the columns; by, in their most advanced form, giving users access over their telephone lines to awkwardly presented huge and hard-to-navigate hierarchies of menus of information of an ill-assorted and uninteresting nature; and to shopping systems that provide poor information about items that cost more. Most of these offerings seem to have been designed on the philosophy that if you could do it with a computer it must be wonderful. But since almost all of these functions can be performed much more conveniently and effectively with the preexisting technology of pencils, paper, calculators, and telephones, it should be no surprise that people find these machines more trouble than they're worth. This diagnosis of the trouble with technology is not confined to computers. Dertouzos, Lester, and Solow (1989) seem to have something very similar in mind in their recommendations for curing the malaise of all of American manufacturing when they say, "The most critical element is the ability to predict early in the product development cycle that a new product will yield superior customer satisfaction in the actual marketplace." Across the board it has come as a surprise to technologists, at least to those who have realized it at all, that just doing something novel and impressive with the technology is not enough.

This condemnation of design in computer technology is, of course, much too sweeping. Often when new systems are designed for business applications, considerable attention is paid to fulfilling the customer's desires and business needs. Sometimes this is done in a satisfactory way, and we'll have many examples later. But more often it is only partly accomplished, with unfortunate results.

A few years ago I went to a carpet store and selected two rugs and two pads. The salesperson began to fill out the sales form, entering my name, address, and phone number; the date and time; his name and employee number; my charge card number; then the particulars for the first rug. Then he pulled out a second form and entered my name, address, and phone number, and all the rest of the same information, then the particulars of the second rug. Two more forms and about twenty minutes later he was done. I asked him why he couldn't put all the items on the same form. His reply, "We used to be able to do that, but we've just been computerized."

I hope that computerization was valuable in some way for the carpet store, perhaps allowing it to track sales, inventory and so forth more effectively. But it certainly reduced the productivity of the sales force and the satisfaction of this consumer. I presume that in designing this system, no one had watched the end users—the salesmen and customers—at work either prior to or after delivery of the system. Believe it or not, this is the standard operating procedure in the custom software business. Even the astonishingly effective airline and automobile reservation systems are guilty of atrocious user interfaces. They take employees a very long time to learn, encourage enormous numbers of errors, and fail to provide many functions that would be useful to customers. When I recently made an auto reservation and asked for a child seat, the clerk told me she would try, but the computer had no place to record the child seat, so she would have to send a separate message. It didn't work; there was no child seat waiting.

It is not only the initial design of computer software that is thus so often flawed. The way in which software is produced and deployed makes it almost inevitable that it will miss its mark in providing the right functions for its users. After the initial specification of a product, which may involve executives and managers of the people who will use it, some of whom may have done the job at some time in their past, software is usually developed by a group of programmers with no further contact with customers until the system is complete. The programmers add and subtract features and functions reflecting their own fantasies of what the job is like and under the assumption that the users are people just like them, which is never true. Systems are only rarely tried out on users in their environment before they are sold.

So far I've been describing large systems specifically made for large industrial consumers. The situation with off-the-shelf software sold in computer stores for PC owners is much worse. Virtually anybody with a PC can compose a new program and try to get it marketed. Scores of programs for any particular purpose compete, and the chance that any one of them has actually been found to be valuable, as compared with doing things the way one used to, is vanishingly small.

When it comes to industry deploying computer technology in the workplace, the situation is also grim. Take the example of introducing word processors into a large organization. The standard technique is to establish word processing centers where letter and manuscript typing is sent. Savings are anticipated from reducing the number of highly trained secretaries who need to be hired, by reducing the typing work load of such secretaries, as well as the interruptions to their other work. Not only are the typists in the word processing center expected to be more efficient because of their new technology, they generally are intended to be lower employment category people at lower pay. Concomitant with the introduction of word processing, it is common to begin centralized answering services—answering machines or voice mail to replace the phone pick-up duties of secretaries. Both of these reorganizations have the effect of reducing the number of staff in the secretarial office as well the variety of work that is left for secretaries to do.

There are, unfortunately, a number of untoward side effects. The important supportive roles of the traditional secretarial staff are greatly diminished by this scheme. There are many fewer secretaries, so commonly only progressively higher management are served by secretaries. As a consequence, the rest of the staff cannot be found by customers, vendors, and managers. The caller is informed only "that she has stepped away from her desk." Professionals and managers have to pass their memos and documents to typists who have no command of the local jargon or facts. And all employees find themselves in a less personal, less knowledgeable environment in which to work, with real morale and effectiveness consequences. Meanwhile, even the boss's secretary cannot be as useful as before, since contact with the rest of the staff diminishes. The direct economies of these implementations of computers are apparent to the managers who institute them, although they are often less real than imaginary. The indirect costs of disrupting smoothly functioning office systems that evolved over a century in American businesses are extremely difficult to measure, but they are surely responsible for some of the disappointment in bottom-line effects of new technology. The root trouble is a lack of mechanism to discover how useful a new technology really is.

Often the "obvious" value of computer technology is asserted on the grounds that where it has been deployed, there have been dramatic changes in business organization. Usually the reorganization of typing and telephone answering into specialized departments and the reduction and reassignment of secretarial forces is part of the evidence. Another part is the formation of large departments devoted to data processing, and their role in the power structure of organizations that have them. These are undeniably real effects, but that they are associated with major productivity gains is far from obvious.

Finally, computers are often deployed in a way that shifts who does the labor, in the economic interest of one of the parties, but not necessarily their sum. I've already given the example of the shifting of typing, compositing, and some drafting activities from typists, editors, compositors, and drafting specialists to professionals. Another widespread example is the employment of computers to implement self-service gas stations; the customer does the work of pumping gas, checking oil, and wiping windshields, while a little computer chip records and transmits the sale data to a centralized clerk who only takes money. This one might be considered a productivity gain, in that the customer would otherwise be wasting her time while she waits and indirectly pays for an attendant to do these jobs. On the other hand, having these jobs done is clearly a service of which drivers are being deprived. Whether there is a net gain in dollars worth of total services (i.e., welfare) delivered per employee hour is not clear. Similar remarks apply to so-called warehouse stores, where the customer does the former "stock boy" merchandise handling operation while the point-of-sale computer takes over the inventory control, and fast food restaurants, where the American public has been induced to wait their own tables and, in astonishing contradiction of their customary behavior on highways and in parks, bus the dishes and tidy up after themselves.

Sometimes large systems have their intended effects undermined by unexpected side effects. Some examples come from the early introduction of operations support computer systems in the telephone companies. When the record keeping of telephones, telephone lines, and bills became oppressive, Bell Laboratories was expanded to produce huge software programs to run on large mainframe computers to do all this record keeping. It was a large and pioneering exercise in the development of complex programs, some of them many millions of lines long. The anticipation was that the work force of people who need to record and retrieve such information would be greatly reduced and the accuracy of records greatly improved. When first introduced, however, two nasty and unexpected complications raised their heads. First, when people entered information directly into the computer, they sometimes made errors. The errors were propagated automatically from one part of the program to another. Finding them later and expunging them was expensive and difficult. The initial solution was to hire extra clerks to check each entry before it was made final, thus largely undoing the expected savings in labor. The impact of this defect was eventually reduced, but to this day accuracy in such systems remains a nettlesome problem. Data are entered from several different sources into several different systems by several different people: the service representative who takes the order, the engineer who plans the service, and the craftsperson who installs the equipment may each have to enter an address, each based on different information. No longer does any human with rich local knowledge look at all the related data together and make sense out of—to a human— trivial differences in spelling, the use of an old versus new street name, the use of St. versus Street versus Ct., and so forth. Keeping the data clean and consistent by computer has turned out to be very difficult.

In the second case, systems were designed to allow the information that service representatives got from customers on the telephone to be entered into a computer database. It turned out that the primitive screen-based terminals that were used for the sake of economy, and in conjunction with the available capacity of the mainframe computers to which they were connected, made it impossible for operators to enter data fast enough to keep up with the conversation with the customer. As a remedy, the service rep recorded the information in pencil on a form and passed it to a entry typist who keyed it into the computer, adding to both the transaction labor time and the opportunity for errors. While these systems became very valuable on margin, their initial design did not achieve some of the most important labor productivity gains for which they were intended.

There are many, many examples of proposed computer uses that seemed to offer obvious productivity advantages but contained fatal flaws that defeated their expected utility. We look closely at several in later chapters.

The Trouble with Computers

The situation sums up this way. Computers are often used to do things that are irrelevant or detrimental to true productivity, such as purely share-shifting marketing functions or excess report generation. And when computer applications are intended to increase worker or process efficiency, they often don't help. There are chicken and egg dynamics here. In the business climate of the last few decades, managers have been so interested in short-term market share that they have not devoted needed resources to making computers do better things. But also it has proved so much harder to make computers do serious work that they have been diverted to easier but more frivolous employment. In either case, we need to make computers into much better tools for work, both for the work of individuals and for the work of organizations. When good tools become available, their use for productivity enhancement will be a potent competitive weapon and will supplant, or at least supplement, unproductive uses. Meanwhile, there are good reasons why it is difficult to make computers effective. Foremost is reliance on traditional design and engineering methods that are not sufficient for the development of tools for intellectual work. Fortunately, new engineering methods are evolving to answer the need. We will delve more deeply into the deficiencies of current computer systems, their lack of usefulness and usability, and then explore the new techniques of user-centered design, development, and deployment.

III

What's Wrong with Them

I have spent more words on computers' defects than on their delights. I intend to continue this crabby theme; my goal is not to praise and promote them but to help them be better than they are. Nonetheless, readers, and especially PC aficionados, may feel that I deal too harshly, and perhaps unfairly, with their beloved boxes. Let me spend a little space tilting the record somewhat closer to straight. First, let me make a clean breast of my personal involvement. I have been a moderately heavy computer user for over thirty years. I have used most kinds of computers and both written and used programs of most varieties. I have designed and evaluated widely used software systems. I have supervised groups of computer science researchers. For ten years I made my living managing research aimed at making computers more useful and usable. Obviously, I wouldn't do this if I didn't think there was a promising opportunity. In truth, I have a very ambivalent relationship with computers. Some of the things they do for me are utterly marvelous and liberating, and I am convinced that they will eventually transform the world for the better. But I often find them frustrating, exasperating, and perplexing. I am most frequently perplexed by finding them in heavy use by people and in jobs where they appear to get in the way more than they help. There is a huge gap between the vision and the reality. This book is an attempt to put in place at least a few trusses, perhaps even a stanchion, for the bridge that will some day span the gap. I want us to get across a bit sooner than we will by just hoping the current will carry us.

4:15, September 23, 1992. I've called my health insurance carrier to request a document. Here's an abbreviated log of the automated transaction and (my responses).

"This is Wanderer's Insurance. If you have a touch-tone phone, press 1, if you . . ."(1)

"To help us process your call, please enter the employee's nine-digit social security number." (nnn-nn-nnnn)

"If you want information on claims, press 1. If you want information on coverage, press 2. If you want to talk to a service representative, press 3. If you . . ."(3)

"To help us serve you better, please enter the first four letters of your last name, followed by the first letter of your first name." (landt)

"We are sorry, the office of Wanderer's Insurance is closed. Our office hours are from nine to four." (unprintable)

I've indicted scarcity of sufficiently useful functions and difficulty of use as the major culprits. I don't claim these are the only troubles with computers. Even if they were wonderful in every way, the social life of business might not be able to adjust to them, inept managers might miss or mess the opportunities, or Wall Street might not ante up enough money for the right things at the right times. Nevertheless, when systems become more useful and usable, the remaining problems will get easier. Needed changes in organizations, managers, and investors will come along faster when large benefits are obvious.

6

Usefulness and Usability

Usefulness

Upscale's department store installed a checkout machine intended for better inventory control and customer service. The screen showed a menu of items for sale. It started with a list of general categories: housewares, men's clothing, and so forth, each represented by a colorful picture, an icon. Choose an icon by touching it with your finger, and up comes a more detailed list—sport clothes, suits, shoes . . . each represented by another colorful icon. And on down to the individual item type. No longer did clerks need to know or enter the item type or number—so long as their interpretation of the icons and categories matched that of the designer. I once tried to buy some candles. Three clerks struggled for fifteen minutes to enter the sale. Candles were under vases under platters under mixers under chairs.[1]

It's easy for a computer to offer operations that don't help people. For example, computer schemes for finding books in libraries and for presenting them electronically make it harder to find the books and harder to read them. Later we'll see how dumb applications have been turned around by user-centered design. For now, let's look at some of the underlying problems.

Phase one computer applications perform the same task that a human might otherwise do. Programming for these applications demands near-perfect understanding of what the task is and how it can be accomplished. In tasks like bookkeeping and gun aiming there are well-defined formulas by which the task can be performed, principles that humans would follow precisely if they could. These can be translated directly into computer programs. It has been said that the first industrial revolution replaced human and animal muscle with more efficient energy sources and that the information revolution is replacing human mental work with more efficient electronic processes. That's the way phase one applications works. Phase one computing has had two effects. First, it has pushed forward the replacement of human motor skills with more accurately controlled mechanical ones. Second, it has largely replaced humans in simple acts of arithmetic and filing. Arithmetic is an easily described skill and one at which no mathematical John Henry would stand a chance.

The second phase of computer application, helping people think, is surprisingly more difficult. Note how shallow are the components of writing assumed by word processors, how superficial the aspects of business decision making taken on by spreadsheets. The mental processes of composing memos and documents, of making medical and business decisions, of negotiating and persuading, of formulating plans, and communicating ideas will not soon be captured and imprisoned in a machine. No one really knows how humans do these mysterious things.[2] Humans have amazing memories from which details can be recalled in response to any hint about any part of the original experience. (What time did your childhood neighbors eat dinner on Christmas?) People have astounding visual and auditory pattern-recognizing ability, can easily identify one among a hundred thousand faces or words. In reading text, a literate adult can guess a missing   from context half the   . And these are paltry feats compared to what goes on in the mind during the comprehension, appreciation, or creation of a serious (or funny) verbal passage. No matter what you may have read in an airline magazine, we can't yet come close to these human abilities in any programmable process.

In services, the role of the computer is to help people help people. Thinking how to do this has proved more difficult than technologists expected. Upscale's worthless point-of-sales device is worse than most others perhaps, but so far not enough are good enough. Reservation and information retrieval systems help people do some important business chores more easily. So do bar code inventory systems, income tax preparation programs, email, and several dozen more. But most department store service has gotten worse since computers; so has the handling of telephone inquiries and dozens more. Figuring out really good things to do with computers in service businesses is difficult.

Usability

I tried to change a character in the bibliography of this book to put in a French diacritical mark. After an hour of reading three manuals (for the text editor, the bibliography program, the bibliography program's enhancement package) and many experiments, I gave up. I hope the Acadèmie Français will forgive me.

A phase two system is unlikely to be useful unless it is easy to operate, although the opposite is possible: a system that is easy to operate but of no value. The division between usefulness and usability is sometimes fuzzy; one can't tell whether a system flunks for one reason or the other. Was the Upscale department store's menu a failure because it was hard to use or because it wasn't useful? Or was it useless because it was hard to use?

Nevertheless, usability is the key issue in thousands of cases. In a system in which you sometimes enter K to "keep" a program and in other cases enter K to "kill" the same program, there is a usability problem no matter how useful the program might otherwise be. Because different programs are written by different programmers at different times and marketed by different companies, such inconsistencies are rife. Even when companies like Apple, and more recently IBM and others, attempt to set up interface consistency standards, they don't always have the desired effect. Sometimes it's impossible to maintain consistency as the functions of a system multiply. Bruce Tognazinni, Apple's erstwhile human interface evangelist, has written, "The Macintosh promises consistency, and it is a promise that is dreadfully hard to keep" (Tognazzini 1992). The Macintosh user interface guidelines say the menu bar (a strip along the top of the screen from which available actions can be chosen by a mouse click) must always be visible. But here comes a program intended to produce a slide show on the screen. Should we leave the menu bar visible on each slide? Of course not.

Standards often force designers to use suboptimal designs; the best way to lay out the screen or structure the user system dialog is not the same for different jobs. For consistency, interface standards say that every computer action should be invoked by the same series of user actions: for example, first click a choice from the main menu bar, then pick one of the subsequently displayed submenu options, and then, perhaps, confirm or type in needed information—like a line thickness or a search term. But use this interface to control a steel-rolling plant and you'd have consistently crumpled metal; all those steps would take much too long. As Emerson might have observed, a foolish consistency is the hobgoblin of little computers.

Another problem is the incredibly rapid change in computer technology. Last year's hot program is this year's dog. Everybody is in a constant state of computer illiteracy. The situation cries out for simplicity, but the cry goes unheard. Instead we get ever greater complexity.

Such problems are not the sole property of PCs. Consider the control of advanced telephone services by a Touch-Tone pad. Transferring a call to another telephone or adding on a third participant can be useful, but remembering to do it by punching 23# is taxing. Thus the familiar, "if this doesn't work, call me back."

The list that follows describes some major phase two applications and contrasts their amazing feats and flaws. If you're not a computer maven, this survey should give you an idea of what a wonderful whiz the computer that's in trouble is.

Mathematics, Science, and Engineering Tools

Computers found their first major applications in doing calculations for scientists and engineers. These have continued to be major phase two applications, taking over the drudgery and increasing the accuracy of computations needed to derive predictions from physical theories and engineering models. Computers can also act as accurate and patient logicians, following a series of deductions through endless boring steps. These capabilities have been used to prove mathematical theorems that were long intractable, for example, the famous four-color conjecture that any two-dimensional map can have its regions distinctly colored by just four colors without any two regions of the same color ever adjoining each other. To prove this one, a ghastly number of cases had to be enumerated and shown to conform. A computer programmed by a mathematician did it.

Engineers can pretend that a bizarrely shaped building is composed of millions of tiny polygons, each vigorously shoving its neighbors, and predict whether it will stand or fall. Power turbines and space shuttle shapes are tested before they're really tested. Simulation isn't cheap; it uses most of the multimillion dollar supercomputers in the world. Simulation isn't enough—NASA has just built a new wind tunnel—but it is a big help.

Data Storage and Retrieval

Businesses need to keep track of bills, accounts, inventories, facilities, personnel assignments, and facts about products. Databases can store information in extraordinarily compact forms and get it back in extremely short times. However, users have to pose questions in extremely cumbersome ways. The query languages in popular use require people to enter formal, logical expressions, the exact words in prescribed order, every bit of syntax and punctuation perfect.

The usability of query languages is so poor that the managers, executives, or salespeople who need the data are rarely able to ask the computer for it themselves. Instead, they ask a lookup specialist, a "systems analyst"—a new employment category needed since computers. I know an applications designer who has invented a wonderful artificial intelligence (AI) program that helps callers find the right employee to talk to at her company. It goes unused because the human effort to extract updates from the corporate database exceeds the resources of the electronic data processing department.

Interestingly, the standard query language, called SQL, was originally introduced to make searching easier, in expectation that end users would ask the computer questions by themselves. Previous schemes had been too difficult. But SQL also failed the usability test and did not reduce the need for technicians.

The latest episode is the development of "natural language" front ends. These AI programs accept questions in near-English (or near-French, etc.) and convert them into SQL. Of course, the necessary words must be added for each database. For example, you might be able to ask about "trousers" or "slacks" but not "pants." And you have to avoid the ambiguities of normal English: "Tell me the salaries of managers who are black and women" may not give you what you want. And you must know what is in the database and what is not. The result is that while such systems have sold well, they need just as many technicians as in the past.

Text Storage and Retrieval

Computer storage and retrieval of text is a substantial industry. Bibliographic records—author, title, category—abstracts of journal articles in the sciences, summaries of legal cases, stock analysis reports, and much more, have been put online. Several large companies provide remote access to huge text databases; instead of libraries with stacks, they operate "disk farms." These services, widely used and handsomely paid for, are useful because they provide rapid physical access to information that people cannot afford to collect or keep on hand. However, the user's chance of finding all and only wanted items is slightly worse than with print on paper.

Like the quantitative databases, these require arcane logical queries. Here is an example:

ABS = (information AND retrieval AND NOT about [range = 3]) AND (text OR data) AND (NOT ((quantitative AND data) OR (numbers OR numerical OR statistics) OR information AND NOT text))

This query is intended to find abstracts about information retrieval, rejecting articles that only discuss databases for numbers. (There are two fatal errors in this query. It wouldn't parse—that is, the computer would reject it because the syntax prevents unambiguous interpretation—and if the syntax were corrected, it would return nothing because the logic is faulty. There are more problems as well. Try to find them.) Such queries make use of Boolean expressions, named after the English mathematician George Boole who invented them in 1847. The skilled user can find all articles that contain the words *common* and *cold* within eight words of each other and do not contain the word *ice* or *snow* and were either written before 1900 or in the interval between 1946 and 1953, and had as one of their authors a person whose middle initial is G. Fundamental theory proves that any text item can be distinguished from any other by statements of this kind and that machines can find the matching items with great efficiency.

Unfortunately the design of these languages was not influenced by the way ordinary people think or by the way people ordinarily use words (Furnas et al. 1987). Most designers in this field have been proudly and steadfastly ignorant of such soft stuff. However, these factors defeat success. Boolean-speak is so difficult, and in practice unreliable, that yet another new occupation, information specialist, has grown up. Not only an expense, this means that questions are translated by someone who always knows less than you do about what you want.

Word Processing and Text Editing

The earliest text editors were invented to help programmers correct programs. At first they just let you march through the program line by line, deleting bad lines and adding new ones. Later editors embodied crafty schemes such as "regular expressions" in which a search for /^[a-Z]..[o,ou]/ will find any word beginning with a capital letter at the beginning of a line in which the fourth letter is an *o* or the fourth and fifth letters are *ou* (in case you're looking for either American or English spelling of *colour*). The UNIX version of such a text editor in an early form, intended for use by secretaries, had a user manual containing the following:

The global command **g** is used to execute one or more ed commands on all those lines in the buffer that match some specified string. For example

g/spellng/p

prints all lines that contain spellng.

Several dozen different commands, each with a nonobvious name (Furnas et al. 1987; Landauer, Galotti, and Hartwell 1983), were listed in a manual. There was no way to look up how to do something without knowing the command name. I was given the dubious honor of evaluating the system for use by legal secretaries. I predicted that they would have trouble; the programmers are still mad at me.

Most modern text editing systems are easier to operate than these early ones, but some are many times as complex and difficult and can be mastered only with a great deal of practice by people with high intelligence and nimble hands. The former have become widespread tools of office workers and the latter important implements for advanced programmers.

Current text editors provide many techniques to correct text, to format it in a variety of type fonts and styles, to rearrange and modify it, to check its spelling and even, crudely, its punctuation, and suggest, again crudely, synonyms or alternative phrases. These features add great power, the characteristic cherished most by developers and gurus, but make them more complex for the ordinary user without necessarily improving the everyday product or speeding the process. The online thesaurus, for example, is tempting but not very good. The most important deficiency is that none of these facilities begins to touch the difficult parts of the composition of memos, letters, and documents, which is just that—their composition. The hard, time-consuming, labor-expensive part, because it is done by high-priced people, is the collection, ordering, and expression of ideas, arguments, descriptions, facts, narratives, and explanations. More help with these would be more useful.

Before we leave text editors, a comment on usability. Documents made with them should have fewer typos. It doesn't always work out that way. The very facilities of easy deleting, inserting, cutting, and pasting that make some kinds of errors easier to correct make others easier to commit. You can tell when a document has been produced with a text editor. It has telltale flaws: missing lines, extra words—as if the typist were stuttering, or like a speaker starting phrases over in the middle—disagreements in number, person, tense. They happen because the computer lets the user make partial changes without typing whole sentences or paragraphs over.

What's going on here here? Computerers are. are wonderful.. **Maybe,** if you're l.ike me flew years black, the very   title of these

book, would did puzzled you, or andm mad. you made. Trouble? rouble indeed! There *must were errors in the meas*urements to productivity .Computerers are fantastic, awe awesome. You love they, I lovethem. They're sell like love the m, I livethem, They're selling like hotcakes:. Úmaybe a little slower that

they used to,, ...but still their the the bigger biggest bright,spit spot on with of by modern perseverance. Everyone has wants one. Everyone has

wants one.Everyone uses wants they, one way or anther. Th*ey'e* hare,
They're everywhere.. Everyone has wants one.

Every accountant, author, secretary, scientist, business person, engineer secretary, scientist, business person, engineer has to has havetoo two
one. They're. making new millionaraires—no billionaraires—all over the
plates ..

Trouble,	what	trouble?

Many professional writers are devoted to their word processors, claiming much greater productivity, and I am loathe to discount their testi-
monies. Conceivably, the 30 percent gains we chalked up earlier are especially important to them; perhaps they extract more value than does the
average office worker or laboratory letter writer.

It is also possible, however, that they are unduly impressed with the
benefits and too easily overlook the costs. One professional writer, Ste-
ven Levy, author of *Artificial Life: The Quest for a New Creation,* stated
the case nicely. In a column called "The Iconoclast" in *Macworld* magazine, he first reviewed Loveman's discouraging analyses of productivity,
reporting that as a fan of word processing he vigorously resisted the conclusion. But then he thinks again. He notes that despite the new technology, he and all the other writers he knows still work all the time. He
recalls just having spent most of his morning installing and exploring a
new minor release, 5.0 to 5.1, of his favorite editor.

*"Back in the old days when I toiled on a typewriter, I never spent a
whole morning installing a new ribbon. Nor did I subscribe to* Reming-
ton World *and* IBM Selectric User. *I did not attend the Smith-Corona
Expo two times a year. I did not scan the stores for the proper cables to
affix to my typewriter, or purchase books that instructed me on how
to get more use from my liquid White-Out" (Levy,* Macworld, *March
1993).*

Spreadsheets

Spreadsheets are the second most commercially successful application for
PCs. With a spreadsheet program, you set up a table of data, for example,
a set of budget categories and dates, with the amounts for each in the

cells. You can change an entry, and the machine will automatically recalculate the sums of each row and column. More sophisticated applications are legion. A typical one calculates the consequences of alternative investment instruments: yield, present value, long-term performance, best- and worst-case outcomes. Financial experiments like this are difficult to perform by hand but useful to clarify people's thinking.

Do spreadsheet programs make users almost perfectly accurate? No. I have seen data suggesting that in common use, over 40 percent of spreadsheets contain at least one error. The computer doesn't add or subtract wrong, but people can't figure out how to get it to do what they want, or they use its power to do foolish or careless things that the programs are helpless to prevent.

Shortly before the publication deadline for this book, I wanted to revise a figure, one I'd done a year ago. After an hour's searching I still could not find a version of the spreadsheet file that the current graph program could work with. I had to start from scratch. (Experts will be tempted to think me disorganized and stupid. That's my point.)

Spreadsheet programs can tempt users into endless puttering—changing this, trying that—of little value. Additional time is stolen by housekeeping: filing results, making disk copies, finding the disks and files later, organizing and cleaning up overloaded file systems, upgrading programs, learning and teaching how to do new operations, keeping the hardware working. Bookstores stock fat volumes about spreadsheet programs, and community colleges offer courses in their use. My first reaction to such books and courses is always that the systems for which they are intended are not well enough designed. The proper goal is that computer systems be so easy to use that people can master them on their own in a short time.

Graphics Programs

Computer chips cannot be made without the systems that let engineers build, see, and test imaginary circuits on their computer screens. The engineer moves and copies parts, or touches a mouse to the screen to apply an imaginary voltage and make an imaginary meter reading. These systems are extremely valuable.

The popular variety of graphics programs, ones like MacDraw and Cricket, allow ordinary people to do on their personal computers what drafting and art departments used to do by hand. There are no data available on the work time or quality of the figures produced by these amateur draftspeople, though. The programs are certainly popular. Where I work, highly educated scientists and engineers spend days producing graphics of much lower quality than drafting department standards. Before every conference, I find Ph.D.s in on weekends running back and forth from their offices to the printer. It appears that people who are unable to execute pretty pictures with pen and paper find it gratifying to try with a computer. This is an important example of a phase two application success, a computer aid that allows people to do things that they could not before. With greater ease and quality, it could be an economic gain as well as a source of personal satisfaction.

"Last year I spent more than fifty hours trying to draw my house in a 3-D graphics program. There is not a wall in that drawing that is properly connected to any other wall. The roof kind of floats here and there, depending on the angle. I eventually abandoned the application and built a model of the house out of construction paper."(Tognazzini 1992, 189).

Desktop Publishing
Desktop publishing means doing type composition, page layout, and laser printing in addition to typing and copyediting on a PC. Desktop publishing has made small-scale publishing ventures, particularly newsletters, spring up like mushrooms after rain. Whether there is a genuine economic advantage over traditional publishing techniques is not so clear. Instead, it could be another case in which person A's time is traded for person B's, in which flexibility is gained but advantages of specialization and scale are lost. Most major book publishers and magazines have not turned to these techniques.[3] A high-placed editor of a major publishing house recently expressed amazement that so many of his authors

turned in copy carefully prettified with such systems. The first thing he does is have the manuscripts retyped for editing according to house standards, discarding all the fancy typography and layout painstakingly created by the author.[4]

A report on desktop publishing in the public relations business, a heavy service industry user, turned up considerable enthusiasm but some additional problems as well (Gordon 1989). According to one informant, "It allows us to do things very professionally and save time. With new business proposals, it helps us generate income, although I'm not sure exactly how I'd quantify that." In previous years, the glitz of a new business proposal was not as important, he explained. Now expectations are much higher. Another said, "Because you're making changes electronically, you have to proof more carefully—watch out for dropped letters. It adds more time at the late stages."

Several users said the number of changes requested by clients had soared because of the perception that changes were easy to make. Nitpicking was rampant, four or five revisions standard. Because the software is so complex, many companies created new specialists for the job. Other respondents thought the quality that resulted from amateur designers using such systems was unacceptable: "It looks like junk," one said. Said another: "I created a newsletter and then wasted days doing layouts without even realizing how much time I was spending. People have so much fun making pretty pictures, they forget they're there to work."

Artificial Intelligence and Expert Systems

Everyone has heard about artificial intelligence. Indeed, the field's leading researchers agree that everyone has heard too much about artificial intelligence. Early workers phenomenally underestimated the difficulty of mimicking human mental powers and confidently expected early sweeping successes. In the 1960s it was predicted that within ten years computers would convert ordinary speech and handwriting to print, comprehend and compose natural language, drive trucks, do housework, and tutor students better than professors could. Thirty years later many proponents see no reason to change these predictions; they still expect them within ten years.

The present stance of the still-confident is that they underestimated the amount of commonsense knowledge used in real life, and that once this is added to AI programs all will be well. A large project under Doug Lenat at MCC has been trying to do that. When it started in 1986, Lenat thought about a million facts (or rules, as the building blocks of knowledge are called in AI) would do the trick. A few years later he upped the number to 2 million, a few years later to 4 million. When last heard from, he was sure his system would be ready to act human around 1997, and by 2004 would have all the 20 to 40 million facts it really needs (Goldsmith 1994).

It is unfortunate that artificial intelligence has been the subject of so much excessive zeal, for some of its products have become, after all, significantly smart and useful. Special-purpose chess machines can sometimes outplay some grand masters, isolated words and handwritten characters can be recognized under favorable conditions with fair accuracy, artificial visual control can guide smart bombs with devastating effectiveness. (Full natural language processing continues to be more difficult than we expected—too much knowledge needed, truck driving is far too complex in both vision and control, tutoring involves mysteries yet to be cracked).

The most important commercial spinoffs of research in artificial intelligence are known as expert systems or "knowledge-based systems." These programs try to put the knowledge of a human expert into a computer routine. Expert systems have been energetically promoted over the last decade and reputedly have found thousands of applications in a variety of different industries (Feigenbaum, McCorduck, and Nii 1988). Digital Equipment Corp. (DEC) was an early user of the technology. One program could choose and list all the pieces needed for a custom installation of one of DEC's computer systems. When first introduced, it reportedly reduced the time and expertise needed for such planning and cut down on delivery goofs and retrofitting excursions. In 1989, it was reported that DEC was using fifteen people and $2.5 million per year updating and maintaining expert systems (Enslow 1989). This represents both the utility of the programs and one of their emerging deficiencies. The systems tended to get out of date rapidly as products and business changed and fell into disuse unless revamped.

Expert system reporting is remarkably prone to the "expected benefit" syndrome: "TI expects the system to reduce cost overruns and preparation expenses by an average of $2 million a year" (Enslow 1989). A 1988 promotional book by one of the fathers of expert systems, Edward Feigenbaum, and two colleagues, begins by telling us it will survey hundreds of successful systems in use, but closer reading reveals that all but a handful are research prototypes being studied in academic labs, not commercially deployed systems.

Point-of-Sale Systems

My wife stopped by the video store. The clerk typed her name into the computer and announced that she owed $27.50 for late charges. She objected, pointing out that the computer had this huge fine posted against a tardiness of one day. The clerk said, "Oh, the computer's got one of those ghosts. Sometimes it just gets confused and keeps issuing these charges. No one knows where they come from."

Perhaps the most commonly met phase two computer applications are the machines that process grocery checkouts. These are quite amazing gadgets. The box or can is passed over a scanner that automatically identifies the product: the computer looks up its current price, rings it up on the register, prints the product name and price on a tape, and stores the data for later use. At least that happens if the clerk is skillful, the scanner glass clean, and all is working well. The usefulness and usability issues are fascinating because of the number of different players involved. Presumably the major recipient of added utility is the store management, which is supposed to get accurate up-to-the minute inventory information, fewer checkout errors, and less theft; save money by avoiding individual price labeling; and obtain valuable marketing information. Of course, it was thought, all of these advantages could be passed along to the customers in the form of lower prices, a more flexible and popular mix of products, speedier and more accurate checkout.

Let us consider the various parties: employees, management, and customers. The checkout job does not look very much different; where clerks no longer do much price entry, they need new skills to make scanners obey and often have to memorize extensive lists of product numbers to key into the system for bagels and broccoli and other weighed or counted items.

A twelve-month observational case study from England reveals some details about what sometimes actually happens (Cutler and Rowe 1990). The scene is a recently upgraded branch of one of England's largest, most modern chains of supermarkets. Store managers reported that since the scanners were introduced, they were able to divert more employees to bagging on busy days, reducing checkout time, pleasing customers, increasing throughput, and decreasing crowding in the parking lot. Staffing records, however, showed a net *increase* in total hours worked and a shift of employment into operating, maintaining, and managing the technology. There was no before-and-after stopwatching of checkout speed, but both observers and cashiers believed there had been no change. When everything went smoothly, scanned entry was fast. But when bar codes were damaged or produce codes unremembered, times could go very much higher than with traditional registers. One response was to pass difficult items through uncharged. Entry errors were supposed to disappear but sometimes increased instead. Employee morale went down, partly due to the physical discomfort of the new checkout setup—a consultant found poor ergonomics in the station design—and partly due to the shift in jobs.

The actual effect on inventory control and stocking was also unexpected. The system produced more detailed records of items sold—brand X toilet paper and brand Z washing powder separately versus just "household goods." The problem was that, for efficiency's sake, goods were still received from the central supply depot in large lots, say a box from Peter Piper's Paper Products containing twenty cases of toilet paper and thirty of paper towels. Thus, the detailed numbers had little advantage over the traditional method of noticing that brand X toilet paper is getting low.

How else do these systems affect customer service? For one thing, they produce itemized receipts. Customers reportedly like these, and they appear to be necessary; rapid, repeated passes over the scanner to get the required beep often causes double charging that customers don't detect from the quickly vanishing item display. (The English investigators don't speculate as to whether items uncharged even out double entries.) Bar codes also make it possible to forgo individual price labels on items; the computer looks them up from the item code, and prices are posted only on store shelves, not on the products. This makes it easier for the store to change prices quickly. From the customer's point of view, however, once the package is in the grocery cart, only memory can help until the item has gone through the scanner and been posted on the display and receipt. A calculator is needed to estimate the current total value of the cart as you shop and a notepad to compare the price of hot sauces in the condiments aisle with those in foreign foods. If you want to keep track at home (e.g., to notice that breakfast cereal prices sometimes increase twice in as many months) you have to search receipts instead of looking in the pantry. (Ah, here's a use for your database program: key in a description of each grocery item and its price.)

My friend Dave remarks that supermarkets these days seem to be out of items much more frequently. He blames it on "not quite in time" inventory control made possible by IT.

Transaction Systems

Computers stand beside clerks who deal with customers by telephone or mail. The burgeoning mail order business has deftly exploited these systems to manage inventory, buying, marketing, and order processing. Using computers, a small staff can run a high-volume operation. Similarly, the processing of payments for everything from monthly utilities to mutual fund investments is handled by systems in which the input clerk does nothing more than enter the amount of payment; the rest comes from the machine-readable portion of the return stub or is fetched from the bowels of the computer.

From management's point of view, these systems save clerical salaries. From both worker and customer's point of view, it depends on how they are implemented. Some phone-order companies give the entire responsibility for an order to a single agent, the person who answers the telephone. With the help of the computer, this person knows about inventory, is knowledgeable about the product, and interacts with the customer from beginning to end. If there is a problem, the single agent can resolve it. Other times, the functions are divided up; one person takes

DILBERT reprinted by permission of UFS, Inc.

requests, another complaints, someone else knows about inventory, and another about customer account status. Salespeople in the former case probably have interesting jobs, ones in which they effectively handle most of the business. In the latter case, the job is as deadly as bobbin loading in a nineteenth-century textile mill.

As a customer in the former case, you are awed and delighted when told that although the store is out of your size sweater in blue you can have one in green or another style, delivered Tuesday, and, by the way, that the correction you requested for the returned sushi calendar has been made, and thank you, Mr. Landauer—pronounced correctly. Or, in the latter case, you can be bumped from ignorant agent to ignorant agent, eventually to be sent the wrong item at the wrong address; you can write on your bill repeatedly, enclose explanatory letters, call thrice and get nowhere, be charged monthly with interest added and collection threats appended. With computers to help, as they say, it all depends.

Desirability: A Critical Combination of Usefulness and Usability

"The application 'unknown' has suddenly quit because an error of type 15 has occurred."

Usefulness and usability, essential as they are, do not quite say it all. A technology will be of little benefit if few use it. When, following a time-honored premise of industrial management, word processors were used to centralize document preparation, typists lost their knowledge of context and jargon, often producing nonsense output, and author and typist could no longer fix problems by quick chats. Departments that needed typing didn't like the situation, and most word processing centers were soon abandoned (Johnson and Rice 1987).

A desirability failure that spoils employees' work lives is especially serious. Centralized word processing had this evil defect as well. Typists and their supervisors usually hated the new style of work—its separation from the real consumer, its social isolation from the life of the office, its artificial work flow control procedures. Many bookkeeping applications have been even worse offenders. They separate the most routine, mechanical parts of the work and assign them to back office employees doing physically stressful and mentally deadening jobs. Computerized workplaces all too easily can become modern sweatshops, modern only in the look of the equipment. Such use of technology is morally repugnant. It is also economically stupid; workers who enjoy their work do it better, stay longer in the face of temptation, and contribute ideas and enthusiasm to the evolution of enhanced productivity.

Other Troubles

"In the world of the computer, we calmly accept limitations we would tolerate nowhere else. The typical monitor is no substitute for the printed page, so we squint at fuzzy, ugly characters we would find utterly repugnant in print. Tiny, blurry, jerky windows of video display that even an inveterate couch potato would scorn are hailed as breakthroughs merely because a computer displays them." Stephen Manes, New York Times, March 29, 1994, B7.

Technical Limitations

Most troubles come from not knowing what functions the computer ought to perform or from our inability to program them to do what we really would want—to help me liven up this section, for example. The problem is rarely lack of computing power. Nevertheless, there are still troubles from this source. For example, although startling special effects for motion pictures are now being created with computers, fully detailed and shaded simulations of realistically prancing bears and dancing people are still a long way off. Somewhat closer to the office, computer screens are not yet up to snuff. People read anywhere from 5 percent to

30 percent slower from computer screens than from printed pages. The problem is the graininess of the display. The characters on a computer screen are made up of little dots of light and dark, just as they are in offset printing. If there are enough tiny dots, as there are in offset, the human eye can't tell the difference. But that takes at least 100,000 dots (or pixels, as they are called on computers) per square inch of surface. Ordinary computer screens have less than one-fifth that many. In addition, the overall size of computers screens is still too small. You don't get nearly as much area to scan by just moving your eyes and head as you do with a full-sized newspaper or with papers spread out on a desk.

Except for very limited uses, you can't talk to a computer. When you type to it, you have to use special language. We don't know how much these limitations reduce usefulness and usability. It is not clear, for example, for what and how much speech recognition would help. Would you want to play a violin or draw a graph by oral instructions?

Unreliability

On March 13, 1993, the Electronic Data System network connecting 5,200 ATMs all across the United States failed because a snowstorm in New Jersey disabled a computer. It took two weeks to restore service and much longer to untangle the accounting mess created by temporary arrangements and transfers of services to other networks (Jones 1993).

One of the most annoying habits of computers is unreliability. How many times have you been told a service is unavailable because the "computer is down"? Compare this with the number of times you've been told you can't get gasoline because the pumps are broken or you can't have your breakfast because the toaster's not working just now. If cars were nonfunctional as often and unexpectedly as computers, we'd probably give them up. I'm constantly amazed at our forbearance.

Computers fail for many reasons. Only a minority of the failures are due to hardware, though disk drives in particular are quite delicate. More common are software glitches. The programs that run the computer, the system software, are extremely complex. They can't anticipate all the combinations of actions and loads put on them, and thus are often surprised and flummoxed into a kind of mental paralysis. They hang, and the user has to start them up again from some point before the confusion began.

Perhaps the most common cause of failure is one that doesn't even get blamed on the computer, though it should: user error. One of the chief virtues of a computer is the flexibility with which it can be asked to do so many things. The unfortunate consequence is that the user can ask it to do things the user really doesn't want. The ability to make unlimited changes with a text editor rests on the fact that the text is stored in an evanescent form. It can go through scores of partial revisions. The user has to keep track of which version is current, "saving" new work at appropriate intervals and deciding whether to keep or obliterate the prior version at each change. It is painfully easy to get confused and wipe out things you wanted to keep. A significant fraction of the times we are told the computer is down results from some such operator error. As I will say again and again in many ways, "operator errors" are almost always the system's fault.

Incompatibility

There is yet another aspect of the complexity problem: computers and their application programs are often designed in staggeringly incompatible manners. Many programs ostensibly for use on the same machine don't function the same way or together. In many places the machines themselves are isolated, not connected together, so that work done in one place can't be conveniently transferred anywhere else. As yet, there is not nearly sufficient connectivity between computers. Documents created in paper can be almost universally shared between people and organizations, not so for electronic versions. It is not uncommon for the same business document or data to be typed separately into three different computers.

And . . .

There are also some widely discussed potential dangers and difficulties of the use of computers, both as physical objects—where the case appears quite flimsy—and as social or work instruments—where more worry is justified. Computers do not emit x-rays or microwave radiation in measurable quantities, despite some early concerns that they might. They do generate some low-frequency electromagnetic energy, as do all other electrical appliances, especially television sets. Although there is no credible evidence of harmful effects, still, almost nothing is known about the long-term consequences. On the other hand, working at a computer terminal for long periods of time can strain eyes, backs, shoulders, and wrists. Resulting fatigue and other painful or disabling symptoms can affect both usefulness and usability and need to be dealt with. Better design of furniture and work practices—for example, arranging frequent short breaks to move around a bit and look at something other than the screen—can help a great deal.

Last, and most, work and social effects of computers are not all always beneficial. IT can usurp jobs. It can diminish satisfaction or remuneration. It makes possible new kinds of covert surveillance and piecework pacing. Computers can deskill and demean work, despite their potential to enrich and improve it.

Well-Known "Successes" and "Failures"

We can get another view of the situation by looking at some major applications of computers—some that are widely regarded as stunning successes, some as catastrophic failures. Three of the best-known success stories are automatic teller machines, airline reservation systems, and the Macintosh user interface.

ATMs Again

ATMs have spread like wild money. They terrorized CitiBank's competitors in New York until other banks banded together and built similar systems. Meanwhile, the head of computing at Chase Manhattan Bank, Elaine Bond, said that ATMs added to the cost of the banks doing business. They are "a convenience that someone has to pay for." It would be nice if computers could offer services that are more desirable than what they replace and at the same time cheaper and more profitable, but perhaps that would be asking them to take us to the moon.

The appeal of ATMs to those who use them is incontestable. They are useful. They improve the convenience of a common chore; users can get cash in many more places, in several other countries, at any time of the day on almost any day, usually without standing in line. And they are usable. The ideal of usability often put forward by human-computer interaction specialists is the "walk up and use" interface. That means the user needs no instruction other than what is on the screen, and the interface results in successful, error-free, satisfying service. Many ATMs have nearly achieved this ideal. Except when the machine is out of order or money, you rarely hear a patron swearing. In some ways, ATMs are even easier to use than a human teller; the patron never asks "To whom should I make the check out?" "Should I sign it on both front and back?" "What is today's date?"

The computer seems to have been used to good effect in most ATMs. The screen presents needed information in a simple, straightforward way, and entry is by a small set of well-labeled buttons corresponding to a few obvious options. The interaction protocol—the series of steps taken by the customer and the machine—is short and sweet. How did it get so good? It's an interesting story.

Machines with the basic functionality—able do the database operations, log the ledger entries, count out bills, issue records—were available from the early 1970s, but they failed to catch on. Only after an intensive design-test-redesign effort to improve the usability of the interface, conducted by a group of human factors specialists at CitiBank, was public acceptance won. I have heard it said that it "was just a matter of ergonomics," as if that were a minor, easy detail. It was neither minor nor easy; it was critical and difficult. What was most difficult about it was realizing that it must be done.

Interestingly, not all imitators have managed to get it right. New interfaces have been introduced and new features added, often, apparently, without benefit of user-centered design methods. One type features a narrow slit that has to be adjusted perfectly for the customer to see the screen. This added feature, probably thought to be a clever security enhancement, drives me crazy. Some models set a maximum allowed withdrawal amount but don't tell you what it is! If you ask for more than the maximum, it rudely refuses, and you have to start the whole procedure over: insert card, type password, and make another blind guess. Why doesn't the line on the screen that offers the option of a withdrawal also state the maximum? Probably because nobody bothered to watch customers use the system before the design was finalized.

Reservation Systems

Airline reservation systems generate roughly a billion dollars in revenues annually. There are hundreds of airlines, thousands of routes, tens of thousands of airplanes, hundreds of thousands of travelers each day. Managing schedules, making reservations and connections, changing them, and keeping track of fares and payments is an extraordinarily complicated job that is virtually impossible to do by hand. Had computerized systems not existed, perhaps a hand ledger system operating by telephone could have evolved. A rather large airline in India operated this way. However, once the records and schedules were computerized in America, there was no turning back. Any airline that wanted to stay in business had to get itself listed in a reservation system, and to serve their function, all the systems had to talk to each other.

The usefulness of reservation systems is obvious. Business efficiency requires keeping track of what seats are occupied, what cars are where, what rooms are reserved, occupied, and cleaned. Customers like having reservations confirmed anywhere instantly. I lived in England for a while before the introduction of networked airline reservation services. To book, I had a travel agent call the airline and ask whether a seat was available on a particular flight. After some delay, a message came back saying no seat was available. The agent looked up another flight, requested a seat, and repeated until an opening was found—sometimes days later.

But now look at usability. Reservation systems are generally a disgrace. They don't appear too bad from a traveler's perspective. One calls the travel agent and requests a point-to-point connection in a certain time slot at a certain service level; the agent does the rest and usually comes up fairly soon with a reasonable solution. True, with the proliferation of flights, fares, and restrictions, one can be puzzled by the different answers that different agents give on different occasions. And, of course, the system may be down or unavailable, requiring a call back and another Muzak hold. However, these are minor nuisances compared to what can happen in an exceptional case. The systems are baroquely complicated and horridly hard to learn. Few agents know how to do much beyond the most routine transactions.

My ticket on an international flight got locked in a secretary's drawer over the weekend I was to leave. When I called, the airline said I could easily get a new ticket and apply for a credit on the old, but I had to get to the counter an hour ahead of time. That seemed like a lot of time, but I complied. As it turned out, no one at the counter knew how to enter the transaction into the computer. The first agent, a trainee, made a few attempts, then called for help. The next agent tried several keyboard incantations, consulted an older colleague at the far end of the counter, tried some more, and gave up. One by one, three other agents appeared, palavered, tried experiment after experiment. The desk supervisor had no better luck; manuals and online help were to no avail. It was over an hour before I had a ticket and a receipt whose legitimacy the supervisor doubted.

The direct users of reservation systems are clerks and agents. Their job is fraught with difficulties. Destination airports, airlines, and service categories are entered by arcane codes. Hundreds of these must be memorized and entered flawlessly. It is an intellectually demanding job, too often filled by people with little experience because of rapid turnover (partly due to the nastiness of the job). The computer systems do a miserable job of helping the agents but are nevertheless successful because they are useful: they do something that both the customer and the supplier want done and do it in a much more efficient and effective way than might otherwise be possible. They are successful despite severe problems in usability. This is all too common. Designers assume that the system only needs to perform its job well; Difficulties in operating it are the employees' problem. Employees should be selected, trained, and "motivated" to cope with the wonderful system.

The Macintosh User Interface
The dramatic market success of the Apple Computer Co. is often attributed to the ease of use of its Macintosh interface. This interface—the way

in which information is presented, the machine is controlled by its user, the screen is laid out—is hailed as the epitome of good usability design, the great breakthrough that brought computing to the masses.

The Macintosh interface is based on the use of windows (different portions of the screen devoted to different functions in a flexible and independent manner), the use of a "mouse," icons, and menus (lists of options to be selected). The design of the screen is quite attractive. The Macintosh employs a consistent interaction style: "pull-down" menus are listed at the top and activated by clicking a mouse, then selected by a further mouse click, and so on. This consistent style is generally followed by people who write application programs to be used on the Macintosh as well as Apple's own designers and has become an article of passionate faith on the part of devoted users and developers. Most of these techniques originated in experiments on interaction techniques conducted in the 1960s at the Stanford Research Institute, further developed at Xerox Palo Alto Research Center, and then commercially exploited by Apple.

The way these elements are combined and used in the basic Macintosh operations (that is, ignoring special applications like income tax programs) created a giant step in ease of use. Tests of users doing basic text editing and spreadsheet operations show 40 to 70 percent improvements in work efficiency over other interfaces.

Often the ease of the use of the Macintosh is attributed simply to the presence of the components listed above, to its GUI (graphical user interface, pronounced "gooey"). This explanation is simplistic and false. It is possible, as many applications program for the Macintosh have made clear, to combine all of these elements in ways that make it impossible to work with reasonable efficiency and accuracy. A recent study compared the use of a variety of functions on the Mac with doing the same things on another widely marketed GUI system. The Mac advantage was almost as big over its competitor as it is over typical non-GUI interfaces. Moreover, there are applications on other systems for which excellent usability is obtained without using any GUI features. The effectiveness of the basic Macintosh's functionality derives from the way in which the elements have been combined, which ones are used when for what purposes, what icons and menu options are used for what, and, especially, the well-chosen set of interlocking functions that have been provided. The way in which the sequence of user actions interacts with how the screen responds has been engineered into a smoothly working whole that optimizes the user's performance of common tasks.

Macintosh's secret of success is the opposite of that of the reservation systems: it is easy to use. Its usefulness is not nearly so dramatic, though. Macs are being used for word processing, graphics, spreadsheets, and databases, but as the superiority of the personal computer for these tasks over their paper and ink predecessors is rather tenuous. It is hard to show that these systems make it possible to do important operations that couldn't be done before or to do old things in a much easier, more effective, or more economical way. Most of their apparent usefulness seems to lie in letting people do themselves what they previously had to have done for them by specialists, though it may not be especially economical or effective to do so.

In the summer of 1991, the National Science Foundation sponsored a conference in Boulder, Colorado, in which researchers were invited to present case histories of systems that had been explicitly designed to help people do mental tasks better and that were proven successes. The participants came up almost empty-handed. They presented mostly designs that were either still in the laboratory or in only limited use. For a real-world example, the participants kept coming back to Macintosh and its sales. We are not swimming in a sea of computer inventions of easily demonstrated value.

Some Not So Successful Examples

Two attempts to build large systems for the U.S. government bombed in instructive ways. One was a system for the patent office, the other for the Internal Revenue Service. A central feature of these two notorious cases is that they are phase two applications, aimed at improving the efficiency and effectiveness of a job done by humans.[5]

Keeping track of the ever increasing flood of patent applications, checking them against the growing mountain of past patents and claims, and processing the new documents is a daunting job. There are about 1,500 patent examiners, over 100,000 applications per year. The main job is searching information files and handling documents, tasks for which computers seem perfectly suited. The project, begun in 1982, was targeted at greatly increasing the efficiency of the examiner's job, a clear case of intellectual augmentation. A decade later, the system was not quite in operation. Online it will have cost most of $1 billion and increased operating expenses by an amount sufficient to add another 1,000 patent examiners. Strassmann (1990) quotes the assistant commissioner of the U.S. Patent Office as saying, "We really get no short-term increases in productivity. The real gains . . . are in improvement in the quality of work." The lack of evidence of quality improvements from other applications of automated information retrieval is cause for doubt as to whether even this claim will be realized.

The IRS awarded a contract for 18,000 portable computers for field tax auditors, with the goal of increasing their productivity and the accuracy with which they could find errors. The delivered system required an agent to load as many as eighteen different diskettes to do an audit. Three-quarters of the agents said they didn't like the new tool, and two-thirds of them refused to use it.

Another report of the value of computers for government comes from France (Fontaine 1992). Information technology applications in sixteen ministries were studied, with uses ranging from automobile registration to statistical analyses of the labor force and inventory control for state-managed pharmacies. Most of the applications involved either automation of record keeping or databases for management information, with a few intended to help in planning and decision making. There were observations, interviews, and analyses of before-and-after output and staffing. Of the sixteen, only three could be counted as clear wins. Seven clearly cost more than they were worth in labor saved. Poor economic results and poor effects on service quality went hand in hand.

We know about these examples only because they were done in public for the public good. There are undoubtedly scores of equally ignominious failures, although perhaps on smaller scales, in the private sphere. But private businesses do not often tell us about foolish investments that they have made.

7

Software Design, Development, and Deployment

The art department at my company once used an expensive and complicated computer-based graphics system. I struggled with it many times. Although it provided plenty of facilities for colors and special effects, lines of all widths and shadings, all manner of lettering fonts and flourishes, it couldn't produce accurate graphs. There was no way to plot data points properly. Providing a list of X, Y coordinates was no help; the system didn't know anything about them. Instead the operators did freehand artistic interpretations of my scientific findings. How could an expensive system be developed that lacks such a fundamental functionality in its intended field of application?

Unfortunately, the overwhelming majority of computer applications are designed and developed solely by computer programmers who know next to nothing about the work that is going to be done with the aid of their program. Programmers rarely have any contact with users; they almost never test the system with real users before release. Once a program is fielded, the programmers get information about bugs that cause malfunctions or crash the system but little information about what aspects of the system help or hinder users in their work.

So where do new software designs come from? The source is almost entirely supply side, or technology push. The designers know how previous similar systems worked. They may know about new algorithms and data structures—new ways to write programs more efficiently or elegantly—and they know tricks they can do to take advantage of the newer, faster processor or the larger on-board memory. They know that they can add features, put more pictures on the screen, offer more

typefaces and colors. I do not want to make light of the skills and knowledge involved; programmers are impressive technologists, and programming the operating system or the interface of a Macintosh or a NeXT
requires brilliance and dedication. But.

Design

Technology push is a wellspring of creative ideas, some useful, some
harebrained. It is too hard to tell the difference. For example, with a
computer and a projection system, it is possible to display all the instruments on a car dashboard against the front window so that the driver
can see them without looking down. Several car companies have proposed such "heads-up" displays, and they have been installed in military
aircraft. The problem is that repeatedly adjusting your eyes between the
artificial display and the outside world causes confusion. In one experiment, a pilot flew into a truck parked on a runway thinking it was only
an icon on the control display. Luckily he was in a simulator.

Implementing a good design is quite different from generating it. Although their knowledge of what can be done at what cost is critical in
planning software development, crack technologists are handicapped in
thinking of what the system should do. Programmers adore computers,
know them intimately, and interact with them comfortably. It's hard for
them to empathize with ordinary users. Star UNIX programmers use a
greatly amplified word processor, with hundreds of convenient commands, each selected by a chord of two or three keys. Watching an expert
at work is like watching a talented organist produce music with ten fingers and two feet. What will such people think natural and easy? Where
will their ambitions lead when they dream up new designs? Rather than
simplifying and fixing annoying details of routine tasks, they will make
new programs soar to new heights.

Software engineers (another name for programmers and system designers) tend to have different personalities, different approaches to the
world, from the rest of us. Programming attracts twice the proportion
of introverts in the general population and three times the number of
"intuitive" thinkers (Tognazzini 1992). Introverts prefer their own
thoughts to social interaction. Intuitive thinkers prefer the products of
their imaginations to humdrum reality; they solve problems by visual

imagery and insight rather than by plodding logic or investigation. These traits apparently suit people for the largely independent, sometimes lonely work of programming and to creating the intricately complex and abstract structures of software systems. It is unlikely that they help a person understand the majority, who would rather interact with co-workers than computers and who prefer to think about simple, concrete problems.

More often than not, the impetus for a new program comes from copying the last product, emulating the way things are done on paper (but doing them on a small and fuzzy computer screen), imitating a competitor's product but trying to do it one better, or from a hunch. A common source is the "wouldn't it be neat if . . ." inspiration. This is sort of like Mallory's famous quote about climbing Mt. Everest; people want to do things just because it's a challenge.

These sources of ideas speed the march of computing, but it's a shame they are the main determinants of its direction. Software-producing organizations have too little knowledge of what the system should accomplish. "Requirements" usually come from an indirect source with limited validity. Programs for personal computers are often produced with no contact with anybody who has the job for which they are going to be used, unless the programmer happens to be one of those people. I have a very popular, highly reputed prereading program for children. Its claim to pedagogical expertise is that one of the two graphic designers who programmed it was a teacher for a few years. The graphics are great.

Sometimes programmers have indirect contact with users through a marketing organization that asks for criticisms and comments. Until quite recently, however, none of the major software companies that published programs for personal computers, and none of those that produced reservation systems, had professionally staffed departments charged with analyzing the tasks and skills of the users for whom the systems were intended.

The situation is a little better at in-house or contract software factories where programs are produced on order for customers. Somebody usually talks to customer representatives, typically managers of data processing departments. But if any of these people ever did the job the program is supposed to aid, it wasn't very recently, and they probably had different talents from the majority of users—who were not promoted. Although many companies brag about customer involvement in system development, they usually mean involvement of people who will sign the check, not those who will use the system.

Typically in software design, a system is developed that performs, in a strictly technical sense, many functions imagined useful. Then an interface, a set of controls by which people can make it work, is attached. If people can't make the system behave, courses are offered and books published. The users are redesigned. Meanwhile, managers are taken to task for failing to rearrange work flows and organizational structure properly.

This is known as "blaming the user." One reason software developers get away with poor usability is that users often blame themselves. No matter how poor the system, users rarely complain that it is badly designed; instead they apologize for their own ineptness. Of course, software is sometimes rejected by the public because of inutility and unusability. Competition in the marketplace will eventually winnow out losers and reward better designs, but this is a slow and painful process.

A few years ago the U.S. Post Office invested in point-of-sales computers for counter clerks. The clerk first enters the postage, or it is entered directly from a scale. Then the clerk enters the amount of money handed over by the customer. The computer computes and displays the change. One result is much longer lines at the post office. I've asked many clerks whether the system is valuable. Some say it is—but for management, not them. Perhaps they make fewer errors, although that is not guaranteed because faulty keying is not infrequent. Change calculation probably is not much faster. Well-practiced keying is slower than mental arithmetic for oft-repeated problems. The worst part, though, is that the terminal gets in the way of handling letters, packages, and change. One clerk put it this way: "If I had another hand or could work with my left hand with my eyes closed to enter figures, this thing would be okay."

Development

Most software development follows a sequence of activities called the "waterfall model." It starts upstream with requirements that feed a tumbling torrent of planning and programming that—usually—plunges into chaos just before it comes to rest. The requirements say what the system will do, what features it will support, the amount of data it will accommodate, how fast it will respond. Requirements may be translated into detailed specifications for parts of the program, which are then apportioned among programmers. Parts are passed to testers, who report bugs that must be fixed. After all the modules work separately, they have to be made to work together. More tests and fixes. By this time, chaos has entered, because parts didn't work as hoped, someone had a better idea, the parts don't fit, and the deadline is tomorrow.

Just about now, work is begun on documentation and instructions for the users. In principle, the programmers interact with the document writers, who are supposed to learn about the system and its intended uses and users. In practice, little of this occurs. It's dangerous to bring documenters and programmers together; each resents the other's encroachment on a job for which they are experts and the others fools. Often document writers are forbidden to talk to the busy programmers and have no opportunity to talk to real users.

Here's a story from a technical writer at a small instrument manufacturing company. The company president told her to write a user manual solely from the written requirements. Rebelliously, she sneaked forbidden moments with a design engineer and tried the product. The president blew his stack. Her instructions told users to operate the instrument differently from the way the president had planned. Never mind that the engineers had altered the operating procedures to make the system work. The instructions were changed to match the president's false conception.

The "get it right the first time" philosophy in software engineering is astonishing and radically at odds with other forms of engineering. Regular cycles of trial and test are an integral part of the development process in the manufacture of automobiles, boats, airplanes, factory machinery, and coffee makers. No one dreams that they can go from design to finished product without test and revision. How the contrary arrogance has gotten imbedded in software development is a mystery. One account runs like this. What software developers test is whether the program runs fast on the computer without overloading, crashing, or producing errors. Programmers focus on what they're good at and paid for—the internals of the system, getting the system qua system to run, without reference to the value of its functions.

In modern systems with graphic interfaces, user interface development can occupy as much as half the total programming effort, but it still usually comes last. Tardy development schedules tend to squeeze out usability testing and fixing, and almost all development schedules are tardy, so even in the rare organizations that have both the will and means to improve usability, it still tends to get short shrift.

Deployment

By deployment I mean the decision to purchase or develop a computer system, the way in which it is managed, the structures of the organizations responsible for its introduction, use, and maintenance, as well as the way in which employees are selected, trained, supervised, and motivated in their work with it. Most important, deployment means the way the computer is used, how it fits into the flow of the work of an organization, the roles it is assigned, the ways it interacts with parts and people in the work process.

These are the computer productivity issues that have received attention from management gurus and business commentators. Stephen Roach, for example, has tagged the failure of management to evaluate whether to install computers and for what as the villain. When he says, "American managers are hooked on computers," he means that they have assumed that computers can cure all ills. Got a problem? Get a computer. Even if you don't know exactly how it's going to help, it will impress your boss, your stockholders, and your customers. Computer companies, the consultants, and the awestruck press regale the innocent manager with seductive tales. (And computer manufacturers and consultants are minting money, aren't they?) So managers make unwise purchase decisions and unwise applications.

Roach and Strassmann say that most computers are bought not for the improvement of manufacturing processes or for cost reduction in operations but in excessive hope that they will improve management decisions.

But weekly piles of detailed reports in place of monthly summaries, the usual output of MIS departments, do not necessarily make managers any wiser. Indeed, too many reports issued too frequently can give misleading transient signals and can easily exceed available reading time or clog the mind. The decision maker needs just the right view of the forest, not a close-up of every tree. Providing the right information has proved much more difficult than providing lots of it.

Truly effective information systems for managers will have to be based on new understanding of how managers make good decisions, knowledge of what kinds of information presented how and when, how shared with whom, and how acted upon helps best.

A central issue in deployment is integrating computer power into work processes. Consider how company A gets a box of floppy disks from company B. It can involve sixty people, ten computers, a dozen manual data entry operations, and forty filed paper records. The principal who needs the disks uses a PC to type a note and company-mails it to her secretary. A mail carrier takes the note to the mailroom, where it's sorted, bundled, taken by another carrier to the secretary who keys in a purchase order form, and makes three copies for purchasing, one for herself, and one for the principal. She files a copy, enters a record in her PC, and mails triplicate forms to purchasing and one to the principal. Six mailroom workers, a porter, two truck drivers, two loaders, two porters, and two mail carriers deliver them. In purchasing, the form is logged into the PC monitoring system, its data entered into another PC to find a supplier, into the accounting department's mainframe to check the budget and the purchasing department's to generate a purchase order and again into the accounting system to register the expense commitment. Three more entries to check the previous ones. Finally, the purchase order is mailed to the vendor. Three mailroom workers, a porter, a truck driver, a loader, nine post office employees, a porter, two mailroom workers, and a mail carrier get the order to the vendor order clerk. Here, entry, inventory database search, customer credit check, order filling, shipping, billing and accounting, and inventory update use three computers and eight manual data entries and checks. Then the box, the invoice, and the bill go back to the ordering company. It logs the box, the invoice, the form from the principal verifying that she received it, issues a check (add five more cycles through the mailroom and some steps at the bank), accounts, budget debits, audits, and double checks.

You might think that a well-designed computer system would obviate most of this mess. The principal would enter a request in her networked terminal and everything would be done by one interconnected, intelligent, error-free system, untouched by human hands, unseen by human eyes. (Well, perhaps a few hands to move boxes and a few eyes to look over nicely displayed records of the entire transaction.) In a very few business settings this has happened. In most it has been postponed, prevented by outmoded business rules, practices and habits, unbudgeable bureaucracy, departmental turf battles, archaic legal constraints, the sheer difficulty of reorganizing a process from start to finish.

A major factor is that business processes evolved over many decades before computers and have yet to readapt. Following the scientific management principles introduced by Taylor and his followers in the early part of this century, work was subdivided according to the handling of the physical objects of the job, and the specialization of the functions people perform with those objects. The wildly successful industrial applications of these principles improved the way cars and bottles and TV sets moved from person to person along assembly lines.

For white-collar office information work, the application of these ideas meant passing pieces of paper between people and subdividing and specializing the jobs of dealing with the information on the paper. Information work was divided into stages of entry, calculation, decision, checking, approving, and so forth. The processing of the information was tied to the handling of the paper on which it was recorded and with which it was moved. Because the information moves only with the paper, to make it handy to all its users multiple copies are filed in many places by many hands.

With the availability of computers and electronic communication networks, paper is no longer necessary to move information. Business jobs, business processes, and business personnel, however, were (and are mostly still) organized around the stages of paper handling. When computers were first deployed, the most obvious way to use them was to make them serve one of the existing stages. Mechanizing one stage at a time made it easy to write the programs, easy to insert the new method into the business process without disrupting everything else, easy to retrain workers because their functions remained more or less the same.

In the Bell companies, for example, early business information systems were actually programmed by managers of line organizations. They intentionally tried to mimic on the computer the paper processes for which they were responsible. They made the computer screens look like the forms workers had always used. Without this strategy, it would probably have been impossible to get the programs written and impossible to get them used. However, it obviously limited the potential impact of computerization, reducing it from a revolution in business process to just one evolutionary step.

Most organizations have computerized in much the same fashion. They have built or bought systems for one business function at a time. The result is that various systems usually can't talk to each other; the mainframe can't use the electronic output of the word processors directly. For example, ordering systems often have buyers print purchase orders from their PCs and fax them to the supplier, where someone types the information into another computer. This is silly. But public standards for electronic data interchange (EDI), the networks needed to transmit it, and compatible systems needed to use it are only now coming on the scene. There have been individual firms, for the most part new, small ones, and a few computer-mature banks and pockets of supplier-manufacturer-distributor combinations, that have gotten their IT acts together effectively, but the fictional case described is still closer to typical than is the ideal.

There has been much talk recently of business process redesign. A central tenet of this movement is that the driving force should not be technology, not the willy-nilly introduction of automation or computers to do whatever a vendor, data processing department, or PC enthusiast proposes, but careful observation, analysis, and planning of work allocation, flow, monitoring and control. Only after the way work is organized is rationalized should anyone even raise the question of computers, it is said. This is an overreaction to the current poor deployment of IT. Computers have much to offer in the integration of business process that can't be achieved without them or without thinking about them deeply at the same time as you think about work design. It is hard to see how anyone could get rid of all the mail handling, paper data entry, and filing operations in the floppy disk order story just by reorganization, but easy to see how it could be accomplished with computers and networks *plus* reorganization.

Another important piece in the deployment puzzle is the management of computational resources. Strassmann, who puts major emphasis here, notes, for example, that traditional DP (data processing) and MIS (management information system) departments often fall victim to their own success. By being too enthusiastic proponents of ever bigger and better computerization, they can overburden an organization with excess computer capacity, excess reports, cost-ineffective services, overgrown DP and MIS staffs and management. Moving to distributed computing, each manager with his and her own PC, has not abolished troubles. Maintenance and upgrading of multiple systems is costly. Integration of all the independent work, making all the budget "as if" experiments use the same data and methods, controlling quality, keeping Joe from shifting the N.Y. sales force to N.J. by a typo, preventing redundancy and conflict between analyses and strategies, avoiding puttering, making it possible for one manager to understand another's work, and keeping the amount of effort spent on fancy presentation graphics within reason are only some of the problems.

Not least among the consequences of introducing computer technology is its effect on the skills and morale of employees. Among the problems are the difficulties of learning new methods, appropriately planning staff requirements, and adjusting work loads and schedules when the work is done differently, the loss of easy, beneficial social interaction patterns, the waste of useful skills.

Ollie Holt, who managed office work design for some of the earliest operation support systems in the telephone companies, used to speak of the need "to go beyond the system boundaries." He was continually frustrated by computer system projects that ignored the human work requirements and skills with which the system had to mesh. Over and over again new systems were introduced that led to unacceptable error rates, produced net increases in transaction processing time, required more employees, raised employee turnover, or made it harder for managers to couple the work supported by the computer smoothly with the rest of the business operation. The trouble, as he saw it, was that designers focused on making the hardware and software work while overlooking the real problem of improving a function of the organization. As we've seen, the telephone companies kept track of what was happening and sent the systems back and back for redesign. But frequently the systems were disastrous at their debuts. Managers who buy entire systems, untested for usefulness and usability, buy trouble.

8

Hype and Broken Promises: or, Why Do We Love Them Still?

Almost all growth in total capital equipment in recent decades has come from investments in computers, telecommunications, and other information technology. Information hardware now accounts for well over $100 billion, or 40 percent of annual equipment spending in the United States and, with software and operating costs, adds up to about 10 percent of GNP (Roach 1992c). Who decides to spend all this money? How are they making their purchase decisions, and what forces are influencing them?

Why Do People Buy Computers?

What They Do Do
A list of computer applications could go on for many pages: programs to run dental offices, video stores, sugar maple plantations. Most applications do something useful, and many provide impressive, clever new ways to do things. With Avis's hand-held terminal, the parking lot attendant can complete a rental car check-in before the driver can get luggage out of the trunk. Telephone repair people carry computer terminals up poles to query distant databanks. With a scanner and onboard machine, the Federal Express delivery person logs each package's individual odyssey, timing its journey from sender's to receiver's hand down to the minute.

Perennially Promised Panaceas
Every few years another major computer advance is declared to be upon us and about to revolutionize our lives. Some, like microprocessors, have

"Excuse me, I'm lost. Can you direct me to the information superhighway?"

Drawing by W. Miller; © 1994 The New Yorker Magazine, Inc.

been true advances in computing hardware. Some, like PCs, have changed the way work is done. However, the tenfold enterprise efficiency gains repeatedly predicted from each tenfold increase in central processing unit speed never materialize. Other panaceas turn out to be mostly wishful thinking; artificial intelligence and speech recognition are good examples. (Right now we are embracing GUIs and breathlessly awaiting handwriting input, interactive multimedia, and group work support systems.)

In the 1960s, we were assured that a large part of education would be taken over and improved by computers. The inroads have been, at best, footpaths. We've been repeatedly told that paper books were on the way out; libraries would be history by 1984. Computer-integrated manufacture (CIM), widely ballyhooed in the early 1980s, has been replaced in management advice columns by prescriptions for human work group reorganization. "CIM Success Depends on People," *Computer Graphics Today* backpedaled in 1985.

Many computer dreams vaporize because mimicking human intelligence is much more difficult than people imagine. Others fail because they aren't good ideas after all. For example, it is not clear that one wants to query databases in natural language. Databases are used for storing and retrieving precisely defined objects, whereas natural conversational language is intrinsically vague and ambiguous ("Twin separated at birth joins parents," a recent headline proclaimed.)

Let's look at one more perennially promised panacea, the paperless office. Any number of seers proclaimed that by the mid-1980s paper would be a thing of the past. Instead, computers generate far more paper than we had before, and the proportion of paper-based jobs that have been taken over by electrons has remained small. Instead, computers have been used to generate more frequent, more detailed reports, endless printouts of indigestible data, even more copies of the same paper orders, receipts, and bills—not to mention thousands of newsletters, brochures, and catalogues. Governments and businesses alike have used the availability of computer records as an excuse to vastly multiply reporting requirements. In embarrassment over the miscarriage of its original mission, the journal *Transactions on Office Information Systems* dropped "Office" from its name.

The paperless office is still a good idea. Access, retrieval, transfer, modification, even security and privacy, could potentially all be managed better in an all-electronic office. However, there are many unresolved problems. Interchange protocols and formats have to be standardized. The systems have to be made easier and more convenient for all potential users. Legal requirements for paper copies and signatures have to be resolved. Reliable, integrated computer systems and effective business processes to go with them need to be developed.

How to Decide?

Suppose you are a business manager trying to decide whether to buy a new software package. Let's divide the reasons into the good, the not so bad, and the bad. A good reason would be that the application is one for which computers are proven tools—perhaps a process control or record-keeping application. Your business might be sufficiently big or complex that there is no other way to run it: a giant telephone company, perhaps, or a mail order house with a staff of two.

A not-so-bad reason would be that everybody else is doing it. In any historical era, the way in which business is conducted is largely dictated by custom. Even today business is conducted in different ways in India, England, France, Japan, and the United States. In India, shop clerks hand customers receipts to be paid at the cashier's stand and brought back to the clerk to claim merchandise. In France, the shopkeeper typically collects the items you ask for, then totes up. In the United States customers carry items to a checkout station for payment. There is nothing in language or national character that makes it necessary to do business differently; rather, business processes, like governments and hats, have evolved differently in different places.

There are also bad reasons for saying yes to computers. The leader is an unfounded hope that the computer, just because it is a computer, is going to do something wonderful. There is prestige, too, in having your business or job computerized. (Otherwise how would people have the nerve to tell you that they have "just computerized" when they can't fix your bill or get your order changed? Would they tell you that they've just started keeping a ledger?) Owning a computer with the latest chip, enormous memory, or a name recognized from the news media is something like owning a BMW or a Jaguar.

Sometimes the decision to plunge ahead is based on insufficient knowledge of the true value of the computer's output. A common example is the installation of computers to provide management information. As Peter Drucker has observed (1988), "People . . . assume the more data, the more information—which was a perfectly valid assumption yesterday when data were scarce, but leads to data overload and information blackout now that they are plentiful."

IT Sci-Fi

Sometimes computers are bought because of their magic, because people think they will do things they can't. Of course, computers are not the only product sold on the basis of unproven claims, but they have their own special brand of insidious hucksterism. Perfectly legitimate, accomplished computer organizations engage in it to an alarming extent. Apple Computer has produced and widely displayed a videotape with a vision of the future they call the "Knowledge Navigator." It depicts a system that interacts with users in natural spoken language, anticipates the user's every need for information, makes appointments, reminds its master of things that need to be done, provides background information, and makes wise suggestions and witty remarks. There would be nothing wrong with this if its viewers recognized it as a "vision of the future"—the goal toward which Apple hopes to move—which is all they explicitly claim for it. But an unsophisticated, unwary customer cannot always distinguish between the vision and reality.

The whole population seems to be having a bit of trouble telling the difference between science-fiction and reality these days. Media fantasy has gotten so realistic, and real technology so fantastic, that the dividing line is fuzzy. I work with people at the cutting edge of computer speech recognition research and know that no machine has come even close to understanding natural large vocabulary connected speech in a normal, noisy environment. Yet I often meet otherwise sophisticated people who tell me confidently that such machines are here.

We have all seen the speech recognition feat for years in movies, read it predicted "soon" for decades, been exposed to ads that almost imply the product does it now. Moreover, machines do perform some speech recognition, just as they do perform some language translation—badly. To the outsider, the next steps seem short. If a vendor claims to have made them, belief is easy. Most of us have seen things that were once only science fiction become reality: people flying rocket ships to the moon, smart bombs aiming themselves toward a single girder on a bridge. How are we to know which ones have and haven't crossed the reality line this month?

The popular press compounds the problem. Journalism needs excitement, and almost every reported discovery in the biology lab, even in botany, is accompanied by a glowing prediction of the diseases it may be applied to (although there is usually a caution from some fuddy-duddy scientist). If one in two thousand "promising developments" panned out as depicted, most ailments would have been eradicated. Newspaper reporting on computers is even worse. Because computers have such an extraordinary reputation, because it's so easy to make them pretend to do things they really can't, and because the field is so lax in evaluation method and desire, reporters find it all too easy to describe visions without warning us of their distance from the ground. Ordinary people can't always make the distinction. I've had several important visitors ask me why our lab has not produced the kinds of human interfaces illustrated in the Apple "vision" video. The tone of voice implies they think us dodos.

Perhaps the danger of the fuzzy line between the fantasy and reality in computer field is best illustrated by a recent issue of *Scientific American*, a magazine noteworthy for the care with which articles are selected and edited to represent solid accomplishments in mathematics, science, or engineering. In the September 1991 edition, devoted to "communications, computers, and networks," almost every article was a wild-eyed speculative description of the author's vision of the future. The closest most of the articles come to what is real now were descriptions of prototype systems in laboratories—prototypes lacking the grace of any empirical evaluation of actual utility. The Apple visionary tape, for example, is described in detail in one of the articles. The entire issue amounts to only slightly more than science fiction (although each paper was clearly identified as speculation). Imagine another issue with similar articles in medicine, one describing how wonderful the world will be when all diseases are treatable with a single vaccination, another telling how micro-machines, coupled with imaging techniques and amazing methods of microsurgery—even now being explored in the laboratory—will make it possible to replace all parts of the body with much better ones. It will never happen. Researchers would never sign their names to its articles. Why does *Scientific American* take on pale *National Inquirer* colors with computers?

It is easier to give the impression that you are doing something that you are not with a computer than it is with other devices. The computer screen is somewhere between the actual interface of a system and a movie or videotape that can be produced with painted Styrofoam sets and special effects. So, for example, the MIT Media Lab often shows a video of a customized newspaper that would be delivered to a person over a computer. The news is selected according to each person's desires. It all looks very nice and is a reasonable illustration of a vision for the future, but the problem of automatically selecting from all and just the articles that a particular person wants is very far from solved. Thus the unwary media reporter sees a system do things that no system can do yet.

Caveat emptor is insufficient when the display is indistinguishable from the real thing it is illustrating. You can't take a shopper out for a spin in a car and have it convincingly pretend to do 500 mph. You can easily have a computer pretend to have translated a spoken question into Japanese.

Assessing Usefulness and Usability

Even harder than evaluating their reality is evaluating the usefulness and usability of computer applications. An ordinary person can fairly easily judge the worth of a supersonic passenger plane that will cut travel time from New York to Paris to one hour. But a hypothetical system that will put a map of the local area on the dashboard of every car is much harder to evaluate. Since the problem of assessing usefulness and usability has already been described at length and its solution is the meat of the next several chapters, we'll just note here that purchase decision makers bear special responsibility for getting such assessment right yet usually have much too little to go on, too little ability to enforce high standards, and, sometimes, too little interest.

Who Decides?

An internecine battle is often waged in large organizations between the centralized DP department and the operating departments as to who chooses computers and software. DP naturally wants to expand, up-grade, and try experiments—or expand, upgrade, and stick with what they know. It responds to pressures of ever greater work loads, requests for more data from management, for faster turnaround and additional service from sales, operations, and research departments. They think if they can only get the money to replace all the machines they bought fifteen—or four—years ago, they can provide better service at a lower price. They know there will be a lot of work switching over to a new system, new bugs to iron out, new training needs. But they are usually assured by their large computer company suppliers that all of that has now been made easy, and they will get plenty of help from the supplier's field engineers.

A new central system is an enormous budget item, usually a substantial portion of available investment funds. Other departments, and management high enough to be above all parties, can be somewhat surprised by this state of affairs. Operating departments question the value they are getting from computing and complain about service. They are told the solution is even more money, but they would like to spend the money on something else. Strassmann (1990) recommends that computers be managed by the operating departments themselves. They can make wiser decisions about how much the investment is worth, are more likely to follow up with evaluations of what they are getting, and forge a tighter coupling between what the system is used for and why it is bought. DP maintains that only they have the competence to select, maintain, and run computers; department autonomy, they charge, would create an anarchic mess of incompatible systems.

The cumbersome decision-making process is not the worst problem. The decision about what systems and software to deploy is never close to, and rarely gets much input from, the actual people who will be using it, not even from the supervisors who will have to orchestrate the work flow in which the computers will take part.

How to Decide?

For all these reasons, buyers are often left largely at the mercy of vendors. The vendors try their best, but they too are handicapped. They usually cannot know the business as well as insiders and have to use their imaginations. They have a strong motive to sell the most complete system they can, one with as many features and functions as possible to cover any unknown buyer needs, one with extra capacity in case the load has been underestimated or grows. They will tend to be more optimistic about the utility of the functions and features of their systems than an unbiased observer.

The Feature Fallacy

In this atmosphere, an interesting competitive dynamic has arisen. First, vendors try to compete on the basis of raw power per buck, though the power may not truly be needed or isn't being applied in the right way. Less obvious is "creeping featurism." To differentiate itself from its competition, a vendor invents a feature—a new trick or function that the hardware or software can do, a new interface widget, a fifth way to cut and paste. Sometimes a feature is suggested by an owner of the previous version or is in response to a user complaint or a reviewer's criticism. Often it's a brainstorm of a designer or developer. There is very little chance that many everyday users have tried it.

The next vendor wants to add the competitor's new feature and raise the ante by one more. One survey found that of the thousands of individual features contained in the myriad products of one large software firm, over one-third were never used at all. Many features in the same package do the same things. Nobody tests, so no one knows which one does it better or how useful or usable any of them are. The buyer wants them all. A common way to make decisions between software products is to pick the one with the largest number of plausibly relevant features.

Added features, however, have costs that can easily outweigh their benefits. Building more features into a software package makes it more expensive and less reliable. It increases the amount of memory and speed needed by the machine. Indeed, a 1994 PC with 100 times the capacity of its 1984 predecessor may have only enough room for the same basic set of programs—an editor, a spreadsheet, and a drawing program—and operate only marginally faster because each program has grown 100 times too. Manuals are much larger and harder to find anything in. Every extra feature carries new opportunities for software and hardware failures.

Additionally, large feature sets usually reduce rather than improve usefulness and usability for individual users. Early features are usually the basic ones that everyone needs; later ones are more specialized, of interest to only a few. Everyone needs some way to correct a typu with a text editor; relatively few want to connect two paragraphs in two different documents so that changes in one will be automatically carried over into the other; even fewer will use five different ways to cut and paste. The more features there are to master, the longer it takes users to learn the system and the more confused they are likely to be. More features make learning harder not just because there are more things to learn but also because the features are harder to discriminate. More commands or menu choices, many of which do similar things, present themselves at each step. It's impossible to think of obvious, distinctive names for all the commands and choices, harder to fit them into obvious menu categories that will make them easy to find. They get jumbled in the user's mind. The more options there are at any step, the longer each will take, if only because the act of choice takes time.[1]

Another common selling point is user friendliness. Most vendors say their systems are easy to learn and use. What's behind such claims? Often purchasers or reviewers make ease of use one item on their wanted-feature lists, and computer magazines rate and weight this aspect. But almost no one has performed a systematic, empirical evaluation of the system's usability. Most often the claim or judgment is nothing more than a subjective opinion based on a superficial examination or a few hours trial by the judge, whose needs and talents are usually unlike any real user and who is unlikely to understand the real user's job. At best, they are based on a survey of opinions of past users who themselves have never measured efficiency effects or learning time in any meaningful way. Imagine assessing vehicle safety or gas mileage this way or the output of a new chemical synthesis process.[2]

Sometimes claims or judgments of superior usability mean merely that a style of interface with a good reputation for usability has been employed. From around 1985 to 1990, menus were the definition of user friendliness. There are still ads that say, "The system is easy to use. It has menus." More recently, systems with windows, icons, mouse control, graphically simulated buttons and sliders, and menus that appear and disappear have taken the fashion lead. Now ads claim, "The system is easy to use. It has a graphical user interface." There has been considerable research into the value and the proper application of these techniques. None of them, by itself, is a guarantee of usability. Systems using menus or graphical techniques can be highly usable—or perfectly ghastly. A good menu can make the alternatives clear and learning easy; a series of ambiguous menu choices among arbitrary categories can lead the user down a weedy garden path to utter confusion. A few good icons can be appealing and save screen space and reading time; two dozen tiny, mysterious, undefined hieroglyphic symbols can turn the user into a cryptographer in search of a Rosetta stone.[3]

Why We Love Them Still

People—especially Americans, I think—love computers because they love gadgets, and no other gadget is as gadgety as a computer. Computers can do oh-so-many, oh-so-cool things. Among the attractions they offer, not the least important is games. It would be a mistake to underestimate the degree to which computer games motivate their popularity. Surveys find games by far the most frequent use of home computers. Businesses that allow games on their computers—and it's hard to keep them off—have sometimes monitored their use. It's always very high. (Those managers working on their spreadsheets, those secretaries editing away, those busy programmers? Creep up behind them and see what's on their screens.)

There are reasons of deeper psychology as well. Computers put enormous power at our fingertips. Most of us can't format a beautiful page of type, produce a pretty illustration, or do the calculations for ten budget scenarios. A computer lets us do these things. The desire to be competent is very basic and starts young; three year olds can be an utter nuisance being competent. An even more fundamental motive is effectance, the sheer pleasure of doing something that makes the world change in interesting ways. A baby shows this pleasure when it drops a cup and laughs as the contents splatter on the floor and walls. Computers can extend personal competence and effectance more widely, more quickly, than any other technology.

Computers are also just plain fun. They're splendid toys. They are interactive, doing things in answer to what you do and, unlike an electric train or model airplane, doing things that you have not explicitly made them do. Unlike a talking doll, their repertoire is huge or even unlimited. They seem to have an intelligence that plays with yours. They pose an endless, graduated challenge. When you've mastered one feature, application, or language, another is always waiting. The toylike fun of computers is always there, even when they are being used for serious business.

Finally, computers are addictive. The basic phenomenon is well known in behavioral psychology (the popular name for the field its Ph.D.s call "the experimental analysis of behavior"). Compulsive behaviors, a form of psychological addiction, can be generated by arranging reinforcement—a food pellet for a rat, a bit of grain for a pigeon, success for a human—to occur on the right schedule. The most effective schedules have success come only rarely and unpredictably. B. F. Skinner did a famous demonstration of the phenomenon with a pigeon. At first, every time the hungry pigeon pecked a lighted key, Skinner gave it a taste of grain. After a while, he began rewarding only every second, third, or fourth peck, gradually increasing the average ratio of pecks to pellets to a hundred to one. That one reinforcement was scheduled randomly; the bird never knew whether the next peck would be the lucky one. At this point Skinner stopped the pellets completely. The bird pecked the key ten thousand times before Skinner gave up.

Psychological addiction explains the success of slot machines, pinball, and video games. Anyone who has tried to use a computer can sympathize with the bird or slot addict's predicament. You accomplish impressive things, but you often fail once or twice, or thirty times, before you succeed. Sometimes a very simple error defeats you. You try again. Nope. You think you see why. You try again. Nope. "I'll try just once more," you say. Nope. You think of another thing to try. You try something you've tried before, just in case the computer wasn't paying attention. Far into the night, you finally succeed. What a wonderful feeling. Thus is a psychological addiction born.

Computers have become a fixture of life. They are thoroughly embedded in the business procedures of large and medium corporations and quickly becoming ubiquitous in even the smallest. They are making inroads into our educational, leisure, and household life. An ancient technology for passing and manipulating information, the use of marks on paper, is rapidly being superseded—or at least joined—by a new one. Anthropologists call the palpable objects and tools that people use their physical culture. The physical culture of Western nations is undergoing a major change.

One way of understanding how computers have permeated our world is to think of them that way—as just another aspect of Western culture. All that's required for a shift in culture is a marginal economic, convenience, or aesthetic advantage, or just the random fashion drift of evolution. Ballpoint pens by the billion have replaced flowing-ink pens. The advantage is only a small one but enough to turn the tide of ink.

Here is the hypothesis. We have taken to computers not because they made us more productive, not because they bring us better products or services, but because we like them. Being able to charge my groceries by swishing a card through a machine that automatically debits my bank account is neat. I get a kick out of it. The store manager does too. We are a world of people who like the new, the cute, and the ingenious. There's nothing to stop us from changing our culture with computers even if it lowered productivity, even if we have to trade wealth and convenience for the pleasure. In this view, computers have been consumer products, not capital goods. We've shifted some of our discretionary spending to computers and the business-life style they afford. If the net effect on GNP is slightly negative because most of the "consumers" involved are business employees using money that managers used to spend on more productive capital goods, so be it.

If this conjecture explains why so many computers are bought with so little measurable benefit to productivity, we might feel less puzzled, but perhaps no less disappointed. That we like computers already need not be the end of the story. These machines are marvelous. It is manifest that they are capable of much more, and we are right to expect economic miracles from them. What we need now are techniques for managers and other innovators to apply to the design and deployment of computer applications that will ensure that they fulfill their promise. They are available. I've called them user-centered methods. The rest of this book describes how they are applied and the gains that result.

IV

How to Fix Computers

So far we've seen that computers haven't had the productivity effects we'd like, and we've looked at some of their weaknesses as work tools. Next we will see what can be done about it. The discussion starts with a picture of progress to date: a stark contrast between incredibly rapid advances in the underlying technology and slow improvement in its application. We look at the special difficulty of improving tools for information work and then at new methods that appear to do the job. We see a score sheet showing substantial gains when new methods are applied. Then we describe the surprisingly simple way in which it is done, give several real life examples, and go deep into one success story.

9

The Track Record So Far

The computerization of America presents a fascinating, mystifying, paradoxical drama. For twenty years, computer use grew slowly and with dignity, serving at first only the mighty and the wise—bankers and insurers, scientists and engineers. For twenty more it has grown with unbridled vigor and abandon, reaching into almost every office and factory, millions of homes, virtually every activity of life. It was led by scores of fundamental inventions bred of modern science, grounded in deep mathematics, advanced by legions of chalk-wielding wizards in gray industrial labs and ivied universities. It was perfected by armies of constantly tinkering hackers in garages, pushed by feverish competition, enormous stakes, and eager money—shaped by thousands of failed commercial ventures and hundreds of successful ones. The march of computers ranks as one of the great technological adventures of history. For sheer speed of technical advance, computers probably have no historical rival. Measured in calculations and bytes per buck, over the last forty years or so they have averaged over 20 percent per year improvement. Compounded, that's 5,400 percent from 1948 to 1970, and another 5,400 percent from 1970 to 1992, for a total of roughly 30,000 percent improvement.[1]

But unlike other major technological triumphs with which it might be compared—the transformation of agriculture, the conquest of disease and trauma, the building of railroads and airlines, the electrification of everything—the information revolution has yet to produce vast and obvious economic benefits or bring widespread and major improvements in the quality of life. There also are some fragments of more direct data. Major productivity gains from computers will come eventually from both individual worker efficiency improvements and from facilitation of work group and enterprise production. For the latter, we are beginning to see reports of impressive achievements. The success stories, growing in number, generally recount productivity gains for particular operations or departments of around 25 percent, and occasionally much more. So far, though, these are minority achievements of large companies based on special circumstances and unusual management insight. They are not yet gains everyone experiences or can expect. Complicating the interpretation of these cases, many get rid of unnecessary functions and reorganize work flow in ways that could be accomplished without a computer. Their progenitors and reporters often attribute gains primarily to the rethinking rather than computerization.

Where worker productivity from phase two computing has been measured, the modal gain over noncomputer methods is around 30 percent. If we amortize these advances over the time they took to come about, the annual compounded growth rate is positive but undramatic. It's a little hard to fix the number of years of evolution that the various systems had when measured. Most grew out of something else and had no distinct birthdate.[2] However, it would seem fair to credit most applications with at least ten years of evolution from the precomputer methods they replaced, putting the average yearly improvement at about 2.5 percent. However, this assumes that the computer systems started on a par with their predecessors; they may instead have started out behind. In that case we're moving forward a little faster than it would appear. For a closer look, we can examine the few cases where efficiency assessments have been made on the same tasks with a progression of older and newer computer aids.

Be aware of a complication in interpreting these data. By my hypothesis, the reason computer applications didn't get better faster is that people seldom study their work value and redesign them accordingly. But the ones for which we have progress data are, obviously, exceptions; someone at least measured their efficiency yield. If I am right, the ones whose progress we know about progressed much faster than the norm. Keeping that in mind, let's see how fast they improved.

Earlier I reported that computer-aided instruction does not seem to have improved much in its teaching effectiveness over its thirty-year his-

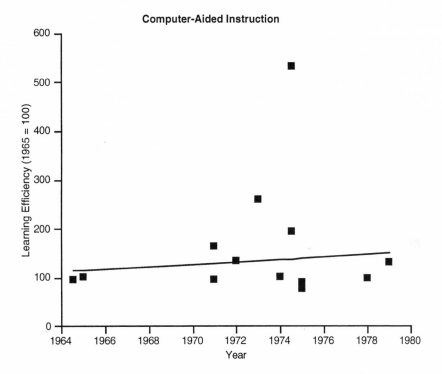

Figure 9.1.
Best-case improvement in the efficiency of learning with computer-based adult learning courses. The statistically unreliable average annual increase is about 2 percent. Data from Kulik, Kulik, and Schwalb 1986.

tory. Both the earliest and most recent accounts show about 30 percent faster learning with CAI. Some of the meta-analyses of CAI have looked at results of studies done at different periods. In the study with the biggest learning differences and largest improvements over time, which involved adult education students, average learning time increased by 2 percent per year over the fifteen years spanned by the studies (figure 9.1).[3] A similar analysis for college courses showed a small decline in learning efficiency (Kulik, Kulik, and Cohen 1980).[4]

Another hope-inspiring close-up is available for text editing. In 1987, two Xerox researchers, Terry Roberts and Tom Moran, tested nine different text-editing systems of various ages on the same set of benchmark operations. The users were all expert with the system of their choice, and

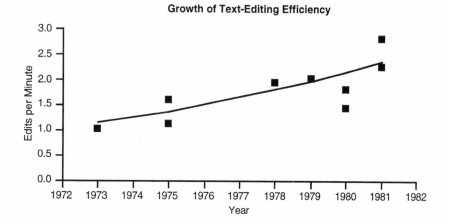

Figure 9.2.
Improvements in efficiency with text editors, 1973–1981. Efficiency is measured in changes in text performed per minute. The average rate of improvement was about 9 percent per year. (Roberts and Moran 1983.) Note: One more data point for editor evolution is available. Egan and Gomez measured the initial use by computer-naive typists of two UNIX editors developed at Bell Labs, an early line editor, *ed,* and a later full screen editor, *ted.* The full screen editor was about 40 percent more efficient. Depending on whether the evolution of UNIX text editing is taken to include the period between its first development and its public release, or only the time during which the larger computing world could have at it, either eleven or six years intervened. That amounts to either 3 or 6 percent per year improvement.

the several tasks fairly represented what people used the systems for. Figure 9.2 gives the results according to the year in which the system was released. Newer designs did not always improve on older ones; nevertheless, on the average effectiveness did improve substantially with time. Between the earliest four text editors studied and the latest three, over a period of six years, the average number of editing operations per minute increased by 61 percent. The average yearly rate of progress from 1973 to 1981 was about 9 percent.[5] If efficiency improvements of this size were achieved widely for individual work components of business operations and continued for several decades, they could bring significant increases in overall productivity.

How general and how lasting these effects are is hard to say in the absence of more data. An editor released by DEC in 1985 was measured on the Roberts and Moran benchmarks and tied for second place with the ones they had tested. If we add it in, the annual improvement drops to 7 percent because it appeared four years after the others.[6] My impression based on this and other indirect evidence is that the rate of progress in text editing efficiency has slowed since 1985. Notice also that these improvements are just in *editing* operations. The whole typist job—input, proofreading, and redrafting—has clearly improved much less.

So far, progress in most computer applications has been based almost entirely on market forces. Better, more productive systems tend, at least on average, to have a sales edge over less productive ones, so in time there are more good ones around and fewer bad ones. But there are many other reasons why people buy one system rather than another: availability, price, advertising, feature preferences that may or may not reflect productivity, and a host of irrelevant political and organizational factors. Systems that succeed in the market may be better on margin than competitors, but they can easily retain many flaws, even ones that less popular competitors avoid. Evolution by market selection of the fittest is fitful. Even if designers of new systems always tried to improve on the currently most popular systems and features, they would still have to wait months or years after a product appears before the market gives guidance. Even then they would get only impressionistic evidence about what makes the better-selling systems better.

For faster progress, we need an engineering and management discipline in which the assessment of progress is brought closer to the source, made sooner and more informative. Speeding and improving assessment accelerates evolution. I call the needed improvement user-centered engineering (UCE) because the assessment that matters is what effect the technology has on its users, taken either singly or as organizations, industries, countries, or in global total. Assessment can be more timely and pointed if done directly by those who design, produce, buy, and deploy the technology rather than by the market. I have divided UCE activities into user-centered design, user-centered development, and user-centered deployment. We start with user-centered design, because it is first in the order of production and is at the heart of the matter. No matter whether advances in productivity come from improved efficiency of individual workers or better integration of the work flow of an industry, it is the way that systems are designed to fulfill the goals of their users that is important.

10

User-Centered Design

Prior to the industrial revolution a highly skilled Indian hand spinner needed 50,000 hours (about twenty years) to produce 100 pounds of cotton thread. A rapid series of inventions between 1868 and 1879 reduced the time to about 300 hours, and another improvement fifty years later cut the time in half again, for a total time reduction of over 300 to 1. In roughly the same sixty-year period, the cost of cotton cloth declined by 80 percent, or five to one. These inventions included the quaint-sounding water frame of Richard Arkright, the spinning jenny of James Hargreaves, Samuel Crompton's mule, and finally Richard Roberts's self-acting mule that moved human skill from the operation of the machine to its mere tending and maintenance. The textile technology story does not end here. There were similar advantages in the processing of wool. Breakthroughs in bleaching and printing contributed. The progressive automation and improvement of weaving, among which the Jacquard loom, a famous predecessor of computers, was an important event, has continued up through the present with dramatic results (Chapman 1972).[1]

The time periods for the invention of computer technology are roughly comparable to the main achievements in textiles, so the comparison does not seem unfair to the computer. But where are the 300 times increases in output per hour, the 80 percent decreases in costs? They are there, and more, but peculiarly misplaced. Hand and pencil multiplication of two ten-digit numbers might take a skilled arithmetician about ten minutes. A very slow computer might take a thousandth of a second for the same job, a fast one much less. So here we have a speed-up of around a million compared to the paltry 300 or so for thread spinning. In graduate school in the mid-1950s, I did numerical calculations with an electric calculator. Each calculation required fifty ten-digit multiplications and adds, and took me, with check, about fifteen minutes. The total cost to my employer was around $1.50 in 1995 money. Even then, we could rent the university's central computer for the same job, charged back to the research project at a piece rate of about $2.00. I'm now doing some quite similar calculations routinely on my workstation at a rate of better than 1,000 per second, and a total cost of about $0.00004 each—for a cost reduction ratio of 50,000 to 1, or 99.998 percent over the prior electromechanical technology, about 300,000 to 1 over brain and pencil. (This figure uses my present inflated salary and assumes that I sit idly by and watch the computer compute, so it even allows for me having to do my own arithmetic instead of hiring an impoverished but highly skilled graduate student, such as the former me my former employer used.)

The computer's primary product, arithmetic and logical calculation, has experienced a phenomenal increase in labor productivity. The problem is that calculations, as such, are not a commodity in sufficiently wide demand. Bomb builders, weather forecasters, aircraft designers, and some scientists use the full power and time of the best computers. Many engineers and bookkeepers can drive their computers flat out some of the time. But they have to take time to formulate problems, to obtain data, and to design the calculations that are going to be done.

Now think about ordinary people. How many calculations do they need to do every day? And how much money would it save them if calculations were free? As cloth became cheaper, it was an enormous benefit to almost everyone. There are many necessary, useful, or at least desirable things that can be done with cloth, things that virtually everyone wants. This is not yet the case for calculations. There is no mass market for square roots, although there *is* a growing niche market for large prime numbers, which are valuable in code making and breaking.

One way to think about this is to consider the impact of making a particular product free. What if all clothing were free, or all automobiles or airline travel? In the aggregate, the overall effect on the economy would be related to the total amounts now spent on such products, grossed up appropriately. Suppose someone devised a method for producing house paint at almost no cost, say one cent per gallon. What would be the effect on productivity, on the overall economy? People would probably use a lot more paint, keep their houses and buildings somewhat brighter, substitute painting for some other kinds of preservation and decoration, and perhaps even invent some clever new things to do with paint. Nevertheless, the overall effect would be quite limited. Paint simply doesn't make up a large part of the economy, and the cost of the paint itself is a small part of the cost of its use. What if someone produced steel at almost zero cost—say ten cents a ton of finished rolled steel? The effect might be somewhat larger, because the cost of this input to a variety of manufactured goods is a significant factor. However, cars, trucks, airplanes, and ships would still have to be designed, stamped, assembled, distributed, advertised, marketed, and maintained, so the cost of transportation might not decrease much or its productivity increase (just as the productivity of transportation did not suffer greatly when the cost of oil shot up in the mid-1970s). The effect on the economy would probably be felt but might not be enormous. And steel is a commodity with a vast number of economically important applications.

Thinking about what free computing would do is somewhat harder, since most computing is done for us indirectly. Nevertheless, the impact would certainly be relatively minor, because little of the necessary cost of our goods and services is arithmetic. Take even the example of the calculations I did as a graduate student. This was a research project in which calculations were of considerable importance, yet its overall budget set aside no more than 10 percent for calculation costs, thus could have saved 10 percent at most if the calculations had been free.

"After you've written a letter, memo or report, the tweaking can be endless. Should it be single-spaced or double-spaced? Bold-face or italic for emphasis? Shadow style section headings? . . . An on-line thesaurus is another productivity wrecker" (L. R. Shannon, New York Times, May 11, 1993).

The future value of ever cheaper calculation will depend on the invention of good, economically important things to do with numbers and information. How will such inventions come about? An important component will be learning to concentrate better on the value of what the manipulations are harnessed to do in addition to how they are done. Consider the difference between spinning cotton and performing calculations. The former produces a product that is directly measurable as a desired end result. The inventor of a new spinning device can easily watch it perform, weigh its output, and see whether it produces more thread in less time.

It may be that it is *too* easy to think of new inventions using computers. They provide marvelous raw materials and tools for invention. The inventor needs very little equipment and relatively little training. Most new software inventions are not the work of people with advanced degrees in computer science. Little experience is required; witness the youth of many major figures in the commercial software world. Bill Gates, the billionaire owner of Microsoft, sold a homemade software program for $20,000 when he was fifteen. Steve Jobs developed the Apple computer in his parents' garage at age twenty-one. Unlike the materials, mechanical devices, and machinery needed for many new technologies, software inventions are made with as little as an easily available $2,000 machine. They are made by the thousands by high school students and hobbyists all around the world. The result is an explosion of software ideas, features, programs, and packages. Surely all of this feverish inventing will eventually give rise to myriad highly useful products through mere trial and error.

But this new technology, though relatively easy to invent, is not nearly as easy to evaluate. The test of good spinning and flying machines is apparent; assessing the utility of a text editor or word processor is a different matter, involving methods from behavioral research, with which most engineers and computer scientists are unfamiliar and uncomfortable. Successful examples show that there are adequate methods available, but they are not widely used.

What Stands in the Way?

The great philosophers Bertrand Russell and Alfred North Whitehead proved that anything that can be clearly described can be expressed with ones and zeros, the native language of computers, so any doable information task ought to be possible to program into a computer. We are looking for ways to help people think, to help them express their thoughts, to help them make decisions. We want computers to shore up service industries. Service industries are largely dependent on processing information in both numeric and textual forms. Shouldn't these be just the right grist for the calculation mill? Yes and no. Few decision-making, communication, and other information-dependent jobs have been reduced to mathematics in the past. Was it just because we didn't have computers? Perhaps. Maybe most legal, medical, governmental, and business management activities could, in principle, be done by arithmetic. But, even if that is possible, today we don't know how to do it.

There are at least two fundamental reasons. First, though any information task that can be done can in principle be done with numbers, it does not follow that any particular job can be done in a practical way. For example, weather forecasting could be done to precision for each city block and hour if only enough data could be collected and enough calculations performed, but the amount of data and the number of calculations is too great. The required number of calculations could not be finished in a shorter time than the weather system itself takes to evolve— the computer would still be whirring when the rain began to fall. So there are some things that we might like to do that we will never be able to do.

There are also some jobs that we already know how to do with calculation but are out of reach of current computers—for example, some complex telephone call routing problems. The long-distance companies' computers don't always have time to pick out the best possible series of office-to-office hops for a particular busy-time call from Boston to Boise, but another thousand-fold increase in computer speed will get them there. University computers can't match up students' desires, class times, professors, lecture hall sizes, and course requirements in the best possible way but should be able to next century.

There is a much more important set of cases: the kinds of jobs that we just plain do not now know how to do with computers. They include most things that people do with their eyes, ears, and minds or with skilled muscle movement, for example, comprehension of speech and recognition of faces. We don't know how to make a machine approach the level of ability of a human. Sometimes it is said that we are getting near to computers with such abilities because their speeds and memories are getting so great. But even with a computer with a million times current capacities, no one would know how to program it to read and write, teach and persuade, decide and plan, paint pictures, compose and play music as well as people can. Despite valiant attempts we aren't even vaguely within reach of adequately translating these processes into computer operations.[2]

It seems, however, that we should at least be able to *help* people do their work better by finding aspects of their jobs to which we can apply calculation and data effectively, but even this kind of success has not come easily or often. A great deal of effort has gone into trying to build computer systems to help people with information work. Indeed, there has been an incredible amount of inventive activity: those tens of thousands of new software programs produced and distributed each year. How many are significantly helpful? It is hard to know. Nielsen and Levy's (in press) survey of forty publication years of seven research journals in computer science netted 2,000 articles about systems or features intended to make some kind of job easier. Among them were 400 for which some kind of data—human performance measurements or preference ratings—on usability was reported. *None* compared usability of a computer system to that of noncomputer methods. Moreover, these studies were of usability, not usefulness. There have been only a few handsful of studies in which systems have been evaluated for effect on the performance of real jobs.

Why Are They So Bad?

That sufficient feedback is lacking to guide the evolution of computers is not quite enough to explain why they haven't succeeded. If good phase two applications were easy to design and build, we might not need much feedback. It appears that it is hard to design useful and usable systems. Why?

Computers Are Hard to Use

Computers are hard to use. Give twenty expert manual typists each the same letter and see how long it takes them to produce a finished, error-free product (figure 10.1). Suppose the fastest takes fourteen minutes, the slowest will probably take about eighteen. Give the same letter to twenty

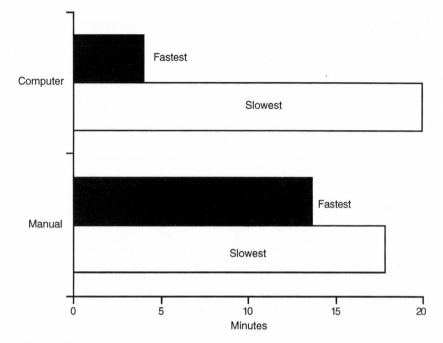

Figure 10.1.
The difference between the fastest and slowest of twenty people is much bigger with computer methods than with manual methods.

expert word processor operators. The fastest might do it in four minutes; if so, the slowest will probably take twenty (Egan 1988; Roberts and Engelbeck 1989).

There can also be enormous variability in the time the same person needs to perform one job and the next. Typing one letter may take three minutes; typing the next one, apparently similar, may take half an hour. Writing one computer program may take a day; the next one, apparently similar, may take a programmer-month. Why? The main reason is that computers make it easy to commit errors that are hard to fix. The same standard profile-based format with which you made that pretty letter lets you undo all its carefully constructed headings, margins and indents, alter the profile itself, and erase the draft on which the letter is based, all with just two badly aimed mouse clicks. A single programming bug—say an incorrect subscript to refer to a cell in a data table—usually is detected by a simple test with example data and can be fixed in a trice. But sometimes the same simple subscript error shows itself only when it changes a special number, and then only on the rare occasions when the special number is needed. Tracking down such a bug, or rewriting a large section of the program in hopes of avoiding the error, can keep four programmers busy for a week.

Computers also can magnify variability by providing many different features and methods. For the first letter you may use Palatino 10 point type font and all goes well. For the second you decide to be minimally creative and use `Monaco 9 point type font` for eleven special subsections, an apparently innocuous change made by a simple menu selection and one that looks fine on the screen. You issue the order to print, then wait twenty minutes. When no output appears, you realize that your printer doesn't know how to do Monaco. To get back to Palatino 10, you have to reformat each segment that you had done in Monaco, avoiding the headings.

The variability among people using a computer to do the same task is colossal. Dennis Egan (1988) reviewed a large number of studies of the differences among people when using various kinds of technology. In computer-mediated work the differences were much greater than in other kinds of work. In computerized text editing, the slowest of twenty users takes three to six times as long to complete a task as does the fastest. In computerized information finding, the ratio is about nine to one. Differences in computer programming proficiency are even greater. In a team of twenty programmers, the best will usually turn out well over ten times as much work as the worst. Egan estimates that after thirty people take a programming course, one student might take a year to finish a program that another could complete in two weeks. In controlled experiments on specific programming and debugging problems, even larger differences are seen. Among twenty programmers writing the same small program or fixing the same bug, the slowest sometimes takes almost fifty times as long as the fastest. Such huge differences are rare in any other kind of work; ranges of less than two to one over twenty people are typical, and even smaller variation is common. For example, the fastest reader or runner out of twenty college students will usually be only about twice as fast as the slowest.

The reasons for the huge discrepancy are quite clear. First, the power and complexity of computers provides greater opportunity for disastrous errors. Second, and equally important, computer-based work makes greater demands on special intellectual abilities: those with high ability may profit from using computer methods, those with less ability can be hurt. Although average performance improves, there is enormous variation between more and less talented users. Two abilities that have been found relevant for a wide range of computer-based tasks are logical reasoning and memory for the location of things in space. Other personal characteristics that have large effects are age and prior experience with computers and mathematics. Personal preferences, such whether a person likes math and mechanics, can also have a strong influence. I have already mentioned the personality traits of introversion and intuitive thinking that are unusually common among programmers. Egan cites several studies in which measured individual abilities were much more important in determining how well people used a system than all design factors combined. For example, the difference between batch and on-line programming is tiny compared to differences between programmers (Grant and Sackman 1967). Other researchers have documented the difficulties of computer work and the influence of differences in individual characteristics and ability.

Researchers at Bell Labs studied the use of text editors by people of varying ages and abilities (Gomez et al. 1983). Seventy-four women from an upscale New Jersey suburb, all touch typists, took part. The researchers measured cognitive abilities with a number of standard tests, and took histories of experience and education. Figure 10.2 shows that young people did well, older people poorly. The poor performance of the oldest people was probably due to the slowing of complex thought processes that affects most of us as we age. Differences in ability to remember where an object was on a page or to do logical reasoning had equally large effects. The top quarter in these abilities performed more than twice as well as the bottom quarter. In these studies, two markedly different text editors were used; one—a screen-based visual editor—was much

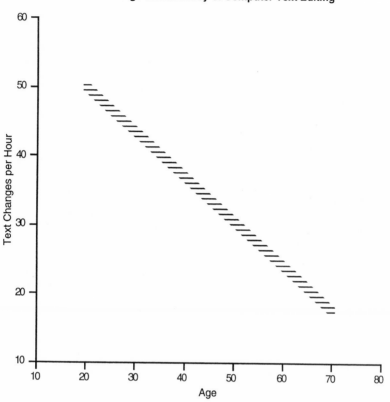

Effect of Age on Efficiency of Computer Text Editing

Figure 10.2.
Only very young people found it easy to operate a computer text editor. Data from Egan and Gomez 1985. Note: The figure shows a straight line fitted to the data after statistical corrections to remove the influence of differences in ability. Raw data points would, of course, be scattered about this line.

better than the other—a command-based line editor. Nevertheless, the researchers could predict how well people would do *twenty times* as accurately by knowing their ability scores and ages as they could by knowing which editor they were using.

In another study, Bellcore researchers (Greene, Gomez, and Devlin 1986) asked ordinary people to try to use the standard query language (SQL) required by most of the databases in which we keep our records. (Recall that this language was explicitly developed to make it easy for end users to find data.) Participants in the study—high school and college-educated women from another affluent New Jersey suburb—took a half-day class in the basics of SQL. Then they tried a set of easy problems in query formulation—ones anyone who hoped to get information from a database would have to be able to solve. Here is one of the problems and its correct answer. Just half the participants got it right.

Problem: Find all the employees who either work in the toy department or are managed by Grant, and also come from the city of London.

Correct SQL query:

SELECT	Name
FROM	Employee
WHERE	(Department = "Toy"
OR	Manager = "Grant")
AND	City = "London"

People with high scores on a logical reasoning test could form most of the queries correctly; those with low scores were almost helpless (figure 10.3). Remember that these were all relatively well-educated, successful people. In this task too, older people were at a considerable disadvantage.

In another study, Susan Dumais, a Bellcore computer scientist, asked college students to enter natural language inquiries in a document retrieval system—the kind of system commonly used in a library or online facility to look up books or references. People with a high degree of verbal fluency, who find it easy to think of words, did much better than the rest, finding documents to answer particular questions in acceptable time. People who scored low on the verbal fluency test took considerably longer (figure 10.4).

Two important conclusions are apparent in all of these studies. First, the average person in each case performed at a disappointing level. Compared to what the most competent people could do with the system, the majority come off badly. Second, in each case, truly adequate use of the system required greater ability or youth than the average person possesses. Indeed, in almost every case, good performance was possible for fewer than one in three suburban women or college students. The very

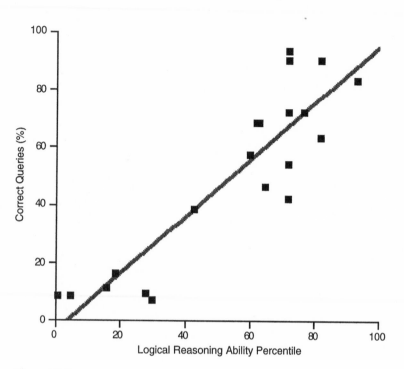

Figure 10.3.
Only people with unusually high reasoning ability find it easy to compose SQL database queries. Data from Greene, Cannata, and Gomez 1990.

young and very able find computer systems easy to use; most others do not. Yet, as we will see later, this is neither an unavoidable sad fact of life nor a necessary property of computers.

Traditional Designers Have Bad Intuition about Usability
We don't know why most computer systems put such pressure on un-common intellectual skills. (Actually some of the needed skills are not all that intellectual. Egan has speculated that one of the most important skills for programmers, and perhaps for other computer users as well, is fast typing.) Part of the problem is that programmers are users too, and often the first users for whom they design their programs. Computer-

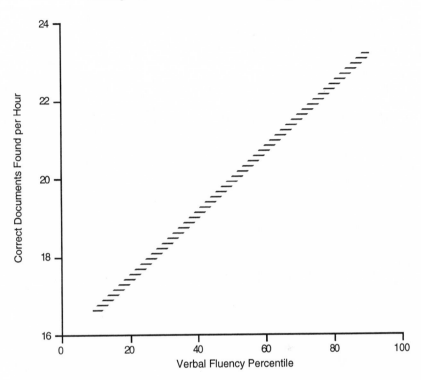

Finding Documents with Natural Language Requests

Figure 10.4.
Even for queries posed in natural language, individual ability differences—in this case, verbal fluency—have a large influence on success with computer-aided work. Data from Dumais and Schmitt 1991. Note: This figure shows a line fitted to complexly analyzed data; the individual points would scatter around it, but the underlying relation is strong.

based tools are generally aimed at information-handling tasks. Programmers are good at information-managing tasks. If they design for themselves, they design to a high level of skill and for a high skill level job. Compare this situation with a designer who designs a chair, house, auto engine, or tea kettle. It's unlikely that the designer has special skills in sitting, house living, engine repair, or tea making.

In designing interfaces, programmers often take a system-centered point of view. They care about how the software works and what parts of it do what. But most users couldn't care less about how the machine works; in fact, this information confuses them. They want to know about the functions they need for their work, file categories from their point of view—perhaps letters, reports and accounts, not the machine's system, floppies, and desktop.

Even if designers concern themselves with the problems of the average user, few are well equipped to do so. Most software designers and developers study engineering, with little exposure to psychology or other behavioral disciplines. Insofar as they want to bring psychology—human information processing abilities and factors—into consideration, they have to fall back on commonsense knowledge. Even the creators of artificial intelligence programs have been accused of relying primarily on folk psychology. Although there are rather few places in which current psychology is up to the task of providing strong guidance to system design, there is enough empirical knowledge in psychology, and in the psychology of system design in particular, to raise serious questions about how good anyone's intuitions are about mind tools.

Once more, please don't get me wrong. Software designers and programmers are smart, talented people who do work worthy of deep respect and admiration. Designing software that does what it is supposed to accurately, quickly, and reliably and performs well despite practical constraints is no small feat. The technical intricacies of the data structures, algorithms, subroutine libraries, protocols, graphical widgets, search engines, and the programming details are dauntingly difficult. The artifacts produced are often stunningly clever and artful.

To fail to appreciate the creative genius, engineering wizardry, and productive effort of software design would be ungrateful. There is no way we will reform computers without the essential contributions of this demanding technical art. Nevertheless, traditional software designers suffer a fatal flaw: their intuitions about what will make a system useful and usable for the people who will use it are, on average, poor. There is a very good reason: programmers and software designers are too smart. (Never mind that their typing speed may be twice a normal person's.) Look at figures 10.2 to 10.4. Where do you think software designers fall on these curves? What part of the population do they come from? Do they have trouble with formal logic? Are their spatial memories weak?

Does math scare them? Are they old? No. Programmers can't graduate without being at the good end of all these scales (at least the first two). They belong to the all the top 10 percent clubs.

Just a couple more factoids. Studies have found that people in technical occupations are faster at text editing than those in nontechnical ones—even if they are slower typists—and spend a third as much time extracting themselves from errors (Card, Robert, and Keenen 1984; Roberts and Moran 1983).

For programmers, computer stuff is easy. That's why they are programmers—and because they are programmers. The systems and interfaces that defeat the masses delight the masters. A programmer hardly ever has trouble operating his or her own program. Neither do his or her friends. Indeed, programmers usually try out their programs on themselves and their colleagues. Other programmers are good at finding technical flaws, at "breaking" the program, at noticing details not done in

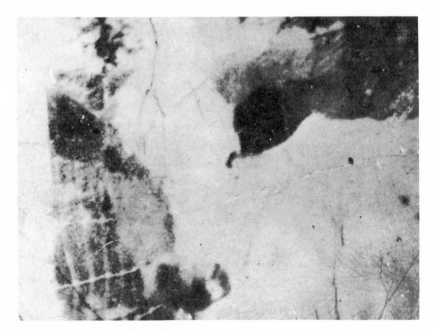

Figure 10.5.
What do you see? An animal? Turn to figure 10.6; then return to this figure.

the latest style or most elegant manner. But programmers are terrible judges of what will be easy, pleasant, or productive for the majority.

Computer intelligence comes not just from natural talent—logical, verbal, and spatial ability—but also from experience, both schooling and job-acquired knowledge of computers and programming and of similar systems seen before, and the more particular experience of the specific piece of software being judged. The decision often faced by software designers is whether the system they have just completed, after weeks or months of concentrated effort, is understandable. A fundamental fact of human judgment is that it is formed out of past experience. Judgment is not just colored by what we know; it is shaped and built, brick by brick, out of the encounters we have with the world. Programmers who have worked day in and night out with a program cannot put themselves in the place of the beginner, no matter how hard they might try and how sincerely.

Here is an example I show software designers to alert them to this problem. It demonstrates the overwhelming, irresistible power of previous experience, even in small doses, on even basic perceptual processes. Look carefully at figure 10.5. What do you see? Do you see an animal? What kind? Now turn to page 221, and look again; then come back to this place. You will never overlook Bossy again.

If a few seconds of looking at a picture can so dramatically and permanently alter the way you see the world, think of what months of work on a graphic interface would do to the designers' ability to see it with innocent eyes. Once they have worked with something intimately—designed it themselves, for example, and gotten accustomed to it—using it becomes easy and natural. They may think they can put themselves in the place of a new nonprogrammer user, may even think that they can do this better than most other people because of their intimate knowledge of the system, but they can't. They cannot think the same way as someone who doesn't know what they know. The human mind is a vast storehouse of richly interconnected facts, perceptions, and assumptions, each one of which can influence any and all of the others. The acquisition of a rich and intricate web of knowledge and skill is a one-way street; you can't go backward by an act of will.

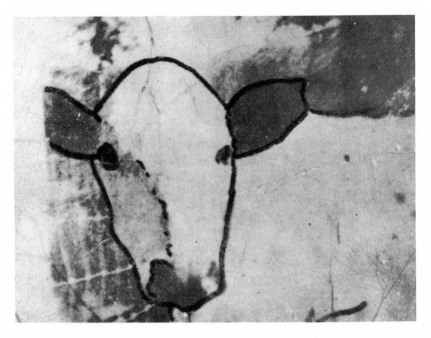

Figure 10.6.
Here's the final part of the exercise. Turn back to figure 10.5, and try *not* to see the animal.

We Can Do Better!

"It is the essence of modern engineering not only to be able to check one's own work but also to have one's work checked and to be able to check the work of others" (Petroski 1982).

An alternative to current standard practice is user-centered design—design driven, informed, and shaped by empirical evaluation of usefulness and usability.

Before diving deeply into how user centered design works, we should see if it really does. Table 10.1 lists results from all the trustable reports I've been able to find. The top part lists outcomes of focused UCDesign efforts—design projects or experiments where some kind of UCD was intentionally applied—and covers a wide variety of systems and a wide variety of UCD methods. The average gains are impressive. Even

Table 10.1
The value of user-centered design

Application and measure	Improvement per UCDesign cycle (%)
Results of explicit UCDesign	
A variety of products of DEC (Whiteside et al.)	30
Mainframe installation (Gould IBM)	400
Data display screens for telephone lines, question answering (Tullis, Bell Laboratories)	67
Transaction system interfaces: transaction, data entry, error correction (Keister and Gallaway, NCR)	67
Data display for space shuttle (Burns et al., NASA)	
Nonexperts	43
Experts	0
Menu-driven multipurpose data processing system (Savage and Habinek, IBM)	219
Text browser for information finding (Egan et al., Bellcore)	100
Text browser for information finding (Instone et al.)	66
Several unidentified "business applications" (IBM)	24
Security log-on procedure for network (Karat, IBM)	720
Enhanced cash register system, clerk tasks (Nielsen)	22
Enhanced home banking system, all types of transactions (Nielsen)	26
Experimental recipe file system: entry and search (Bailey at Church of LDS)	30
Results of simple test two and pick	
106 cases from performance time comparisons reviewed by Nielsen and Levy	19
9 text editors studied by Roberts and Moran	35
A famous case: GUI versus old style	
Comparison of Macintosh-style GUI versus command-based PC applications (Temple, Barker & Sloane)	
One application, editor or spreadsheet, new users	48
Two applications, editor and spreadsheet, experts	78
Supervisor's time card system (Dayton, Bellcore) GUI system versus "dumb terminal" version	58

Note: Where measured and reported, evaluation and guided redesign have almost always led to substantial improvement in user work efficiency. Simply measuring efficiency with two comparable systems and picking the better also works but not as well. The gains produced by graphical user interfaces are within the range produced by UCDesign, of which they are an instance.

counting the one case with no benefit, the median efficiency improvement is around 50 percent.[3]

There are a few much larger gains. At least one of these can be explained by the difficulty of defining a design cycle.[4] The Bellcore text browser originated as a research prototype. It went through two fairly distinct revisions before it was made available to anyone outside the research group, but I've collapsed those into one cycle. If they are separated into two cycles, the gains were 53 percent and 31 percent (which compound to 100 percent). If we were to include additional UCD-based improvements over the two succeeding years when production versions were released and counted the most recently measured application, an all-electronic chemistry library, the overall efficiency gain would mount up to almost 500 percent for one primary user task. Something of the sort may lie behind the other big numbers cited in the table. The sources are a bit shy on the necessary details.

A more exciting explanation of whopper gains, ones much bigger than the standard 50 percent, goes like this. The standard gain comes from cleaning up the interface without doing anything fundamental to functionality. Many of these reports bill themselves merely as interface redesign, even just screen redesign. As we will see, without UCDesign, a user interface typically has around forty flaws that can slow users and lead to errors—for example: one choice on a banking system menu reads "Transfer money," another "Move an amount"; the last screen for a complex spreadsheet function omits the "cancel" button, so a mistake at the end can cause a huge mess to clean up. Suppose, not unrealistically, that half of design flaws are this easy to detect and fix and that UCDevelopment usually does so. That's where 20 to 80 percent gains come from. Much bigger gains may require innovations that reconceptualize the user's task and provide new tools to do work in new ways—for example: provide a way to copy data entries from one screen to another instead of typing them over; put all the data needed by a transaction clerk in one place, reached by one search instead of four. UCDesign can also yield up that kind of advance—and much fancier ones—but it is not as automatic; it demands insight and creativity and, occasionally new hardware or algorithms.

Small or zero gains can be explained in some similar and some different ways. Some small gains are probably the result of incomplete cycles, quick and dirty UCDesign activities. Indeed, in several accounts, efficiency sometimes declined from one iterative fix to the next during the period before freezing and release. Evaluation without insight does not necessarily lead to better design. In other cases, redesign may fail to improve performance because users are so expert on the old system that any change is likely to hurt for a while, and no superficial change may be of much value. For example, NASA trains astronauts so long and so hard that their every action is reduced to reflex. They reach enormous proficiency on interfaces that would totally defeat a person with only a few days' practice. However, redesign is not always less effective for experts than for novices. Where the job uses several interacting or alternating application programs, only an expert may be able to profit fully from smoother methods of transition. Such may be the case in the larger benefit of GUI interfaces for experts shown in the last section of table 10.1.

The cleanest, most compelling data in the table come from the controlled experiment by Bailey. He induced a number of developers to each design and redesign a recipe file system until they were satisfied with their products. At regular intervals he had test users try each system. The developers saw videotapes of the tests. Systems designed with videotape feedback had 30 percent higher efficiency scores than those produced without it. Bailey probably somewhat undermined the feedback effect by not letting the UCDesigners talk to users or see detailed data on their problems; he wanted to keep them from "designing to the test."

Now look at the second part of the table labeled "Results of simple test-two and pick." These studies suggest what would happen if we used evaluation only to choose the best version and not to also guide design. Think of this as the most primitive (but not the most economical) form of UCDesign: design in the usual way, but always design two versions and test to see which is better. The numbers here are my best estimates of how much difference there would usually be between version A and version B. The estimates are derived from reanalyzing data from Nielsen and Levy's (1995) survey of system comparisons and Roberts and Moran's (1983) studies of text editors, then doing some statistical maneuvers.[5] The data suggest that this very simple form of UCDesign might yield about 25 percent efficiency gains each time it is applied. This may be an overestimate. The Roberts and Moran study included designs evolved over eight years and that were the subject of unusual amounts of research attention, if not direct UCD as such. The systems compared in all of Nielsen and Levy's reexamined studies were probably more different from the average randomly picked applications for the same purpose. After all, someone thought the comparisons were worth publishing. (It's likely that there is bias of the same kind in the explicit UCDesign numbers too; the professionals who do UCDesign are probably more eager to tell when things go well.) [6]

The bottom section of table 10.1 is also very interesting. Perhaps the most famous event in the history of computer usability is the Macintosh interface, which has often been hailed as a great breakthrough, credited with enormous commercial success, and widely copied. The German interface experts, Ziegler and Fähnrich (1988) say, it "was considered by many specialists as being the starting point for a new era in human-computer interaction." Much has been written about it, and various principles of design have been proclaimed on its example, most notably the ideas of metaphor in interfaces, direct manipulation, and the importance of object-oriented approaches. How much of an improvement in user work efficiency did it bring? To what should its success be attributed?

The commercial popularity of the GUI would seem ample proof of its attractiveness, but it is not easy to separate novelty and aesthetic qualities from work efficiency effects, the focus here. A study of user productivity with GUI and CUI (command-based user interfaces) interfaces was sponsored by Microsoft and Zenith and performed by Temple, Barker & Sloane, a human factors consulting firm. Here GUI refers to the constellation of features and interaction styles incorporated into the Mac or Windows interface and exercised in word processing and spreadsheet tasks. Although the distributed report of the study is not entirely adequate— there is no mention of the number of users in the tests (but one can infer that there were probably four to six users in each group from the statistical footnotes)—the study appears well designed and competently executed. There were both novice and experienced users doing seven different exercises on either IBM-compatible PCs running the DOS operating system for CUI, or GUI on Macs or PCs running Windows. The tasks were text editing and spreadsheet problems using "the most popular" application programs of corresponding genre. As shown, the overall efficiency advantage of GUI was 48 percent for novices' mastery of basic methods after a few days training and 78 percent for experienced users doing mixed task exercises with both applications.[7]

The unpublished report in the last row was slightly different. It started with a GUI interface for a telephone company application that had been subject to UCDesign. The functionality was transferred to a terminal with only character lines and command keys, with cursor movements controlled by holding down a control key and striking one or more letter keys. The comparison non-GUI interface was not subjected to UCD, and the test users were all experienced GUI users. The difference is in the same range.[8]

"And then we actually implemented two or three of the various ways and tested them on users, and that's how we made the decisions. Sometimes we found that everybody was wrong. We had a couple of real beauties where the users couldn't use any of the versions that were given to them and they would immediately say, 'Why don't you just do it this way' and that was the obviously the way to do it. So sometimes we got the ideas from our user tests, and we all thought 'Why didn't we think of that?' Then we did it that way" (Larry Tesler, as quoted by (Morgan, Williams, and Lemmons 1983, 104).

What, then, lies behind the Mac interface's actual accomplishments? Though ill fated in the market, the Lisa computer was where the Mac interface was born. Larry Tesler, manager of the Lisa user interface development team, personally tested new variants of the design with naive users two or three nights a week and passed the results back to his programmers (Morgan, Williams, and Lemmons 1983; Tesler 1983). Tesler's efforts did not start from scratch. Many of the techniques in the Lisa interface had been developed at Xerox, and at SRI before Xerox. There had been "friendly-user" trials and presumably comments from the many leading interface and usability experts at both places. Nor did UCDesign end with Tesler. Apple established and regularly used a usability testing lab. Bruce Tognazzini, Apple's long-time user interface design guru is one of the fiercest advocates of usability testing.

The superiority in user efficiency of the Mac style graphical interface over predecessor command and menu systems is, as shown in table 10.1, in the middle to high range of advances regularly achieved by UCD. The Mac was a recipient of extensive user-centered design. Should we believe that UCD is all there was to the Mac's success, or is the graphical user interface, independent of UCD, the possessor of usability magic? An unpublished study comparing several basic Mac user operations with a similar medley from a PC-based windowed GUI line from a major competitor—one with no reputation for good UCD or usability assessment—is suggestive; it found Mac usability just about as superior to the competing GUI as it is to competing CUIs. My guess is that some of the innovations in GUIs are quite helpful, some neutral, and some sometimes detrimental. Unfortunately, we don't have a good understanding of which are which.[9]

Summing Up What UCDesign Can Do

So far we've looked just at the direct work efficiency effects of improving software design by evaluative feedback, an appropriate focus since productivity is our principal target, and efficiency gains from using the computer as a tool are the first order of business. However, other effects have been reported when these methods have been applied, and some make indirect contributions to productivity. Here is a list of such side effects.

• *Reduce training costs.* Systems designed with usability testing have typically reduced the time needed for learning by around 25 percent. If interaction is sufficiently simple and trouble free, sometimes formal training can be eliminated completely and users can teach themselves with an online manual. High school graduates were able to learn a UCD-perfected text browser that way in about forty minutes. One company reported eliminating a training video after a UCD effort, another a dramatic decline in help-line calls.

• *Reduce human error.* Reductions in error rates have always accompanied UCD-based reductions in work times. In fact, a large part of the efficiency improvements reviewed came from better menu labels, less complexity, improved help facilities, and repairs to "black holes" that trap users in errors that take forever to fix. Errors can have other effects than slowing individual users. Putting the wrong data in the database can lose a customer's record or an airplane, send field staff on a wild goose chase, ripple through dozens of operations and cost many labor hours to backtrack. Errors in checklist use, preventable by better interface design, have caused plane crashes. Errors in reading warning signals, preventable by better usability engineering, have caused nuclear reactor accidents. UCDesign typically cuts errors in user-system interactions from 5 percent down to 1 percent; one of the listed redesigns reduced mistakes by a factor of twenty; the NASA redesign slashed errors even for experts.

• *Reduce employee turnover.* Employees sometimes divorce unloved computer systems or are kicked out for failing to get along with difficult ones. Well-designed systems can multiply employees' competence, equip them for broader responsibilities, help make interactions with customers more satisfying, reduce boring work, improve work schedules, and make supervision fairer. It has been estimated that turnover usually costs from half to one and a half times an employee's annual salary (Schlesinger and Heskett 1991). Analyses by one large hotel chain showed that a 10 percent reduction in employee turnover would double profits. Another large company reported a 20 percent turnover reduction as a result of UCD.

• *Increase customer throughput and service value.* A department store or restaurant whose system helps employees serve customer needs more fully and accurately not only increases the productivity of its employees but also decreases the waiting and shopping-around time of customers and adds to the value of the services they receive. UCD, with customers as the users, can contribute to these effects.

• *Reduce maintenance.* If it costs $10 (five or ten minutes) to make a program change during development, it will probably cost $400 to do it after the system is in the field (Pressman 1992). It's expensive to wait for customer complaints; it's much cheaper to get them from usability test subjects. Experience with UCD projects is that maintenance expenses are lower, help calls less frequent. Xerox found that service calls plummeted after user-centered redesign of its machines. The machines weren't broken before; the users just couldn't figure out how to work them (Brown 1991).

• *Increase satisfaction.* Occasionally users who are made more efficient by redesigned machines resent the change; they prefer the more leisurely pace of yesteryears. However, much more often, UCD systems have gotten considerably higher marks than their usability-neglected counterparts, especially if the design takes direct aim at desirability. How are user satisfaction and productivity related? One simple but important way is that if users don't like a system, they may not use it. If an efficient computer operation is added to a business process but the old paper process is retained, a loss, not a savings, results. Real life examples are legion. I did most of the calculations for table 10.1 with a hand calculator and a sheet of paper instead of my more efficient spreadsheet program. I prefer the paper because I can draw lines through trial numbers without deleting them, add comments and check marks next to them, draw arrows and circles and put little notes to myself on top of the numbers. I know of a large inventory system that goes virtually unused solely because the password procedure is too cumbersome. The IRS field agents mentioned earlier preferred their pads and pencils, the grocery checkout clerks passed items through uncharged. Service reps on commission at DueTel keep paper records of their transactions because they don't trust the computer.

The tight security system of Gigantic Information Systems assigned each user a new ten-character alphanumeric password each week. (Here's yours: G*379537h8.) They needed it to log into their terminals to work. Passwords could be found attached to the front of many terminals.

• *Synergize business process improvement and reengineering.* Rarely are business operations independent of one another; the functions of one rely on the effectiveness of another. If you want to eliminate matching invoices with orders by having receiving dock personnel check and enter orders, the system they use had better be usable. A change in one system can either help or hinder another. A dispatch system for a large service company automates the record keeping and prioritizes the repair jobs it assigns to field workers. But someone forgot to put addresses on the computer screens, and the dispatcher spends an extra hour each day to fetch them. A $10 fix would have made the process redesign $ millions more valuable.

• *Breed new useful uses.* Most of the UCD effects I've listed concern themselves with increasing the efficiency of computer-based tools already born. Where do computer tools come from? To date they've mostly been conceived more or less by accident, bred in the fertile imagination of a programmer who has met a function in the line of work. Text editors evolved from schemes to alter programs more easily. The progenitor of the spreadsheet line, Visicalc, popped out of Dan Bricklin's head when, as an MIT computer science graduate, he found himself doing account ledgers at Harvard Business School. It was a brilliant idea, one of those breakthroughs that are obvious in hindsight. Something like necessity was the mother of both editors and spreadsheets.

Needed now, though, is some more intentional, directed breeding: the thoroughbred race horses and cocker spaniels of computing. New animal breeds are the result of a speeding up of natural selection, accomplished by watching the offspring more closely and taking steps to produce desirable traits. Modern evolutionary theory has added the idea of "punctuated equilibrium." A well-adapted species changes very little until suddenly small variations couple with new opportunity in the environment; then major transformations rapidly suit it for a new niche. The leap forward in text editor efficiency with the availability of screens and mice in the late 1970s—a new environmental niche for software applications—was such an event in computer land. Luckily, in technology we can do Lamarckian evolution (named after the French scientist who proposed the theory that acquired traits can be inherited) instead of waiting around for chance mutations to change the design. Nor do we have to wait for chance events like Bricklin's accounting course to stumble onto new niches (Landauer 1992).

Getting from Here to There, How Fast? Very.

How much progress in work efficiency and productivity can we expect in the future? My projections combine the available numbers with my own judgment of which of them can be trusted most, which are likely to be high and which low, which probably apply to many other systems and processes, which are limited to their original venue, which effects are local and transient, which promise to self-multiply. My judgment is based on much more research and case study literature than I have dared bore you with, much of which has no efficiency numbers as such but bears qualitatively on what can be made of the numbers we have. Hundreds of studies, for example, don't measure efficiency but do assess percentage success on problems or report subjective value. My impressions are based as well on my thirty-five years of watching computer technology get invented, developed, deployed, used, and evaluated.

Staying the Present Course

How will we do in improving work efficiency if we just keep on keeping on? Let's limit the discussion to information work and workers. The evidence is thin but discouraging: less than 1.5 percent per year improvement in service sector work productivity in the last twelve years, with 1992 looking a lot better, and 1993 looking slower again. We found measurements for just two phase two computer applications over time, CAI and text editing, both badly out of date. CAI showed little or no improvement over time; text correction posted 9 percent annual gains. I see lots of activity and new directions in computer-based education but no reason to believe any efficiency gains have been made. In fact, my guess is that most of the newer approaches, were they measured, would show less than the stable 30 percent advantage of traditional CAI. Text editors showed reasonably healthy gains in the 1970s and have probably gotten marginally better since. However, text editors require another caveat here. During their period of advance, text editors were the object of intense usability research. The earliest efforts in trying to understand, model, and engineer the human factors of computing systems concentrated heavily on text editors because they were then the most widely used, and obviously improvable, computer applications. The first theories and principles of computer use were tested against text editors. The first benchmark tests for computer usability were initially tried with text editors. Nothing like this quantity or quality of effort has gone into any other application, with the possible exception of information retrieval. For example, there has been very little usability research or comparative evaluation of spreadsheets or reservation systems. Most of the text editor usability research was aimed at discovering general principles of human-computer interaction rather than redesigning the systems themselves, so the degree to which the gains in text editing can be credited to UCD rather than to market evolution and old-style engineering is unclear. My guess is that the world would have gotten about a half the gain anyway had the researchers stood aside.

There is much hoopla this year (as always) about new management strategies—things like work flow analysis and process reengineering—promising to change the course, to make computer technology finally pay off. I believe some of this and am certainly all in favor, but many of these ideas are not new. Managers have always tried to improve their operations both by incremental streamlining—earlier American and current Japanese industry's claim to fame—and radically, by substituting machines for human processes, as the proponents of reengineering now hammer in. I'm not persuaded that we are doing it very much faster than before.[10]

Efficiency Prediction sans UCD

I predict a little faster improvement, at 3 to 5 percent per year, in the work efficiency effects of computer applications over the next ten years even without increased efforts in UCD. The graph in figure 10.7 is plotted with the generous value of 5 percent.

Using UCD to Its Fullest

The *mean* (or arithmetic average; notice I've been talking about median, or midpoint, before, but the mean is relevant here) UCD efficiency gain in table 10.1—167 percent—is undoubtedly unrealistic. Many of the studies put their best feet forward, reported only aspects of jobs that the process affected, or applied the process to only parts of jobs. The average effect on whole jobs can't be expected to be nearly that good. Many of the studies concentrated on first-time users or first-time use. Often system differences diminish with practice. Many of the studies were done in the lab with prototypes. Real settings have a way of diluting advantages seen in the lab; the "extraneous" factors of motivation, social complexities, interruptions, bottlenecks, and task mixes rear their ugly heads. Most of the quoted results are from one cycle; only a few tell us what happens when a system gets UCD improvement, then starts over for another round. Note, however, that we are talking about percentage gain. If a system goes from one operation per minute to two, a 100 percent efficiency gain, it means the user took one minute before and thirty seconds after revision. To get the same 100 percent efficiency gain on the next round, we don't have to cut off another thirty seconds, which would be impossible, just another fifteen. Nevertheless, it seems likely that even the percentage gain obtainable may decrease from one round to the next for many systems. We might also wonder whether UCD efforts will cease at product release or pause while awaiting a new round of development. However, UCDesign efforts can be continuous, and, in fact, some of the

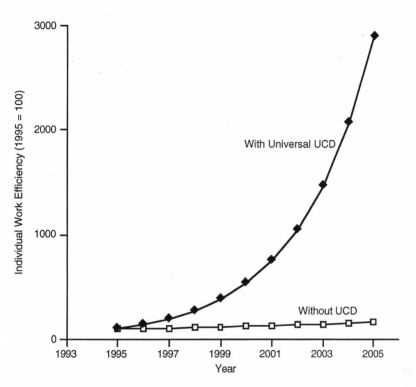

Figure 10.7.
Predictions of computer work efficiency improvements from universally applied UCD and from business as usual: 40 percent per year with UCD and 5 percent per year without. (Author's estimates.)

most significant changes come between releases, when deep functionality can finally be altered based on things discovered too late in the last cycle. Putting all such considerations together, my conservative guess is that real effects will average not 167 percent, but only 20 to 40 percent. On the other hand, these numbers don't take any credit for the many indirect effects, listed above, which may be substantial. Moreover, UCDesign advances don't take a year. Sometimes evaluation and redesign can be done in two weeks; rarely need it take more than a few months. However, because UCDesign often has to wait on ordinary software development for its expression, a figure of six months per cycle is probably realistic.

Efficiency Prediction cum UCD

Figure 10.7 shows my guess for annual efficiency gains if every computer application is subjected to thorough UCD: 40 to 80 percent; (the plot uses the lower value of 40 percent per year). If the magnitude of these predicted efficiency gains seems large, remember that they are not unusual in the history of technology. The real surprise is that computers haven't brought them before now. (Of course, the UCD prediction assumes that all software development projects started using these methods on January 1, 1995, and *that* is surely unrealistic.)

Predicting Overall Productivity

What will UCD do for productivity in the service sector? Estimating overall productivity effects, as shown in figure 10.8, takes several more steps, each a bit uncertain. First, there are a few more corrections needed in the improvement figures before they can be used for this purpose. In the downward direction we have to take into account still another problem in many of the measurements. Usually quantitative evaluations set up particular discrete tasks for test users—benchmark operations—and measure how long they take. But in real life users don't spend all their time doing focused tasks. They also talk to customers and coworkers, plan their day, think about what message to type next with their word processors, what amounts to juggle with their spreadsheets, what data to fetch from their databases, and spin their wheels in various ways. We've made much less progress so far in helping them with these activities (except, perhaps, for spinning wheels, for which computers supply superlative opportunities; someone may need to invent computer games that take less time and screen savers that are less engaging.) I believe UCD is the best hope here, but it would be unrealistic to pin too much on it. I'm guessing the next decade's UCD efficiency improvements apply to only half the work time spent at the computer. In the upward direction, we need to take into account all the indirect effects, especially the promise of better usability to enable process redesign that would otherwise fail. One of the text browsers listed in the table provides a case in point. In one application, the direct work effect on looking up information saved only fifteen minutes per week per worker because information search in documents was only a minor part of the job. But because the new tech-

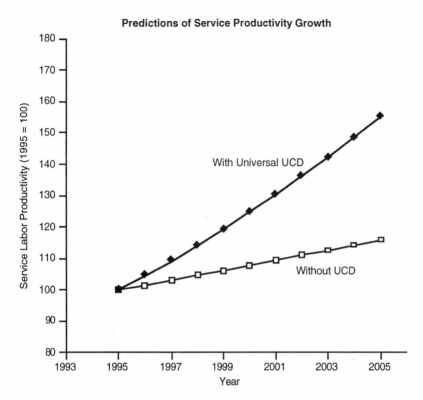

Figure 10.8.
Conservative predictions of service industry productivity improvements with UCD and with business as usual. (The graph assumes all software projects used UCD as of January 1, 1995; change the dates and proportions to taste.) (Author's estimates.)

nology was good enough to replace paper, it was possible to eliminate all the costs of production, distribution, and manual updating. The total savings was about four times the direct efficiency effect. Such synergies may at least double the average benefits.

"Packaged with a hot selling version of Microsoft Corp's Windows program, Solitaire [a computer game] proved so distracting that Boeing Co. and other companies removed it from all their PCs. 'It sure blew people's productivity', admits Wes Cherry, the Microsoft programmer who developed it" (Business Week, *June 14, 1993, 76).*

Next, we have to convert gains in work efficiency of individual applications into productivity. Part one of this exercise is how much of total work time computers influence. On this I've found no reliable data. I take a conservative guess: 10 percent of American work time is spent in front of a computer. This chops the gain from 40 to 80 percent down to 4 to 8 percent. Part two of the exercise is how the computer's share of work will grow. If it goes up by 12.5 percent a year, it will reach just under 25 percent by the year 2000. That certainly doesn't strike me as too high and nudges the total to 4.5 to 9 percent overall productivity growth per year with UCD.[11]

The plot again uses the lower value, 4.5 percent per year. The magnitude of this growth may seem surprising, but it is not a historical oddity; Japanese productivity growth from 1950 to 1973, for example, was higher. Again the real surprise should be the lack of growth we've actually experienced.

11

Here's How

"Without testing, a user interface cannot be expected to work very well"
(Good et al. 1984, 1043).

How is this new technique employed? It is embarrassingly simple. Designers study what users need help with and what might help them, then try solutions and test to see what actually helps. Before expanding these themes, let me tell some stories.

A Story about Maps

In 1982 some Bell Labs researchers had a notion to put intelligent electronic maps in automobiles. The map would keep track of the position of the car and plot the best route from where it was to wherever the driver wanted to go. Lynn Streeter, a computer scientist newly retreaded from a human factors specialist, was asked to look into how the maps ought to be displayed. Streeter invited potential electronic map users into the lab, among them local homemakers, engineers, and college students. She had them trace routes on standard road maps for the area and asked them a number of questions about how they usually found the way from one place to another. She inquired about their education and work background and gave them some standard tests of cognitive abilities. She was surprised at how many made serious errors in plotting routes. They planned to drive along county lines, rivers, and railroads and to get on and off superhighways where there were no exits. They penned grossly roundabout paths or simply got confused. When asked, the majority said they really didn't like maps or use them much. They preferred verbal instructions: go left on Main Street until you get to the church, right on Maple past the fire station, and on to the freeway north.

The next step in Streeter's analysis was to compare the navigational utility of a customized map with a well-designed set of verbal instructions, and both with the preexisting technology. She sent people out in a heavily insured car to find their way from the lab, X, to somewhere else, Y. About half the participants were professional drivers and half amateurs. A research assistant rode along in the back seat to record where the cars went and how long it took, and to bring them back when they got lost. Some of the drivers were given specially designed maps of the area. Unnecessary details were suppressed and the best route was marked with a wide red line, much as might be offered by an electronic display. Other drivers were given a cassette tape that read off a new instruction each time the driver pressed a button. It told which way to turn at streets, landmarks, and trip-meter mileages. A third group of drivers were given both map and tape; a fourth made do with standard road maps and their own resources.

Verbal instructions worked best. Drivers with the tape made 40 percent fewer errors, drove 10 percent fewer miles than those with custom maps, and were happier with their aid. Interestingly, giving people the map in addition to the tape resulted in significantly more errors. Overall, both enhanced navigation aids were better than traditional road maps (and stopping for directions, which was allowed); the tape users surpassed their old-fashioned competitors by 29 percent in both mileage and time spent on the road.

A computer that would calculate the optimum route between point X and Y would be indifferent to how the user was told about the route. Provided the necessary information was available in a database (as it was for Streeter's experiments), the best route would be determined by a search algorithm. The system could use speech synthesis to build an audiotape and graphics techniques to construct a map. An audio system would be much cheaper to install and safer to use.

Many applications simply take what was done before and put it on a small screen on a box. There's some logic in that, of course, considering that computers can store and rapidly fetch vast amounts of data. However, the assumption is that quantity and speed are the most important factors, and often they are not. The average student is better off in the local school library than in the Library of Congress. The average checking account balancer is not better off with a calculator that can do imaginary numbers and trigonometric functions but might be aided by one that searches out inconsistent figures in the checkbook and bank statement entries.

The check checking feature is a good example of a pure thin air idea. I have no way of knowing whether it addresses the real problems people have or would really help them. How would I discover real problems and real aids? Streeter's work offers an excellent example. Before computers, maps were the best, perhaps the only, way to provide a guide (other than a human) that would help you get from *any* X to *any* Y. A book with verbal instructions for each possible combination of start and end point wasn't practical to publish and wouldn't have been practical to use. A computer can easily compute such instructions on the fly. But traditional design habit meant using the computation to do the same old thing a little worse but quicker: mark the route on a map. It took a study like Streeter's to reveal that most people would profit more from having the computer put to a new purpose.[1]

Finding out what to invent is the first step. Making it work well for people is the next.

Two Tales from DEC

A group of researchers led by John Whiteside at Digital Equipment Corporation (DEC) has contributed greatly to the development of UCD methods. One of their techniques, a user-derived interface, illustrates the value of gathering data on what users really do as a foundation of design. In a delightful example, Dennis Wixon pretended to be the computer as test users in an adjoining room struggled with a series of miniversions of an electronic mail system. The first version, a better-than-average first stab, was based on a melding of features and commands found in popular email systems. Test users, professionals or professionals in training, were given a brief tutorial and a set of eight common email tasks to accomplish in an hour. For example they were to "see that Mike Good gets the message about the keyboard study from Crowling." With the initial version, none of the four test users was able to do any of the tasks without help; Mike never got his message. By the end of the project, many novices could do all eight on their own (Good et al. 1984).[2]

What happened in between? The big problem at the beginning was that users tried to type words to the computer that it didn't understand. For the test problem about sending messages to Mike Good, users tried commands containing the words *memo, from, about,* and *copy,* none of which the computer understood. Here's how that was fixed. After every test session, Mike, who was actually the project's chief designer-programmer, did get one important message: a list of all the words and phrases users had tried. He analyzed these and made changes to the system's parser, the part of the program that interprets what users type. The majority of changes were just adding synonyms for the words needed in commands—*memo* and *note* for *message,* for example. The team kept track of how many of the users' commands got by the parser. At the outset, the system recognized only one of fourteen inputs; the rest were turned back with reports like "Stopped understanding at 'memo' in message." Figure 11.1 shows how the proportion of successes grew as more changes based on user behavior were added. At the end of the project, three-quarters of the commands offered up by inexperienced users were handled correctly. Additional tests showed that the ultimate design was easy to use for both novices and expert users and that it was more favorably rated than the standard system used at the outset.

Edison read every scrap of prior science and technology possibly relevant to a problem before stepping into his lab. Then he did literally thousands of experiments on the way to each major invention. So did Bell, and the Wright brothers, who built a novel wind tunnel where they performed over 200 experiments on wing lift and drag, to add to their hundreds of experiments with kites and gliders, before they did scores of experiments with powered airships. Incandescence, speech acoustics, and aerodynamics are certainly no more complex and mysterious than human thought. We need wind tunnels for mindships too.

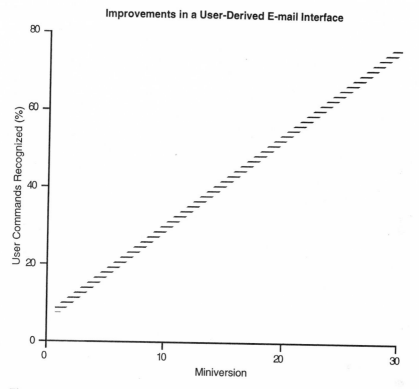

Figure 11.1.
At DEC, the interface to an email system was improved by changes that made it accept commands in the way test users spontaneously entered them. The initial version was similar to existing programs. Changes were made in a series of thirty slightly altered versions as data were collected. (Good et al. 1984.) Note: The authors do not provide data separately for each miniversion and probably did not test sufficiently to plot the percentage recognized for each. The figure depicts the overall improvement from the first to the thirtieth version, which they do report.

The second DEC story is from the same group and is about the development of the text editor EVE. The email program was an experimental prototype explicitly developed for the purposes of designing a single product. The UCD effort for the text editor was aimed at improving its usability in parallel with a larger project of which it was a component. The UCD activity was constrained by both the overall development schedule and the congealed functionality of the larger system. The strategy was to make an early version of the editor available within the company, to seek users and use, complaints and suggestions. As usability problems were identified, they were corrected. When suggestions for changes looked valuable to the usability specialists and if they were not contradicted by other suggestions, did not overload the complexity of the interface, and were technically feasible, they were tried. Over 200 suggestions were received in the first four months, almost half of them in the first month after wide distribution. Of the 200, about 140 were implemented. After the fifth month many fewer suggestions were made and almost none implemented. The system's usability was measured in the eighth month and found adequate, well before the project's final deadline. This was the editor that, despite being nongraphical, tied for second place against those in the Roberts and Moran tests.

These three examples illustrate a kind of progression in the placement of UCD in the design life cycle and correspondingly different purposes. The map story shows how first studying the intellectual difficulties of a practical user problem—in this case way-finding—and evaluating possible solutions can help to formulate the *what* of a computer system, and steer design toward the right functions.

The email example shows how, given a decision of what the system is for—electronic text message exchange, in this case—the details of design can be greatly improved by careful study of the behavior of users trying to use a mock-up or prototype.

The text editor example illustrates the perfection of a system that already exists, albeit in a still malleable form. The text editor was put out for real use and the experience of users harnessed systematically to pull its usability forward.

The IBM 1984 Olympic Message System

At IBM's Yorktown Heights, New York, research lab in late 1983, a team of five, led by Steve Boise and John Gould, were handed a formidable job: to design a totally new communications system for the Summer Olympics to be held nine months later in Los Angeles (Gould et al. 1987b). The system would make it possible for athletes housed in Olympic Village dorms to send and receive recorded voice messages to and from each other, to coaches and staff outside the villages, and to friends and relatives in all parts of the world. The system would have to accept input from any kind of telephone anywhere. Arabic-speaking parents in Marrakech, Mandarin-speaking friends in Hong Kong, Norwegian coaches in Los Angeles, as well as the Olympians, would have to learn how to use the system.

In 1984 there were almost no public voice message systems operating anywhere. Not everyone in the United States, and hardly anyone in Kiev, had used an answering machine. IBM had built and experimented with a voice store and forward system in the 1970s but had not imagined using it in this way. In Los Angeles, the system would be set up at two dozen kiosks in the villages connected to a dozen national Olympic Committee headquarters. Olympians would operate the system themselves from the kiosks. Non-Olympians would leave messages by calling into committee headquarters, where an operator would connect them to the system.

Design of the system was wide open and daunting. What functions should it provide: forwarding, message editing, distribution lists, nicknames, or just bare bones? What kind of interface and what sorts of instructions could make the system easy enough to use for such a constituency under such conditions? The stakes were high: the competitors would care a great deal; the prestigious Olympic Committee, the press, and the public would be watching. The system would operate for just four weeks; if it didn't succeed at first, there would be no try again.

The team started by composing a set of scenarios—detailed descriptions of imaginary users interacting with the system, engaging in dialogs with its prompts, exercising its intended functions. These documents provided concrete examples for potential users—the Olympic Committee, parents, programmers, and operators—to think about, discuss, and criticize. On the basis of these comments, the distribution list feature was dropped before ever being designed, as was a facility to verify that a message had been received and another to place calls to Olympians with waiting messages. Simplicity and manageability began to take center stage.

The next step was the production and test of user guides. Versions of these instructions for both the athletes and for their families and friends were produced. They were written *before* any code was programmed and shown to potential users. Comments and questions about the instructions shaped the features and functions of the system, not vice versa; for example, an easy method for headquarters operators to switch the language of the prompts was discovered to be necessary. In response to suggestions from readers and tests with system simulations, 200 modifications were made to the Olympian version of the guide, over fifty to the family and friends version. The brief user guides became the definitive design requirement documents for the project. The fact that the guides had already settled a vast number of design questions meant that many fewer changes would be made in the working prototypes.

Only a few weeks after the project was begun, computer simulations of the system and interface were tested. An experimenter read the prompts—instead of the eventual recorded-speech module—and typed the received voice messages into a file for later reading aloud to recipients. The researchers used a rapid prototyping and interface building kit that made it easy to transfer successful trial programs to the final system. In the early stages, lab personnel and visitors were the test users, not world-class athletes or their cousins, but they were nevertheless able to show up glaring errors: that four alternatives in an audio menu were too many—"Press 1, listen again; 2, listen to another new message; 3, send a message; 4, hang up"—and stated backward, "To listen again, press 1 . . ." is better.

Demonstrations and test trials with users from outside the United States began as soon as a working audio prototype was available and turned up many problems. The foreign users, less accustomed to computers and electronic interfaces, were more easily overwhelmed. Some functions that had been integrated already were dropped, for example, a facility to insert material in the middle of a message. The team also interviewed Olympians to see what life, schedules, and desires would be like. Over objections of the officials, who thought maps and expert opinions should suffice, they toured the site, making critical discoveries, for example, that classroom training would be impractical—users would have to learn as they used—and that smog, heat, and desert bugs would create hardware problems.

They tested the system overseas with overseas users and telephone systems, learning yet more lessons about the virtue of simplicity: functions for reviewing and revising messages were dropped, an example interaction added to the guide pamphlet. They tested the kiosk design in a hallway of the IBM research center, starting with a huge hollow cylinder with pasted-on concept drawings of the interface. Passersby edited and commented, and changes were made. Plans posted on the wall led to suggestions from strolling craftspeople. Moving on to a working prototype system in the still-changeable shell, they posted received messages for fellow workers on the computer screen, much as they would later for competitors. Layout, scanning rate, colors, translations, wordings of the official French and English instructions were improved. Intensive, systematic usability tests were conducted with about a hundred people. Interactive interface bugs were caught: prompts that misled, improper handling of time-outs for pauses. They held contests for employees to see who could find a problem, who could sign on most and send the most messages. More bugs were caught. They invited local computer science students to come by in the evenings and try to destroy the system.

Next came field tests at a pre-Olympic event with competitors from sixty-five countries. In five days the team discovered fifty-seven more usability items too severe to ignore. Despite the translated pamphlets, the videotaped mime demonstration, the international symbols, and the instructions in the kiosk in French and English, competitors from Oman, Pakistan, Japan, and Korea were helpless. Two new translations were added, then eight more. The problem of names from other cultures, where the first, middle, last name convention is not honored and for which equivalent English spellings are uncertain, was addressed by referring to badges and providing a reply function. A nest of problems with logging in and passwords was uncovered and beheaded.

And then 2,800 people were connected to the system at Yorktown and another 1,000 in Los Angeles. They used the system in their work and tested the robustness of the hardware and software in the face of connections to four different telephone companies and the stress of real loads.

Was the project a success? The system, with its six central computers and three dozen user stations, was never down entirely. Used at least once by 4,000 of the 10,000 Olympians, it carried one to two messages per minute day and night. Competitors received almost 12,000 greetings and good wishes.

This case powerfully illustrates the variety of ways to do UCD. There are many ways to maintain user focus and to obtain empirical data on what does and doesn't work. UCD consists in doing some of them. In table 10.1, almost no two projects did their UCD the same way, and, unlike this example, none used more than one or two techniques.

A Scene from Xerox

In the early 1980s, Xerox's copier business was slipping (Brown 1991). Strong new competition from Japanese manufacturers like Canon was only part of the problem. Service calls and customer complaints were up and rising. Customer interviews and service personnel reports suggested that the machines were not breaking down any more often than before, but that customers were having more difficulty operating them. A user would attempt some job and run into an obstacle—perhaps a paper jam or low toner or, worse, a complete mystery. The user might try to fix the problem—or not—and give up, abandoning the machine in a nonfunctioning condition. The next user would find it "out of order" and call for repair.

To find out why customers were having such difficulty, Lucy Suchman, a Xerox researcher, put a video camera over one of the copiers in the lab building and recorded interactions between people and machine. To the amazement and alarm of executives who later saw the tapes, their own employees had enormous trouble operating the device. In one segment, two renowned computer scientists stand by the machine in obvious frustration, try one thing, then another, reason together, then give up.

Instructions and trouble-shooting procedures for Xerox copiers of the era were contained in packs of flip cards attached to the machine. When the machine failed, a code would light on the machine, and the user was supposed to find the corresponding flip card and follow its directions. As machines added more features, the flip card packs waxed, and the users' temptation to consult them waned. Based on analyses of the videos, the copiers were redesigned. In new versions, the flip cards are gone. Instead, a small computer-driven screen displays instructions related to the function being used and shows icons and diagrams. When something goes wrong, a picture of the machine appears, showing where the problem is and illustrating how to get at it. Typical downtime for a paper jam plunged from twenty-eight minutes to twenty seconds because customers were much more willing and able to fix their own problems.

The SuperBook Saga

This story traces an extended user-centered design project from its origin in a series of applied research studies and inventions through prototype experiments and evaluations to software products. The SuperBook story is chosen for special treatment not only because I was involved but because it illustrates well the gold standard of usability engineering: user testing. It also will provide a much closer look at an actual phase two application system than we have had up to now.

Electronic Documents

Part of the dream of the paperless office is that tons of documents now stored and distributed at great expense could be replaced by efficient electronic storage and transmission. A document would be stored in just one computer file instead of piles of copies in a warehouse. It would be distributed when and as needed to only those who needed it. Updates and revisions could be done instantaneously. The cost of producing and distributing paper documents is between two and ten cents per page, depending on the size of the run and the fanciness and efficiency of the production. Hundreds of billions of pages of business documents are produced and distributed annually, at a cost of tens of billions of dollars. It's a tempting target. The hardware technology has been available and cheap enough for some time now. Magnetic disk storage sufficient to hold 1,000 books the size of this one cost about $2,000 in 1994. CD-ROM storage is even cheaper. Such devices occupy about one-fourth of a cubic foot of physical space. With electronic distribution, dozens or perhaps thousands of people could share a single copy. Whole buildings would go empty.

There are many schemes available for electronic document distribution. Floppy disks and CD-ROMs can be sent by ordinary mail, then mounted either on individual PCs or on server machines attached to a network. Another option is to send the electronic information directly over telephone lines or optical fiber or microwave networks. By any of these routes, the distribution cost is a tiny fraction of the expense of printing, boxing, shipping, handling, and unboxing. So with all these advantages, why is electronic delivery not here?

One of the barriers to widespread adoption of electronic document delivery is that much useful text that was produced before computers is still in use; converting it into electronic form is expensive and a bother. Although most new text now originates in an electronic form, as word processor output, it is not easy to use in that form. Each system has its own set of convoluted conventions by which the computer keeps track of type fonts, line widths, heading levels, figures, and footnotes, and each has its own incomprehensible set of invisible codes to mark up the page format and layout, and its own ways to organize and store the codes. There are scores of different format schemes for word processors and several hundred more for the automatic typesetting machines used by printers. To get between one of these formats and another, or to some standard, is seldom easy. Still, it is doubtful that these barriers would have remained if getting text in electronic form had been really desirable. The world has mechanisms, both formal and informal, for arriving at standard information exchange formats. They have been quite successful in international telephone message exchange, computer programming languages, and a host of other examples. The cost of retyping an old document would be approximately offset by the savings in printing and distribution costs if 100 fewer paper copies were made.

Electronic documents would have long since arrived if it were not for one stumbling block: people hate them. In almost every trial of providing electronic documentation, users have found the documents so unpleasant to use and so unsupportive of the work that they are needed for that they have refused to surrender their paper. The result has been that where electronic documents have been introduced, the paper documents that they were supposed to replace have remained. Thus instead of doing away with expensive paper and substituting cheap electrons, the organization ends up providing both. Since work with electronic documentation is usually less efficient than with paper, it's a lose-lose situation.

What's wrong with electronic documents as we have known them? First, reading text from a computer screen is perceptually difficult. People read more slowly from text on a screen than from text on paper. John Gould and his collaborators (Gould 1987a) at IBM's Watson Laboratory have tracked down several contributing factors, but almost all of them could be overcome by much better computer screens—screens four times as big and with four times as many pixels per square inch.

Another reason why reading from a computer is often slower stems from the computer's own power. Right-justified computer print—with lines made to end at the same place by filling in white space between words and letters—takes about 10 percent longer to read than the alternative, print with a jagged right edge (Trollip and Sales 1986). The reason appears to be that the jagged edge makes it easier for the eye to find the next line, so the reader doesn't waste time starting over. Unlike typewriters, computer text editors give the author the choice. Aping the aesthetics of print, authors are strongly tempted to right justify. The result is that most *printed* business letters now take longer to read than they used to.[3]

Slow reading is only one of the disadvantages of online text. Limited screen space makes it hard to provide sufficient context. In paper, you can keep two or three different pages open at once, refer to a table of contents or an index or look at a graph, and still keep the corner of your eye on the print. Books provide techniques that help readers move from one part of the story to another and to understand where they are. Over the centuries, writers and printers invented many aids: pages to replace more cumbersome scrolls, then page numbers—at one point printers re-peated the last line of one page as the first line of the next—tables of contents, indexes, footnotes, chapter divisions, section headings. These accessories and conventions serve two purposes. First, they help to main-tain the context needed for comprehension. The word *run* takes on differ-ent significance in discussions of shoes, hosiery, and advertising campaigns. The comprehension of every sentence and paragraph in a text is affected by its placement in the stream of discourse and in the overall structure of subsections, sections, and chapters of a book. Imagine your puzzlement if this paragraph had been inserted in chapter 1.

Second, print conventions provide methods for search. Much reading is not beginning to end; the reader wants to find a particular discussion, a particular set of facts, the opinions of a particular authority. Indexes and tables of contents, coupled with heading structures and page num-bers, help such search. Computer text, at least in its most frequently en-countered form, has taken us straight back to the scroll. At any one time you can see only a small part of the text, there are no page numbers, and headings slide quickly out of view. As a result, people reading long texts on computer screens quickly become disoriented. They don't know where they are in the text; they can't get back to where they want to be. They have trouble locating the information they want and comprehend-ing it when they find it. (I am *not* proposing that we mimic all paper book features on the screen; there are better uses of computer power.)

The end result is that people work less efficiently and less satisfyingly with online text and prefer paper documents. There have been nine scien-tifically satisfactory studies comparing online text with a paper and print equivalent. Most looked at the ability to find answers to questions based on information in the text. In almost all cases, users were quicker and more successful using paper and print than with the electronic form. This conclusion seems surprising, since search and retrieval would seem to be the place where computers ought to provide an advantage. Also, remark-ably, the inferiority for information finding was greatest for systems with all the features of hypertext. Hypertext, one of today's hot computer technologies, is a technique of presenting information in small modules that are connected by easily traversed links. The screen shows a word or other "hot spot" or "anchor," which when clicked leads instantly to some other related module of information. The intense interest and enthusiasm for these systems is motivated by the belief that they will greatly improve peoples' ability to find just the information they want.

Perhaps the most telling experiment was done by McKnight, Dillon, and Richardson (1991). Because it is sometimes asserted that the benefits of hypertext will accrue only to documents that have been written for the medium, these researchers studied a small reference text that had been explicitly written to be delivered on a popular commercial hypertext platform. The text had never appeared in book form, so they produced a paper version by printing out the computer text files left behind by the authors. They established a set of questions representing the information people would want to find by reading this work and watched and timed students as they used the material in the paper or electronic form. Students were significantly faster and more accurate with the paper form. When asked, they said they preferred it.

Bellcore's SuperBook was the first online text presentation system that was demonstrably better than paper. As such, the story of how it got this way is instructive.

SuperBook's Research Foundations

During the first part of the 1980s, the cognitive science group at Bellcore had been doing research on the finding and presentation of information from a psychological point of view.[4] They had discovered a few basic phenomena, had reached some understanding of the major difficulties that people have, had generated some ideas on how to overcome some of the difficulties, and had implemented and tested several computer-based instantiations of these ideas. Some of the ideas had proved themselves in the laboratory, making it easier for people to find information, find their way between one part of a document and another, and formulate database queries. Others proved worthless or worse.

The Trouble with Information Retrieval

The most important fact of nature this research group discovered was that people call the same thing many different names. In both paper-based and online retrieval systems, it has been typical to index documents or portions of documents by a single category label or perhaps by a handful of selected key words. The researchers collected the words that people used in referring to an object that might be stored in a computer file. If a hundred people were asked, they would typically propose thirty different names. On average, the most popular word for an object was used by fewer than a third of the people. Overall, if you ask someone else to assign a label to an object, then try to guess the label, you will be right less than one-sixth of the time. If you keep guessing, you'll usually come up with three or four more candidates. The chance that one of them matches will still be less than fifty-fifty.

Not coincidentally, the typical success rates for finding something in online catalogs and text databases is less than one in six on the first try, and less than fifty-fifty by the time a determined searcher gives up. Most of the words the searcher tries are unknown to the machine; most of the objects a searcher would like to find are not indexed by any word the user thinks of.

Unlimited Aliases

But there is an obvious solution. If we know that there are thirty words that people might try for an object, why not just give each object thirty labels? In print, this solution would be cumbersome and expensive; half the book would be index. However, for a computer, there's no problem. The Bellcore researchers tried doing this, and it worked like a charm. Simulations showed that by collecting names from a large number of people and putting them all in the computer, the likelihood of finding something a person wanted could be pushed up to almost 80 percent, way above the 10 to 20 percent of current technology. What's more, doing it this way did not seem to have an intolerable effect on the noise problem. While the proportion of wanted things found went up by a factor of five, the amount of junk that came along only doubled or tripled, so the ratio got much better. The Bellcore researchers called the principle that fell out of this finding *unlimited aliasing*: don't limit the number of terms by which an information object is known; give it all the names any user wants to call it (Furnas et al. 1987).

Direct experiments confirmed the principle (Gomez, Lochbaum, and Landauer 1990). In one, a file of 188 recipes for home cooks was put in a simple interactive online search system. In various versions the number of key words assigned to each recipe was varied from a low of two—typical of better paper indexes and many online systems—up to a high of over thirty. The local homemakers who used the system conformed perfectly to the predictions of the principle. When the system had only two index words per recipe, they found only about 20 percent of the recipes for which they hunted. When there were thirty index words per recipe, they found almost 80 percent. The time it took them to find a recipe was slightly shorter with the richer indexing vocabularies.

The main drawback to the unlimited aliasing technique is the difficulty of collecting all the terms that people will use. One approach is full-text indexing. In this method, which works for finding text objects, things made of words, all of the words in the object itself are made into key words by which it can be found. In the recipe experiment, full-text indexing was as effective as using the sets of thirty words collected from real searchers, although 120 words had to be assigned to each recipe on the average rather than 30. (There are many words in a text that no one will use in searching for it but no easy way to tell which they are.) However, even with this very large number of words, the time to find recipes was about the same. People have sometimes feared that full-text indexing would find too much that users didn't want. There is some justification in this concern, and we will discuss how SuperBook deals with the problem. Unfortunately, most previous methods that reduce the amount of unwanted junk reduce even more the amount of relevant material returned. You end up with the choice of getting a little that you want and too much that you don't—or nothing at all.[5]

An online retrieval system accesses the catalogs of all the libraries in the immense University of California system from anywhere in the world. Forty percent of all user queries return zero hits. The other 60 percent return an average of 700 apiece.

An Index that Learns

Another approach to harvesting all the right words was a scheme called *adaptive indexing* (Furnas 1985; Furnas et al. 1987). The system keeps track of the words that users try that don't succeed. If and when the user finally finds a sought item, the system asks whether some of the words that didn't work ought to be added to the list of index terms for that item. If the user concurs, it is done, and the new key words remain available for that and other users in the future. Suppose there is a directory of services for your organization online:

You type: *Reproduction*
It responds: ? [It has never heard of Reproduction.]
You type: *Xerox*
It responds: ?
You type: *Copying*
It responds: ?

You give up, and go down the hall to a knowledgeable coworker. She says, "You want *reprographics*." You go back to your terminal and

You type: *Reprographics*
It responds: **Reprographics Department. Reproduction, copying done on Xerox machines, while you wait or by special order. Room G311, x9567.**
You type: *q* [for quit]
It responds: **Should "Reproduction" be added to the index for this service? Y/N**
You type: *Y*
It responds: **Should "Xerox" be added to the index for this service? Y/N**
You type: *Y*
It responds: **Should "Copying" be added to the index for this service? Y/N**
You type: *Y*
It responds: **Thank you, good-bye.**

The next time you or anyone else asks for *Reproduction*, the system will display the Reprographics Department listing. Of course, nothing prevents someone else from making *Reproduction* refer to the Art Department instead of Reprographics. This is not really a problem. After extensive use, when you ask for *Reproduction*, the system responds:

"Reproduction"
has been applied to (1) The Reprographics Department by 28 people.
(2) The Art Department by 6 people.
(3) the Medical Department by 1 person.
Which listing do you want to see (1, 2, 3) ?

A test of this scheme with the online directory of services at the University of Texas found that it increased students' success in looking up telephone numbers by 50 percent after only a few weeks of use.

Navigating in a Sea of Words

Another step forward came from studies of the way people think about large, structured sets of information. The human mind is able to think about only a small field of view at a time. In reading, we actually take in only one word at a time. Our working memory maintains only about two seconds worth of spoken information. Such small bits of information are almost useless by themselves. Words are given full meaning only by the sentences in which they are imbedded. Sentences achieve much of their import by the way they combine with other sentences in a paragraph. One paragraph sets the stage for the next. Paragraphs in a subsection or section need to be taken together and in the right order to develop the topic or message of a chapter, and so on.

A reader dropped suddenly into a single paragraph, or even a single page of a text in the middle of a long document, can share the sensations of a person dropped at night into the sea in a lifeboat: you don't know where you are, where you came from, or where you're going, and you don't know which way to paddle to get to someplace nicer. Full-text documentation systems typically show a list of paragraphs or pages that they think you might like to see. Going to one of them can leave you at sea, because you don't know where you are in relation to other things you might want. You'd like to climb a tree and look around, but there isn't one.

A typical hypertext system can impart much the same disoriented feelings. You're reading along in a piece of text that interests you and find an anchor for a link. You follow the link and find yourself in another piece of text that the author thought you might be interested in, but you discover you're not. You are not sure why you are at that spot, given your own reasons for having been where you were before. Worse, many such systems don't let you retrace your steps. Instead, you have to wend your way rather blindly from link to link hoping to return, or you have to start over again. By the time you get back to the place from which you started the detour, you may have lost the train of thought or forgotten needed background information.

How should you get from place to place in text? The traditional route is to follow the path chosen for you by the author; start at page 1 and read until "The End." But often, especially in large reference books and manuals—the kinds of documents used in business, engineering, science, and education—you instead want to find your way to the bits you need right now. When you get there, you want to know you're there, and you want to be able to understand what you're being told.

In paper books, some guidance is provided by a table of contents, an abbreviated, structured view of the way topics are related and organized in the document. Students are often urged to read the Contents pages carefully before reading the whole book. It's good advice, and it's known that people get more out of books when they follow it. But confess: do you always study the Contents pages carefully? I don't, and videotapes of students reading books confirm the suspicion. It appears that a standard table of contents is not an attractive tool. It is either too long and detailed, and therefore difficult to use, or too short and abstract. The information it gives about the contents is rather thin. Titles of chapters and sections are limited to a few words or phrases, which may not tell readers much, especially if they don't already know the material and aren't familiar with the concepts and terminology.

Fisheye Views   Can computers offer a better way to help people get from one topic of interest to another? George Furnas put forward a model of the perceptual and thought processes that go on in such situations. You need to know the details about matters at the focus of your attention. Things that are at the center of your "mind's eye" but closely related to what you're thinking about also need to be available but in less detail. You only need to know the most important aspects of them. And so on. As information moves away from your current focus, you need to know less and less detail.

Furnas likens the situation to the famous *New Yorker* cartoon of the Manhattanite's view of the world. The streets and buildings of Manhattan are shown. The Hudson River is there, as are Newark and the rest of New Jersey. Next are Chicago, Los Angeles, the Pacific Ocean, and Japan. This is more than just a joke. To understand the geography of Manhattan, you need to know about its streets and buildings in detail. You also need to know that Manhattan is bounded by the Hudson River and has Newark on the other side; otherwise you're likely to go there by mistake. However, it's unlikely that you'll need information about the insides of Newark or of Chicago either. But you'll want to know that you could drive west to Chicago in a pinch, that you'd want to fly if you had to go to Los Angeles, and that Japan is out of the question without an increase in your travel budget. You couldn't draw a single map of the United States this way because the information you need to provide depends on where the person is who is using the map. You would have to supply a different map for every different standpoint. With computers, we can do that.

Let's go back to text. The static table of contents of a paper book offers the same view no matter where in the book you are or want to be. Therefore, it offers either too much detail or not enough. With a computer, we can construct a table of contents with an unlimited amount of detail but show only as much as is useful at any one time. Furnas's model describes what is most useful to show: specific information about material near our current point of interest and more and more general information as the context widens. This is called a fisheye view, after the kind of lens in which a high-resolution narrow focus at the center gradually widens into a low-resolution broad focus at the edges. In the online document version, the segment of text currently displayed on the computer screen is linked to the point in the table of contents where it appears. A dynamic view of the table of contents opens to different parts depending on what section you are reading. The title of the section you are in and the titles of all sections at the same level under the same superordinate heading are all shown, and so forth. An example should make this clearer; see the fisheye table of contents in figure 11.2.

To understand how this affects your sense of orientation in the text, first look at *fisheye views* in this view, then compare it to locating your current place (here) in the traditional table of contents in the front of the book.

An additional advantage of fisheye views for online documents is that they overcome the lack of real estate. If you put a thorough table of contents for a large, complicated book on a screen, users would have to scroll through it, which would make it even more difficult to use than

- I The Productivity Puzzle
- II Solutions to the Puzzle
- III What's Wrong with Them
- IV How to Fix Computers
    - 9 The Track Record So Far
    - 10 User-Centered Design
    - 11 Here's How
        - A Story about Maps
        - Two Tales from DEC
        - The IBM 1984 Olympic Message System
        - A Scene from Xerox
        - The SuperBook Saga
            - Electronic Documents
            - SuperBook's Research Foundations
                - The Trouble with Information Retrieval
                - Unlimited Aliases
                - An Index that Learns
                - Navigating in a Sea of Words
                    - ▶ **Fisheye Views**
                    - Menus
                    - ANDs, NOTs, and Ors
            - SuperBook Version 0
            - Evaluations
            - Further Applications and Tests
            - SuperBook Lessons
        - User-Centered Design
    - 12 User-Centered Design Methods
    - 13 User-Centered Development
    - 14 User-Centered Deployment
- V What Then?

Figure 11.2.
Fisheye table of contents.

usual. The fisheye view squeezes the important parts into a small region on the screen. Even in paper, the full structure of sections and subsections is often too much for the front-of-book listing, and lower-level headings are not shown (which is why you couldn't find Fisheye views in the one for this book.)

Furnas tested fisheye views as a way of finding information in text. He gave students problems of finding one piece of information and then another in a book of legal codes and observed how well they did using either an online fisheye view or a traditional table of contents. They were significantly faster and more effective with the fisheye view.

Menus The Bellcore researchers also did laboratory evaluations of several other tools that have been applied to information finding. For example, they studied the use of spatial filing, a technique that shows information as objects arrayed on the screen; often the objects look like tiny file folders. The idea is that humans store things in physical locations around offices so this must be a useful way to locate information. The experiments were quite disappointing. If there were more than six folders and each was marked with some sort of meaningful label—as little as a two-letter name—arranging the labels in a single alphabetic list was just as good as allowing users to place little folders wherever they wanted on their screens. (The same thing happened in "real" offices: provided that real manila folders had a label, letting people place them wherever they wanted in their own offices didn't help. Folders in a single pile were just as easy to find. The fact that people leave things lying around their desks and offices apparently does not prove that it is a useful habit for information retrieval (Dumais and Wright 1986; Jones and Dumais 1986).

The researchers also did extensive studies of the use of menus, a close relative of tables of contents. Menus have been widely regarded, and advertised, as the heart and soul of user friendliness. They are supposed to let users merely recognize the right choice rather than having to recall a name. However, these researchers—and many others before and after them—found that for finding particular pieces of information in large, heterogeneous sources, or in long documents, menus don't work well. The problem is that the segments of text that occur in nature are hard to categorize and its hard to label the categories; everybody does it differently. Take all the listings in your local Yellow Pages and divide them up into five categories. Give each category as good a name as you can. Pick a listing at random, and ask ten friends to guess its category. If more than six get it right, you're just lucky. (We did the experiment. (Dumais and Landauer 1984))

Menus are certainly useful for many kinds of computer operations, ones with a small number of well-defined alternatives that are either obvious from their labels or used so often that they are easily remembered (but not so often that a typed-in command would also be well learned). However, as an access route to information in large collections where each item is infrequently sought, they are not very effective.

*ANDs, NOTs, and ORs**   There were other studies of the usefulness of traditional logical query languages, techniques similar to database query languages like SQL but for expressing Boolean combinations of content words to tell the machine what text objects are wanted. As we've seen, most people find conversing in the language of logic rather forbidding. (Do you OR (your mother AND your father) AND NOT your aunt have trouble with Booleans?) The main aim of these techniques is to cut down on all the unwanted junk—documents or paragraphs you don't want— that often gets returned in full-text searches.

Suppose you were interested in the topic we are now discussing and you wanted to find all the sections of this book about it. If you searched for all occurrences of the word *search*, you'd get over 100 hits, most of them irrelevant. The Boolean approach is intended to help. Let's do a simple AND, the easiest and most natural kind of query beyond the one-word search. We need to think of a combination of two words, both of which are in paragraphs about text searching: this paragraph, the ones around it, a couple back in a previous section, but in as few other places as possible. What word can we AND with *search* to get the desired effect? How about *search* AND *text?* That would match this paragraph and a few others but miss the one just previous and the two to follow this one.

A story famous among reference librarians tells of a user who asked the online system for titles containing Navajo AND Indian. *Getting no hits, the user then asked for* Navajo AND Indian AND Arizona.

---

* Read note 5 in the Notes section.

Notice that here we had the immense advantage of knowing exactly what we are looking for; we had target text right in front of us. Ordinarily searchers have to guess what words the author used in relevant text. Yet the chance of guessing one word that someone else uses for a topic is about one in six. If you have to guess two different words both of which the author used in every relevant paragraph, what do you think would happen? About one in thirty-six relevant paragraphs would match. You cut down the extraneous material but drastically reduce the chance of finding everything you want as well. Unfortunately, it's easy to see when you are getting unwanted text but almost impossible to tell when you are missing items you want. This less-is-more illusion often seduces people into designing and using retrieval tools that are good at rejecting the bad but bad at finding the good.

In a case study of a legal text search system, the lawyers kept sending the professional searchers back until they were satisfied they had found at least 70 percent of the relevant material. Later exhaustive examination showed they had really gotten less than 20 percent (Blair and Maron 1985).

The Bellcore researchers were hardly the only ones active in search research prior to SuperBook.[6] Hundreds of active, publishing researchers are exploring the field of information retrieval. As they investigate the value of various information access techniques and interfaces, several have watched users struggle with current technology and tried to understand their difficulties. Chris Borgman (1986), found that only a quarter of students at Stanford could use the library's online catalog system after a day's instruction, and most of these were engineers who hardly ever used the library. Others have been making steady, incremental advances in automatic indexing and search methods, but even the most advanced experimental methods, even those using artificial intelligence and the most powerful massively parallel computers, still don't break the 50/50 limit—50 percent of what's wanted found, 50 percent of what's found wanted.[7]

SuperBook Version 0

By around 1985 some of the Bellcore group thought they were ready to design a better book, an electronic version that would put the power of computing to work. Most workers in telephone companies have to consult monstrous, sometimes rapidly changing manuals full of information on service features and codes, tariffs, technical and business procedures. Bellcore alone delivers almost 300 million printed pages of this stuff a year to the regional telephone companies. Hundreds of thousands of employees had networked computer terminals on their desks. Storage and transmission hardware was already adequate and getting faster, cheaper, and more capacious all the time. Electronic document delivery appeared to be economically desirable; it promised to obliterate the expensive printing, delivery, and updating of paper binders. However, as in other businesses, previous attempts of which we were aware had not been successful. Online documents were unpopular and often ignored; paper ones were still demanded. Moreover, we calculated that the rejection of electronic documents was economically rational. Given the problems just reviewed (and data to be described shortly), it appears that online documents would have reduced worker efficiency and that the resulting increased labor costs would have exceeded paper production savings.

We hoped to change the balance by applying what we had learned from research. Joel Remde set to work on an experimental prototype that would embody as many of the new principles and techniques as possible. Let me describe the system, the original of which we call Version 0.[8]

SuperBook appears with several windows. The one on the right contains a segment of text waiting to be read. The one on the left displays a dynamic table of contents; that on the bottom left, a search dialog area; and a thin window across the top contains some control menus. Windows can be moved around and new ones opened for additional text segments, figures, footnotes, and, in recent multimedia versions, animations and video clips. Text windows and table of contents can be paged and/or scrolled depending on the version.

The software has three parts. One part accepts text just as it comes from word processing programs. This part gets the text in shape for presenting on a screen, constructs a dynamic table of contents from the headings in the document, and prepares the full text indexing. These functions are done only once, before the document is put aboard for use. On current hardware, it takes about a minute to process a 1-megabyte book—the size of *Moby Dick*. The second part of the program stores the text and the index and does the work of looking up searches, fetching, and arranging text and figures. The third part is the user interface: it accepts mouse clicks, navigation button commands, and search requests from the user and displays results and text on the screen. In recent versions, all three parts can be on one machine or on different machines and do their work by passing messages around a network in what is called a client-server arrangement.

When a user starts up SuperBook on a document, its first page appears in the text window. Four levels of headings are shown above the text and are updated as the user scrolls or jumps through the text. The left-hand window contains a dynamic table of contents, an approximation to a fisheye view. When it first appears, it shows only the highest-level headings of the document. The user can open up to the next level at any point by clicking with the mouse. A mark on a heading signals more detail below.

When the user clicks on a point in the table of contents, the page of text is replaced with the first segment of text in the section so indicated. A third click in the same place closes the section. No matter how the user moves from one section of text to another, the cursor indicator in the table of contents keeps pace. Thus, the user gets information about the text segment's document position in two ways: the updated headings over the page of text itself and the cursor position in the table of contents. This gives a great deal of orientation information. SuperBook users rarely get lost.

Full text search is provided in the following way. If the user types a word in the look-up window, the system finds all paragraphs that contain that word. Users can also invoke a search by clicking on a word in the text window, and they can search for any word beginning with a particular string of letters, say *infor*. If the user types two or more words, SuperBook looks for paragraphs that contain all of the words, without regard to what order they occur in or how far apart. In information retrieval jargon this means that the search is treated as an AND with paragraph-level scope, but the user doesn't know anything about all that and doesn't have to. The user doesn't consciously construct Boolean search strings.

This default for multiword queries was chosen because it is a simple compromise believed to be the most effective for ordinary users. The most common and effective Boolean queries, where they are used, are simple ANDs. Trying to be more precise about the order and spacing of occurrences is both too difficult and too likely to lead to wrong answers. It is not often that two words, say, *retrieval* and *information,* occur in the same paragraph but convey a distinctly different meaning than they would if they were right next to each other, say, as *information retrieval.* It does happen but not with enough frequency to be worth making users learn a query language. On the other hand, it is not uncommon, in a full Boolean scheme, for a search that requires two words to occur adjacently, say, *information retrieval* again, to miss targets of interest, say, *retrieval of information.* It is easy to think of phrases that you would surely want if found but difficult to imagine phrases that would be all right but you haven't thought of. Such refinements are usually added to increase precision, that is to reject unwanted items, but this desire is at war with increasing recall, that is, getting more of what you want. Experience shows that providing these methods is detrimental for most users. In any event, SuperBook has another technique for increasing precision.[9]

Almost certainly the most important innovation in SuperBook is *structured feedback.* When a search is done, the user is first told the total number of paragraphs containing the query. The user *could* search through the document looking at each of these paragraphs in turn, by clicking on the search arrows in the text window, but this can be a slow and tedious process. Moreover, it is a rather hit-and-miss procedure that tends to get the user to a target in the absence of good context knowledge. SuperBook provides a different way. In addition to showing the total number of paragraphs containing the query, the places where the hits occur are posted against the table of contents. The user can track down the paragraphs that are truly of interest by looking for ones that have both hits on the query terms and appropriate titles and positions in the overall structure of the document.

This powerful combination allows the user to search for general, easily remembered terms that are likely to appear in any paragraph on a desired topic (and many others) and then to narrow the possibilities by recognizing which parts of the displayed and labeled text structure are most likely to be using the word the intended way. We thought this would be easier and more effective than having to think of all the right words and combinations. However, I have gotten somewhat ahead of the story. While initially we thought that this structured search feedback technique had promise for some of the reasons outlined, it had never been tried and it wasn't until well into the testing that its value was appreciated.

The SuperBook system has a number of other features, bells and whistles. For example, it allows people to leave notes behind whose content can be searched like any other part of the text.[10] It allows users to leave bookmarks, to extract pages and sections and send them to files, email, or fax. It accommodates several or hundreds of different books all indexed together, if that is something the user wants. The user can have as many different pages of text open at the same time as wanted, even from different books. Figures, footnotes, tables, videos, audios, animations, and so forth are handled automatically by a program that inserts an icon in the margin of the screen page at the place where they occur, allowing the user to click when the diversion is to be viewed. (Many previous computer-based text systems did not support graphics or did so in a difficult and awkward way. Graphic figures were an important requirement of several of our intended applications. Additional experiments, not reported here, were done to try to understand how best to do it. We now think we have it right.) Users can declare synonyms by clicking on words they earlier looked up. There are history mechanisms for both the word look-ups and pages of text seen, so that the users could go back and see what they had searched for, repeat searches, and march backward through the series of pages that they had previously viewed.

Evaluations

When shy, mild-mannered Joel Remde emerged from his programming booth to show us his first prototype, we were so awestruck we immediately named it SuperBook. We thought our ideas brought to life were even better than they had seemed in the brainstorming sessions that hatched the system design. We were confident we'd licked the electronic text usability problem. Luckily, however, we were honor bound to

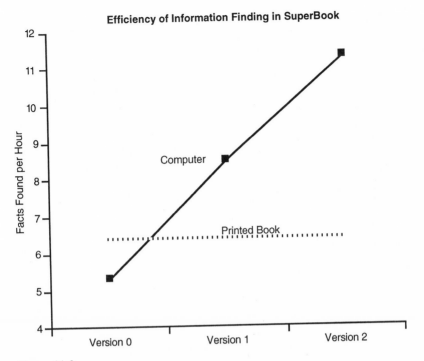

Figure 11.3.
Efficiency of finding facts in a technical document with the original printed version (print) and with three successive versions of the SuperBook text browser.

follow our own advice—we were preaching UCD even then—and give it a test trial (whose results are shown in figure 11.3).

For a trial book we chose a combination textbook and manual for an online statistics and graphics package called S (Becker and Chambers 1984). We thought this well-written and indexed 550-page technical book would be typical of a kind of document that SuperBook might be used for and had subject matter that would be of interest to the trial users, university students who had had at least one statistics class.

The book was automatically converted by SuperBook from its original UNIX text files. A set of twenty-four questions was constructed whose answers could be found in paragraphs dispersed throughout the book. The questions and paragraphs were selected so that there were systematic variations in the degree of overlap in the language used in the questions and the language used in the paragraphs or the subheadings under which they occurred so that we could compare different questions and assure ourselves that any results were not an accident of wording that made them particularly easy to find. Here's an example of a test problem: "Find the section that describes the first thing you have to do to get S to print pictorial output." The section that answers this question has no words in common with it, as would usually be the case if someone had thought of the question without having memorized the book.

Test users, who had no previous contact with S, learned to use SuperBook, then answered questions either with SuperBook or the standard paper version.[11] The SuperBook program was modified so that everything any user did was recorded. It was possible to play back the program and have the computer do just what it had done under user control, with all the same time intervals. In addition, test users were asked about their preferences and reactions. Other tests were also run.

Figure 11.3 shows the principal results for three successive versions— 0, 1, and 2—of SuperBook. The data shown are measures of user efficiency, the number of questions answered per hour of work with the system.[12] Perhaps the most interesting finding is the poor results of Version 0. SuperBook started out *worse* than paper. Information finding efficiency, the intended forte of electronic text, especially of SuperBook, was about 15 percent *lower* than with the manual technology it was intended to replace. Users were somewhat more accurate with SuperBook but much slower. Yet this was a phase two application with everything in its favor: it was built of proven parts, the designers had a deep research base, both from their own experimental work and from an unusually user-oriented subspecialty of computer science, information retrieval; their goal was a system that would make users more productive; the team included both psychologists and computer scientists, people with considerable usability experience and interface design expertise; the system ran on powerful, sophisticated machinery, operating systems, and window management software. (It used a Sun workstation, the UNIX operating system, and an extremely fast, homegrown window manager called MGR.) If this effort did not succeed on the first try, what would?

Perhaps a more important and deeper question is why a design with such a good foundation failed to achieve strong productivity gains. Were the proven parts and the presumed better understanding chimerical? Were we just fooling ourselves? I think not. I think the good results obtained later were largely due to the presence of these factors. What was wrong is something that is likely to be wrong with all first attempts: humans are complicated, computers are complicated, computer systems to aid humans in difficult tasks are quadruply complicated. There are literally hundreds of decisions in a design: in the way the interface is laid out, in the kinds of operations users need to do, in the dialog between the user and system. All must be right. A few, even one, that is seriously wrong can spoil the whole thing. It is impossible to get a significant computer-based cognitive tool right on the first attempt. Version 0 was no exception; it made errors on many fronts.

Analysis of the log data for Version 0 revealed that users were often waiting as much as twenty seconds for the system to return with a new page of text or with an update of the table of contents. Part of this was because the original programming language, LISP, is slow. We knew that, but many systems, including many widely honored and ballyhooed ones, are built on LISP.

Moreover, Version 0 was no slower, indeed somewhat faster, than other online text systems that we had seen. We had no way of knowing that the slowness of response was going to undo the productivity advantage. In addition, we didn't know when, with what urgency, and how often actions that were slow would be invoked by users. We didn't know what they might do while waiting, and whether the wait would materially disrupt the performance of their job. Indeed, we were genuinely disappointed when the results showed that people found information more slowly with Version 0 than with paper. Our own examination and use of the system had suggested that although we were sometimes annoyed at having to wait, we were still getting to things remarkably quickly.

There was more to the slowness of Version 0 than just the sluggishness of LISP. Even had we speeded up the processing so that pages were replaced almost instantaneously, as we did for succeeding versions by reprogramming in the C language, there still would have been a time differential favoring paper. In addition, over four sessions of practice, user times decreased greatly. How was that happening? As analysis of the data comparing Versions 0, 1, and 2 eventually revealed, the rest of the difference—approximately half the excess time for version 0—came from users' inefficient strategies. Version 0 actually operated in slightly different ways from the description given, which applies more nearly to Version 3. In Version 0, many of the individual operations, like posting hits against the table of contents or getting the first page of a section into the page of text window, took an explicit action on the part of the user. This was done partly in the belief, widely shared in the human-computer interaction (HCI) community (but not by us since our experience with SuperBook), that users should be given great flexibility and opportunity to use the system in the ways they want. The upshot was that many users tried to find material either by searching one by one through the list of hit paragraphs or by exploring the table of contents without doing word look-up. People who did that were much slower than those who used the structured feedback technique: search and post first, then hunt in the table of contents. Most users got considerably more efficient as they practiced with the system, and the main thing that changed was more use of this superior strategy.

We redesigned, making structured feedback happen automatically on every search. There were some other smaller but worthwhile changes made to add speed. For example, analyses of users' actions showed that they often had to move the mouse cursor a long distance across the screen. By rearranging the position of windows and buttons, we were able to reduce these motions and gained some small bits of time.

The same suboptimum strategies that cost users time also cost them accuracy. Using structured search feedback more often led to the right answer. Automating it, and adding highlighting of the found words in the table of contents headings as well as in the page of text, contributed to a substantial increase in accuracy across the three versions in the graph.

Again, observations showed that the users were sometimes having trouble locating the highlighted words in the text, which in Version 0 were made into bold type. Substituting inverse video (white letters on black) improved matters. There were a number of other minor changes, most of them motivated by analyses of the log data, observations of the users, or responses to their comments and suggestions. The result was a system that was substantially better than paper. User efficiency with

Version 2 was more than twice that with Version 0 and 67 percent better than with the paper book.

It turned out that users were more effective with SuperBook in some other ways as well. One example is writing an essay based on the contents of a book or a small library. In the first such test, statistics students were given an open book essay exam in which they were to compare and contrast several of the functions performed by S. Correctly answering the question required combining information from several parts of the book. Some of the students used the online version and some the paper and print. When they were done, the essays were scored blind by a statistician who knew the book and the system. The average scores for the SuperBook users were much higher than those of the print book users. In a college course the SuperBook students would have averaged an A− and the paper book students a C+. Such large differences are rarely found in controlled experiments on educational techniques. As an indication of just how big this difference is, consider that it is larger than the difference between an average Ph.D. and an average high school student on an IQ test.[13]

Detailed analysis found that the essays of SuperBook users were better primarily because they contained several facts found in a particular paragraph of the manual. The same facts were missed by almost all the paper book users. At first, we jumped to the conclusion that the computer search tools had led SuperBook users to a pertinent page not indexed in the original. Wrong. True, the logs showed that all SuperBookers got to the relevant part, but videotapes revealed that all the paper book users found the same page too. Indeed, they had the same paragraph open in front of them and looked at it just as long as did the SuperBook users, but they missed the facts. Apparently getting to the paragraph in the SuperBook manner—searching for words, then going through the table of contents—helped get its contents off the page and into the essays. It literally made the important words stand out; after a SuperBook lookup, the paragraph would be at the top of the window, the search terms highlighted. In paper, the telling paragraph was near the bottom of a page, and other aspects of the page were emphasized by the original layout and typography; the critical part was easily overlooked. The SuperBook style search may also have helped establish context for noticing and understanding what the paragraph had to say.

This finding also speaks to a another hotly debated question in electronic text delivery: should the text on the screen look exactly like the text on paper, follow well-worn print conventions, and take advantage of the compositor's art, or is it useful to do it differently in the new medium? We contend, mostly on philosophical grounds, partly on this shred of evidence, that one should harness the power of the computer to do better than paper. We have even dignified the position with a name: *dynamic text reformatting and layout*. The idea, not enough exploited yet, is that the way the text is arranged on the screen—its white spaces, heading indents, typographical flourishes—should be tailored to the instantaneous needs of the user, not set in lead.

Further Applications and Tests

We tested SuperBook with several other books, reading tasks, and user groups to be sure we hadn't stumbled on idiosyncratically favorable cases in the first evaluations and to learn more about how to design future generations. Every test save one confirmed SuperBook's efficiency advantage over paper, although not always by a wide margin. Several customers and commentators, especially some academics, worried that emphasizing direct search would undermine the serendipitous discovery of unexpected gems of knowledge. Therefore we also tested SuperBook for browsing through a book with general topics in mind rather than specific questions. SuperBook had a significant edge over paper here as well; readers still happen upon the unexpected, only faster. We always asked users what they liked. SuperBook was rated much easier to use than paper. SuperBook users usually had a higher opinion of the document itself. We asked the statistics book subjects if they'd like to take more courses in statistics. Significantly more of the SuperBook users said yes. (But people sometimes say things like that to please the researcher.)

When given an exact citation, author, article, publication, and pages, however, SuperBook users, although just as accurate, took longer. Analysis of log files showed that they used the usual word search and table of contents strategy, and ignored a special look-up feature that limits search to authors or titles (no one ever told them about it). As a result, on author names like *Gold* or *Green* they had to wade through articles about metals and plants, or ones that cited Mr. Gold or Dr. Green, on the way to articles written by these stalwarts. Once again, a tiny detail. Full citation search, where paper won its only race, is the mainstay of traditional library reference. Refined over centuries, it works well within the constraints of paper, provided users are looking for material someone else has already cited.

From a productivity perspective, the two most interesting new applications were an evaluation in a business setting and one in a university library with a larger set of documents. The business case was at Pacific Bell, which wanted to put a 4,000-page manual online for first hundreds and eventually thousands of service representatives. Producing and distributing the document and its 50 pages per week of changes was a seven-figure expense. The service reps used the manual daily for short but critical reference to product codes and setup procedures. They spent almost half an hour a week inserting updated pages into their binders—at least they were supposed to.

Pacific Bell followed a strategy that all other businesses would do well to copy for all computer applications. Before adopting the SuperBook approach, they tried it out with their own documents and their own experienced workers on their own premises. They composed a number of test questions that sampled the kinds of use to which their document is put. Randomly chosen service reps taught themselves the system in thirty minutes to an hour, using a short instruction booklet, then were timed and observed as they did the problems. Others worked the problems using the familiar paper document.

The speed and accuracy advantage of the online version was almost identical to that in the lab tests. The test takers loved it. Pacific Bell revised the interface to merge with their other online systems and put it to work. The real users love it; they are more efficient and no longer spend time making inserts. The information is accurate and up to date. Most important, the users are happily doing without the paper; it's not being printed any more, not a single copy.

The university application was mounted by Cornell with the help of the American Chemical Society. Before replacing its chemistry journal collection with online text, which the ACS has wisely kept for the last dozen years, the library wanted to see if users would use the new system. As a test, one year of the flagship chemical journal was offered to advanced chemistry students and faculty over SuperBook. The faculty devised tests like the ones we've looked at but with difficult chemistry research problems (e.g., "What's new in the synthesis of the antibiotic streptolydigen?"). Volunteers worked with SuperBook or with bound chemistry journals plus the normal sets of indexed abstracts used by scholars in the field. In this case, the efficiency gain for fact searches was enormous: SuperBook users answered questions at a rate of 4.8 per hour; users of the conventional paper research media answered only 0.7 per hour—a ratio of seven to one, or a 586 percent improvement in efficiency. Probably the improvement was so large because of the large amount of text—over 1,000 articles and 4,000 pages—and the demanding chemistry problems. Whether the difference will be even more lopsided when the full collection—about twenty times as large—is in place, we cannot say.

From the perspective of UCD methods, a recent report of a separate effort on a different online text system is intriguing. A group at Bowling Green State University in Ohio developed and tested paper and online versions of an encyclopedia of facts about Sherlock Holmes (Instone, Teasley, and Leventhal 1993). An encyclopedia made up, as this one was, of 3,400 independent short fragments connected by 10,000 cross-references, should be just the stuff for hypertext. A popular commercial hypertext building system was used for the computer version. The researchers were shocked that their first attempt tested worse than paper and set out to improve the interface and functionality on the basis of problems encountered by test users. The original users spent excessive time with overlapping windows, constructing overly complex queries, and, particularly, following links that got them lost. The researchers reduced the number of features, removed most of the search options, fixed the windows in separated tiles, made orientation views more prominent, and deep-sixed a major method for following blind links. The result? Searching for facts was 66 percent more efficient with the second version than the first and 58 percent more efficient than with the paper counterpart.[14]

There's still work to be done on SuperBook and its cousins and offspring. In the chemistry experiment, some types of questions yielded meager efficiency advantages for the online version. No one has tested online books with material that readers want to read from front to back or compared online books on palmtops and laptops to their paper equivalent. No one knows just how far we can get even with the efficiency of basic fact search; so far it looks like roughly two doublings have been achieved, at least tentatively (counting paper to SuperBook Version 2 and then on to the chemistry application). So far, graphics sometimes work better on the computer and sometimes in paper.

SuperBook Lessons

Foundation research and its resulting understanding and proven piece parts were certainly important to the success of SuperBook. The components, correctly combined, turned a good idea, electronic documents, into a qualitatively new mental work tool. However, the new power tool initially lost out to its John Henry. I think of the situation as akin to a pile of ore containing a few gold nuggets. The whole thing is not much good until you wash away the dirt. In the end, both the nuggets and the washing process are essential.

User-Centered Design

Successful UCD projects have all engaged in two or—usually—all three of these basic activities:

1. *Analysis*. Before starting to build a software system, the designers watched and talked to the prospective users. They explored what users were trying to accomplish and how a system could get them there.
2. *Idea evaluation*. While they were designing, they found some way to try out their ideas that showed how to improve them. They tried possibilities out on people like those who would eventually use them, doing the operations they would do with them.
3. *Testing*. When they got something working, they tested to be sure it worked with the prospective users doing the operations they would do with it.

Is it really that easy? It should be. However, the Nielsen and Levy (1995) survey found that only 20 percent of published accounts of new systems and gizmos reported any kind of systematic evaluation. Worse, when Nielsen plotted the number of evaluations over time, he found a slight downward trend.

Apple interface guru Bruce Tognazzini tells this story. The in-box tutorial for novices, "Apple Presents . . . Apple," needed to know whether the machine it was on had a color monitor. He and his colleagues rejected the original design solution, "Are you using a color TV on the Apple?" because computer store customers might not know that they were using a monitor with the color turned off. So he tried putting up a color graphic and asking, "Is the picture above in color?" Twenty-five percent of test users didn't know; they thought maybe their color was turned off.

Then he tried a graphic with color names in their color, GREEN, BLUE, ORANGE, MAGENTA, and asked, "Are the words above in color?" Users with black and white or color monitors got it right. But luckily the designers tried a green-screen monitor too. No user got it right; they all thought green was a fine color.

Next he tried the same graphic but asked, "Are the words above in more than one color?" Half the green-screen users thought white and green qualified. So he asked, "Are the words above in several different colors?" The result was better: only a quarter of the green-screen users flunked, by missing the little word in. Finally, "Do the words above appear in several different colors?"

Success.

Many designers seem to be genuinely uninterested in testing. When the SuperBook evaluations were submitted to a conference on hypertext, one of the reviewers said that it was an excellent paper for what it was but questioned the idea of publishing evaluations. Said this referee, everybody knows how to do evaluations; he wanted new designs and implementations.

Perhaps he is right; it's not that people don't know how but that they think it's not necessary, or not very important, or that someone else will do it. The data and examples presented here show that evaluation makes a big difference but that it isn't being done. In case some of the reluctance stems from fear of the unknown, from doubts that usefulness and usability can really be assessed and analyzed objectively, the next chapter describes in more detail some of the specific methods that have been used successfully in UCDesign.

12

User-Centered Design Methods

One usability engineer watched while a new user tried to insert a floppy disk into a crack in the front of the computer housing instead of the proper disk slot. Then there was the user who when told to press any key, pressed the break [halt everything] key and brought the system down. Said the user, "It said press any key."

Traditionally, a lead sentence right about here says that of course a single chapter like this won't make you competent; you'll need to read many other books, go back to school, hire the author as a consultant. In this case, I have my doubts. Experienced experts will do better evaluation, but they won't know the application as well as those who are responsible, and they may not be listened to as respectfully. This chapter says most of what needs reading before getting started. The best next step is doing. Nobody has a magic formula beyond the general kinds of activities in which to engage. Little extra knowledge is essential. Certainly once a particular aspect is in focus—say, screen design for a form filling inter-face—reading up on what others have done and said will provide useful guidance. Practice, however, appears to be critical; every one of the cited successes came from an experienced team. Here is a list of techniques that have been involved in significant achievements.

Task Analysis

Chapters and books have been devoted to task analysis. They set forth pseudo-formal methodologies and structured sets of activities with specific reports and analyses, and they make very boring reading.[1] In practice, task analysis is a loose collection of formal and informal techniques for finding out what the job is to which the system is going to be applied, how it is done now, what role the current and planned technology might play. Probably the most important aspect is identifying the goals of the work. This means not just the goals of the computer system but the goals of the business or entertainment activity for which it is contemplated. The most effective attitude is that a noncomputer solution is equally welcome.

The first step is always to go the place of work and see what is being done now. Analysts watch people and ask questions; they talk to executives, managers, supervisors, and especially to the people doing the work. The way work is actually done is seldom the way it is officially prescribed; real workers find better procedures. Analysts hanging about the workplace at Xerox discovered a rich underground culture of job knowledge passed by example and word of mouth that was nowhere in the supervisors' descriptions, the official job specifications, or the training materials. Such observations directly suggested solutions ranging from furniture and office architecture to electronic message facilities to facilitate informal communication rather than suppress it (Brown 1991).

Many analysts try to get workers to talk aloud as they work. The context of actively performing the job brings things to mind that aren't thought of later or mentioned in an interview. The opportunity to delve deeper and ask what might help is greater. Some analysts make videotapes and find footage of struggling workers valuable for converting unbelieving executives and designers. (Whether extensive taping is worthwhile as a supplement to live observation is debatable. It is very labor expensive.) The analyst looks for tasks that might be done better or not at all and tries to determine if a reorganization of the work, or even a change of goals, is called for. Thinking about computer function and design comes very late in the game.

Task analysts always take careful notes about how much work of what kind is being done. They measure how long people spend doing what. They stick around long enough to find out what the major problems are, not just by asking supervisors but by watching and asking many workers. They notice what kind of errors workers are urged to avoid, the "stupidities" on the part of workers about which managers complain. (Worker errors and stupidities are usually due to bad procedures and systems.) How much time does each part of the work or process take? How much variation is there in that time? On what does the variation depend? Are some workers much faster than others? Are some kinds of jobs finished much faster than others? How could slow jobs or slow people be converted into fast jobs and fast people? All of this investigation takes time, typically several full days.

No one set of methods or activities characterizes all successful task analyses. Almost every situation in which a new computer system is contemplated is different in important respects from every other. What appears to be required is a questioning approach that puts its emphasis on finding the relevant facts and keeping an open mind about how improvements are to be realized.

All consultants know "how much of their sustained employment they owe to the fact that few managers actually know what goes on in their workplaces" (Zuboff 1991, 164).

Here are some more specific techniques that have often been successful:

Learn the Job.   On learning to do a job, experienced computer designers see all kinds of ways in which it can be improved. Effective task analysts never stop there. They ask users whether the improvement would be worthwhile; as often as not, the users will have thought of the same ideas and will have rejected them for good reason. The analyst is not the only smart cookie on the block.

Consult the Users.   When it comes to jobs, it's hard to be wiser than the people doing them. Opinions and suggestions are collected both informally and formally. One formal method is the questionnaire, but most questionnaires are misunderstood by the people who answer them and provide uninterpretable or misleading data. In this aspect of task analysis, expertise is important. An expert analyst never writes a questionnaire before doing observations and never administers one without testing. A questionnaire is a user interface and is never gotten right the first time. Involving users in the design process increases the chances that they will like what they get. The so called Scandinavian school of system design prescribes going out into the work environment in which the system is to be used and bringing users into the process at every step. The emphasis is on personal, social, and organizational factors in the introduction and use of new technology. Spending time with workers in the workplace and involving them in design helps ensure that the system will promote rather than interfere with important aspects of work and work life, essential work habits of individuals, and communication patterns of groups. For example, if the normal communications among the nursing and medical staff of a hospital are maintained through the bedside chart, replacing the chart with a computer could have disastrous consequences for the exchange of informal news about patients and the maintenance of good working relationships.

Use Subject Matter Experts.   An indirect sort of observation and questioning is often achieved by using a subject matter expert, someone with extensive experience of the work in question. A talkative low-level supervisor is the usual source. The wise analyst never takes the information extracted from a subject matter expert as gospel. Experts have a tendency to think things fine and easy that aren't. They have a fish-in-water view. Information from subject matter experts is best used to guide and interpret field observations.

Conduct Time and Motion Studies.   The old technique of time and motion studies is still used to good effect. The analyst first categorizes the various subparts and activities of a business process, then applies an inconspicuous stopwatch. These measurements call attention to time-consuming activities that can be reduced or eliminated. Whiteside, Bennett, and Holtzblatt (1988) report a case in which people spent significant time accessing an online help system when they didn't need any help.

Consult Normal Business Records.   Measurements that most businesses keep as routine data (even though they may never use them) are often helpful. The amounts of money spent on consultants, training, overtime for error correction, and the like can be revealing. The budget tells where important gains are to be made. The analyst measures the number of whatever per day and asks what makes there be so much or little. Xerox homed in on its usability problems by counting service calls.

Formative Design Evaluation

"Engineering design shares certain characteristics with the positing of scientific theories. But instead of hypothesizing about behavior of a given universe, . . . engineers hypothesize about assemblages of concrete and steel that they arrange into a world of their own making" (Petroski 1982, 43).

The terminology *formative evaluation* is borrowed from the development of instructional methods, which often contrasts it with *summative evaluation*. Formative evaluation is used to guide changes; summative evaluation is testing to determine how good something is. Unfortunately, most usability testing for computer systems is summative: somebody wants to check that the finished system works or to produce data for marketing purposes. Such evaluation rarely produces useful design guidance.[2] In formative evaluation, by contrast, the notion is not just to decide which is better, system A or system B, but to produce detailed information about why system A is better or what is good and bad about both systems—what needs fixing, amplification, or replacement. The Olympic Message System, DEC, and SuperBook iterative development stories were about formative design evaluation. Formative evaluation can run a gamut of techniques from simple observations and questions to elaborate laboratory experiments. Some of the deeper methods are described in a later section on performance analysis. Here we focus on quick and practical approaches that have been successfully applied in ordinary software development settings.

The Gold Standard: User Testing

We want information that will help us make what people do with a system more productive. Only by studying real workers doing real jobs in real environments can we be sure that what we find out is truly relevant. User testing tries to get as close to this ideal as possible. The Olympic Message System trials and the Xerox video vignettes were the nearest we've seen. Field trials with finished systems can get even closer.

Usually practicalities get in the way. Real workers and real designers are busy in different cities. Measurement and observation is too cumbersome, intrusive, and slow in the real workplace. The real system can't be tested until there is a real system, but much earlier guidance is much better. Compromises and approximations are necessary. The most common compromise is to test people like those for whom the system is intended with tasks like those they will most often do, using a prototype or early version in a laboratory setting that is vaguely like the intended office or other place of use. Experience suggests that such compromises are usually good enough. Information gained from user tests has been the most frequent source of major usability improvements.

User testing is straightforward. Someone—it has been most successful when the person was a specialist but also a full-fledged member of the design team—thinks up a set of tasks for users to try with the system, and gets test users to come in or goes to them. While users try, the tester watches, notes errors, measures times, and later asks questions. Many practitioners urge the test users to talk aloud as they work so that their conceptions, misunderstandings, and suggestions can be gathered and discussed. Others prefer the greater realism and more accurate measures of work efficiency afforded if users don't try to divide their time this way.

Mike Grisham at Bell Labs worked the bugs out of instructions to operate a voice messaging system by having volunteers come into the lab and try to operate a crude mockup of the system. With the initial, professionally written instructions, the majority of users made fatal errors of one kind or another. For a few weeks, Grisham tried one wording and procedure sequence after another, modifying each on the basis of what he learned from the previous ones. In later field tests, fatal error rates were less than 1 percent.

It is a good idea to start formative evaluation before building the system. Rapid prototypes that can be quickly built, then thrown away or changed, are extremely useful. Unfortunately, it is often either impossible or too expensive to build them. Moreover, it is best to get an even earlier head start, to evaluate how to build the prototype. A variety of techniques have been devised for testing user-oriented systems before they exist.

Wizard of Oz Experiments. The DEC email system, where Dennis Wixon played the part of the computer, was an example of this technique. Another is provided by John Gould (Gould, Conti, and Hovanyecz 1983), who wanted to see how well businesspeople could use a typewriter that took dictation using automatic speech recognition. Since no such system existed, he faked it by having a human sit behind a wall and translate. The idea is to test function and interface without having to build it first.

A Good Second Best: Heuristic Evaluation

In this technique real users, and sometimes real systems, are replaced by expert judgment. This distinctly doesn't mean just letting the boss or a consultant take a look. Rather, it means a systematic, disciplined inspection by several specially trained evaluators working independently. Jakob Nielsen, working with Rolf Molich at the Technological University of Denmark, evolved a set of ten heuristics for judging the quality of a computer's user interface. (A heuristic is a general principle or rule of thumb that is usually but not always effective.) His heuristics represent a consensus of usability guideline wisdom (Nielsen 1993c).

People already knowledgeable about computers spend a half-day to a few weeks learning the meaning of the heuristic rules and their basis and practice applying them. Then they spend an hour to a half-day examining the system, either real, in prototype, or as a set of written descriptions and drawings. They search for usability problems, aspects of the system's user interface that violate the heuristic rules.

Here are Nielsen's ten heuristics, briefly paraphrased:

1. Use simple and natural dialogue. Tell only what is necessary, and tell it in a natural and logical order. Ask only what users can answer.

2. Speak the users' language. Use words and concepts familiar to them in their work, not jargon about the computer's innards.

3. Minimize the users' memory load by providing needed information when it's needed.

4. Be consistent in terminology and required actions.

5. Keep the user informed about what the computer is doing.

6. Provide clearly marked exits so users can escape from unintended situations.

7. Provide shortcuts for frequent actions and advanced users.

8. Give good, clear, specific, and constructive error messages in plain language, not beeps or codes.

9. Wherever possible, prevent errors from occurring by keeping choices and actions simple and easy.

10. Provide clear, concise, complete online help, instructions, and documentation. Orient them to user tasks.

Evaluators need to know quite a lot more to cash these principles out in practice. Catching wordings that are computer gibberish is relatively easy, but knowing what wordings are truly communicative for intended users takes experience (indeed, may not be possible without repeated user tests). In one case, Nielsen (1992) found that usability experts, people with training and professional experience in usability engineering, noticed almost twice as many problems, on average, as programmers who had had a half-day introduction to the method. The more sensitive detectives weren't just being pickier; once identified, the problems they found were judged to be just as real and bad by evaluators who had missed them.

Nielsen has found that a single evaluator typically finds only about a third of the lurking problems—sometimes more, sometimes less, depending on system, experience, and luck. But different evaluators find different problems. In fact there's very little correlation between the 20 percent that one expert finds and the 40 percent that the next one detects. That means that more and more of the bugs can be detected by sending out more and more experts to look.[3]

Nielsen also found enormous variation between one system and another; you never know how many usability bugs to expect, although there are usually a lot of them. Over one set of eleven user interfaces subjected to exhaustive evaluation, the number of problems ranged from 9 to 145, with an average of 42. Of usability problems found this way, perhaps half are both easy to fix and well worth fixing (Nielsen 1993a). No matter how many problems there are, a single evaluator finds about the same proportion of them, usually around a third.

The number of usability problems found by heuristic evaluation is roughly the same as the number found by user testing (Virzi 1992). That is, one expert examination will find about the same number as one test user will tumble over. (And different user tests expose different problems, just as different experts do.) However, the kind of problems found by the two methods may not be the same. Those found by testing appear to be somewhat more severe, and more frequently occurring problems tend to be experienced first. More important, user testing seems more likely to reveal why users are doing well or poorly and to offer insights into how to improve usefulness and polish usability. Heuristic evaluation is aimed primarily at catching common interface design errors rather than analysis of the adequacy of a system's functionality for getting a job done. User tests have more often led to significant innovations. One of Nielsen's studies suggests that the best approach may be a combination of two to four expert examinations and a like number of user tests at each iteration.

Paper, Pencil, Plastic, and Palaver

Another shortcut method is a sort of brainstorming session held over a cheap mock-up of the interface. People try to simulate a new interface and mimic the operations they would do with it. This method is particularly useful for initial designs of screens for information input and display. Recently it has been expanded into a cute technique for designing graphical user interfaces. In the PICTIVE technique a design team sits around a table with a drawing of a computer screen. Using a number of common interface tools—icons, menus, and cursors—in the form of plastic overlays or glued note sheets, they arrange and rearrange interface components and act out work activities done with the interface, attempting to design layout, dialogue, and functionality for a system they have in mind. If the design team includes actual users as well as usability engineers and programmers, the first try will be closer to the best (Muller 1992).

A related technique is called a cognitive walkthrough. A group of experts reads the specs, then gathers round to imagine going through the same mental steps a user would, discussing and commenting on the good and bad. In all, these group design methods appear to find fewer problems than Nielsen's heuristic evaluation but perhaps different ones (Jeffries et al. 1991; Muller, Dayton, and Root 1993).[4]

Engineering Models

More formal methods rely on explicit models of human task performance; the best is the so-called GOMS model (Card, Moran, and Newell,

1983). Skilled tasks are broken down into atomic components consisting of goals (what the user is trying to do—say, change *this* to *thus*), operators (the actual action needed—a thought or a keystroke), and methods (the strategy chosen—for example, deleting and replacing the whole offending word or line or just editing one letter). Careful observations are made of the use of a system, and the time for each kind of operation is measured. To estimate how well people would perform with a variation of the design, the engineer specifies the new sequence of operations that expert users would execute. The time required to achieve goals with the new system is estimated by adding up the times for all the component actions. The predicted times for different strategies are compared, and the expert user is assumed to choose the best one. For the kinds of systems and tasks to which it is applicable, GOMS analysis is sometimes sufficiently accurate to substitute for heuristic evaluation or user tests (Gray, John, and Atwood 1992; Nielsen and Phillips 1993).

GOMS works best when the operators are simple perception-motion sequences like keystrokes. Its major deficiencies are the incorrect assumption that experts always choose the best of the available ways to do something and the lack of a good way to predict errors, which often eat a large share of a user's time and patience.

Another form of analysis has been tried for cases in which the action is mostly mental. In cognitive complexity analysis, the thought processes are simulated by an artificial intelligence program. To measure the difference in difficulty between two designs, the number of steps in the program is counted. Similarly, the proportion of common steps in the two predicts transfer of training between one and the other. The authors, Kieras and Polson (1985), have had some luck predicting which systems are easier to learn for people who already know which other systems. The method, however, is labor intensive and difficult to apply successfully.

Performance Analysis

Performance analysis refers to the kind of systematic experiments and observations that were illustrated in the SuperBook project; in contrast to the methods reviewed so far, their main goal is deeper understanding on which to base innovation and initial design rather than assessment and improvement of existing designs. Performance analysis is more likely to be found in an industrial or academic applied research organization than in the usability assurance group of a software house. Broadly, performance analysis studies people doing information processing tasks in an attempt to understand what they do well and poorly, where help is needed, and, if possible, what might help. Performance analysis is done either in the laboratory with somewhat abstracted tasks, such as suggesting titles or key words for information objects, or explicitly with an existing technology for the performance of some job. Performance analysis, when successful, leads to the identification of a human work problem that a computer can ameliorate. Computers are so powerful and flexible and there are so many things that they can be made to do that finding the right problem is often harder than finding its solution. An example is the unlimited aliasing technique already described. Once it had been discovered that many more names were needed, providing them with a computer was easy. There are a variety of aspects of user task performance that can be observed and used in performance analysis.

Time Is the Essence

In striving for work productivity, we fundamentally want to reduce the amount of time that a user needs to spend to accomplish a given amount of work. Eric Nilsen, in his 1991 University of Michigan thesis, measured the time users took to make selections from menus of different design. He discovered that the popular walking menu results in excessive selection times because it requires carefully aimed curved movements with the mouse. These movements are difficult for people. By substituting two short, straight movements for one long, curved movement, Nilsen found an alternative that saved substantial time.

Errors Are the Villains

Errors are the main thieves of time (and satisfaction). In an early and influential book on the psychology of human-computer interaction, Card, Moran, and Newell (1983) presented detailed analyses of the actions involved in using text editors. The data showed that the largest source of wasted time was errors. Finding what causes errors and getting rid of the cause (or at least providing more than a beep or secret code number to help the user recover) has big benefits.

"Beep," System has quit due to error 593.

Learning from Learning
Learning time is both a diagnostic and a design object in its own right. In some software development environments, standard operating procedure is to assume that usability is the exclusive province of training; just design a powerful feature, then let someone figure out how to teach its use. The bigger the training manual, the longer the time required to learn a particular function, the more redesign is needed. (Beware a 400-page manual beginning, "This application is very easy to learn and very easy to use.") Analysis of what aspects users find hard to learn illuminates both how to change the system and how to write the instructions if all else fails.

Variability Is a Source of Progress
In Darwinian evolution, natural genetic variation provides the opportunity for change. Something similar applies in usability design. Looking where there is the most variability between one task and another, or between one user and another, can reveal paths to progress. If some people do things well that others do poorly, the more efficient may have found a strategy that everyone could use. The power of the structured search feedback technique of SuperBook was discovered this way.

The flip side is that especially slow or error-prone users may have discovered an especially poor way to perform the task that deserves extinction. These kinds of situations occur most frequently in powerful, feature-rich systems that offer users many ways to do the same job. Some users are sure to compound enormously complex, and sometimes enormously poor, procedures. The same comments hold for variations across task problems. If some problems are dealt with quickly and others slowly, an opportunity may be hiding or a soft spot in system design may be at fault. SuperBook again offers an example—this time a flaw. With

SuperBook, chemists did very well on most information search problems, much better than with paper technology. However, when the problems required information from pictures of chemical structures, they did quite poorly. Analysis disclosed that students using the online version often failed to bring up the pictures.

The Talent Search

Productive technology for the service sector multitudes should not require rare talent. Yet as figures 10.2 to 10.4 showed, many, and perhaps most, do. Tracking down the special abilities needed can unearth hints about what needs to be done. In the case of each of the problems illustrated in these figures, ways to reduce the dependence on special abilities were found. In text editing, when so-called full-screen editors were introduced, older people found them much easier. Young people got better too, but the older people improved more. Designers of full-screen editors had believed that it was the WYSIWYG (what you see is what you get) visual nature of full-screen displays that accounted for their superiority. Gomez and Egan showed that, instead, it was the way the user specifies a place in the text that mattered. The hunt that found the reason was guided by looking for parts of the task that required special abilities. Gomez and Egan discovered that people with poor spatial memory couldn't think abstractly about positions in the text so they had to point. Older people had trouble formulating complex statements. Replacing complex commands with simple syntax or arrow keys reduced the need for youth and talent.

In the case of the database query languages studied by Greene and associates, the analysis suggested that some method of querying that did not require logical reasoning was needed. Other experiments showed that people, regardless of logical ability, can identify the cells in a table that contain the data they want. (They may not know much about data, but they know what they like.) Greene, and coworkers devised an interface in which the computer provided the tables and the users had only to mark the cases they wanted. As figure 12.1 shows, this interface made everyone almost equal, again by bringing up the laggards without hurting the champs.

Query Language and Talent

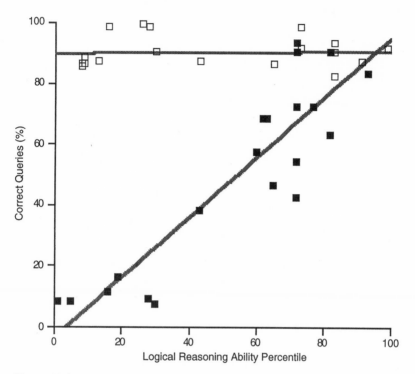

Figure 12.1.
After discovering that standard query languages require special logic expressing abilities but picking the right cell in a data table doesn't, a new query language that everyone can use was invented. Data from Greene, Gomez, and Devlin 1986.

The final example, shown in figure 12.2, comes from Susan Dumais's work on text querying and makes a similar point. Even when people could say what they wanted in their native language, their verbal fluency—the ability to remember words of a particular meaning—had a large impact on success. In an alternative search technique, once users find examples of desired documents, they can ask the system to find similar ones. When they are using this technique, the need for high verbal fluency virtually disappears.

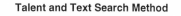

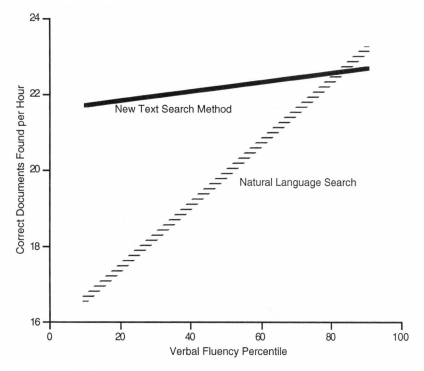

Figure 12.2.
Telling the computer what you want, even in your own words, demands high verbal fluency. When people instead can provide examples of the documents they want, everyone does well. Data from Dumais and Schmitt 1991.

An Aside: Different Strokes for Different Folks?

The fact that some interaction styles can be easy for one person and difficult for another has not been lost on software designers; as the two previous figures show, it's hard to miss. However, some have drawn from this a dangerously incorrect conclusion: systems should provide a wide variety of ways to do the same thing, so as to fit all comers, and to make interfaces reconfigurable so users can more or less design for themselves.

This conclusion has several problems. First, while it is often true that a particular method is much easier for Jill than for Jack, it is rarely true that some other method will be much easier for Jack than for Jill. In virtually every case I know of, the real situation is like the one depicted in figures 12.1 and 12.2: those who do well with method A will do well with method B too, while those who do poorly with A may sometimes do better with B. If a method is found that helps Jack, it will not hurt Jill—it just equalizes the two of them somewhat. There are techniques that few can master and techniques that all can master—not different easy strokes for different folks.

The only exception, and even it is often overestimated, is the difference between novices and experts. What the user can be expected to know or needs to be told obviously depends on experience. It's not a good idea to make beginners memorize eighty-eight arcane key chords before they can get started, even if chords may be helpful after mastery. Advanced, powerful techniques are best reserved for experienced users. However, the line can be fuzzy. Many menu-and-mouse-driven interfaces provide alternative keyboard accelerators—keystroke chords that have the same effect as a menu selection. These are intended, and believed by most expert users, to make those who are willing to learn them faster. Tognazzini (1992) claims the advantage is illusory. He says timing studies of experts invoking commands by key chords and mouse with menus find them equally fast. He claims the keystroke method just *seems* faster because of a perceptual phenomenon by which time appears to run slower when it is occupied by things you consciously see and think about, such as menu alternatives and cursor movements on the screen.

The absence of cases where different methods are optimal for different people would not surprise educational researchers. Despite a widely believed myth, decades and hundreds of attempts to show these kinds of effects in teaching methods—that one method is best for one kind of learner and another for others—have generally met with failure (Cronbach and Snow 1977). Most graphs of learning speed for different teaching methods used for students with differing aptitudes, say verbal or spatial abilities, look like figures 12.1 and 12.2. One method stresses the ability more heavily than the other; the other makes all students more nearly equal, but there is no flip-over. In the rare cases when there is a flip—student type V does better with method 1, student type M with method 2—the effect is always small; a tiny percentage of all students change places in the ranking because the teaching method changes. Again, the major exception to this generalization is experience. An advanced text is more helpful for advanced students than for beginners, and an introductory text the opposite. Interestingly, when students are offered a cafeteria of learning methods, having choice sometimes helps, but only for the top-ranking students. Only the most able are able to take advantage of using different methods at different times (Cronbach and Snow 1977). Perhaps we have a parallel in computer systems. Perhaps the most talented—the programmers and power users—do profit from a wide variety of alternative methods and features. This could explain why designers and data processing department gurus are attracted to variety and self-tailored interfaces. On the other hand, as we will see later, given a choice between two interfaces, one of which is objectively quite superior, most users, even programmers, may have little better than a fifty-fifty chance of choosing the more effective. Thus, providing both would make half the users less efficient than necessary.

The second problem with variety is that it is confuses and delays. The more techniques there are to learn, the longer it takes and the more likely the learner will mix up the options and actions of one with another. The more options available at one time, the longer it will take to choose—it takes twice as long to decide among eight alternatives than between two—and the greater will be the chance of choosing wrong. One popular spreadsheet program offers more than eight different ways to move from one cell to another. Even highly expert users of the system often select the less efficient method for particular tasks (Nilsen et al., 1992)

An additional problem with user tailorability (letting users design their own functions and interfaces) is that usability engineering is not an amateur sport. It's easy enough to be done by any software development team but takes much more than tinkering by average users, who will not know what's best or even how to tell. Making users design their own interfaces is not much more sensible than making drivers design cars or highway bridges. In summary, Jack Spratt and wife are not a good model for productivity software design.[5]

Guidelines, Standards, and Examples

When iron was first used in bridges, there were very frequent collapses— one in four bridges by certain accounts. In 1847 Queen Victoria appointed a commission to find out what was going on and charged it to look into the situation and propose rules. The commission came up with some useful strictures, though the theoretical reasoning behind them was entirely mistaken (Petroski 1982).

A final way to go about user-centered design is to heed good advice. Advice based on wisdom gained from experience, the best guesses of experts, and the results of research, both basic and applied, have been codified in compendia of design guidelines. These how-to books range from the minutia of one company's suggestions for one product type to Noah's arks covering all species. Collections of general guidelines range from 162 to 944 entries; a catalog of all the separate admonishments plausibly relevant to a single system can easily exceed 1,000 (Brown 1988; Marshall, Nelson, and Gardiner 1987; Mayhew 1992; Smith and Mosier 1984).

Undoubtedly, careful attention to applicable guidelines would improve usability over current norms. Clear violations of clearly established principles are rampant in commercial products: commands like **A3492-Q6,** yellow letters on gray backgrounds, missing help information for incomprehensible menu choices. There are, however, severe limitations to the value of guidelines. First, in the current state of the art and science, their validity is often questionable. Pick any specific guideline from any collection and ask three experts; at least one is likely to disagree or qualify its application. Like commonsense aphorisms, usability guidelines are sometimes contradictory: "provide alternate accelerators for experts" but "always keep it simple." The guidelines all say to make instructions specific and clear, but clarity can be assured only by user testing. Second, guidelines are hard to follow. There are so many of them that finding all the relevant ones is difficult. Many are vague: for example, "provide feedback"—but about what, when, how much? Third, guidelines provide little support for the critical analytic and creative parts of design. In practice, guidelines are infrequently consulted and inconsistently obeyed

(Bellotti 1990). Most designers appear to copy their designs from predecessors and competitors, not a bad idea. Nielsen's ten general heuristics are easier to apply than 1,000 specific guidelines but are successful for evaluation of designs, not for their creation. He has found that the same training in heuristics that makes programmers into reasonably good interface critics has virtually no effect on the quality of interfaces they produce before inspection begins. A principle that helps you recognize problems does not necessarily proffer the skill to avoid them.

Standards differ from guidelines in being more specific and in being enforced, or at least agreed in some official manner. Their main goal is consistency. Provided they do not cast in concrete bad elements of design—a real concern at our current stage of knowledge—standards can make it easier for users to go from one application or system to another. As I write, companywide and international committees are laboriously negotiating standards for human interfaces for computers. Luckily for all of us, many are concentrating most heavily on urging user-oriented methods of design rather than specifying detailed solutions.

Science

It is tempting to think that cognitive psychology, human factors and human engineering principles, and the newly emerging field of cognitive science might provide theory and fact to steer this effort. They can, but only to a modest extent. Psychological science has provided some real advances in understanding human behavior but only in limited domains, usually attached to narrow problems that have been brought to the laboratory. A few "laws" and principles are available that speak to system design. For example, the Hick-Hyman law says that decision time is proportional to the log of the number of equal alternatives. Useful in designing menus, it implies that a single screen with many choices (well organized and laid out) is better than a series of screens with a few choices each (Landauer and Nachbar 1985). Fitts' (1954) law tells how long it takes to point to an object depending on how large and how far away the object is. Fitts' law helps in designing pointing devices and laying out the icons and buttons on a screen. Yet another law, the power law of practice, tells how response speed increases over time. Given appropriate user tests, it could predict by how much and when experts with a new system would outperform those using an old system. There is knowledge about how much people can remember from one screen to the next and about how long it takes them to do most of the simple stimulus–response things they do when interacting with a computer. This knowledge forms the foundation of the GOMS method.

Knowing all this, plus immersion in all the lab lore and rules of thumb enshrined in guidelines, combined with experience, is unquestionably valuable. In the Bailey experiment cited earlier, half the designers had training and experience in computer system human factors. Their designs for the recipe file system tested out significantly superior to those of programmers lacking such backgrounds (although it took them longer to write the programs). In fact, their initial designs were better, in terms of flaws and user efficiency, than the final versions arrived at by unwashed programmers.

Nevertheless, as a foundation for design, cognitive science is up against a tough, possibly impossible problem. The human mind is an extremely complex information processing device. Physically it is based on a brain that has hundreds of billions of mysterious parts that interact in extraordinarily complex and almost completely unknown ways. It uses enormous amounts of information from enormous-squared amounts of experience; we ingest billions of bits of perceptual information every second. Its complexity is similar to what one bumps up against trying to predict weather or model the turbulence of air flow around an airplane wing. Like other such dynamic physical systems, the brain is vulnerable to chaotic disorganization. The mind—the brain's function—may be at least as complex. There have been repeated expressions of hope that mental activity and behavior will somehow be subject to simpler organizing principles than the physical machinery on which it rests. Such occurrences are not without precedent in nature; the heart beats in finely conducted rhythms despite the fact that its cellular systems for neural control are of vast complexity. However, the hope of discovering simplicity in mental function has so far gone mostly unfulfilled. (I hear psychologists and AI proponents screaming. They want to voice confidence in one or another theory. But read their literature. Every theory has serious holes and ever-changing countertheories; almost none has the validity, generality, or precision needed as a base for technology.)

We cannot rely on scientific theory for answers; however, all is not lost. The same situation applies in most areas of engineering, and where it does not apply today, it certainly did in times not long past. There's a great deal of debate over the relation between science and technology. Some knowledgeable commentators, such as the philosopher of science Kuhn (1977), go so far as to argue that technology progresses faster when science is in abeyance. Technological advances most often come from accumulated practical wisdom. People try things, see what's wrong with them, try to fix, and so forth. Only at occasional critical points does even a modern field of engineering such as electronics need to renew its scientific principles to solve a problem or to suggest new directions. It is said that the interplay between science and technology is, despite common belief, much more often in the opposite direction. Problems raised by technology raise curiosity that drives scientific research.

"We have not had a thousand failures. We have discovered a thousand things that don't work." Attributed to Thomas Edison.

Here is an illustrative example of both the success and limitations of science as so far applied to computer usability. Early research efforts focused on the design of command languages. The question was what words to use and what syntax when stringing them together. Some authorities assumed that "all natural" words would be a big advantage, as would consistent, natural syntax. Experiments comparing ways to choose words made several discoveries. First, for small systems, say a basic text editor, and frequent users, the choice of words didn't make much difference. Total nonsense strings were a problem, but using the words *allege, cipher,* and *deliberate* instead of *omit, add,* and *change* was inconsequential (Landauer Galotti, and Hartwell, 1983). Why? In the first place, new users were so busy learning about the system—the very concept of a typewriter that did mysterious things behind the scenes—that the added difficulty of learning a new meaning for a few words in special context didn't slow them down. Second, humans have many names for the same thing, and computer actions don't fit known word meanings perfectly, so there isn't an enormous difference between one word and another as a choice for a computer command. Investigations of syntax had a similar upshot. Using "normal" English word order sometimes made a difference but not a great deal. Using a consistent word order—verb before object, for example—sometimes was helpful. However, sometimes, as in natural languages like English, it is more useful to have different orders for different kinds of functions or activities (Barnard and Grudin 1988; Barnard et al. 1981). The language research with the best payoff was on how to construct abbreviations. It turned out that using a consistent rule was more important than what rule was used (Streeter, Acroff, and Taylor 1983).

Although I am pessimistic about basic science as the main basis of usability engineering, nevertheless it can do good. We are surrounded by bad design decisions that could have been better guided by existing knowledge about perception and cognition; for example, screen color is often used in ways that science says confuses and slows. Perhaps some such knowledge helped Bailey's sophisticates, and perhaps all designers would profit from better training in usability-relevant science. Moreover, the examples we have seen show that research aimed at better understanding of the cognitive underpinnings of information system use can pay off. However, it will take time, and much greater volume than the current trickle, to make a major contribution.

Now, the most-needed aspect of science may be its skepticism. Current design of information tools is largely based on intuition and art. It is popular among practitioners to compare computer interface design to architecture. The problem with intuition as a basis for design in this realm is that intuition about human thought is unreliable. People do not understand their own minds, nor can they predict their own behavior or that of their best friends. There is endless evidence for this assertion. Here are some examples. Remember the numbers 2, 4, 3, 7, 1. Got them?

Do this in your head only, and don't look back at the list.

Quick, was the number four part of that set? How did you determine that it was? Most people will say that they compared four with 2, then with 4, decided it matched, and answered yes. The evidence is overwhelming, however, that they ordinarily do nothing of the sort. Instead, they unconsciously compare the target with all the numbers in the set before deciding. The evidence is that the time to make such a decision increases by 35 milliseconds for each additional number in the set; it doesn't matter if the added numbers come before or after the matching one (4 here) or even if none match.

You meet with a group of people for a day, or live with them in a dorm for a semester. Then you try to judge which ones think that you like them and which don't. If you are an average person, you will be quite confident in your predictions, but you would do almost as well by flipping a coin.

You talk to somebody for an hour, then try to rate his or her intelligence or honesty. You would have done almost as well without ever having met the person. You probably don't believe that. Your intuition tells you otherwise, largely because your intuition has never had a chance to test itself against truth in such situations and therefore goes on supporting your self-confidence.

Here is one of my favorites: almost everyone's intuition tells them that if they want to remember a telephone number permanently, they should repeat it over and over to themselves right after they have heard it. This method will keep the memory fresh as long as they keep repeating it, but it has virtually no benefit for remembering it half an hour or more later (Landauer and Bjork 1978).

The point is that the same complexities and uncertainties that plague the science of human interaction with computers plague our intuitions about such matters. The analogy to architectural design is both apt and inappropriate—apt because architects rarely do the kind of upfront task analysis that their products deserve. (Thus the almost universal provision of the same number of toilet facilities for men and women in public places, despite the painful differences in queue length at every public event.) Like current software designers, architects have very poorly developed mechanisms for feedback of usability results into their designs. The sense in which the analogy is inappropriate is that architects are largely concerned with aesthetics. People, but especially architects, care a great deal about the beauty of their surroundings and are manifestly willing to trade some comfort and convenience for eye appeal. Although eye appeal in computer screens is certainly something users like, it seems unlikely that they would knowingly trade much usability or usefulness for better looks in their work tools.

This overview of the available technology for doing user-centered design has demonstrated that the quiver is far from empty and provides almost enough instruction to get started. For readers who are interested in more how-to, the chapter by John Gould in the *Handbook of Human Computer Interaction,* edited by Martin Helander (1988), followed by the recent book *Usability Engineering,* by Jakob Nielsen (Nielsen 1993b), will take you a long way down the path to being as much of an expert as book learning alone can promise.

13

User-Centered Development

"Who the hell thought of this? It doesn't make any sense. Nobody has talked to any users." Supervisor of an order department after installation of a new system.

Usability and Development

After design comes production. Right? Wrong. Neither ideally nor in practice does it work that way for software. With automobiles and television sets, a good design is just the starting place. The critical factor is devising an economical manufacturing process to spew out millions of near-identical copies. With software, the copying part is trivial; the critical step is completing the first model. Doing that corresponds roughly to the combined design and development stages in automobile manufacturing. Ideally, since it is impossible to get usability right without iterative prototyping and testing, software design must evolve throughout development. In practice too, design evolves throughout development but for different reasons. As a system is implemented, the original plans frequently turn out to be too hard to execute; its parts get in each other's way. Often usability-related aspects—what screens will look like, how error messages will be worded, what action options will be in which menus—are not specified in advance. Usually programmers get new ideas as they work. This means that opportunities for UCE continue to abound. It quickly gets harder to change what the system does, its basic functionality, as implementation progresses. However, if the architecture—the overall organization of the software's components and how they interconnect—is planned appropriately, changes in the user interface can remain possible right up to the end.

In IBM's Olympic message system project, user-centered engineering started well before the system's functions were settled. In Bellcore's SuperBook project, user-centered engineering started long before there was a project, however, in common practice, usability isn't addressed until sometime in the development game's fourth quarter. By then the question of what to build has already been settled, while the details of user interfaces and interactions have been postponed. The problem set before the development staff is how to achieve the functionality. Careful analysis, tightly knit organization, and rigorous testing are focused on the how. The how focus becomes dominant. As the programming staff struggles to stay afloat amid the inevitable storm of unexpected difficulties, all opportunity and desire for UCD slips beneath the waves of delivery deadlines.

Usability Evaluation for Software Development

Ensuring usability requires a shift of focus. The development process itself has to be reengineered so that it will be driven primarily by usefulness and usability rather than by the sheer need to get something done on time. The success stories recounted in chapters 10 and 11 show that early and regular usability testing is extremely effective, but it hasn't become standard development practice, for two reasons tied together in a vicious circle. First, software developers are uncomfortable with this soft, people stuff. Although many have been introduced to UCD, they remain shy. Gould and Lewis asked 450 production programmers at IBM to describe the important elements in creating a computer system for end users (Gould and Lewis 1985). Only one in six included early user focus, usability testing, and iteration in their answers. A more recent survey in Denmark, where industrial democracy reigns, found only 6 percent of software developers trying out interfaces with users before release (Milsted, Varnild, and Jorgensen 1989). An excellent recent book on the management of software development stresses the importance of frequent and careful measurement of almost all parts of the programming process and outlines many measurement techniques to ensure that software is fault free, fast, meets requirements and specifications, and more. It mentions usability just twice, suggests that programmer inspection of conformance to requirements and standards is the only needed usability engineering activity during development, and shows usability testing occurring only at the end of the process, when coding has been completed. Usefulness is measured only by customer questionnaire responses (Grady 1992).

The second reason is a perception that usability testing, and UCD in general, is too expensive and takes too long. Given that their central problem is getting the system to work at all, programmers greet proposals to add boring, lengthy steps with understandable suspicion. Without usability evaluation, getting the thing to work is the sole goal. And around it goes.

Can we break the cycle? The way to start is by asking how difficult, expensive, and time-consuming user-centered development really is. Maybe the perception is correct that nothing would ever get done using UCD. Perhaps it requires skill and training that is in short supply. Perhaps it delays projects unacceptably in a rapidly changing market. Perhaps it costs more than it's worth for the average project.

Is It Worth It?

Let's start at the bottom. How cost-effective is usability assessment? Nielsen and I (1993) analyzed data from thirteen software development projects that included either user testing or heuristic evaluation and compared the extra cost of the assessment activities to the expected economic benefits. (Earlier, I inveighed against judging success by predicted rather than measured benefits, and I apologize for this lapse. However, there aren't better data, so the best we can do is to estimate with caution.)

For cost estimates we took the range of values we have seen in both our own and others' projects, the number of dollars worth of experts' and users' time appropriately grossed up for overheads. For benefit estimates we started with the number of interface problems discovered, discounted by 50 percent to reflect the usual experience about the net number that end up fixed. We then guessed at the dollar value of the fixes by averaging the work efficiency gains experienced in well-measured cases and multiplying by typical loaded salaries for the types of workers who use the systems. To bracket the target, we looked at projections for

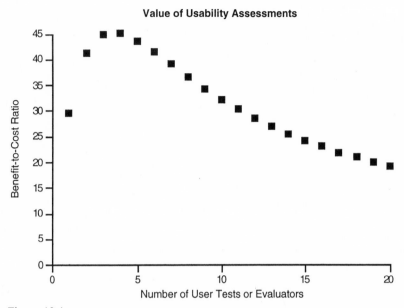

Figure 13.1.
Estimated ratios of benefit to cost of usability evaluation for a typical software system to be used by about a thousand people. The maximum ratio of forty-five to one is obtained with three to five tests or evaluations, but many more assessments are valuable. Data from Nielsen and Landauer 1993.

small, medium, and large systems, by which we meant ones intended for around a hundred, a few thousand, or many tens of thousands of users, and multiplied accordingly.

Figure 13.1 shows a typical result. For a system to be used by a thousand white-collar workers, it shows how the ratio of expected gain to extra expense depends on how many evaluation sessions are conducted. As it turned out, it made little difference overall whether assessments were made by heuristic evaluation or user testing, although variations in one-time overhead expenses and differences in consultant fees can tip the balance in individual cases. The benefit-to-cost ratios are rather large. Indeed, I know of no other software engineering techniques with anything approaching these payoffs (Brooks 1987). Using the most favorable number of evaluation sessions, usability assessment is worth upwards of 500 times its cost for large systems and 5 times its cost even for very small ones. Even with much more extensive testing than would be worthwhile—enough to catch every last usability bug before each revision—the ratio can stay positive. For the small system scenario, we estimate that over sixty assessments could be run, on average, before a testing program would cost more than it was worth![1]

The benefits we counted go directly to the users of the software, not to its producers or sellers. If our goal is increased labor productivity, this is entirely appropriate. However, there has to be something in it for providers, or they won't bother. We might hope that superior productivity effects will earn higher sales and profits, but given the difficulties of measurement and the allure of computers, this link is often weak. I'll suggest some ways to strengthen the connection in the next chapter. There are also potential benefits for developers in the form of simpler programs, fewer retrofits, and lower maintenance costs. The first question to answer, though, is just how difficult, disruptive, and expensive usability assessment is. Over and above historical inertia, how high are the objective barriers?

Some Barriers

Although sixty user tests or inspection sessions would produce compensating productivity gains for users far down the road, they would be seen as incredibly excessive detours by developers. If done one after the other, sixty tests could take more than a month, including setup time, scheduling delays, and data analysis. Perhaps this is the specter that has frightened developers away. In fact, some overenthusiastic beginners, fresh out of graduate schools where truth rather than pragmatism is the grail, have been known to test well beyond reason. There are even published reports and recommendations for usability evaluation methods costing ten times the optima in our analyses (Jeffries et al. 1991; Mantei and Teory 1988). Until recently, unfortunately, many usability test groups have not known when enough was enough.

One persistent problem has been widespread misunderstanding of the proper application of the concept of statistical significance. Statistically half-sophisticated testers and development managers have often assumed that the object of testing was to establish beyond reasonable doubt—that is, with "statistical significance"—that one version was better than another. As we have seen, there is large variability between one test user and another. As a result, comparisons based on having one group of users tested on each of two versions are not very sensitive. Demanding that such a difference be significant by standard scientific criteria, usually a 95 percent confidence that the difference is not just chance, could take twenty-four or more tests for two systems that have not been iteratively perfected (although, as we will see, it is usually much easier to prove that a well-designed system excels over its predecessor). Nielsen tells of talking to a high-level manager at a major software company who took a dim view of testing because of the large number of subjects required for statistical significance. (Whether he thought it was possible to avoid this problem by using just one test, his own opinion, was not reported.)

There are two different critical flaws in this view. First, even if we conceive of the goal as testing between two versions, the traditional 95 percent confidence level is not appropriate. The development organization has no choice but to pick one version over another. Suppose we run only three tests with each. For two typical unimproved versions, the difference would have a 67 percent confidence level instead of the classical 95 percent or 99 percent. But a 67 percent confidence level means the odds are two to one that the better version is really better. That's not a bad bet, and certainly better than the fifty-fifty chance of choosing right we would probably have without testing.

The second, and more important, flaw in this manager's view is conceiving of testing as a two-choice comparison. This is analogous to testing each car off an assembly line to see if it is better, overall, than the previous one. A more pertinent goal is the detection of defects to be fixed. The probability that a particular usability problem will be found with one test is usually around a third, and testing with six users will find it with odds of eight to one. Put differently, the typical user interface has forty usability bugs. Testing with six users, or six expert evaluators, will reveal thirty-six of the forty on average. With 95 percent confidence, it will find from fifteen to forty.[2]

Thus, UCDevelopment practice may have often overshot its target and spoiled its reputation. Another overindulgence has been videotaping. The procedure seems to appeal especially to inexperienced usability engineers, perhaps because its high technology and objective appearance calms their fears of rejection. The expense of video begins with special equipment and a special lab room. It continues with an operator to record each session and is redoubled by the time it takes to go over and over the tapes. Experience shows that video recordings are not especially helpful for detection and diagnosis of flaws. One survey of software engineers found twice as high ratings for live user tests as for tapes of similar sessions (Perlman 1988). While details on particular issues can sometimes be resolved by reviewing and analyzing tapes, the most useful information is garnered by watching and talking to the trial users.

On the other hand, videotapes can be enormously effective for persuasion. Stories are common of endlessly ignored usability tests that finally got attention when developers or managers were shown videos of struggling users. A human factors specialist at Apple once told me that her most potent tool was the lab's one-way glass testing rooms. She didn't use them herself; she sat with the test users. The hidden observation room was reserved for programmers watching users try out their latest efforts. She said videotapes had a similar effect, which was not to show *what* was wrong but to convince developers and executives that *something* was wrong.

Perhaps the most famous case comes from the Xerox story told in chapter 11. Arnold Wasserman, who directed a well-regarded human factors group at Xerox, asserts that the copiers studied by Suchman at Xerox research had been thoroughly evaluated before release and had not passed: "We conducted extensive usability tests and delivered reports predicting every one of the difficulties users eventually had understanding these machines in the field. Our reports were ignored, rejected, and in some cases, deliberately suppressed by the product engineers rushing to get the machines into production!" (Wasserman 1991). However, when Suchman showed her videos to top executives and designers, things changed. Seeing famous computer scientists fail and fume had an emotional impact that dry error data from human factors tests could not touch. Once management will to change was created, the detailed observations showed what to do.[3]

Some Problems

The point of usability testing during development is to find defects to fix. How efficient is this process? The idea is to test, fix, test again, fix again, until the final product is as near to flawless as practical. Unfortunately, usability fixes don't always take. The same difficulties that plague the original design afflict each successive miniversion. Each fix removes old flaws by replacing some feature or part with another. Sometimes the needed change is obvious. If an error message was absent, adding one can remove the problem. Sometimes the solution is not so easy. If the error message was confusingly worded, the next try may or may not be better. If the problem was how to organize a set of complexly related choices into a simple, meaningful menu structure, there may be no way to effect real improvement. In Bailey's (1993) multiple iteration design experiment, average quality improved, but almost as many new and serious problems were introduced at each stage as were removed.

Especially if the basic design concept is bad, tinkering with the interface may not solve the problem. A car with a poor turning radius will be hard to parallel park no matter how many times anyone redesigns the steering wheel. A database query language that depends on Boolean expressions will baffle users no matter what kind of screen buttons are used to construct them.

Nielsen (1993a) reports an experiment in which he measured usability after each of four revisions and found that efficiency improved a meager 24 percent over the whole series. There were two problems, neither unusual. One was that each new version was designed by a different person with minimum knowledge of what others had done and of the specific effects of earlier changes. The second designer knew that the first design hadn't worked well and tried changes. The third designer knew the second design fell short and tried other changes, sometimes returning to earlier ideas. Wisdom did not accumulate.

The second problem was that the original specification of the system functionality was poor. The system was supposed to allow users to set up profiles for accepting telephone calls and forwarding them to different places according to the day and time. The specification demanded an elaborate scheme in which a basic profile covering all calls had to be filled out, then specialized profiles for different conditions. Because of the way the guts of the initial version were programmed, there were additional constraints. For example, the designers were not allowed to consider a table of times and places or a calendar for accepting and presenting the individualized data. They were required to make the user specify the area codes from which collect calls would be selected depending on the day, time, and place where they would be received. As one of the designers, I thought that the basic design would not fit the way many people think about their communications needs, that its view of scheduling would be very hard to understand. I felt that the built-in constraints tied my hands in trying to think of ways to make the task doable.

Other projects have suffered the same fate. For example, as successive versions of SuperBook have been designed to deal with increasingly large collections of documents and a wider variety of input formats and as the size of the project has expanded, new designers have gotten involved. Unmindful of the history of test-based revisions, several have proposed adding features, such as AND queries with range arguments, that early on were replaced by easier, more efficient search methods. The same sort of difficulties inhibit market-based evolution of better usability. The innovations of producer B can easily be the flaws removed by producer A. Many of the imitators of SuperBook have reintroduced complex Booleans. The constraints of preestablished functionality rear their ugly heads here too. The ever-expanding list of features demanded by marketing prevents radical redesign and simplification of the next product.

Separate Interface from Functionality?
Remarkably, one impediment to progress is a principle much espoused by software developers interested in human interface construction: that the functionality of a software system—what it does and how it does it—should be kept independent from the user interface. The idea is that interface designers should be free to make changes based on usability needs without having to rewrite all the rest of the programs. So far as it goes, this makes good sense. The difficulty is that usability and usefulness depend critically on functionality. It takes iterative testing to figure out what the machine should do just as much as to figure out how the user should operate it. Even the choices for operations, such as filling in a calendar versus making a series of menu selections, as in the Nielsen

experiment, can be limited by what functions the underlying program supports. So although it is a good idea to make the sorting algorithms and communications facilities independent program modules or objects, it is a mistake to cast the functionality in concrete before designing the user interface.

Clearly, the most effective usability testing programs are going to perform many quick tests, each just sufficient to guide alterations, the sum of all of them providing enough opportunity for experiments and cumulating wisdom, none taking so long as to hold up progress. Remember Tognazzini's story about color monitors? It took five successive tiny tests to get it right. Each showed that the last good guess was wrong, and each added a jot of understanding.

How Many Tests?

Can we expect to get enough information from a small enough number of tests at each iteration? Figure 13.1 shows that four to eight assessments is optimal in the sense of yielding the most work-efficiency dollars per test dollar, but whether such a small number is enough to guide design well is a different matter. From case studies, we have suggestive evidence that usability testing, in the framework of formative evaluation, can lead to good fundamental design, the important starting places that are necessary for large gains from iterative fixing. We have more solid evidence for the effectiveness of testing for detecting flaws in interfaces. By looking at the data used for figure 13.1 from a slightly different angle, we can estimate the average number of flaws that will be found by a certain number of tests. It turns out we can do even more than that; we can provide a practical method to predict the total number of problems waiting to be found and how much time and money it will cost to find them.

Figure 13.2 is based on the thirteen cases analyzed by Nielsen and me. It shows the proportion of the total flaws that were found by one, two, three, and up to twenty different assessments. Again, I averaged heuristic inspections and user tests. Across the thirteen cases the number of total problems varied from a low of 9 to a high of 166, with an average of 42. Knowing nothing about a new design, you can guess that its interface will contain around forty flaws; however, the number could be four times that large or only a quarter. In general, the larger the system is and the

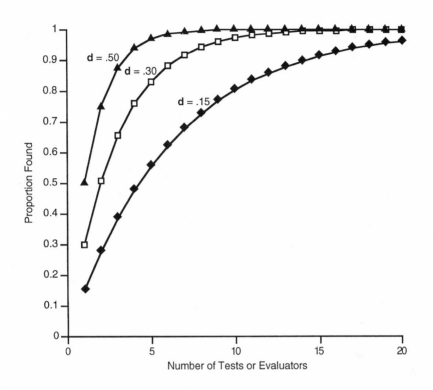

Figure 13.2.
The proportion of usability problems in a user interface that are found increases
as more assessments are done. This regular relation makes it easy to estimate the
total number of errors and plan the most effective testing program. The three
curves are for interfaces with very easy, average, and very hard to detect usability
bugs: **d** = detectability, the probability that the average test will find the average
flaw. Data and model from Nielsen and Landauer 1993.

more that the interface does, the larger is the number of errors, but it is very hard to predict without testing. Fortunately, a modest number of tests will provide a fairly accurate prediction.

In figure 13.2 the total error numbers are not shown, only the proportion of the total that is found depending on the number of evaluations. Three different curves are plotted: one for the average case, one for a case where the problems are very hard to detect, and one for a case where the problems are very easy to detect. In the average case, a typical assessment finds 30 percent of the defects. In an easy case, an average assessment finds 50 percent of the flaws but in a hard case only 15 percent.[4]

The smooth curves shown in figure 13.2 come from a simple theory that matches the data extremely well. The theory says that each evaluation, on average, has the same chance of finding any problem that hasn't been found yet. If a single test finds one-third of the flaws, a second test will find one-third of the ones that were missed. Together, two tests will find one-third plus one-third of the remaining two-thirds, or five-ninths.

A rough rule of thumb is that each pair of evaluations finds half of the remaining problems for the average system ($0.3 + 0.3 \times 0.7 = 0.51$). This handy rule makes it easy to know when to stop. If the development project finds it convenient to make frequent fixes, it can stop after two tests knowing it probably has found about half the problems. After a round of fixes, it can test again and expect to find half of the still remaining problems, plus half of the ones it failed to fix, plus half of any new flaws it has introduced while trying to fix the old ones.[5] If the project has time and inclination, it can add two or four more tests in each cycle, thus halving and rehalving the likely errors that remain undetected. With six tests, the average user interface version will have shown around 90 percent of its usability bugs. Making this strategy even more attractive is an observation that serious flaws tend to show up earlier than others (Virzi 1990). If a flaw is likely to show itself often in use, it is likely to show itself often—and therefore early—in user testing.

If the project wants to be very safe, the theory also tells it how to be sure it has found all the problems. For the average case, it says that if testing is continued until eight tests have failed to find any new problems, the chances are twenty to one that none is left to find. This might be a good strategy just prior to release, when, presumably, no flaws are left.

If a project tried to test with this much certainty at the outset, it would have to run almost twenty tests for our average case, and over fifty for the worst.

To predict the total number of flaws in an interface without that much testing, all you have to do is find out whether you are on the lower, middle, or upper curve of figure 13.2, or perhaps on one in between, then do some easy arithmetic.[6] Six evaluations is enough to come within 15 percent of the correct number with high confidence.

Where does all this leave us? In very good shape. A small number of evaluations can catch the majority of errors. With an established testing procedure in place, a development organization could get valuable feedback within as little as a day—using two or three tests or inspections—and for very little money. What's more, it would be easy to estimate how many errors there are and how many more tests may be needed; six evaluations would give quite accurate estimates. This means that a development project can afford to test frequently and that it will learn a great deal from the tests.

The next question, whether the project can correct the flaws it finds, is not as easy to settle. Its answer will depend on the particular system, its basic design and function, the talent of the programming staff, the availability of rapid prototyping tools and techniques, and the flexibility of the organization. An attempted fix may even make things worse in some respect; another reason to use many short test-and-fix cycles.

Clearly testing and trying to take advantage of the results has great potential. Let us put together what we've just found out with what we learned about the average results of UCD in earlier chapters. Intensive UCD efforts have typically improved efficiency effects by about 50 percent. We can assume that these efforts fixed about as many of the bugs they found as is usually practical. To be conservative, assume these projects found twice as high a proportion as will be typical. We can conclude that a typical development project should be able to improve user efficiency by at least 25 percent on the basis of just one day of tests.[7]

In summary, Larry Tesler at Apple had it right. When he ran two or three tests on each minor revision of Lisa, as often as twice a week, he was probably following the ideal strategy.

Who Are the Testers?

Does it matter who does the evaluations? It would be very convenient if it didn't, if any programmer, development manager, or executive could examine each version carefully and report the flaws. Unfortunately, it doesn't work out that way.

Again we have Jakob Nielsen to thank for evidence on how things really are. Following one of his early consulting efforts, Nielsen subjected his redesign to a rigorous comparison with the original he had set out to improve. The interface in this case was a set of twelve bank account statement forms. At issue was how well customers would understand the information on the statements. Nielsen had gone through eight versions, testing each with one or two potential users and revising (Nielsen 1989).

To verify the superiority of the final version, he ran a classical double-blind experiment. Each of thirty-eight computer science students tested two subjects with the original version and two with the final revised version. The subjects tried to find information on the statements, such as the size of a recent deposit, the current interest rate, or the credit limit of the customer. Neither the student experimenters nor the subjects knew which of the two versions was the original and which Nielsen's redesign (and as we will see shortly, they probably couldn't have guessed).

Users of the original version answered only 56 percent of the questions correctly; users of the final version got 76 percent right, a highly significant difference.[8] However, that's not the point here, except to show that there was a large, objective difference. In the next part of the experiment, twenty-one fresh computer science students examined the two versions and were asked which they would recommend to management for adoption. These judges were all programmers of modest sophistication, perhaps at the level of beginner development staff. None had yet learned about usability engineering or heuristic evaluation. As shown in figure 13.3, they divided evenly in their choice of interface: ten chose the original, ten chose the new version, and one couldn't decide. Finally, Nielsen asked the thirty-eight students who had done the user tests to pick the winner. Remember that each tester had observed just two users with each version. Twenty-six picked the objectively better version, six picked the worse version, and six waffled.

These results say two important things. First, examinations by people with no usability evaluation training may be worthless. Without testing,

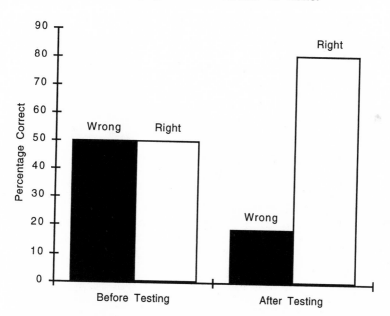

Figure 13.3.
Programmers examined two interfaces for the same purposes either before or after testing two users on each. Of those who had an opinion, half chose the better one before testing, while eight out of ten chose it after testing. Data from Nielsen 1989.

their chances of making the right choice were fifty-fifty. Second, even without usability expertise, someone who has tested just four users, two on each version, can usually make the right choice. In this case, the odds for the testers—counting those who had no opinion as just guessing—were three to one. Other studies have gotten similar results.[9]

In another experiment, Nielsen (1992) compared the number of usability problems found by heuristic evaluations when they were done by people with differing backgrounds. The system in this case was an interface for activating special telephone services. There were three kinds of evaluators: computer science students, professional usability specialists with degrees in behavioral science and two or more years of UCE experience, and usability specialists with experience in telephone systems (dubbed "double experts"). There were large differences between the groups. People knowledgeable about computers but not about usability on average

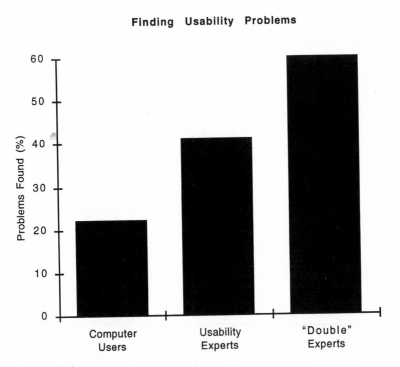

Finding Usability Problems

Figure 13.4.
In one study, the average double expert, someone trained in usability evaluation who also knew the application domain, did much better at finding interface bugs than did an average computer programmer (users). Usability specialists without domain expertise were in between. Data from Nielsen 1992.

found 22 percent of the problems in the interface. Usability professionals found 41 percent. Double experts averaged 60 percent (figure 13.4).

Could a development project succeed simply by finding the right expert to do its evaluations? Maybe, but maybe not. To catch more than 60 percent of the bugs would require more than one double expert (and I suspect that Nielsen's 60 percent was atypically high). Double experts are hard to find; ordinary experts are more available. Unfortunately they vary considerably in how well they do. Even the same expert may find most of the bugs on one occasion and very few on the next (Nielsen and Molich 1990). Trying to pick a single expert or two could be a hazardous strategy. On the other hand, obtaining multiple evaluations from multiple experts will almost inexorably lead to identification of as great a proportion of the flaws as need and patience dictate. Better still, user testing will accomplish the same thing, and, unless they are astronauts or presidents, users are even more available.

User testing profits from a skilled tester but the same one or two people can do all the testing. The only truly bad strategy to emerge from this line of research is relying on programmers without UCD training to evaluate user interfaces by inspection. What about software development managers and software company executives? No one has studied their abilities as bug catchers. In my experience, they usually have clear and confident opinions. Indeed, executives are often as sure of the relative merits of user interfaces as programmers without UCD training.

Who Are the Users?

My friend Don, a high-priced software management consultant, tells this tale. A substantial software company he worked for produced programs for running small businesses. It didn't sell the software packages directly but supplied them on contract to a distributor. Don was called in because the company was about to go under. The distributor said customers complained that the programs didn't do what they wanted. For example, a billing program for dental offices might not have the standard treatment categories required by insurers. Don discovered that none of the system designers had ever talked to a manager or employee of any of the businesses for which the software was intended or visited a place of business. The supplier told the designers the type of business they wanted programs for and nothing more.

The assessment procedures we have discussed all center on end users, the people whose productivity the systems would help, as they should. Still, two components are missing in the techniques I have described. First is the social and organizational context in which the system will be used, often as critical a factor in success as ease of use. Both proper functionality and interface design must take into account how the system will support the work of organizations as well as individuals and of individuals in social settings as well as in lonely office cubicles. Second, end users are not usually the buyers of work-related computer systems, and even when they are, their purchasing decisions are rarely based on actual experience with the systems. Thus a development organization has to find some way to assess and improve the value of its product in real use and as an attracter of purchase. Moreover, I will assume it wants to do so in ways that rest on and promote productivity, not mere hucksterism.

The early design stage of task analysis has these matters as its focus, going out to the workplace to find out what is needed and wanted. However, if the effort to stay in touch does not continue throughout development, the danger of slowly drifting away from reality is significant. Cries of "this isn't what we wanted at all" greet many software deliveries. The developers have followed one clever idea to the next, only diverted here and there by insurmountable implementation difficulties. No one has gone back to check that the system is doing what it should. That UCD has made the system easy and fun to operate is now irrelevant.

John Gould (1988) tells of a case in which designers were working on an artificial intelligence system to help operators of mainframe computers. They had no intention of watching current operators or talking to them. Apparently they thought such interactions would distract them from their real business.

The first line of defense against this ill is to increase contact between developers and customers. Some software shops invite customer representatives for frequent visits to approve what's happening. A few take their prototypes out into the field for criticism and admiration. This probably helps, but if what we've learned about the limits of usability assessment by undisciplined inspection holds even halfway in this more difficult situation, it is unlikely to help enough.

It should be possible to devise tests of use in context to complement individual usability evaluation. We have been scared away from such attempts in the past by the assumption that usability assessment requires a large number of tests. Inducing a working organization to assign twenty new workers every few weeks to a new version is usually out of the question. However, asking to have two interacting workers or one or two branch offices assigned for a day or a week a few times during a year might be acceptable. If what we've learned about the efficiency of individual testing applies, the value for the adopter could be many times the cost.

What about purchasers? The closest marketers usually come to helping developers know the users is to run focus groups. I have grave doubts about focus groups evaluating new computer systems. Asking people what they would like in a system as complex, as technically difficult to get right, as hard to evaluate by inspection or intuitions as we know software products to be seems manifestly futile. Focus group members asked to tell what features and interaction techniques would be desirable can only talk with any knowledge about ones they know, not about innovations. They cannot possibly be wise about the complex combinations that constitute real systems, the ones experienced designers can't get right or even evaluate without test. True, they may reveal something about the prejudices they hold that will affect their purchase decisions. But I think we should respect our consumers more than to design to their untutored superficial inclinations. My guess is that if asked, most people would prefer to base their decisions on knowledge of how well the system will eventually help them work.

To help them, I propose taking prototypes to the people. Describing a system verbally won't do; even expert evaluators fare badly when given only detailed descriptions (Nielsen 1993a). The new restaurant dishes I sometimes choose from menu descriptions often fail to please my palate. Software systems are more complicated than pasta primavera. Why not let potential buyers try out trial systems and mockups, and *then* ask them what they like?

What about managers and executives? There is a tradition of taking design advice from experts in the customer organization. Doing what the customer wants is sacrosanct. However, again, I don't see why customers can't be asked better questions. Asking accounting executives, or even chief information officers (CIOs), to design their own systems or their own user interfaces is like asking readers to write, or at least plan the plots, of their own novels. It's not even a case of "I don't know anything about usability design, but I know what I like." A potential user can't look at an interface and know whether it will serve and please. But developers can get much closer to this goal as well, and by the same familiar route. Why not let executives try using the thing? Better still, since they are likely to be wise enough to know how different they are from their average employees, let them watch usability tests. Remember Suchman and Xerox. I think we can move experience forward in time from failure in the field to success during development.

The Value of Usability for Software Development

Speeding the Process

The Xerox story tells it all: field failures are expensive and sometimes fatal for a company. Often they are fatal for what would otherwise have been a good idea. About 80 percent of software life cycle costs occur not during development but during the maintenance period. In turn, 80 percent of these maintenance costs are a result of problems users have with what the system does, not programming bugs (Boehm 1981; Martin and McClure 1983; Pressman 1992). Boehm estimates that a problem discovered in the field costs 100 times as much to fix as one discovered during development (Pressman puts the ratio at *"only"* about forty to one). Although the ratios are probably not as steep, discovering a problem early in the development cycle is much cheaper than discovering it later. The more code has been written, the more dependencies are created and the more difficult it is to change. If a problem has become so deeply enmeshed that it can't be fixed, the whole project is jeopardized.

In addition, usability improvements usually mean simplification, with fewer features rather than more: fewer screens, fewer menus, fewer options and actions, fewer icons and help boxes, fewer error messages and instructions. Various estimates put the amount of programming effort devoted to the human interface at anywhere between 30 and 60 percent and rising over time (Myers and Rosson 1992; Smith and Mosier 1984; Wixon and Jones 1991). If simplifying design changes are made early, they cut development costs not only by the expense of perfecting and testing the omitted features but by savings on underlying data storage and algorithms and in the complicated programming of their interactions with other parts of the program. Contrary to fears, changes dictated by usability testing usually reduce rather than increase the programming effort. Common experience has been that development efforts are not delayed by usability efforts. Good's tale of finishing the DEC editor improvements well ahead of the deadline for the full system is typical. Now that we have discovered that testing can be much more rapid than we used to assume, the balance is even more favorable.

Is There an Easier Way?

Sometimes software development managers want their usability people to just get on with the job. Just design it right in the first place; to hell with all this testing and fixing. It can't be done. Bailey's experiment did show that good usability engineers can get a design off to a better usability start than other people, but they can't do it well enough to skip the iteration. Even they find it impossible to produce good systems; science, principle, and guidelines are not up to the task, not accurate or consistent enough, not nearly capable of dealing with the fundamental complexities. Interface standards and tool sets may increase consistency, and consistency may usually, if not always, be desirable. But there is no evidence yet that standards and consistency make a very large difference.

Programmers Are Users Too

One special target of productivity improvement is software development itself. Software is getting bigger and bigger (perhaps too big) and the software development problem is getting bigger even faster. There have been both intermittent and incremental improvements in the labor productivity of software developments. For example, companies that produce large software systems for running businesses have tracked the number of program lines per programmer over two decades. It has gone up 3 to 6 percent per year. That's not terrible, even if it doesn't come near the productivity gains in mips and bytes of computer hardware per person-year.

Unfortunately, the size of common application programs has been going up about five times as fast. The largest programming productivity gains have come from better programming languages, ones in which more and more of the repetitive details are filled in by the computer itself. However, this source appears to be drying up, and attention has shifted to tools—programs that help programmers program other programs. Universally, so far, these have been written by programmers without help of usability assessment. Earlier I pointed at programmers' designing for themselves as one cause of the usability problem. The problem is probably less severe when the users actually are programmers, but even the best cook cannot, without testing, create a recipe that she is sure to like.

Summing Up User-Centered Development

Have testers, not customers, find the flaws.

Usability testing during development improves the efficiency effects of software. Getting useful functionality requires early empirical guidance. It seems obvious that the best strategy for software development is to test early and often. Such a strategy would allow designers to learn what is needed, to carry out series of small experiments, which are often essential for solving interface issues, to keep track of progress, and to ensure that systems do not go into the field with defects that are much more expensive to fix later. The motto might be, "Have testers, not customers, find the flaws."

Despite these obvious advantages, the vast majority of software development projects don't do it, apparently in the belief that testing is too slow and expensive. Partly, this reflects deficiencies in past practice. However, recent evidence from a large number of studies by Jakob Nielsen and others has changed the picture. Analysis of these studies shows:

• The average interface has around forty defects in need of repair.

• Two usability evaluations or user tests usually will find half the flaws; six will find almost 90 percent. This work will take only a day or two.

• After six tests, one can estimate accurately the number of remaining flaws and the rate at which they are being found.

• Usability assessment has very large benefits relative to cost.

• The work efficiency effect of a software system can be expected to improve by around 25 percent as a result of a single day of usability testing.

• While specialists are better at usability design and at finding flaws, both systematic inspections and user tests can be done effectively by people with modest training.

• These results, and experience as well, indicate that usability testing can reduce the difficulty and time for development while contributing dramatically to quality.

14

User-Centered Deployment; or, What to Use Them For and How

"Fleet Financial Group, a Providence, R.I. bank holding company built a consumer service center . . . to handle all customer inquiries from any of its seven subsidiaries in six states. Operating 24 hours a day, it gets 1.5 million calls a month—80% entirely handled by computer. Despite the longer service hours and wider range of inquiries handled, it now has 40% fewer customer service people than the separate banks did" (Wall Street Journal, *March 1, 1993).*

In its June 1993 issue, *Business Week* ran a feature article, "The Technology Payoff," trumpeting a turnaround in IT's contribution to productivity. They cited Brynjolfsson and Hilt (1993) to support a thesis that industry had finally learned to use computers effectively. A table showed how the top forty-six "productivity champions" among major manufacturing firms had improved their sales revenues per employee in the previous five years. Indeed, many firms showed much better growth on this measure from 1987 to 1992 than they had in the previous five years, and the average growth rate for all Fortune 500 laureates was up a notch. Unfortunately, the same data show that half the champion firms improved their productivity more *slowly* in the last five years than in the previous five.[1] Were the most successful ones just lucky, or were they doing something better, something we can identify and other firms can imitate? In particular, were they using their computers better, and, if so, how?

The *Business Week* authors suggested that many of the improved results followed business process redesign in which IT played an important supporting role. This is a common theme among business consultants of the nineties. They are telling managers to worry about the way they run their operations first, and *then* think about new IT.

What Can You Do with a Computer?

After managers finish redesigning, what should they think about using computers for? There are four ways to use computers to increase productivity:

1. Reduce unnecessary and duplicate work by storing and transporting information electronically.
2. Improve the coordination and synchronization of work by better planning, monitoring, tracking, and analysis.
3. Support new high-productivity products and services that depend on powerful information processing.
4. Help individuals perform information work more efficiently.

Almost all the widely reported successes have gone down route 1. Typically, close examination reveals a processes in which many paper records are produced for one basic transaction, say, the purchase of a truckload of oranges. There is an order, a package list, a bill, an invoice, a payment, a receipt, each in multiple copies, routed to different file cabinets and later compared with each other. A new process is designed that requires fewer entries and fewer comparisons. The computer helps by storing all the information in one place.

Success by the other routes appears to be less common. There are examples, though. Airlines optimize their routes and schedules so that planes are full and get the pilots and cabin attendants to their starting places with minimum shuffling, a nice bit of coordination—route 2. Perhaps the most widespread computer-based reorganizations have been centralization of functions. By using telecommunications and electronic data storage, all the bookkeeping for a multibranch bank can be done in one low-rent place, saving facilities and managers—a combination of routes 1 and 2. Federal Express has made a business of delivering packages in a shorter time than the post office imagined possible; Dialog and Lexis offer scholarly journal abstracts and court decisions instantly to every college library and law office—route 3. Engineers can design computer chips and airplane bodies much more quickly—route 4.

Reengineering and Eternal Hope

Across America meeting rooms are fully booked. Teams of suited executives are feverishly plotting radical revolutions. The Karl Marx of the movement is Michael Hammer, and its rallying cry, "Don't automate: obliterate." The revolutions, when pulled off, are radical redesigns and reorganization of parts of a business. The Fleet Financial group story is typical. More examples are cited in a compelling book by Hammer and James Champy, *Reengineering the Corporation*. They have convinced CEOs everywhere to take a new look at how their organizations operate.

The coordination of ocean shipping is an ancient nightmare. One company operates dozens of huge ships, collects thousands of items from hundreds of shippers in scores of ports, and tries to pass the right ones on to hundreds of importers scattered across the globe, all the while keeping holds as full, sailing as little distance, and moving cargo as infrequently as possible. SeaLand contracted a computer network to replace the manifests, bills of lading, and ledger sheets. A $1 million annual tab is said to save $25 million in labor expenses. (Source: The CEO of the network company, an anonymous seat partner on a flight from Pittsburgh to Newark.)

The time is ripe for such soul searching and reform. Most business processes, developed before electronic data handling, were evolved to make people and records regular and efficient when the only technology was ink on paper. Jobs were subdivided into specialties that would maximize practice on what each person had to do and minimize what each person had to know. Information was collected and distributed through a tree of paper reports by subordinates to superiors and memos from superiors to subordinates. At least half the work merely copied, checked, compared, or approved what other people had already done. Each person was another opportunity for a typo or sick day. Between people the paper stood in stacks for hours or weeks.

Many poor business processes are ingrained in habit and tradition, entrenched in the self-interest of departments and their managers. Rethinking can work wonders, especially in time of economic distress when upper management has the nerve to face down internal imperialism. If the route to success is process reform, only small additional IT investments may be required.

Process redesign as being practiced is not all that's needed. Certainly the redesign movement is likely to have substantial effects as more and more companies revise their information handling methods, but the movement is likely to play itself out rather quickly. While there are many places where reducing duplicate paperwork and information handling delays can contribute to increased productivity, experience suggests that the usual gain is modest and local, confined to one or a few component operations.

Moreover, sadly, most reengineering efforts fail. One candid consultant told me that less than a third of redesign efforts are able to identify and exploit opportunities for significant improvement. More often, the old process was pretty efficient after all, or the new process ideas are organizationally, politically or technically impractical. Indeed, even its most ardent proponents, Hammer and Champy, come up with only a small handful of cases with large effects. Others are a quite mundane one-time 10 to 30 percent efficiency improvement. Many of the examples that Hammer and Champy cite—Federal Express, Ford, Taco Bell—have previously been advertised as examples of other management fads like total quality or lean manufacturing. Others, insiders tell me, were still in the "we expect" stage when written up. Certainly some companies have turned themselves around, but as Hammer and Champy themselves make clear, many have failed, and each success has been accomplished differently.

However, there is one common denominator of success: where IT is used, it is used well rather than blindly. So far, in almost all the widely advertised victories, IT's main role has been to help reduce duplicate work. Each worker turns out the same amount of work, but there are fewer workers because work gets done once instead of thrice. Centralization is the usual method. It has been widely employed by telephone companies, which is why the operator who helps you charge a call from

Brooklyn to Oakland may have a Texas accent. Blue Cross and Blue Shield of Virginia deployed a system that let insurers send payments directly to doctors and hospitals. One hospital, the University of Virginia Medical Center, reduced the number of people keying in payment requests from 14 to 7. Salomon Brothers revised its record keeping system so that traders in New York key their own trades into a computer in Tampa rather than handwriting paper tickets to be copied in—with added errors—by an entry clerk.[2] Centralization of another sort is also mentioned often: making it possible for a single worker to handle more of the business so there are fewer handoffs, less confusion and error, smoother service.

Few of the success stories tout improvement of individual worker efficiency as such. Hammer and many others assert that simply automating jobs is futile; trying to make individual workers more efficient has no effect on the firm's performance. They have drawn a false conclusion. From the fact that vast computer application to individual jobs has not paid off, they have inferred that individual worker productivity gains don't help. Their reasoning assumes that computers have actually improved individual worker efficiency materially, they are unaware of the meager effects that IT usually produces. None of the analysts refer to the direct evidence on work efficiency reviewed here. Few mention the striking exception of telephony where greatly improved worker efficiency produced impressive productivity gains.

The second National Research Council report (1994b) falls into the same trap. Although accepting the productivity paradox as real, its authors focus on the linkages between individual work and the productivity of organizations. They insightfully analyze ways in which slack, inability for one part to use the output of the last, efforts misdirected to unimportant problems and unproductive uses, negative motivational consequences, high training costs, social barriers to information sharing and cooperation can keep gains in individual productivity from getting out the door. The theory is that computers have strong productivity shoulders but are pushing rope.

Two problems undermine this position. One is that other individual productivity inventions have had big effects: electric motors, textile machines, farming methods, telephone switches, and telecom databases. We are being asked to believe that things are totally different in the services now using computers. Perhaps transforming worker efficiency into enterprise productivity is harder in offices than factories; the special issues are certainly worth thinking about. However, the fundamental problem is that there are no big shoulders, at least not very big and very many. So the weak linkage explanation of productivity failure isn't needed just yet.

I claim that the reengineering movement is both right and wrong. It is quite right in calling for a reexamination of business processes and looking for better methods of dividing and coordinating work with the help of computers. It is right in placing emphasis on the team activities where communication and data storage have been roadblocks. However, it is dead wrong in giving up on worker efficiency. Improved worker efficiency has been the great engine of progress for two centuries. Moving from muscle to information work need not—and should not—mean that we cannot help each worker do more and better work.

Finding a Road from Here to There

Computers that multiply work efficiency can be designed through UCD. So that better systems are used, and used right, the people who buy, use, and manage IT must be able to choose and deploy wisely. As things stand, they are severely handicapped. Purchasers are given too much information about hardware and features, almost nothing reliable about usefulness and usability. They have few effective tools for finding out whether what they've bought has helped. Some big businesses do hypothetical cost-benefit projections before computer purchase; almost none do serious evaluation afterward to check their assumptions (National Research Council 1994a). On the other hand, we know that empirical testing, measurement of success, observation of accelerators and inhibitors, and revisions can bring large improvements. The problem is to get them applied and extended into the practical world of business.

An Underwriter's Lab for Usefulness and Usability?

Some popular trade magazines, ones with "PC" in their names, have recently begun doing their own user testing. For years, benchmarking has been part of the process on which they have based the opinions and quality ratings in their product reviews, but their empirical measurements have been exclusively concerned with speed, size, and features. The average product review mentions usability twelve times, but there is no objective evaluation behind the remarks. Instead there is the opinion of an overqualified user—a reviewer who has tried dozens of different products and therefore has a seriously warped view of how easy they are to use. Readers of these reviews, mostly managers of work groups who use computers, increasingly demand firmer information about usefulness and usability; they want to know how the product will affect productivity, not just how it operates.

The most dramatic tests reported so far were evaluations of notebook computers by *PC World* in its May 1993 edition. With the cooperation of American Airlines and its usability staff, they had six representative users try a variety of tasks on each of five different laptops while seated in coach seats of an airline training simulator. One test user found the passenger in front trying to recline his seat too far for comfort. He tried to jam his machine between the arm of his own seat and the encroaching back. It didn't work—and it added a new feature to the desiderata list.

Insiders at several computer companies say that management and marketing often reject proposals for efforts to measure and improve productivity on the grounds that neither reviewers nor buyers can tell the difference (as figure 13.3 shows, they're probably right). The introduction of trade magazine tests may push the manufacturers toward paying the same attention to usability that they give to raw speed.

So far the tests have been minimal. They have not included whole jobs of real people. They have been done in artificial situations; even *PC World*'s simulator tests did not include air turbulence or large seatmates with weak bladders. Another magazine's standard evaluations use only three subjects. Fortunately, as we've seen, that's enough to tell a UCD-perfected system from one that's not. The head tester says flaws of the latter simply jump out.

I have great hopes for reviewer testing. More objective reviews will help to filter what gets into use and thus gradually improve the efficiency of computer users. But the backstream effect on design, development, and peddling will be even more important; it will force manufacturers to do UCDdevelopment, if only to avoid embarrassment.

Still, much more is needed. The functional adequacy of trucks, beams, and milling machines, not to mention drugs, condoms, and TV sets, is appropriately tested by manufacturers. Wise purchasers will find ways to enforce customized testing of the usefulness and usability required by their own firm or their own customers. Tests will be done by the suppliers, on the model of drug companies, by consulting groups, on the model of structural engineering firms, or by the buyers themselves, on the model of the telephone companies.

Better Management?

An aircraft instrument manufacturer installed a computer-based resource management system. The goals were clear, the economic analysis sound, the implementation thoroughly planned. Ten months later, there had been no efficiency gains. The problem? Use of the system was rigidly governed by management rules. Workers were reluctant to override the system's decisions even when manifestly wrong. Local shortcuts and workarounds remained secrets. "Learning from mistakes was limited because effective job performance for the system designers was measured by adherence to best technical practice, not to shopfloor reality."[3]

The most popular diagnosis of the ills of computers, aside from under-rug sweeping, has been improper management of their use, and the favorite prescription is that upper management pull up its socks.

Clearly, successful reform needs to make each process mesh with the rest and contribute to the right overall outcomes. Dertouzos and Thurow go even further.[4] They propose that computers will boost productivity only when they are integrated in a national and international fashion. Banks need to get rid of checks, not just read the maker numbers automatically. Important goals like these require organizational decisions and negotiations by managers with clout.

But the good management that is so easy to urge is not so easy to do. Take the admonition that rather than simply automating jobs, managers should first reorganize work flow in efficient ways. If managers could make business operations much more efficient, what's kept them? If you have to do it before you bring in the information technology, why didn't you do it before there was information technology? I know companies that are on their third try at redesigning the same processes.

The task requires teams of creative people that combine thorough knowledge of the functions of the organization with knowledge of hardware, software, and, particularly, evaluation techniques. Getting people and teams to do this work is not easy. There are virtually no stars to hire or emulate; few if any have had repeated successes sufficiently impressive to assume that they could do it again. But neither is the task impossible. There are many superb computer programmers and computer project managers, many managers who truly understand the work of their own organizations and are open to change. And there are a growing number of usability specialists. The experiment of bringing them together in effective teams has only begun.

Automating Old Jobs

A West Coast clothing company introduced an advanced computer system so sales representatives could enter orders directly in handwriting, using new OCR technology to shortcut the labor-intensive card-punching operations that had slowed order delivery and caused customer complaints. The system "works"; there are actually fewer input errors than expected. But questionnaires answered by sales reps before and after the change indicate significant decreases in the quality of order filling and customer service, which in turn are associated with lower job satisfaction among the sales people (Lucus 1978).

We can also expect to get some help directly from the technology itself. I strongly disagree with the notion that old jobs should not be automated. With proper design, jobs that are time-consuming or error prone can be made much less so. We've seen many examples. If the jobs that are improved have important economic consequences, so will their improvement. The pundits have erroneously taken the fact that augmentation for individual jobs has failed so far to mean that it is hopeless.

Better Uses

Yesterday my wife, a lower-upper manager in a giant company, was late for dinner. She'd neglected to save a long memo she was typing herself, and a bug hung the program, forcing her to redo the work.

Strassmann estimated that 64 percent of total IT costs went for management information but was unable to show any general benefits of computers in productivity or competitiveness, despite valiant and imaginative efforts. Weill (cited by Attewell 1994) estimated that only 22 percent of IT goes to support transactions, despite the fact that these were the only uses he could show were significantly useful. Pentland (cited by Attewell 1994) found that IRS agents with their infamous laptops believed that the quality and authority of their work was better. Objective studies found no such effect—but did find much diminished productivity. Attewell himself reports a survey showing that average internal output per hour went up by 78 percent but that internal work volume, mostly reports, went up by the same amount, while the output of the firms he studied apparently stayed constant. Attewell also remarks that the huge increase in what-if experiments by spreadsheet users is not justified; a large literature shows that the resulting decisions are usually no better. The use of paper in offices has gone up twice as fast as GNP. Many observers have commented on the increased aesthetic appeal of carefully formatted casual memos and charts and the explosion of unnecessarily detailed business cases.

We need to find service business activities where computers can help people do things that help more. Weill's hint about transaction applications (point of sale and order taking), a similar finding by Strassmann, and the successes of the telephone companies suggest that more concentration on operations and customer service applications and less on toys for professionals and managers is in order.

Augmentation and the Organization

Many experts have been predicting that computerization would revolutionize organizations. The most popular prediction is flattening of management hierarchies. The claim is that hierarchy is obsolete. With local area networks, each person can communicate with each other almost instantaneously. The CEO can ask every one of her hundred thousand employees a question and get an answer in minutes. "I'm going to Sweden. Anyone know a large customer in Stockholm?" Computer databases give every employee access to the same information. To find out how many T-shirts Bob Jones Inc. ordered last year, neither the salesperson nor the boss needs to ask anyone.

Peter Drucker and MIT's Tom Malone say that the increasing technical depth of most organizations means that managers and troops alike have much more need of each other's expertise. Thus, not only does modern technology bring the means for more direct communication between people but the necessity as well. The CEO needs the advice of a computer expert, a financial analyst, and an engineer and can make better use of them without the delay and distortion of intermediaries. Since modern business work is so fast paced and information dependent, access to information, in employees' heads or in databases, needs to be much more rapid and cannot, it is contended, put up with creaky old hierarchies.

This analysis is all very compelling—so compelling that it must have come to pass. But the total number of managers doubled between 1972 and 1988, and there were *more* middle managers in 1992 than ever before. The prophecy failed for three reasons. The most benign is that a chain of command is an efficient way to allocate responsibility, make decisions, and divide expertise. A less cheering reason is that command chains maintain political power that is not easily surrendered. A last explanation is that computerized information sharing is just not good enough. It is still too hard to use and insufficiently useful. Most large organizations do not yet have electronic mail networks that reach all employees, so the kind of communication that requires a permanent readable, processable, storable form cannot yet be sent electronically by everyone to everyone. Where such facilities exist, they are too cumbersome to attract all the crucial players. Few high-placed executives have terminals on their desks. Few employees have direct access to either databases or electronic messaging systems other than the telephone. Most message systems are too difficult to use for people who use them only sporadically. Even when they are usable, their usefulness is diminished by awkward addressing and by the information glut they can spew out. (A contrary view is expressed by Attewell. He says IT is too good; it tempts managers to spend too much time, money, and attention on messages and numbers.)

Interestingly, another prediction about computers and organization seems to have come true: that IT would produce smaller companies because electronic coordination lets firms turn to others for general functions like maintenance and travel. Brynjolfsson et al. (1994) have found evidence that using more IT is associated with subsequent decreases in firm size, an especially interesting finding because it is mostly large firms that have appeared to improve productivity in recent years. Is it possible that IT encourages forms of organization that miss out on economies of scale, specialization, and control?

Overcoming Problems
Part of the job of improving productivity returns from IT will be to overcome some long-standing sources of ineffective deployment. Let me mention a few.

Piece-Wise Design
Most software packages are invented and sold one at a time. They address one task—seldom the whole job of any one person, never all the work of a whole organization. But effective information workers don't spend their whole day at one task. Well-used secretaries make appointments, answer telephones, make records, find information, and type. Software companies do try to make different programs compatible, so that the output of one can be the input to another, and some icons and commands have the same meaning in different places. But whole systems that aid the full activities of any one person or the full functionality of any office or factory are rare.

Specialization and Information Work
Piecewise development has also pushed management into dividing jobs into specialties that use the computer facilities, often physically separating interrelated workers. This blind mimicry of the labor specialization of the first industrial revolution saves steps and maximizes expertise in manufacturing. But in information work it can increase communication costs, delays, misunderstanding, error, and duplication of work.

Sometimes, as in database applications, and especially in computer-aided design, specialization happens because computer systems are so hard to learn. Once somebody has been trained, management doesn't want to waste her time doing anything else. But the tail is wagging the dog: systems should be designed to fit efficient labor division, not require inefficient new specialization.

We got a request to design a graphical user interface for a system that helps dispatchers schedule field repair jobs. A visit to the workplace revealed that dispatchers spend most of their time making telephone calls to get needed information and copying information from one system into another. This results in frequent errors, like wrong IDs for faulty equipment, that can compound themselves into a gummy mess. Did the clients need a GUI? Maybe. Did they need a less error-prone, less time-consuming information collection scheme? Certainly.

The essence of information work is the assembly of knowledge. When information workers are overspecialized, they lose command of what is going on. Information about the boss's schedule is unknown by the pool wordprocessing typist who is writing an answering letter to someone who wants an appointment, and thus an error—not a typo, but an error in judgment—goes out in an envelope.

Worst of all is what piecewise specialization does to work life. The wordprocessing typist who knows nothing about the writers' goals or even how to spell their names garners little satisfaction. It's worse than an auto assembly line, where workers at least know what their parts do, whether a job's done right, and what is being built. Maximizing the number of words someone types during the day is an indecent goal. We have to keep the kind of productivity effects we are really after in sight. The true goal is not productivity in dollars per hour just to have dollars per hour; somewhere we need to factor in the satisfaction and pleasure of the working day. To put a crass economic slant on it, disaffected employees tend to goof off, call in sick, and work elsewhere. Thus even the most uncaring Henry Ford ought to care that phase two makes employees like their work.

Piecemeal application also causes problems for customers. If the billing function is taken over by a different program on a different computer from the order entry function, then it is tempting to have different people enter orders and manage billing. The person to whom you complain that you never ordered the clown nutcracker responds disdainfully that it is "in the computer." The checks and balances of the amazing human brain have been denied to the organization. *Quality,* the business buzzword just before *reengineering,* has not been served.

Piecemeal specialization also brings extra coordination. One large corporation has a special office to handle complex orders. There are seven databases. A customer's name and addresses often don't match. (T. K. Landauer, Tom Landauer, Thomas Landauer—a human knows they're all me.) The company employs order shepherds.

Fragmentation

Consider a large university. The accounting department computer has data on salaries paid and tuition bills due, the registrar's on courses and students, the personnel department's on faculty particulars. Is scholarship money going only to students who maintain a B average, who are not also employed by the university in high-paying jobs or getting faculty family benefits? To find out, you need to run all over campus, log into a computer in the administration building, another in the accounting department, and still another in the registrar's office. With luck, each one hands over a fat paper printout that has to be compared by eye and pencil.

This fragmentation happens not because someone is stupid or because management is on holiday but because it is an almost inevitable consequence of the way computer applications are, or at least have been, deployed. To get a system in place requires a whole battery of resources: funding, staff, space, management, techie stuff. Doing something compatible and good for even two different functions is probably four times as hard as for one.

Nonproductive Uses

A popular business case taught at Denver University's business school is about the demise of Colorado's once-proud Frontier Airline. The story runs that Frontier pioneered computerized reservation systems and used its IT effectively for internal accounting, route, and personnel management. United buried Frontier by using the information in its reservation system, Appollo, not just for efficient booking but to pry business away from its competitors. United made it easier for customers to book their own flights, searched out its competitor's best customers and offered them deals, analyzed everyone's usage patterns, and tuned their own routes, schedules, and fares to appeal to everyone's passengers.

To prepare for the writing of this chapter, I immersed myself in the management literature on the use of information systems. Innocently, I had assumed that the primary goal is to produce better goods and services at lower prices. But for every article that even mentions that aim, there are at least ten whose sole ambition is to tell how one company can take business away from another. A favorite example is American Hospital Supply, which beat its competitors to the punch by installing direct-order terminals in hospitals. The scheme gave the organization a kind of de facto monopoly but did nothing for productivity.

I find this style of advice especially puzzling. What is the point of telling everyone how to compete unproductively with everyone else?

The examples given earlier of successes in the telephone businesses point a better way. Could it be that the regulated monopoly telephone businesses, which by law could not be interested in taking business away from competitors, were better motivated to deploy computers productively? Under rate-of-return regulation, public utilities were told how much they could charge. The rates were set every, say, five years. Between rate settings, the companies keep increased profits from improved productivity. Thus, they were motivated to make their service workers' salary dollars and equipment purchase funds go further, and they did it.

Learning

OOPS, I MUST BE ON MY HOME MACHINE<NOW WHERE IS THAT "CAPS LOck," oh there it is!

My son-in-law, Tom, a high school special education teacher, wanted to produce a simple form to record student grades—a page with columns and dates. He thought his easy-to-use computer should be just the thing. But when he tried to print out the sheet of columns, they didn't line up. It seemed easy to fix so he tried again. At 1:00 A.M. he surrendered and did it by hand.

Fortunately there is somebody in his school to whom Tom can turn for computer help—Joe, the local computer guru. This unofficial job is found everywhere except in budgets and BLS statistics, usually performed by a computer amateur who is supposed to be doing something else. (I know a world-famous statistician who has taken on this role. He spends most of his time writing useful small programs for his colleagues, leaving little for the intellectual pursuits for which he is famous.)

Computer systems are rarely easy to learn. An average engineer takes over nine months to be proficient on a CAD system. My graphic artist says she's still learning two years into her latest formatter. Because of equipment changeouts, job switches, and software improvements, most computer users learn a new system every few years. I'm on my *eighth* text editor. In the olden days, vast numbers of employees knew how to operate a standard typewriter that was the same everywhere. Not so anymore. The QWERTY keys are still in the same place. But where is the Enter key? Or do you use Return instead? Where is the Backspace key, or is it called Delete? People can't jump into each other's shoes and often can't advise each other. The cost of training and retraining is substantial. In today's constantly reorganizing firms, this friction is significant. And because systems change so fast, education can't help much.

Unintended Consequences.

My wife picked out a dress at Upscale Department Store and took it to the checkout. The item number made the terminal display "Belt $17.50." No cure was found; she had to take the dress at $17.50.

Remember the English supermarket chain that installed a state-of-the-art point-of-sale device? The intent was better inventory control, speedier check-out, fewer employees, a smaller car park. Throughput at checkout counters was improved, and more personnel were assigned to bagging, but none of the other expectations was fulfilled. Equipment maintainers and managers replaced the redundant stockers and markers. Inventory couldn't be improved because it was more efficient for suppliers to send mixed lot cartons and too much trouble to count in single products. Because produce requires memorized codes, operators often put courgettes in the customer's string bag unrung (Cutler and Rowe 1990).

Cost
While the price per megathing has plummeted, the cost of computing has oddly stayed nearly constant. An equivalent machine today costs a frac-

tion of what it did just ten years ago, but you couldn't buy one, and your employees wouldn't stand for it if you did. Instead you get one with ten times the flops and bytes at about the same price. The price of software has not dropped much either, partly *because* the hardware has become so much more powerful. It is now possible—and irresistible—to write very much bigger programs with many more features.

There are also disastrous expenses. The literature on computerization is filled with stories of companies that computerized at great expense, only to find that their system never got up, had terrific overruns, or didn't do what people wanted. A $4 billion transaction processing facility for Bank of America was much bigger than needed and too expensive to operate. The officer in charge resigned and the CEO retired. The system included a vast array of new services that customers didn't like.

And Back to Test-and-Fix

"The Tone for this chapter has been set succinctly in the internal memorandum of the International Center for Information Technologies: '. . . How to measure the business value of information technologies is one of the most difficult problems management faces in planning for computer investments. Information technology budgets have exploded over the last few years even if other cost elements are flat or even shrinking. . . . These conclusions are increasingly echoed by executives trying to deal with economic justification of computers. A 1986 survey of 71 chief executive officers from leading U.S. corporations considered information systems (IS) the most difficult corporate staff to manage and the most likely to increase in cost' " (Strassmann 1988).

Proponents of quality, such as Juran (1989) and Deming (1982) emphasize measurement and feedback. Juran's definition of quality, "fitness for use," is very close to what I mean by usefulness and usability. The urgings of this book could be fairly restated as a special case of the quality approach, the case of phase two computer applications.

All concerned believe that the sine qua non of progress in IT is better measurement of value. Strassmann, citing an IBM source, says that less than 20 percent of data processing costs are supported by business case analyses. The business cases, in turn, represent MIS justifications of new computer costs, not analyses of what computers have been good for, where they have failed, and how to make them fitter for use.

Purchase justifications always include auspicious assumptions about outcomes, about work and process efficiency. Cases of successful applications are marshaled. In one how-to book (Meyer and Boone 1987), the authors report that an error was committed in preparing a proposal for a Defense Department allocation. The error was discovered using a spreadsheet program, saving $10 million. They claim the $150 program was worth 60,000 times its cost—but the same program was used to make the mistake.

What is missing here is a control group. The only way to be sure that technology has helped is to compare performance with and without it. This is neither as easy nor as hard as it might appear. It's deceptively easy if one just looks at a bottom line before and after. But business is never so simple. When systems are introduced, many other things usually change too, either intentionally or by chance, and people react with enthusiasm or resistance. To get beyond such problems, it's necessary to do the experiment several times in several places and to give the organization time to settle afterward before judging the outcome.

People often contend that controlled studies are impractical in real businesses, but this is just knee-jerk pessimism. Most changes are too expensive and difficult to do all at once in large organizations so are instituted one or two departments or branches at a time. Add to that appropriate measurement, and, if possible, pick which departments come earlier and later by rolling dice, and you've got it.[5]

I once participated in a marketing study done this way (Doob et al. 1969). We wanted to know whether low-price introductory offers lead to brand switching and lower total sales when the price goes up, as certain psychological theories predict. The CEO of a chain of discount stores let us pick half the outlets for this kind of promotion on a series of house-brand introductions—items like razor blades and cookies—leaving the other outlets to start them at the regular price. The result was clear proof that the low price offer *caused* lower sales in the long run, a question that had been fruitlessly argued ad nauseum before the experiment.

The study by Kraut, Dumais, and Koch (1989) of introducing automation in telephone company business offices was done the same way. It produced much more reliable conclusions than anecdotes, individual case studies, guru impressions, and surveys of manager opinions ever can. The investigators were able to show that the particular automation actually caused increased output per hour, and, more important, to discover that there were other effects and determinants. For example, the new technology caused more work and headaches for managers in most offices and was associated with good or bad changes in quality of work life depending on whether the technology was used flexibly with employee input or according to rigid top-down rules.

Just what and how to measure are very important questions. Two slightly contradictory principles reign. The first is that what we really want to know is the overall result—the bottom line on dollars of stuff sold for hours of labor toiled. I call this end-to-end measurement. It's easy to measure the number of sheets of paper coming off the printers in word processing, the number of transactions handled by ATMs, or the number of service calls scheduled. But if, as often happens, the sheets of paper are minor revisions that don't really matter, the ATM transactions are for smaller amounts in addition to, not instead of teller activities, the service calls the result of new kinds of database errors, the good-looking results are mere mirage. We want to look instead at how much is brought in by the whole operation with how much effort, before and after.

But the second principle is that end-to-end quarterly bottom-line figures say almost nothing that will help improve purchase decisions and deployment methods. Deming complains that American managers are preoccupied with numbers about final results, to the exclusion of paying attention to the people and processes that produce them. The point is that two kinds of measurement are critical. Only end-to-end bottom-line figures can show whether the whole effort has succeeded, test whether apparent local improvements have synergised each other or have been thwarted, diluted, or frittered away. But only detailed measurements of component processes, and all the right component processes, can illuminate what's happening.

The difference is exactly the contrast we saw earlier between summative and formative evaluation in usability assessment. Summative evaluation determines whether the goal has been reached; formative evaluation tells what is going well and badly and informs the designer—here the manager—about what to change. And just as in UCD for individual usability, in UCD for organizational deployment, close observation, both formal and informal, is the secret of turning evaluation into understanding and creativity.

In the Kraut, Dumais, and Koch studies, the summative evaluations of number of customers served showed overall success, at least of one kind. Simultaneous surveys of employees and managers, and observations and conversations, unearthed hypotheses about the management styles correlated with varying degrees of success and about the workarounds that effective employees used to improve the value of the technology. For example, where not forbidden, productive service reps subverted the system design by using fake customer records to pass notes to each other, thus overcoming a serious barrier to cooperation that the system had unwittingly imposed. Clearly the next release should provide a usable useful message facility, and supervisors should encourage its proper use.

The techniques for UCDeployment mirror those for UCDesign and UCDevelopment. Start with task analysis, then design, then try, then design again. The only difference is that the task analysis needs to be of the total task of the organization, or at least of complete functional groups, and the evaluations need to be observations of activities and measurements of their inputs and outputs, the fixes aimed at improving waste control, coordination and transfer as well individual efficiency. The process engineer or manager has to look closely at what people are doing and what is being produced, and exercise judgment about its value. The check on those judgments is the end-to-end evaluation.[6]

A New Scientific Management?

I am urging the application of the scientific method to business decisions—not the scientific management of Taylor but the more fundamental scientific method of controlled comparisons. In IT deployment we find ourselves in an arena where intuition and experience have proved poor guides. We have not done well at predicting the consequences of IT investments aimed at productivity. The way out is to improve our ability to know what works. The surest way to such discovery is the controlled experiment, and the time has come to use it. We want not deep truths about physical nature but merely little practical truths about what helps people and organizations do better work faster. We're after engineering experiments like the ones the Wright brothers did by the hundreds, to see if new designs help us fly farther, but also, and more important, to garner observations of where they wobble or need better controls, so that the next attempts will be better.

V

What Then?

I really do believe that computers are wonderful and will be harnessed to increase productivity and the quality of life. Some speculation on the might-be of it all may help us think about what we want.

Suppose we do succeed in doing to service work what we did to farming and manufacturing. What then? What will be left for people to do? How will they fill their time? Undoubtedly, a large part of the answer will be still more leisure activities, more spectator sports, more reading and watching, more concerts, movies, and television, or whatever multimedia formats overtake them. There will be more modes and manners of social interaction, more games, more communication. And, of course, there will be more shopping, more browsing through the increased abundance and variety of things. However, there is only so much time for those activities. How much more time can people spend watching television? How many more hours can they peruse catalogs and prowl malls? So far, people seem to want to divide their time between leisure activities and something else, usually work or study. Predicted further extrapolations of the historical workweek decline have not come true; indeed those who are working now are working more hours than in the recent past, at least in the United States, often at more than one job. It seems safe to believe that some balance of work and leisure, perhaps with more merging, will continue. It seems nearly as safe to predict that more work will be devoted to providing for nonwork activities and for supporting the activities of less worklike work. With the important exception of health care, work itself is losing some of its survival seriousness as it produces less food and shelter, more portable telephones, videos, credit lines, and personal beauty. The line between competitive games and work grows fuzzier. The popularity of gambling as part of both work (high-risk business strategies) and play (lotteries and river boats) rises.

There is talk of computers bringing more need for worker expertise and education. In the large, the opposite seems as likely. While there is modest growth in high-tech occupations like computer programming, thousands of highly experienced executives and Ph.D. physicists are out of work, and low-wage, low-skill jobs, like feeding prepackaged gunk into automated taco-making machines, account for most new employment. In the far future, most people may need more education for their leisure, family, and social life than for their vocations.

These present and predicted shifts in activities and interests are part and parcel, both cause and effect, of the transition to a service economy. Information is at the heart of the service economy and of the pleasure and people-oriented life of the coming world. Computers are about and for information. I take seriously the rosy productivity projection in figure 13.3, or at least some approximation to it. With proper design, development, and deployment we can make the immense potential of this technology pay off immensely.

What will computers contribute to the new world they create? What will be their role? My speculations are divided into two groups: first, in a slightly practical vein, are some ideas for fantasy business systems, and then are some thoughts on what might happen to individual people's lives.

15

Fantasy Business Systems

I claim the UCD will bring new and useful IT, but the world has so far offered up few proven examples. If I hypothesized some and implied that they'd surely work, I would undermine the most important point I've tried to make. On the other hand, I have been studying work augmentation for some time and I've been primed to think of things that might stand trying. So—with cautions—I offer here some ideas for systems that might be explored on the way to improved productivity. They fall into two genres: work efficiency enhancers and new products.

Work Efficiency Enhancers

An Empowering, Integrating, Obliterating Intelligent Order Processing System

Let's start with an imaginary order processing system that could function with some modification in a variety of organizations, from telephone order lingerie companies, to service offices for cable companies, to direct-from-factory sales offices for Ukrainian pickup trucks.

At Frau Frocks in Detroit, service representatives sit facing each other in a circle inside a large room, each with a computer terminal roughly four times the size of present ones (four times is the maximum visual space a person can use without getting up to walk around). The resolution on the screens is about ten times what it is on current computers so that the tiniest print of the maximum quality useful to human eyes can be displayed. In addition to individual workstations, there are large projected displays on the walls.

Customer Jane Jones rings in from Toledo on an 800 number. Her name and face appear on the wall and on the terminal of her personal sales rep, Bob (unless Jane wants anonymity, in which case she gets the level of privacy she desires). Names for others who have ordered from that telephone also appear, and a slot for visitors. All records possibly pertinent to a forthcoming transaction are instantly available: a classified list of everything Jane has ordered lately (June 3: three pairs size large black tights), notices of any complaints (June 12: Jane said she was billed for four tights: credited, apology call made) or returns (April 2: one yellow polka-dot bikini), account status (paid up), credit line ($5K), and an expert system–derived summary of her sizes (dress 12–14, shoes 9C) and tastes in colors (black, pink, white, NOT yellow polka dots), styles, prices, and terse advice on interaction ("likes to chat about new fashions; doesn't like styles suggested by Amy").

Bob asks what Jane wants and chooses a type of interaction with his mouse: *purchase, complaint, inventory inquiry.* The computer leads Bob through the questions and entries needed. Bob doesn't know what shoe size Jane's four-year old niece is likely to need. He searches the database by typing "four-year old girl shoe size" and follows marked paths of likely choices. Jane wonders what to wear to a brunch at her Korean boss's house on Saturday. (It's Tuesday afternoon now.) Bob clicks for help from the other service reps. They can all see the suddenly enlarged transaction record for Bob's customer and listen in on the conversation if they want. A conference ensues.

Jane thinks she wants some black silk slacks. Bob discovers that there is one pair in Jane's size at supplier Hao-Long's shop in Hong Kong. The computer tells him previous experience with Hao predicts a fifty-fifty chance of delivery by Friday. As a backup, Jane picks out a long white skirt, available in one day from Dow's in Detroit. A click instructs the computer to order the slacks, keep in touch with their progress, cancel the order if not shipped by the last minute it can get there on time or the last time the skirt would probably be successful, whichever comes first (the computer knows all about this stuff and figures it out itself).

Now the order is sent on to the next stages, electronically, of course. It appears on the hand-held device of Soong in Hao's stockroom. The device shows Soong graphically what shelf the slacks are on. When she picks them up, she scans in the bar code, as does the shipping clerk to whom she hands them, and the rickshaw driver who gets them next, and so forth. Billing happens automatically as the box goes out Hao's door, and receipt is acknowledged automatically as it comes in Frau's, by changing a 0 bit to 1 in the electronic order database that all the parties share over Worldwide Bussinette.

Meanwhile, back in service central at Frau Frocks, the computer is keeping score and reporting the play-by-play. Each order has a life of its own within the computer—it is an "object" in computer-speak. The object knows when it (the order) is supposed to have done what. On the big screen, every item under order at Frau's is shown as a dot that moves from place to place, from service central (a smiley-face icon) to supplier (that's Hao this time), back to Frau's, out to Fly-by-Night Express, to customer, all the while marking itself removed from inventory, billed, received, debited, complete.

Usually the order appears on the wall only as a little gray spot that moves across the screen as it goes normally through the process. Among all the other normal orders, it looks like part of a smoothly flowing river. If anything goes wrong—if it fails to get onto the rickshaw when it should or the electronic debit finds Jane's cash drawer empty—it gets first bigger, then red or blue or spotted, depending on what ails it, then starts flashing. It shows Bob's name, puts itself on his screen, and speaks to him: "Hey BOB," it says. "Your order for Jane Jones is stuck in Honolulu, and Dow's has screwed up again—help!" Versions of the same display are mounted in warehouses, shipping and receiving centers, parcel–service control rooms everywhere.

An intriguing possibility would be to turn the exception handling into a kind of group video game. The first person to grab the troubled order (by a mouse click) and succeed in fixing the problem scores.

What's nice about all this for productivity is its possibilities for coordination, redundancy elimination, error reduction, first-time-right orders with fewer returns and higher customer value, and, especially, the provision of detailed data to be used in process improvement. There is but one record of everything, and everyone involved has access to it. No paper records change hands or get filed anywhere. Bob knows all about the order start to finish and can do what is needed to fix problems and talk intelligently and helpfully to Jane. When the problem is out of Bob's hands, time, or expertise, it can pass smoothly to someone else.

The computer can keep track of how long each order takes, where it waits how long and how often, what errors occur, which handoffs are slow or unreliable, which suppliers, service reps, or shippers are overloaded. It can calculate better work load distributions. Managers can use the data to see what to change. After changes, they can keep track of what happens.

A fascinating article in the *Harvard Business Review* (Shapiro, Rangan, and Sviokla 1992), titled "Staple Yourself to an Order," makes a case that many organizations can be fruitfully analyzed by careful description of what happens to an order as it goes through its life cycle. The fantasy system would deal with all of the problems these authors encountered in many field studies.

Note two other advantages. First, the system allows each worker to be treated as an individual. Up to now, the organization of information work has blindly followed in the footsteps of factory work design. The task is divided into discrete steps, and each worker performs only one step. Workers on a given job are treated as if identical. But human workers are not identical. As we have seen, differences between people in information work are huge. The traditional solution is to make many jobs, each narrow and routine, and train the workers carefully, a cruel and wasteful system.

Information work begs for and makes feasible a better way of organizing and assigning work. Our fantasy system attacks the problem in two ways. First, by UCD it makes all parts of the job easier for everyone, improving performance and evening out the effects of talent. Second, knowing that at any time each person will still have different skills and different knowledge from any other, it tries to use each person's abilities optimally by smarter, more flexible process coordination. Workers handle as much or as little of each order as they can. The electronic sharing of access to each order, its tracking of its own progress, the shared display of its status, the easy communication among workers, the gamelike and hopefully friendly competition to serve each order optimally could provide great flexibility in the amount and kind of work that each person does.

A second advantage is that the physical location of workers becomes relatively unimportant. If individual workers had the wall display on a large-screen personal computer and access to the same databases and communication network, they could do their parts from home, office, or community work center. Almost certainly most people will still want to be together while they work, when and if they can, but the extra flexibility could provide new opportunities for both efficiency and satisfaction. Greater flexibility in who can do what work and where can lower training requirements, reduce labor costs, and do so humanely, and boost productivity.

Sounds pretty good to me.

Disclaimer: It won't work—not until it is based on thorough task analysis in a realistic setting, not until it is mocked up and tried and revised, then again; then prototyped and tried and revised, then again; then experimentally implemented and evaluated and revised, then again.

The Perfect Professional Private Personal Workstation
Now let's dream up a workstation for an independent professional. Imagine a stockbroker—a securities customer representative. Jim sits at a desk and interacts with investment centers like the New York Stock Exchange, and school bond, and porkbelly markets. He talks in person or over the telephone to clients. He gives advice, makes buy and sell orders.

When investor Jane Jones calls, her full record comes up on a large screen. First is an overall summary of her account. Behind each category—her holdings in tax-free municipals, her positions in blue chips, her cash accounts—are clickable details listing each investment entity, and behind those, in a scheme similar to SuperBook, information about the company, the issuing institution, the price history, opinions snatched from the online Dow Jones and *Wall Street Journal* wires, Jim's company's own analysts. Also on screen are the names of Jane's family members, her work life, hobbies, and interests, notes from Jim's last conversation with her, and a summary of what Jim has done for Jane lately, and how well what Jim has done for Jane has worked. Jim can be very friendly.

Jim can access broad and deep information about all kinds of investment instruments and their markets. The same seven-to-one advantage in information retrieval reported for the chemists would be realized by

Jim. Of course, the workstation also helps Jim enter, record, and follow orders for all trades. Everything is kept track of and monitored by an object-oriented system similar to the one described above. In this case there is a nested set of objects, the individual orders being children of Jane's parent portfolio object, which knows about all its descendant investments. When anything exciting or dismaying happens, the computer tells Jim, who tells Jane, whose telephone number magically appears and dials itself when clicked. It uses an expert system to monitor how Jane's portfolio is doing relative to her goals and compared to other potential options that it suggests Jim talk to her about. Jane has an "agent," a computer program that acts as an individual adviser, keeping tabs, doing simulations, searching the markets for opportunities to Jane's taste, looking at what changes or shifts are in her interests and which ones not. All of this could be done quite reasonably.

How does this help productivity? It reduces the labor overhead of stockbrokers. Extended to lawyers and accountants, it increases the efficiency, decreases the billed time per customer problem, of a large population of very expensive knowledge workers.

Sounds good—but read the disclaimer above.

The Paperless Office

Let's reconsider that old favorite, the paperless office. As reported by Thomas McCarroll in the August 12, 1991, edition of *Time* magazine, the Reliance Insurance Company of Philadelphia set out to get rid of paper by 1983. It had (paper) posters on the walls saying, "Paper-free in 1983." It reportedly invested millions of dollars in computers and telecommunications but was unable to make the goal. Reliance employees shun the electronic mail system at the heart of the operation because it is excessively cumbersome. An executive responsible for such things was quoted as saying that maybe they'd get there by 2003, some twenty years after the original target date.

I don't think the idea of a paperless office is anywhere near dead or need be as far off as 2003. The critical element in the paperless office is avoidance of paper. All documents, bills, all reference manuals, all company procedures, all memos, notes, and letters, are in electronic form.

Every employee has a computer hooked to a network. Where people are peripatetic, this will be hard. Where everyone does most of their work near a desk, it will be easier. Portable computers with wireless communications will help but not suffice. To support complex information work, people need good, big screens and full-sized keyboards. Otherwise paper is more efficient and pleasant, and people rightfully hang on to it. That is the hardware end of the deal, except for high-capacity highly reliable networks.

Useful and usable software is even more critical. We need better word processing, text editing, spreadsheet, and database programs. We need full systems that support all the work that a person does in an integrated fashion, where the spreadsheet, the text editor, the database, and email work together effortlessly. We need office systems that help the various people in an office communicate, share, and cooperate. Computer-supported cooperative work systems, shared filing systems, messaging systems are on the market but aren't useful and usable enough yet.

Still, we need more. My fantasy system helps you know what to write and how to write it well. You type something close to what you think you want to say. It goes off to a store of a hundred million well-written paragraphs and brings you back ten that closely resemble what you tried to say. You pick the three best, and it returns with ten like their average, or three like each of them. From each you borrow inspiration. The system also helps you make good decisions and in the same way. You type a description of your problem. It finds the ten most similar cases among 10 million and lets you see what other people have done. Both schemes are what you've always done, but very slowly: learned what to say and do from examples, from experience. Now you have a power tool to concentrate and accelerate the process. We need such inventions.

An essential component of our paperless office is much better information retrieval methods because much of the day of an office worker is spent in trying to find information. The productivity advantage comes from typing documents only once and finding them once typed (estimates have it that less than half of filed paper document are found when needed). Memos, ideas, recordings of meetings, and so forth get to the people who need them when they need them. Telephone tag doesn't happen. Delays and false starts while everybody waits for desk-to-desks disappear. The information necessary for better coordination and more flexible work sharing is provided.

There are a host of reasons to think that this environment will be more efficient and will provide a foundation on which many new inventions and processes are mounted. The system will keep track of itself, of how often people are unable to find things, how many memos never get read, how many bills go astray. The same kind of object-oriented monitoring that we imagined for customer and client orders will track the pieces of unpaper that flow through the office. Bad linkages, excess versions and recipients, redundant spreadsheet analyses, cued or idle work will be easy to detect, thus much easier to correct.

Will all of this happen? Standard caveats.

New Products

Cost reduction is only one part of productivity improvement. Arguably, a more important part will be the development of new information products—new useful information, new usable packaging and delivery of information. Current online database systems are just a beginning.

All-Electronic Messages

People are intensely social animals; with few exceptions they'd rather sit around in groups and talk than do almost anything else you might name. (What is a party? Why do powerful executives who can do whatever they want go to so many inefficient meetings?) Services to help people communicate with each other better look like a promising investment.

Good home communication stations will support vastly improved, more flexible, more functional, more effective means of interpersonal communication. Now you can have telephone conversations, if and when you find the other party, send written letters with two- to ten-day delivery. Some of us have answering machines or voice mail services. A few have faxes. Eventually we all will be able to send messages easily and comfortably in voice, print, handwriting, pictures, videos, animations—depending only on need and mood. Messages will be automatically stored, easy to find, and ready to forward, no matter what the medium.

Despite great utility—most users believe it a totally new and better medium for many purposes—current text messaging (electronic mail) is implemented in such a curiously arcane manner that it is often rejected by ordinary people. However, it is avidly used by 25,000 workers at CitiBank, 15,000 students at the University of Colorado, and 30 million computer programmers, scientists, and engineers around the world. Once across the difficulty barrier, most people find email a marvelous addition to their lives. Email need not be complicated and hard to use. We programmed a much simplified interface for a prototype version, a telephone with a simple screen and keyboard attached. Like the ordinary telephone, the system is always on, always ready to transmit messages. Unlike a PC, there is no logging on, no disks, no commands, no requesting messages from a mailbox, no choosing from menus, no learning. You just sidle up, type a telephone number or a name, peck out a message, and press the Send button. That's it. When you receive a message, the system automatically prints it out, simultaneously saving it in its memory. You don't need to ask.

To test this email without a computer idea, we gave experimental prototypes to top executives in a big company. They used it with no training, no problem, and loved it. In another test, we gave prototypes to thirty-six women over the age of sixty-five, the most technology-averse part of the population. They liked it so much that they got together for a reunion a year after the experimental system was removed.

Different kinds of messages appear to go best in different media. The telephone spans distance cheaply. It also is a way to trade short messages quickly. In this respect, email goes the telephone two better. Not only is there no transport time, but there is no lost time trying to find the other party present to receive. It also removes the telephone's conversational pressure to ask about the family and say good-bye ten times. Sometimes you want to send a shopping list—much better in print. Sometimes you want to send a map; neither voice nor print will help. Sometime you will want to send Grandma a video of the baby. The universal message center will help you.

I think this will be useful enough that people will pay enough to make it a productive industry.

The Home Shopping Supermall

Predictions of dramatic expansion of shopping at home via computer have been made repeatedly over the last fifteen years but have not materialized. On the other hand, home shopping without a customer computer, by mail and 800-number telephone order has exploded. Cable television shopping programs have also taken off, although they still account for far smaller volume. Why has computer-based shopping been relatively unpopular? What could be done with home computers that would be more useful?

Computers have failed as a shopping medium because they are too hard to operate and offer too little extra. Contrast them with the Yellow Pages, an enormously successful businesses and a tremendously popular avenue for buying. Let's combine the power of computation with the Yellow Pages. Each household has a television-sized console with a screen, loudspeaker, and keyboard, our home communications station again. It is as easy to operate as our experimental email. (There's no need to worry about typing skills. Such a device requires only the most rudimentary typing, and the majority of adults now type at work.)

This system does everything the Yellow Pages now do, only faster and better. You can scan the listings, categories, and ads, just as now. But pick a listing or an ad, and up comes more description, as much as the lister has provided, including pictures, sound, or videos. Pick one and have the machine automatically dial the telephone.

Better than that, you can search. Type a word or phrase: "dentist with an opening today," "Levi Jeans size 33/36," "broccoli and feta cheese pizza by the slice." It comes back with ten supplier options and tells you whether each is a guarantee, a likely bet, or just a hunch. The system is integrated with inventory databases of cooperating businesses, so it can show what's in stock and the price. Asked, it gives hours, location, and driving instructions from wherever you called. If you and the seller agree, it lets you place an order. If you want, it automatically fills in your name and address and debits your bank account. (The Minitel system in France already does part; it can bring up the menu for a restaurant and place a home delivery order.)

Let's be bolder. How about simulating a mall in interactive video. You start with an aerial view of a virtual mall, zoom in on its halls, a store, look closely at its wares, rummage through its stockroom, then do your ordering, or mosey on. Clothing stores could keep computer models of your body, and put a suit on virtual you to model for your consideration.

With these schemes we create an incredible new free market, the economist's darling candidate for efficiency.

Let's go a step further. Suppose I don't know exactly what I'm looking for, except that I'd like, shall we say, a movie (over my telephone line, of course, starting when I'm ready). I ask the machine for suggestions. I have rated 100 movies 1 to 10 for it, and it knows what it has showed me before. It has similar data on millions of other people around the world. It searches out thirty with tastes like mine, a virtual community of like-minded movie watchers (it might also look for peculiar people who always hate the ones I love). Using some computational magic, it picks the top ten movies I haven't seen but probably would like. It could then give me a bit of information, perhaps a preview of each.

Again, we've actually tried this one in a small way. We did it with people on Internet, all by plain email. Our predictions were pretty good—much better than ones based on movie critic ratings and significantly better than mere popularity.

The same kind of scheme could be applied over the whole spectrum of consumer goods and services. It would generate efficiency by connecting consumers more easily, with fewer ads and catalogs, with products they want. I know half the population *likes* to shop, and wouldn't pay extra to find what they want faster. But the other half might.

The standard disclaimer applies.

The Electronic British Library of Congress Française

How about a true electronic library? For decades we've been told that the Library of Congress, the British Library, and the Bibliothèque de France rolled into one was coming soon to our living rooms. Part of the delay has been technological. Storage devices for that much material aren't here just yet. Additionally when samples of this idea have been tried, they have not been very popular. I *think* the reason may be usefulness and usability. What is needed is a system that will easily fetch all and only those things that you want. I *think* a lot of people would pay if the system found them just the right article from any encyclopedia, a perfect quotation from anywhere in the Bible or the *Congressional Record*, a short story they'd love from anywhere in the British Library—and did so with no hassle.

I have this recurring experience. I go on a vacation trip. I try to find out what to do, where to go, what to do and see. I never quite succeed. Guidebooks are written by someone else; friends who've been have different interests and tastes. I don't find out what I'd really like to know until I've been there. There's always much more useful information there than I can get here. How about putting it all in one easy-to-use electronic collection? How about putting a live local expert on every topic on the net and providing me with a search system for finding the right one anyplace? Would I pay enough for the service? Might be worth a UC try.

16

Life, Love, and Intellect

Information and communications tools ought to be just the thing to improve intellectual and social life. For the 20 million of us worldwide, and growing 20 percent a month, electronic mail offers a way to interact with other people that is fundamentally different from any that we've had before. Virtual friends ask a thousand of each other what to do to make comfortable a child with chicken pox, how to cook a rattlesnake. They take advantage of expertise spread around the globe, ask advice on buying truffles in Paris (bring francs), camping in Morocco (don't). This week a gang of professionals is having a long debate on email on whether long debates on email are any good. When the technology comes home, you too will send electronic notes to your lover, your sister, your next-door neighbor, and your child's teacher.

Math

Sadly, the majority of the population avoids mathematics like herpes. But math is really good stuff. With algebra you can figure out how much sugar you need in chocolate mousse for eleven when you have a recipe for six. With calculus you can calculate how much you'll have for college in thirteen years, five months if you save $117.60 a month at 3.62 percent. People used to have trouble with simple arithmetic. Most don't anymore because calculators help so well. The same thing will soon happen to algebra and calculus.

Calculus, like other mathematics, is a kind of tool for doing mental work. With a set of rules and tricks, pencil and paper, a person can do wonderful things. But the tools are so hard to use that only very smart, highly trained persons find them useful. I think that all can change.

The spreadsheet is a harbinger but not good enough yet. For figure 9.1 I wanted to fit a standard growth curve, like compound interest, to my data on the efficiency of eight text editors introduced at various times, so that I could calculate the average improvement per year and graph the result. My spreadsheet program contains such a facility, but here's an (only slightly unfair) excerpt from its instructions:

Syntax

GROWTH (**known_*y*'s**,*known_x*'s,*new_x*'s,*const*)
...

The array *known_x*'s can include one or more sets of variables. If only one variable is used, *known_y*'s and *known_x*'s can be ranges of any shape, as long as they have equal dimensions. If more than one variable is used, *known_y*'s must be a vector (that is, a range with a height of one row or a width of one column).[1]

I couldn't make it work in an hour and a half of trying, so I did the problem with a calculator in ten minutes. I maintain that the difficulty isn't necessary. My fantasy version does something like this:

Put the numbers you already know in two columns, one for the X values, one for the Ys. Here's an example:

Year (X)	Accumulated Savings (Y) at Unknown Rate
1990	$100
1995	$163
1992	$117

I do one just like the example. It says "OK."
It asks, "What's the smallest X you want a Y value for?"
I say "1973."
It asks, "What's the largest X you want a Y value for?"
I say, "2000."
It says, "The average growth rate was 9.4 percent. Do you want a plot?"

I have another hunch. I think most people would find simulation programs easier to use than regular math (Landauer 1988). For example, instead of using calculus to find out how much of your mortgage payments for the first ten years was interest, the program lets you type in the amount of the loan and the percentage interest, then click a button once for each payment period to have the program multiply by the percentage, cumulate the interest payments, and subtract each from the balance. It would be much easier to set up the problem, the operation most people find hardest. If you tried to do it this way by hand, you'd have to do 120 multiplications and subtractions for a ten-year period, and you'd probably make mistakes. The computer won't.

Standard Disclaimer: It won't work—not until it is based on thorough task analysis in a realistic setting, not until it's mocked-up and tried and revised, then again; then prototyped and tried and revised, then again; then experimentally implemented and evaluated and revised, then again.

Education

How many times did teachers tell you that all you need to know is how to use the library? Did you believe them? Did you stop studying textbooks and just rely on visiting the library? No. Using the library is too hard, slow, and unreliable. Someday we'll solve this problem, and on some fronts we've made exciting advances. Recall some of the SuperBook experiments. Statistics and chemistry students taking open computer exams scored A's while classmates with traditional books got C's. Chemistry students found needed facts seven times as fast with the computer. The balance for them had already shifted. Given the availability of such tools, students will rely on finding more and learning less. Just how much of this we can get away with is a deep question for research. You can't learn much chemistry without knowing much chemistry. But you certainly can do more chemistry without knowing as much as you do now if you can find out what you need to know more easily. Where will it end? I don't know, but somewhere different and better than where we are now. For analogy, look at what calculators have done to arithmetic. Soon, people with their computer partners by their sides will be much more knowledgeable than people have ever been before.

Creativity

The mind things that computers will amplify won't be limited to boring scholarly activities like math and chemistry. Most kids love to draw until they find out they're not good at it; grown-ups love to invent tunes when no one can hear. So far, we have computer-aided tools for drawing, composition, and performance that are sometimes interesting in the hands of experts, but they don't do much for the average person. These systems have received almost no UCD, no performance analysis of what it is that ordinary people want to do, what they find hard, and what would help them, almost no iterative design.

When it happens, you and I will be able to draw lifelike portraits of our cousins, animations, and cute cartoons of our pets. We'll produce decent home movies. We'll be able to compose, God forbid, rap songs and set them to what passes for music and play them as loud and often as we want.

Entertainment

Engrossing games by, through, and with computers are already here, captivating millions of players, filling billions of hours that might otherwise be wasted. They will get even better. Commercial versions of chess programs play as well as most human opponents want them to. Email schemes let you find a pick-up game of GO or gin rummy with a human (or so you think). Dungeon and dragon games, endless adventures and mysteries in the bowels of the computer's imagination, amuse masses. Versions that involve multiple players and multiple machines interact with each other day and night across the Internet. Here, if anywhere, the programmer inventors have found things for people to do with computers that can't be done without, that are truly original, popular, and profitable (especially in the guise of video games). So far, most of the players tend to be young, nerdy, and male. The future, with easier computers used by more people, will see more games loved by the average kid and grandma too.

Books and entertainment will change too. A book will spring into life, it's illustrations animated and singing, showing videos of helicopter flights over the Amazon basin where great trees are bending and characters are developing. But I don't know, really, how much of the envisioned multimedia, over our 500 channel interactive cable, is going to be really nice. People know a lot already about how to string the fibers and chop the data into bytes, but there is precious little knowledge of what will please. Following that tradition, here's another little idea.

People have already started writing computerized books,and the *New York Times* has started reviewing them (apparently by hand). Some take advantage of the fact that the computerized plot can go 4, or 512, different ways, depending on which menu button the user clicks. Here's my idea. (I don't know if it's original.) In my computer-based murder mystery, you the reader choose anyplace in the world to be, any character to be watching and listening to, like a fly on the wall, at any time during the story. But you can't be two places at once, and you can't go back. Reading such a story would be fun because your chance of solving the mystery would involve constant active decisions and luck. Writing such a story would be also be a lot of fun—and work. It could be realistic and engaging with graphics and multimedia; place your alter-ego character in pictured places, and the computer lets you see and hear only what you really could. Computers can do stuff like that. The publisher could make these books profitable by charging you again every time you went through it. Someone could rewrite *War and Peace* in the same style. Follow every one of the dozens of characters for every hour of their lives during the Napoleonic Wars. It could expand to 20,000 pages, maybe more, still easily stored on the hard disk of the computer I just bought.

Standard disclaimer.

Enough

I won't go on. The story of the human race is one of ever-increasing intellectual capability. Since our early cave-dwelling ancestors, our brains have gotten no bigger, our hands no more nimble, but there has been a steady accretion of new tools for intellectual work—how to grow crops, domesticate animals, build shelters, paint paintings. It includes governing and inspiring and, unfortunately, waging wars. It includes how to build and operate airlines, television sets, and football teams. This shared capacity was first manifest in language, later in writing, math, and science, and in the huge collections of experience and discovery stored in books and libraries. By comparison with our forebears, each of us has become a genius. The human mind is not housed in an isolated block of tissue in a person's skull. It draws on the whole wealth of stored human knowledge and the whole power of our shared mental tools. The growth of this mental power is not over. In relative terms, it has probably just begun. Computers offer so much more than mere language and mere marks on paper. They will make our mental powers appear to our great-grandchildren the way those of chimpanzees appear to us today.

Standard caveat.

Notes

Chapter 1

1. For the U.S. national account, we should also debit a substantial sum for the education and public research support of the academic computer scientists and engineers who have invented and developed much of the technology, although a large portion can be assigned to presumably valuable military applications. [15]

2. There was a large jump in productivity in 1992—a growth rate of 2.9 percent for the year—followed by a collapse in the first two quarters of 1993 and a jump forward in the third. It is too early to tell if we are seeing harbingers of the long-awaited turnaround or temporary fluctuations resulting from massive layoffs. What the world is after, of course, is sustained productivity growth coupled with high levels of employment and total output. If the measure is output per person or output per dollar of capital goods, the bad news continued unabated through 1993. Thus the apparent improvement, if permanent, reflects a greater ability to sustain the same output while working less. Previous productivity gains have both increased output and decreased work hours, thus improving standards of living. [15]

3. Maddison and Thor apparently used different measures of prices for the same goods in the various countries to equate GDP figures. Figure 1.3 combines data from these two sources to extend the years covered. As a result the absolute numbers could have small errors, but the overall pattern is not affected. Using 1990 price indexes, productivity in France and Germany had surpassed that in the United States in 1990 (McKinsey Global Institute 1992). However, Thor (1994) concludes that the United States is still ahead in purchase power per work hour although trailing badly in product per person measured by exchange rate dollar values. [18]

4. The recent report by McKinsey Global Institute (1992), coauthored by a blue-ribbon group of economists, looked closely at international differences and concluded, with apparent surprise, that the overall lead of the United States in productivity had not narrowed significantly in very recent years (the 1990 data in figure 1.3 come from this report). In 1950 France and Germany averaged only

67 percent of the U.S. proportion of employment devoted to services, whereas by 1987 the proportion had grown to 84 percent of the U.S. figure. In the United States in 1987, 70 percent of the work force was in services. [19]

5. Because the productivity of computer manufacture is calculated in an unusual and, as we will see later, questionable way, one might want to exclude it in any event. [23]

6. Data cited in this and the following paragraph were taken from Baily and Gordon (1988). Readers may notice some apparent inconsistencies in the numbers variously quoted here for productivity and other economic variables. The measure of productivity (whether labor or multifactor productivity) and subtler differences within these types, the periods covered, the way different businesses are grouped into larger categories, the sources of data (e.g., from BEA, BLS, census, or nongovernment surveys), and the corrections made for inflation or measurement gaps vary from one authority and report to another. For example, Baily and Chakrabarti, in another 1988 publication (Baily 1988), show multifactor growth rates in a slightly different category, "nonfarm-nonmanufacturing," declining from 1.7 percent a year in the 1948–1973 period to a negative 0.3 percent for 1973–1985. Insofar as possible, I've tried to capture the central tendencies of the sources in the data presented here and to concentrate on labor productivity. [24]

7. The industries with large accumulations of IT capital in 1987 were not Johnny-come-latelies to the technology. There is very strong consistency in the relative size of IT investments across industries over the successive years of this period. Those that were doing the most in 1987 had been doing the most for at least fifteen years (Baily 1988). [24]

8. Of course, this is a small number of cases, and one could imagine ways in which a small increase in IT could be more effective in one industry than a large one was in another. But note that these are percentage increases, each industry relative to its own 1981 baseline. The industries varied considerably in productivity growth, and the differences were negatively correlated with the degree to which they expanded their IT. The correlation coefficient is $-.57$; the odds against such a strong negative relation among seven cases are approximately nine to one. [27]

9. Roach's (1989) diagnosis: "U.S. business is simply hooked on computers." [29]

10. Part of the reason is a shift toward more information workers and fewer production workers. If total output for all workers combined did not change much during such a shift, the amount per worker would obviously go up for the declining number of production workers and down for the increasing number of information workers. [29]

11. This ambiguity appears in my previous comparisons of whole industries, countries, or time periods only to the extent that some spent a higher proportion of their IT on competition than others; it is virtually absent in the individual worker effects we will consider later. [32]

12. Some other relatively small, unpublished econometric studies of IT and production are cited by Brynjolfsson and Hitt (1993) and the National Research Council (1994a, 1994b). One by Morrison and Berndt in 1990 found a negative relation, $.80 returned for every dollar invested, in manufacturing industries. A study of thirty-three strategic business units by Weil in 1992 found no effect of overall IS spending. Barua, Kreibel, and Mukudpadhyay found no correlation with return on assets. Brynjolfsson finds fault with all of these, and with the Loveman study reviewed here, on the basis of their small number of cases. However, the consistently negative results over several different and independent small studies add up to strong evidence of no general and big positive effect. Another study that could be included in this genre is an analysis of employment effects (mixed) by Osterman that is reviewed later. [33]

13. Brynjolfsson and Hitt acknowledge this defect but sidestep it by assuming that hidden computer costs are perfectly correlated with known ones. Given their bang-for-buck deflator, this means they are assuming, at least in part, that software, maintenance, and labor are exactly proportional to mips and bytes. Undoing these two interlocking problems—the questionable deflator and the badly underestimated costs—would be very difficult and require new data and new analysis. Meanwhile, the correct size of the imputed return on investment is unknowable. Indeed, if there are several different components of overall computer costs that are nearly but not quite perfectly correlated with each other, and each is treated as a separate variable in the econometric equation, their colinearity could result in one being assigned a very high coefficient and the others very low coefficients. If instead the components had been added together into a single variable, the coefficient would have some intermediate value. [35]

14. Baily and Chakrabarti caution that the size of an input factor coefficient in an econometric equation cannot be interpreted safely as return on investment, as Brynjolfsson and Hitt have done, but that return on investment can't be positive unless the corresponding coefficient is. [36]

15. Anecdote. To analyze the printed mass of 254 points I needed to convert each to X-Y coordinates, a nasty job if done by hand. At lunch I mentioned my problem to my boss, Mike Lesk, a UNIX superhacker among other accomplishments. A few hours later he sent me a newly written C-language program with which, after I digitized a photocopy of the page, I could put a cross-hair on each point, click my mouse button, and enter each X-Y directly into a file; our local statistics package did the rest. Computers are wonderful.

However, for one of the Strassmann plots, a smaller one, done some months later, I found myself working at home on a different computer. Should I drive into work, find where the plot pick-off program was filed on my office workstation, and refresh my memory on how to use it, the scanner and digitizer system and the statistics package? Instead I drove to the neighborhood stationery store and bought a drafting triangle with a millimeter scale, added a grid with a pencil, and read the numbers off by eye and hand. The whole operation took about forty minutes. [39]

16. The relation depicted here is quite weak, but it is statistically reliable. It implies that the average firm in Strassmann's largest sample lost just over 3 percent in overall return on assets as a result of using information technology. [40]

17. Taken at face value, figure 1.15 implies that the average firm lost just over 1 percent in returns as a result of using computers. The negativity of the relation is not nearly trustworthy on statistical grounds. [40]

18. At face value, figure 1.16 implies that the average service firm lost 1.4 percent in stockholder returns by investing in computers. However, this strong a relation appears in completely random data over half the time. [41]

19. Taken at face value, figure 1.18 implies that the average bank may have added about 2 percent to shareholder returns through the use of computers, not a statistically reliable difference. [44]

20. Strassmann did find much higher return on management (ROM) for Japanese than for American firms. Japanese firms, he and others report, are less computerized than American. But one suspects that ROM is higher in Japan because employees work longer and harder for the same pay, a hidden variable in the numerator of Strassmann's ROM ratio. [44]

21. Unlike the accounting practices of most firms and government agencies, I consider a large part of the expenditures for maintaining computer equipment and producing and maintaining software to be investment rather than expense, for several reasons. First, the whole enterprise is the provision of a strictly capital good, a "factory," which is then used by the rest of the business in its production process; second, software is just as necessary a part of a system as hardware, just as expensive, and has similar durability; and, third, some of what a computer provides is information that can be used over and over again to help run a business. For the purposes of this calculation, however, we want a figure that is comparable to the capital input numbers used in the econometric and business success studies from which we take estimates of relative returns on investment. While the authors of these studies are not always entirely clear about just what is included in computer or IT investment, most of the associated labor and software inputs are apparently not counted. If we were to include some or all of these extra costs, the percentage shortfall of return from IT investments needed to explain the productivity slowdown would be smaller. My hunch is that an appropriate adjustment would bring the necessary IT return deficit to only 8 to 11 percent, but there are too many indeterminacies to make more refined estimates worthwhile. Alternatively, if we assumed that the inferior returns inferred by Loveman, Franke, Strassmann, and the others for "computer" investments applied to software and utilization costs as well as hardware, computerization would explain more of the slowdown than just the "residual" category that Denison and Baily and Chakrabarti couldn't fill, for example, accounting for the lower quality of capital or management that has received some of the blame as partialed out by Mohr and others. [45]

22. Returns in the absence of IT investment were estimated by fitting a straight line to Strassmann's largest data set, for 254 firms. The far left side—the zero

intercept of the function—supplies the estimate, which was actually 13.3 percent (plus or minus 3 percent). [45]

23. One might try to see if there is a similar match between overall capital returns and the whole growth slowdown. Average capital returns decreased roughly 2 percent between the periods in question (Baily and Chakrabarti 1988). Using values from the previous calculations, about 40 percent of the decrease is attributable to the large deficit on IT, though it involved a shift in only about 6 percent of capital stock (Roach 1988). The other 94 percent of capital thus would have produced roughly 1.25 percent less output than previously. By the hypothesis I am proposing, this part corresponds to the familiar forms of capital—buildings, machines, inventories—that participate in the part of the slowdown that traditional factors were able to explain. In other words, it appears that capital "switched" from traditional forms to IT lost over 13 percent of its productivity, while traditional forms lost a little over 1 percent. These numbers, however, are very crude approximations.

Because the available economic data and analyses do not have a consistent focus, use different measures and definitions of measures, aggregate components differently, and are sometimes imprecise or unclear, I have had to play a little fast and loose with these calculations. In particular, the distinction between IT and computers as such is not always respected in the various sources. Some of the data and results apply to one, some to the other, and I have jumbled them. Certain considerations mitigate the likely consequences of this sloppiness. First, since the mid-seventies, computers as such, or as components of communications and office equipment, have been a large and growing part of IT, probably a large majority in dollar terms. Second, it is hard to separate computers from other IT cleanly. Which is a FAX machine, for example, or a copier? Third, if the productivity of all IT is nearly the same as that of computers as such, mixing conclusions from one with the other will not necessarily be an apples and oranges affair. For example, using Strassmann's observations of nil return on assets as a function of number of PCs per employee as part of the evidence about how much IT returns differ from those of other investments is probably fair, at least within the degree of precision needed here.

Note that withholding money from IT and spending it some other way would not necessarily have rescued productivity. We don't know if there were any substitutes available that could have added another $30 billion output per year. [45]

Chapter 2

1. Between 1970 and 1980, there was a 32 percent increase in clerks, a 24 percent reduction in communications operators, and a 147 percent increase in computer equipment operators (Hunt and Hunt 1986). [47]

2. There is a striking difference in attitude between labor-oriented and productivity-oriented economists. The labor focus sees increases in employment in a computer-affected category (e.g., more managers) as a positive outcome; the

productivity focus views them as symptoms of inefficiency. Obviously, the best result would be increases in real wages (and, thus, output) across the whole population (and economy). [48]

3. I get an efficiency gain of 267 percent, not 340 percent, from the worker numbers. The author apparently did not count the word processing center supervisor. But never mind, 267 percent is plenty. Maintenance labor, training, equipment, and operations costs were not reported. [49]

4. The most astonishingly favorable case report on text processing that I've come across is from an unpublished U.S. Air Force report from 1979, for which I thank David A. Potter of AT&T Bell Laboratories. The Maintenance Policy and Procedures Division Directorate and Supply Headquarters (sorry, that's the way they talk; no wonder large efficiency gains are possible) produced new versions of standards documents. In one application of their old method, 150 people gathered in an off-site hotel for 100 days to compose, cut, and paste a draft that then took eleven more staff-years to polish. All told, the cost was $3,126.46 per published page for a 643-page manual. With the introduction of an early text editing system, 20 people working 20 days in their own building, plus just two staff years of editing, polished off a 240-page manual, at a cost of only $287.69 per page, including equipment. That's a 987 percent efficiency gain. I can't imagine what 150 people did for 100 days to *revise* 643 pages, or what the text editing system could have done to help them this much. I suspect this is a dramatic example of the potential benefits of process reengineering preceding a reorganization to accommodate computerization, an approach now being widely advocated and that will be discussed in later chapters. It may also be an example of Brooks' law: if ten people can do a project in ten days, one hundred people can do it in one hundred days (Brooks 1975). [50]

5. There is some argument about this. For example, Jorgenson, Gollop, and Fraumeni (1987) contend with great econometric show that capital accumulation is much more important than technological progress. I am strongly inclined to follow Solow (1959), Mokyer (1990), Baily (1988), and others in believing that capital can be applied productively only when there is the right technology available in which to invest. [53]

6. Peers are probably more appropriate if you want to know about practical implications of the results. [55]

7. Suppose, in all these studies, that the noncomputer letters had been done with a typewriter instead of by handwriting, perhaps with later pencil editing before transcription. Since even moderately skilled typing is faster than handwriting, which averages slightly over twenty words a minute, the time differences between precomputer and computer methods might have been less favorable to computers. [55]

8. There is one more controlled experiment on text editing versus handwriting in the research literature. It studied the use of text editors by low-aptitude first-year college students who had taken a one-semester course in computer-aided writing as a hoped-for remedy for their poor writing skills (Vacc 1991). They

either used the machine or wrote by hand to compose a series of letters of different style and content (with the handwriting later transcribed character by character by someone else; the time required for this was not reported). In this case there was a significant difference in quality (although the author does not report the appropriate statistical tests, the published numbers made such an analysis possible). As judged by writing instructors, letters written with the computer received an average quality rating of 5.5, those written by hand only 4.8. (Eight out of eight students received better ratings for their computer-based compositions than for their handwritten ones; the odds are more than one hundred to one against this happening by chance.) However, computer letters took much longer as well; sixty-four minutes with the text editor, only forty-two by hand. The author of the study took this to be a favorable outcome; the students were spending more time—mostly correcting spelling, it would appear—to do better work, something the educators were trying to encourage. However, from a productivity point of view, these results are equivocal. Is the quality difference worth the extra time for students writing letters? Such a question is difficult to resolve. We would clearly be on firmer footing in declaring text editing a success if the quality was better and the time needed less as well. If we include transcription, how do the two methods stack up in terms of efficiency? If we assume transcription took two-thirds as long as the handwriting, as it did in the Gould experiment, adding in transcription time gives total times of sixty-four minutes for text editing and seventy for handwriting plus transcription. So we are left with a modest advantage for text editing on the basis of these data as well. [55]

9. Extrapolating a bit from figures cited by Clark, at least 600 studies have evaluated computer-based instruction (CAI). Of these, some 150 meet reasonable research standards and were the basis of the meta-analyses reviewed here. Experts distinguish computer-aided instruction (CAI), in which the computer interacts continuously with the student; CMI, in which the computer is used for diagnostic testing and advice on which individualized lesson module or review to study next; intelligent tutoring systems, sometimes called ICAI, that try to model the knowledge possessed and needed by the learner; and yet more acronymic variants. I've lumped them; there's no evidence of markedly different effectiveness. [56]

10. The total amount learned was also better, on the average, with CAI, but only by a modest and quite variable margin (Clark 1985; Kulik, Kulik, and Shwalb 1986). The average CAI student scored at the sixtieth percentile in college courses, and at the sixty-sixth percentile in adult education courses, on examinations where traditionally taught students defined the fiftieth percentile. CAI had a similar advantage for elementary students but a much smaller effect for high school students. [57]

11. This assumes the familiar normal (bell-shaped) distribution of learning times. [57]

12. In comparison studies in which the same instruction method is followed with and without the computer, the advantage of CAI all but disappears (Clark 1985; Orlansky and String 1979). [57]

13. Meta-analyses of CAI studies show no significant improvement in effectiveness from the late 1960s to the early 1980s. Many later efforts have employed techniques from the field of artificial intelligence. Few have been evaluated against standard teaching methods. However, evaluations were made of a computer tutor developed by John Anderson and his students at Carnegie Mellon that is designed to teach the LISP programming language. This system is widely regarded as the most practically effective of the new genre. It produced a 30 percent reduction in the time students spent on practice exercises before mastering lessons (Anderson and Reiser 1985). Thirty percent efficiency improvement over twenty-five years, the approximate time since the first CAI, amounts to a net gain of only 1 percent per year, compounded.

This calculation, however, assumes a constant cost for instruction. A hope of CAI was not just to improve effectiveness but to reduce instructional costs. Traditional elementary or high school classroom instruction is a tough competitor here. Suppose the average teacher had twenty students for six hours per day. To match the teacher's output, a school would need twenty PCs, programs for 1,000 hours of instruction, plus floor and desk space, maintenance of hardware and software, "principal training," and someone to help students with hardware, software, social, and personal problems—a capital outlay on the order of $100,000 per classroom and continuing costs of at least $30,000 per year. The costs for college instruction are higher, and students more independent, so the balance is probably more favorable. Some estimates for CAI come out significantly less than traditional instruction in terms of dollars per contact hour (Eberts and Brock 1988). [58]

14. Between 1973 and 1982, the number of library attendants and assistants increased 7.5 percent. This compares with increases of 25 percent for keypunch operators, 21 percent for bookkeepers, and 3 percent for billing clerks and with decreases of 7.5 percent for typists and 34 percent for telephone operators (Hunt and Hunt 1986). [59]

15. The productivity effect of early entry is limited to the increased value over input compared to previous products for the number of units of the product sold before they would otherwise have come to market. Thus, if the product itself is not more valuable for the same production cost—it isn't going to contribute to increased productivity in the long run—its early entry isn't a productivity win either. [62]

16. Unpublished results from a recent study by L. A. Streeter, R. E. Kraut, H. C. Lucus, and L. Caby, sponsored by Bellcore and France Telecom, of electronic network use in French and American businesses (Streeter et al. in press). [64]

17. That is not to say that telephony has been the only industry with good productivity gains since the mid-1970s. There have been others. Agriculture has continued to improve at a brisk pace; among goods manufacturers, textiles and computers have been the major exceptions. Of these three, only the computer industry is heavily computerized. In the service classification, however, telecommunications is a clear standout. The insurance business had reasonably strong

productivity growth for a while after its early introduction of computers but the trend does not appear to have continued. Productivity in the telephone business not only maintained a traditional growth rate but by some measures grew faster than ever from 1973 up to the latest data. The telephone business was and is an intensive user of both phase one and phase two computing. [65]

18. Suppose we followed a "hedonic" productivity measurement approach similar to the one now used for the computer industry, which counts the product as the peak number of calculations the average computer can do. For the telephone business we might compute the number of potential point-to-point connections per employee and arrive at a gargantuan productivity gain of 10.2 percent per year from 1970 to 1990. It might seem somewhat more sensible to use telephone calls completed per employee; that would result in a gain of 7.6 percent per year from 1970 to 1987. [66]

19. By contrast, across the rest of private industry, wages in constant dollars decreased steadily during this period, by a total of 7.5 percent from 1970 to 1980, a predivestiture decade for which comparable data are available. In retail trade, FIRE (finance, insurance, and real estate), and direct services, the 1970 to 1980 decline was 12 percent. During the 1970s, the total labor force increased by 22 percent, telephone employment by 12 percent (Wright 1992). [66]

20. Other factors distinguish the telephone industry and may have contributed to its success. Regulation by federal and state governments encouraged intensive R&D aimed at productivity improvement. First, because prices were controlled, the only way in which telephone companies could get higher rates of return was to improve productivity between price settings. Second, regulators allowed the companies to count most R&D as necessary cost rather than deducting it from profit. Along with the sheer size of the Bell system, these factors produced Bell Laboratories (split after divestiture into Bell Labs and Bellcore), the largest concentration of industrial research in the world, which was an invaluable resource for analysis and innovation. [71]

Chapter 3

1. Up to here, these ideas are not new. For example, Lester Thurow (1981) put forward the hypothesis that productivity declines were due to a shift to services, and Baumol and Wolff (cited by Baily and Chakrabarti 1988) pointed out that many service activities did not or could not use technological amplifiers to produce growth. Moreover, Baily (1986) says that he and Gollop (1985) showed that "mix" effects, changing the proportion of labor in different sectors, did not explain the late 1970s slowdown. However, the analyses presented here put the matter in a somewhat different perspective and bring this line of explanation back to first place. [74]

2. The numbers are probably not too far off. My guess is that from 1973 to 1987, the service sector spent on the order of $1.5 trillion on computing. The

total of new value-added because of the sector's expansion was about the same. A sizable portion of the new workers in these industries was employed directly in supporting computer operations rather than in production. More precise calculations would not be worthwhile because data on such labor costs of computing as training time and intermediary services are not available. [75]

Chapter 4

1. The most noteworthy and prestigious example of explaining away the problem has come in one of the two reports published by the National Research Council. Its Committee to Study the Impact of Information Technology on the Performance of Service Activities had the participation of thirteen representatives of large computer-using service corporations and seven economists, sociologists, and computer scientists. Citing all of the excuses enumerated below, the committee decided to dismiss the productivity paradox as a nonproblem and to concentrate on developing advice on how to use the technology well. Readers who want a different view and conclusion from the one offered here can do no better than read this report. I find it wanting. In reviewing negative data, the authors are quick to claim irrelevance because of any possible flaw. In citing ostensibly positive data, they overlook most of the problems I have raised. In two examples reviewed here—their seven service industry analyses and their supermarket variety data—they fail to note clear implications of their own data that are at variance with their conclusions. There are minor lapses of the same kind in citing others' data. For example, they summarize the Cron and Sobel study of hospital suppliers as saying that some big users of IT did quite well and others poorly—a small effect—and neglect to mention that nonusers did better than users. They give a good deal of attention and approval to nonproductive competitive uses, which I find disappointing in an institution chartered to advise in the interests of the public. While calling the report a whitewash would be too harsh, I see in it a bias at least as strong as industry proponents will undoubtedly see in this book. Nevertheless, the report provides interesting new observations by industry spokespeople. Their reports, discussions, and recommendations on how to use and improve IT are thoughtful and informative. [83]

2. Since I have had some arguments with economists on this point, let me beat it just once more. Suppose Bresnehan had used the weight of computers in pounds (akin to wheat or cotton thread) as the measure and calculated the area under the demand curve—cumulative pounds of computers bought as the price per pound changed over time. The result would have been extremely different; it would look as if consumers had contributed mightily to the computer industry rather than vice versa, a vast "welfare spill-under." Now, of course, megapounds of computers is not the right measure. And that is the point; neither are megaflops or megabytes, and the choice of the right index for utility is both critical and extremely difficult. [86]

3. Weizenbaum (1976, 92). [88]

4. My hypothesis that computers made possible the continuity of employment during the decline of manufacturing is not incompatible with this argument. Computer-facilitated services are what we did for more work, not necessarily the only thing we could have done. Instead of more stockbrokers, programmers, and flight attendants, we might have decided to have more teachers, artists, actors, and strolling musicians (just as we decided to have more lawyers). [88]

5. Seventy-three percent of the companies said they had gotten acceptable to high returns on IT investments; the other 27 percent said that returns were negative or indeterminate. If we combined them roughly, we might estimate that the average for this group was modestly positive. Remember that this is for reports by people responsible for IT success in companies likely to be relatively successful (National Research Council 1994a). The committee notes that measurement problems were serious. [93]

6. Especially interesting is their critique of IT (in this case, computers and office machines) prices. In historical comparisons, the usual methods underestimate IT's share of purchases in early years and overestimate it in later years. [97]

7. Out of a total that they give here as 1.5 percent—thus, less than one-seventh of the problem. [98]

8. To get this number I started with the 1.25 percent residual shortfall in productivity growth described in chapter 1, that is, the amount by which the economy grew less rapidly postcomputers after taking into account all the usual factors, including estimates of some measurement errors. Compounding over twenty-one years, current GNP would be about 30 percent greater if growth had continued at the old rate.

Another way of getting this estimate is to tote up the money spent on computers since 1973 and ask what current earnings would be on the accumulated capital if the money had been invested in bonds instead of computers. Given the estimated zero marginal return on IT, that would give the amount we are forgoing for the pleasures of computing. The number is approximately the same. Both methods assume that there would have been some better capital to invest in all this time, which is not obvious. However, that is not the issue here; rather, the question is how much quality improvement we are talking about if we think IT investments were at least as good as others but simply went unmeasured. If we were to take Bresnehan's or Brynjolfsson's conclusions seriously, the unmeasured improvements would mount to many times as much; you would be receiving the vast majority of your "real" income in this form. [98]

9. These data come from *Information Technology in the Service Society: A Twenty-first Century Lever* (National Research Council 1994), which in turn cites annual issues of *The Supermarket Industry Speaks*, from Super Market Institute, Chicago. The earliest period, 1950–1957, well before computer impact, showed a 12 percent annual increase, while the latest three years in the series, 1982–1985, showed a 10.1 percent annual expansion. Interestingly, the NRC report uses these figures to argue that IT brought a "huge increase in the variety of products offered." [99]

10. Information on cereal varieties and ingredients cost from Chip Simons, "A Very Rich Food," *New York Times Magazine,* March 6, 1994, 13. [99]

11. Telephone companies have long employed an extensive and sophisticated attitude survey method for tracking customers' perceptions of the quality of services. Many other large businesses have begun to follow suit. However, I suspect that the matter needs a quantum jump in both magnitude of effort and sophistication. Suppose the BEA could find out that every 1 point increase in consumer satisfaction ratings translated into, say, a 9.5 percent increase in the market price for traditional easily counted products such as automobiles. They could then apply the same correction to the value of having ten varieties of checking accounts available instead of two. More sophistication is also possible at the psychological level, in accurately measuring value to the individual consumer. Considerable strides have been made in both theory and empirical knowledge in the relevant fields of behavioral measurement, and much of it has not yet found its way into practice. Indeed, economists generally ignore the matter entirely and obtain measures of utility only indirectly, by making it a variable in complex equations based on abstract—and questionable—assumptions fitted to gross economic data. [101]

12. But should we count Babbage's loom controllers the equivalent to Watt's engine? In that case computers have already had over a hundred years to succeed. [102]

13. I'm bending way over backward here. The first design of an automatic calculating machine was described by Babbage in the mid-1800s. The partly electrical (and fully "digital") punched card sorters and tabulators developed by Hollerith (whose company evolved into IBM) were used in the 1890 census to analyze data on 63 million people. These machines might easily bear comparison with Edison's dynamo as their bloodline's progenitor. The electromechanical telephone switches of the 1920s certainly could. The first machine *called* a digital computer was doing real war work at the University of Pennsylvania in 1946. Another comparison is with the first crude electric motors driven by hand-cranked electric generators, which were demonstrated in the early 1870s, only fifteen years before Hollerith's first hand-cranked tabulators. If we equate these two events, computers should have been having significant effects on productivity by 1940 if they were perfected and deployed as rapidly as electric motors. Moreover, by this equation, the two technologies shared some of their youthful growing period. David gets his comparison by counting as computers only those that use the latest generation of electronic technology. Following this strategy, we'll have to start the clock again when all-photonic devices appear. [103]

14. David also claims computers have still hardly started their diffusion because less than 10 percent of the businesses in the world have them. But we're not trying to explain a paradox in China. [103]

15. To be precise, in David's model it isn't how many firms have adopted the technology but what proportion of its potential output has been reached that determines when its maximum effects will be felt. Just as it took a long time to

apply electricity effectively almost everywhere that power was needed (it still isn't driving cars), it could still be a while before 70 percent of IT's latent output benefits are realized. Indeed, one reasonable view is that learning how to get there is the issue. [103]

16. The tendency of managers—and many economists—to consider computers as single, all-purpose tools, to be bought rather like electric motors and put to work wherever needed, rather than evaluating which particular application programs do useful things, is an important part of the problem. [104]

17. Below, I show that efficiency effects of text editors appeared to improve by 9.5 percent per year over one six-year period for which data are available. On the other hand, computer-based instruction showed almost no improvement over time following its first introduction. By contrast, the compounded change in cotton thread production over the fifty-two-year-period of 1838–1890, after the "perfection" of spinning machines, was about 12 percent per year, the improvement between 1868 and 1879, at the height of innovation, was over 50 percent per year (Mokyr 1990). [105]

18. Imagine asking a telephone company if that industry's government reporting activities, including reports to regulators, are lighter than average. [106]

19. An audience member at one of my talks even suggested that the common denominator for most of the period of slow productivity growth has been Republican administrations in Washington. David suggests that the baby boom that began hitting the labor force in the late 1960s was hard to absorb and may have diluted the output-to-labor ratio. [106]

Chapter 5

1. If all business files could be stored exclusively on computer, the saving in floor space alone could sometimes pay for the equipment. A typical 1990 disk drive held the equivalent of 10,000 to 500,000 (depending on the amount of graphics, font, white space, coding scheme, etc.) pages of text in the volume of a shoebox and cost under $3,000 in quantity. Not only do accounting practices make it hard to justify computer purchases against building rental costs, but various factors have conspired to make it necessary to continue to store many records in paper even when they are also available electronically. [117]

2. Some will argue that speech or handwriting recognition will eventually replace typing. I doubt it, for several reasons. One is that handwriting is slower than typing and unlikely ever to be as accurate; consider how well humans can read each other's. Writing is probably harder to learn than typing; if we forgo one of them eventually, it may be handwriting (just as we are gradually surrendering arithmetic skills). Second, speech is faster at full clip—perhaps 150 words per minute versus 75 for a current well-trained citizen. At ordinary operating speeds, when you are thinking before speaking, the rates are much closer. Moreover, we can reasonably expect computers to help more with typing in the future. For example, as everyone learns computer-based typing, shorthand-like shortcuts can

easily be added to everyone's repertoire, the machine can learn to predict the ends of the long words you most frequently type, and so forth. Third, given the past rate of improvement in speech recognition technology, it will be a long time before its speed and accuracy approach that of skilled typing (and accuracy may never be as high for fundamental reasons such as the choice between homonyms). Before it gets close, most people may be typing fast enough. [121]

3. See Strassmann (1990, 447–451) and Baily and Chakrabarti (1988) for further discussion and examples. [124]

Chapter 6

1. You're beginning to think I have special talent for defeating service computers. I don't think so; I think I just notice more and am less tolerant than most people. [142]

2. Some of my artificial intelligence and cognitive scientist colleagues will take umbrage at this. No insult is intended, only realism. We have some interesting theories and can do some cool stuff, but let's not kid ourselves. [142]

3. Except in the too-prevalent use of "camera-ready copy" for the pasting together of ugly, low-legibility budget textbooks and scholarly publications. [151]

4. In a stunning example of how lack of end-to-end integration can defeat the value of IT, the printers to whom this publisher sends manuscripts (*manuscript* comes from Latin for "handwritten") key them into one the special formats needed by "automated" printing equipment. [152]

5. Strassmann cites these same cases as failures of proper management of computer development, without even mentioning the deficiencies of their design. Indeed, in general, his book offers a rather different diagnosis of the computer productivity problem from mine. He is primarily concerned with computers as business tools for maximizing competitive advantage and profit, so he focuses on the relative advantage to a single firm rather the overall productivity of the world. In addition, he believes it is all a problem of management. He tacitly assumes that the computer systems will always do what they should; there are no fundamental problems in design, only in how the deployment process is managed. My view is that deployment management is only a part of the problem. Moreover, management wisdom, hints, and exhortations will not be sufficient to cure even that aspect; a more rigorous approach is required. [166]

Chapter 8

1. A well-established psychological principle, the Hick-Hyman law, says that, other things equal, the time to make a choice is proportional to the logarithm of the number of alternatives. [190]

2. Given the way purchase decisions are being made, basing advertising claims

and product reviews on reputation, subjective impressions, and opinion gathering may be appropriate. Such measures might reflect sales potential and future customer satisfaction ratings better than accurate measures of usability or work efficiency would. Sad. [190]

3. In a serious sense, icons are a throwback to the early forms of writing used in Egypt and Central America. There was a good reason that these were replaced in later writing systems. The new medium of computer screens seems sometimes to cast designers into a state of grace from which they start back up the evolutionary path of symbolic communication, reinventing abandoned forms in turn. We already have icons in place of words, scrolls instead of pages. Colored illuminations in the margins should be here soon. [190]

Chapter 9

1. It's difficult to make accurate comparisons with earlier technological advances on a bang-for-buck basis. However, the earlier example of cotton thread manufacture is suggestive. The gain in yards per worker hour was about 30,000 percent over fifty years, but the spinning machine supervised by one worker was very much more expensive than the simple spindle of the Indian hand weaver or the wheel of a European cottage. Moreover, the megabit, megaflop machine on my desk is (usually) operated by just me, whereas its much more expensive mainframe forebear needed extra tending when operating at full clip. [199]

2. PC-based text editing evolved in the late 1970s out of magnetic-tape typewriters and time-shared computer system applications introduced in the late 1960s. Spreadsheets were invented in 1979. Computer-based instruction started in the mid-1960s. [200]

3. What is shown in the graph of figure 9.2 is improvements in the total time to finish a course. There was also about 6 percent per year improvement in the amount learned as assessed by exams. [201]

4. Neither result was statistically meaningful. Figure 9.1 shows the best results, the adult learning learning curve. Oddly, more recent papers on computers and instruction contain almost no quantitative evaluation. For example, a recent edition of *Communications of the ACM,* the journal most widely read by computer professionals and researchers, was devoted to computers in K–12 education. With virtually no exceptions, the closest to evaluations in the twenty-one papers by leaders in the field were glowing anecdotal reports of the accomplishments of projects selected because they were reputed to be successful and recounted by their sponsors and proponents. The history of educational methods is full of techniques that have dramatic results in the hands of their devotees but fail when passed on to others. Good teachers can make most methods succeed. [201]

5. Statistically, the upward trend is significant despite the small number of cases measured. A correlation this large (.79) would occur by chance less than one time in a hundred. On the other hand, we can't take the exact percentage gain too

seriously; there is a good chance that it would be off by half if we had many more cases to go on. [202]

6. As we will note later, this character matrix editor is an especially intriguing data point because the other high scorers were all more "modern" GUI types. It was developed using iterative test-and-fix user-centered design. [203]

Chapter 10

1. Important individual technologies in mechanical agriculture, scientific crop improvement, and rational medicine had similar life histories. Once the fundamental scientific and technical innovations were accomplished, 50 to 100-year periods of application had hundred-fold and greater impacts on their immediate targets. [205]

2. I won't mention playing basketball. We don't even have a robot player who could sit on the bench effectively yet, but the productivity consequences of having an automated nine-foot center, though it would certainly be a service industry employee, are unclear. [210]

3. The efficiency gain estimates in the top portion of table 10.1 have a mean of 167 percent and a median somewhere between 43 percent and 66 percent. These numbers should be interpreted cautiously. They apply to a wide variety of tasks, often to only selected parts of jobs, mostly to relatively unpracticed users. Some come from studies of laboratory prototypes rather than systems in use. They should be taken to show the potential of UCDesign more than its actual accomplishments in full-scale working systems. Estimates were calculated from data in the following sources: Burns, Warren, and Rudisill (1986); Egan et al. (1989); Gould, Boies, and Lewis (1991); Instone, Teasley, and Leventhal (1993); Karat (1990); Keister and Gallaway (1983); Nielsen (1993a, 1993b); Roberts and Moran (1983); Savage and Habinek (1984); Temple, Barker, & Sloan (1990); Tullis (1981); Whiteside, Bennett, and Holtzblatt (1988). [223]

4. The concept of a design cycle is somewhat fuzzy. Even if formal evaluation is going on, development projects rarely wait for a system to be finished before making alterations based on reports and suggestions. In trying to pin down some numbers, I've been mostly interested in how much gain can be expected from the UCDesign activity that can be built into a development project. Thus, if a system is developed in a series of releases or versions and each profits from a good evaluation and feedback process, I'd count each version or release as a UCDesign cycle. This roughly distinguishes a design cycle from small, ongoing incremental development changes on the one hand, and on the other from the kinds of redesigns that occur after systems have outlived their markets and are revised in response to competition, saturation, or obsolescence. The criterion may seem vague, but the point is to understand what UCD can accomplish over and above market evolution. [223]

5. The Nielsen and Levy survey found 106 reports of objective measures of per-

formance time for two comparable computer systems, features, or methods. The things compared were a mixed bag of input devices, menu arrangements, screen layouts, and so forth. Which of the two compared was newer or believed to be better was often not clear. Nonetheless, overall, there was an average efficiency difference between one and the other of 28 percent. However, the analysis cannot stop here. Work efficiency measurements are not perfectly accurate. Some of the differences must have been due to chance factors such as which test subject was assigned to which system. To correct for this, I used measures of the variability between subjects that were available for fifteen similar studies in the literature. The average of these led to an estimate of how much the means for each system would vary because of measurement error. Assuming that such errors come from a normal distribution, the expected difference between the larger and smaller of two observations that differ only by chance was 9 percent. Thus, it is reasonable to suppose that 9 percent of the 28 percent was chance and should be subtracted out, for the 19 percent shown in the table.

(To be brutally technical about this, I first computed mean absolute differences on the main sample. Then, because there were no within-treatment variances available for that sample, I took the mean standard error from another, presumably comparable but smaller, sample of studies as an estimate of the population standard deviation. Then I multiplied by the expected difference between the smallest and largest observation in a sample of two as found in a table of order statistics for the normal distribution to get the correction factor. I did the same with Roberts and Moran's measurements of nine text editors. In this case, the variability of subjects was reported, and was similar to the previous estimate, so fewer assumptions are needed. However, the text editors Roberts and Moran studied are probably considerably more different from one another than the average two systems picked at random and differ partly through something closely akin to UCDesign effects. [224]

6. The Bailey experiment cited above probably had no "pride of publication" bias. Not only would Bailey probably have published it no matter how it came out, but it is the only controlled experiment of the kind, positive or negative, that I know of. [225]

7. Some of the efficiency effects of individual component features of the Mac-style GUI have also been evaluated. Card, Robert, and Keenen (1984) found pointing with a mouse to be about 60 percent more efficient than the worst device, step keys, with which it was compared, with other types giving intermediate values. Others have found less advantage, depending on task and design variations (Greenstein and Arnaut 1988). The use of menus has a checkered evaluation history, without a clearly defined win over the preceding command or function key approaches; menus probably have an advantage for some tasks and users and a disadvantage for others. (Paap and Roske-Hofstrand 1988). The advantage of the graphical nature of the interface has been the subject of considerable claims (and acclaim), but there is little direct evidence of its influence on task efficiency, as distinct from user appeal, where it is a clear winner. How about windows?

One study suggested that windows are not an unmixed blessing; some tasks are slower and more error prone in a windowed interface (Bury et al. 1985). The windowing system in this study appeared to be relatively primitive and poorly designed from a usability perspective. But the point here is that windows versus no windows may not be what matters in GUI so much as getting the windowing system and interaction right (Whiteside et al. 1985). [226]

8. There are other data on GUIs versus CUIs. Some show similar differences, some larger, some smaller. Roberts and Moran report that the display editors in their study averaged about twice as fast as the nondisplay editors. Egan and Gomez, after the study shown in figure 10.2, found about 60 percent greater efficiency for a new display version of the editor, but their analysis showed that the advantage was due to easier means for indicating the location of an intended change and that it could also be achieved in a redesign of the character-based line editor. By applying UCD, Michael Good at DEC was able to produce a non-GUI text editor that scored as high on their benchmarks as all but one of the GUI editors measured by Roberts and Moran. The worst result came from a recent European cooperative project that measured professional secretaries' use of a GUI word processor compared with a menu-driven version of the same program. Some measures were better with the GUI version, but costly errors were more frequent, and the authors report that "there is no overall difference in the total task time" (Houwing, Withoff, and Arnold 1993). Nevertheless, as in many other studies, users expressed a distinct preference for the graphical interface.

The variation in efficiency effects between studies is quite large and the reasons for differences unclear but one might guess at this point that GUI techniques offer a technical base that has the potential for improvements in the 50 to 100 percent region, depending on the application, but realizable only when they are properly assembled and polished. [226]

9. The mere presence of any interface technique or feature does not necessarily increase usability. That is not to say that good interface elements cannot be used to good effect; they can. However, just as sodium must be properly combined with chlorine to make table salt, interface components must be put together right to make usability. Just being menu based or graphical is not enough. Interface designers and marketers, and users as well, have been sold on windows, menus, icons, mice, and graphics largely by the success of the Macintosh. What about these techniques as such? There have been several laboratory studies of the use of menus versus typed-in commands (Paap and Roske-Hofstrand 1988). The surprising result is that commands have usually won. Both novices and experienced users were not only faster with commands than with menus, but having tried both for the same task, tended to prefer commands. A similar surprise comes from research on icons. For some tasks that have been studied, correctly selecting an option described with a single word or a short abbreviation was easier than picking the right icon. Results of experiments comparing the mouse with keys for pointing are more ambiguous but also don't show a clear and universal advantage (Greenstein 1988). Such experiments have been limited; they may not have used the best-designed menus and icons, and they have studied only a few user

tasks. Nevertheless, they make my point clearly enough: menus, icons, or mice do not equal usability.

Nevertheless, WIMP (window, icon, menu, pointer) interfaces have great sales appeal. Without doubt, the availability of these elements gives interface designers a richer palette. With them they can fashion more aesthetically appealing screens and novel and interesting modes of interaction. Icons have the advantage of taking up less screen space, so more functions and features can be made available at once. Windows offer the user quick access to several different applications. Mice provide an alternative selection and editing device that many people like. Many user interface experts have proposed that the ability to move pictured objects about on the screen or to interact with them by pointing is more natural and appealing than telling the computer what to do in words. Properly put together, these parts can be used to fashion very good tools. Even if the end result is not greater work efficiency, it may still be a significant style advantage. Style matters. Autos and clothes are bought for style as well as function; why not computers? But don't assume that because an interface draws more customers it is necessarily more productive. [227]

10. Some of the proponents of reengineering want to combine it with the measurement aspects of the quality improvement movement. This could make it almost indistinguishable from UCD, at least with regard to figuring out what to do with technology, as compared with how to get the necessary technology designed and developed. I've counted doing what they urge as part of the promise of UCD; someone else might want to claim that doing so is what will make a rosier prediction than mine in the absence of UCD. [232]

11. A different way of arriving at an overall productivity guess is to extrapolate from the history of how individual process efficiency gains translate into labor productivity. There's not much precedent. I keep falling back on textiles because it offers a clearer case than most. From 1973 to 1985 there were 65 percent annual efficiency gains in some central processes but only 4.5 percent overall productivity gains—a ratio of fifteen to one. A perhaps more relevant success story is the telephone business, where the greatest efficiency gain was in the operator's job. Annual improvements in calls per operator averaged 15 percent between 1970 and 1980. Overall labor productivity growth in the roughly comparable 1973–1983 period averaged about 5 to 6 percent a year, a much more favorable ratio of only two and a half or three to one. Applying textile's fifteen to one to the 40 to 80 percent range would give 2.7 to 5.3 percent; jacking it up with indirect effects and expected expansion of UCD's sphere of influence would get us into the same ballpark we just left. Applying the telephone companies' ratio would hit the ball out of the park. [236]

Chapter 11

1. This is a prototypical phase two mental aid; it doesn't steer the car, just tells you where to go. [239]

2. "During early prototype testing . . . it was discovered that typical initial users could not read even a single mail message no matter how hard they tried during an hour's use of the system" (Good et al. 1984). The report does not give quantitative data on how well users performed at the end. However, I have an idea of the possible end point because we followed their example in designing an easy-to-use electronic mail interface called POMS (for Plain Old Message System). Almost every user has been able to send and read an email message within about two minutes of use, with no instruction of any kind. [240]

3. You wonder why this book is right justified? The publisher would be ashamed to do otherwise. [249]

4. Bellcore is a research, development, and engineering organization formed to serve the regional telephone companies after AT&T's divestiture in 1984. [251]

5. Writing this section provided an interesting example of the promise and problems of hypertext. The main previous method referred to here is Boolean search, and it would have been better to discuss it here rather than blithely brushing it aside as inferior. However, that would have interrupted the flow of ideas about solving the vocabulary mismatch problem. So I put Booleans later, in a section on navigation, where they don't really fit. Suppose you were reading this book on a computer (I hope you are, actually). If there were a link to take you from here directly to the section on Booleans, would you have followed it? Would it have been a good idea for me to provide it? If you want to try it, jump now to the main text beginning with an asterisk (p. 260). Was putting this note—or a link to it—here, a good idea? [253]

6. An unusual and admirable characteristic of the work in information retrieval is that many of the techniques have been subjected to an empirical test that comes close to measuring the actual object of the systems. The ideal is for users to be able to find all and only those documents that they want. Researchers have assembled collections of documents, obtained genuine queries from real users, and then gone through the documents one by one and decided which ones are relevant to which queries. Techniques for matching a query with documents can be evaluated by how many relevant and irrelevant are returned. As retrieval systems have moved from batch versions operated by information specialists to interactive online systems for end users, this test method has become inappropriate, and nothing has replaced it. Another unfortunate aspect of the situation is that many of the workers in computer-based text delivery have been, at least until very recently, unaware of or at least uninfluenced by all of this work. Indeed the node and link organization of a database, as used in hypertext, was one of the original schemes tried for text storage and search but rapidly abandoned as unsuitable. [261]

7. Bellcore researchers have developed a technique based on a sophisticated statistical analysis of large bodies of text that somewhat gets around the vocabulary or synonym problem. The synonym problem is one of the main barriers to achieving better success in information retrieval. The Bellcore system improves the overall ability of users to find information by around 20 percent over the previous state of the art. To illustrate what that means, if you make a query with a current

top system and ask for its ten best guesses, you'll typically get four items you want and six that you don't. With our big advance, you'll get five and five. That still leaves a lot to be desired. [261]

8. The SuperBook text browser has gone through many changes and currently exists in many forms for different applications and platforms. To simplify, I've described here its common, basic features and illustrated an implementation that doesn't exactly match Version 0 or any other. For a more detailed description of version changes, see Landauer et al. (1993). [262]

9. In recent product versions Bellcore has responded to customer requests for the Boolean operators they are familiar with from other systems but have kept users out of harm's way by providing Booleans only as indirectly invoked options that are invisible in normal use. [264]

10. **tkl June 2, 1994 02:32:37.** If you had clicked on the little foot icon in the SuperBook version of this book, it would have popped up a window with this note in it. I left it in my SuperBook copy of this book on June 2, 1994, by clicking in the margin, then typing the plain text part of this text into an editing window that appeared on my screen. You could have found the note by searching for any word or words in it, say, *note*. The text of the note was added to the index immediately, my log-in and the date entered automatically.

(Aside: The foot icon violates a guideline forbidding visual puns. Tich.) [265]

11. A remark for the experimentally fastidious. The figures for the paper version baseline are based on data from the Version 0 and Version 1 tests combined. For Version 0 we used a within-subject design; counterbalanced halves of the subjects used the online and paper versions first, then the other. For Version 1, each group used only one of the methods. Results for the paper users were similar and statistically indistinguishable in all conditions and orders, as they have been in replications done subsequently. [267]

12. I've combined data from the various question types here. For rawer, more detailed data, consult Landauer et al. (1993) and its references. [267]

13. Keep in mind that this result is based on just one exam question for one group of students. But does it mean that average Ph.D.s would exceed average high school students on the same S manual exam—using the paper book—by the same amount? I can't say for sure, but it's not out of the question. The reading comprehension and problem-solving skills required by this open book essay exam are similar to those tapped by the major parts of IQ tests.

Does this mean that SuperBook has turned its users into Ph.D.s or raised their IQs? Hardly. However, for the half-hour spent answering this question, SuperBook users were much smarter, in the same way that anyone is smarter if he or she knows arithmetic and has a pencil when faced with a math problem. The temporary increase in ability seems to have had about the same effect on performance as a twenty-five-point gain in IQ.

Some of the subsequent SuperBook usability tests also included essay exams. SuperBook users have always surpassed paper book controls but not always by such a dramatic margin. Unsurprisingly, the benefit seems to depend on the amount and kind of material and the particular question. [270]

14. Here are a few more details about the Bowling Green study. Think of this, and most other notes, as much like the kind of blind outgoing links that are the major feature of hypertext, ones that lead you to a surprise chosen by the author. Between the unsuccessful first and successful second versions of HyperHolmes, the use of such link features went down by half, while the use of keyword search doubled. All questions in the Bowling Green tests included words that appeared in the title or text body containing the answer. Since these questions are easier than ones for which users have to come up with the matching words themselves and are more directly aided by computer keyword search, the advantages may be slightly overstated. [273]

Chapter 12

1. For a task-analytic approach to dialogue design, see Phillips et al. (1988) and Drury (1983). [278]

2. There have been a few honorable and brave reports of sequences of iterative tests in which each successive design did more poorly than the one before. If these efforts had stopped too early, the total gain from UCD would have been zero; the developers would have chosen the first design. I suspect that the problem in these cases was that the evaluation was done in a summative fashion; no guiding detailed data were produced. After each test, the designers simply started over and did it some other way. With nothing more to go on, the designers' first guess was probably better than their second guess. [281]

3. There is some difference among experts in their ability to catch usability bugs. Hire ten experts to evaluate the same interface; the best will find twice as many problems as the worst. But almost half the difference will be due to luck, so picking consultants this way is likely to be expensive (Nielsen and Molich 1990). [284]

4. This is no surprise. Research on group problem solving has repeatedly shown that when a problem requires expertise, the best individual in the group usually would have found a better solution than the one arrived at by consensus (while the consensus solution is better than the average individual's). Consensus builds cohesion, commitment, and morale but does not always use information in an optimal way (Taylor, Berry, and Block 1958). Just so, expert evaluators in a group will probably not find as many total problems as they would working independently. [285]

5. The matter of variety raises a sticky conflict between marketing and productivity. Programmers and feature-list happy reviewers are not the only ones who like lots of alternatives. Users themselves often profess such a preference. In one study, 94 percent of users said they wanted both keyword entry and menu choice (Lee et al. 1986). Yet as we have seen, there is ample evidence that some methods are significantly more efficient than others, that extra choices confuse and slow both learning and performance, and that even experts do not always choose the best method for a given task (Barnard 1987; Nilsen et al. 1992). [293]

Chapter 13

1. The point at which the next test costs more than its expected payoff comes earlier. Nonetheless, even in the small system case, this doesn't happen until the tenth test. Thus, nine assessments are optimal in terms of total dollar benefit derived. For larger systems the optimum number is much larger. For example, in the hypothetical case illustrated in figure 10.1, forty-seven tests would return the greatest total value. However, there are usually good reasons to stop earlier. [305]

2. See Landauer (1988) for further discussion of statistical methods in usability assurance. [306]

3. Wasserman (1991) says the eventual redesign magic came from linking his group's human-performance model of the user with Lucy Suchman's model of human behavior in social context and the creation of the Trillium rapid human interface prototyping tool by Austin Henderson. [307]

4. The hard and easy curves are for the expected fifth and ninety-fifth percentile, respectively. Precise numbers from fitting a theory to the data and then predicting on the basis of the normal distribution are 30 percent, 51 percent, and 13 percent; round numbers have been used in the text and figures. [312]

5. By this point, there will be enough data to estimate the total number and the proportion being found per test with considerable accuracy. [312]

6. Which curve a testing program is on can be determined with sufficient accuracy by the following simple procedure. Make six assessments, either heuristic evaluations or user tests—three of each if feasible. Classify and tally all the different usability problems found in any assessment. Then create a table with a row for each problem and a column for each assessment. Next compare each pair of assessments. There will be fifteen comparisons, each column against each of the others. For each comparison, mark and count all the separate problems found by the two combined. Then mark and count those that were found by both assessments. Divide the latter by the former. Average these numbers for all the pairs, and divide by two. This yields the average proportion of the problems found by one assessment that are found by another. By theory this is also the proportion of the total that is found by each assessment. The number, **d**, is given for each of the curves in figure 10.2. If the calculated **d** is not close to one of the pictured curves, it's probably enough to sketch a similar-shaped curve interpolated in the approximately correct position on the graph.

This much will tell how many assessments are likely to be needed to catch any desired proportion of the total errors. The last step is to estimate the total itself. An easy approximate for this step is to divide the average number of problems found in one assessment by **d**. Thus, if the foregoing calculations led to the conclusion that each assessment found an average of one-quarter of the problems and single assessments found twenty problems on average, then there were probably $20/0.25 = 80 +/- 12$ (the 15 percent margin for 95 percent confidence) total problems. In other words, if the average assessment finds a quarter of the problems, then the total is four times what the average assessment finds.

Once **d** has been estimated, some of the other approximations mentioned above can be improved. For example, the number of tests needed to halve the remaining problems is seven if **d** is .1, and one if **d** is .5. The number of tests with no new problems needed to conclude—with 95 percent confidence—that there are no more to be found is 28 if **d** is .1 and 5 if **d** is .5.

There are some minor errors in this procedure due to simplifying assumptions. For a more rigorous derivation and more accurate estimation methods see Nielsen and Landauer (1993). [313]

7. While there are obviously some unstated assumptions here, they are not hard to accept. The successful UCD cases enumerated earlier seldom relied on more than two or three rounds of testing, so it is unlikely that they found more than twice the number of flaws a single series of, say, four to six tests would have revealed. I have already noted that the first flaws found tend to be more serious. There is no reason to believe that early detected flaws are harder to fix than the average. Moreover, quick testing should lend itself to application at earlier points in development when changes are easier. [313]

8. Nielsen was not aiming at user speed; accuracy was the goal. However, the experimenters did record times. A rough estimate of the efficiency gain is the number of correct answers per minute. It increased by 41 percent. Of course, this is just the efficiency of reading the statement. We would really want to know the effects on peoples' efficiency in managing their finances. Correct versus incorrect reading of a bank statement could be a trivial matter, or it could snowball into an enormous productivity loss. [314]

9. For example, Nielsen and Phillips (1993) looked at how well the better of two designs for a particular interface could be chosen by different usability assessment methods. The system was an integrated front end intended to allow telephone office personnel to access data in several different database machines in a coordinated fashion. They found that it took two user tests of each version, three heuristic evaluations or two expert calculations using the GOMS keystroke model, which was nicely applicable in this case, to pick the winner with 95 percent confidence. [315]

Chapter 14

1. To make matters worse, the measure—sales per employee—counts longer work hours resulting from the recent layoff epidemic as productivity gains. [323]

2. *Wall Street Journal,* March 1, 1993. [327]

3. C. Ciborra and L. Schneider, paper at Technology and the Future of Work Conference, Stanford, March 28–30, 1990, as cited by Majchrzak (1992). [330]

4. Talks to an MIT industrial affiliates conference in 1992. [332]

5. This is an informal description of a lagged panel quasi-experimental research design. By having different before-after experiments at different but overlapping times, it is possible to separate changes due to time and extraneous changes in

the world from ones attributable to the experimental variable. This powerful and robust method often can be surprisingly easy to apply. [340]

6. Controlled studies are rare in the business and economics literature. There have been several that looked at morale and worklife effects, with mixed results (Kling 1991). Strassmann (1985, page 38), says, "Morale and a positive attitude had a greater effect on the final outcome than did technology" in a case of office automation. Strassmann reports two comparisons between an office that gets a system and one that doesn't, finding benefits of around 30 percent. [342]

Chapter 16

1. *Function Reference, Microsoft Excel,* Microsoft Corporation, 1992. [362]

References

Anderson, J. R., and Reiser, B. J. (1985). The LISP tutor. *Byte* (April), 159–175.

Attewell, P. (1994). Information technology and the productivity paradox. In D. H. Harris (eds), *Organizational Linkages: Understanding the Productivity Paradox*. Washington, DC: National Academy Press.

Attewell, P., and Rule, J. (1984). Computing and organizations: What we know and what we don't know. *Communications of the ACM, 27*(12), 1184–1191.

Avner, A. R. (1979). Production of computer-based instructional materials. In H. F. O'Neil (ed.), *Issues in Instructional Systems Development*. New York: Academic Press.

Bailey, G. (1993). Iterative methodology and designer training in human-computer interface design. In *INTERCHI'93 Conference on Human Factors in Computing Systems* (pp. 24–29). Amsterdam: ACM.

Baily, M. N. (1982). Productivity growth slowdown by industry. *Brookings Papers on Economic Activities, 2*, 423–454.

Baily, M. N. (1986a). Productivity and the electronics revolution. *Bell Atlantic Quarterly, 3*, 39–48.

Baily, M. N. (1986b). What has happened to productivity growth? *Science*(234), 443–451.

Baily, M., and Chakrabarti, A. K. (1988). *Innovation and the Productivity Crisis*. Washington DC: Brookings Institution.

Baily, M. N., and Gordon, R. J. (1988). *The Productivity Slowdown, Measurement Issues, and the Explosion of Computer Power* (No. 1199). Cambridge, MA: National Bureau of Economic Research.

Baran, B. (1987). The technological transformation of white collar work: A case study of the insurance industry. In H. I. Hartmann (ed.), *Computer Chips and Paper Clips: Technology and Women's Employment* (pp. 25–62). Washington, DC: National Academy Press.

Barnard, P. (1987). Cognitive resources and the learning of human-computer dialogues. In J. M. Carroll (ed.), *Interfacing Thought: Cognitive Aspects of Human-Computer Interaction*. Cambridge, MA: MIT Press.

Barnard, P. J., and Grudin, J. (1988). Command names. In M. Helander (ed.), *Handbook of Human-Computer Interaction*. Amsterdam: North-Holland.

Barnard, P. J., Hammond, N. V., Morton, J., Long, J. B., and Clark, I. A. (1981). Consistency and compatibility in human-computer dialogue. *International Journal of Man-Machine Studies, 15*, 87–134.

Becker, R. A., and Chambers, J. M. (1984). *S: An Interactive Environment for Data Analysis and Graphics*. Belmont, CA: Wadsworth.

Bellotti, V. (1990). A framework for assessing HCI techniques. In *Interact '90* (pp. 213–218). Amsterdam: Elsevier Science Publishers.

Benoit, C., Cossette, A., and Cardillo, P. (1984). *L'Incidence de la machine à traitement de textes sur l'emploi et le travail*. Ministère du Travail, Canada.

Blair, D. C., and Maron, M. E. (1985). An evaluation of retrieval effectiveness for a full-text document-retrieval system. *Communications of the ACM, 28*, 280–299.

Block, J. H., and Bums, R. B. (1978). Mastery learning. In L. Shulman (ed.), *Review of Research in Education, 4*, Itsaca, IL: Peacock Publishers.

Bloom, B. S. (1984). The 2 sigma problem: The search for methods of group instruction as effective as one to one tutoring. *Educational Researcher, 13*, 4–16.

Boehm, B. W. (1981). *Software Engineering Economics*. Englewood Cliffs, NJ: Prentice-Hall.

Borgman, C. L. (1986). Why are online catalogs hard to use? Lessons learned from information-retrieval studies. *Journal of the American Association for Information Science, 37*(6), 387–400.

Brand, H., and Duke, J. (1982). Productivity in commercial banking: Computers spur advance. *Monthly Labor Review, 105* (December), 19–27.

Bresnehan, T. F. (1986). Measuring the spillovers from technological advance: Mainframe computers in financial services. *American Economic Review, 76* (September), 742–755.

Brooks, F. P. (1987). No silver bullet: Essence and accidents of software engineering. *IEEE Computer, 20*, 10–19.

Brooks, F. P. J. (1975). *The Mythical Man-Month*. Reading, MA: Addison-Wesley.

Brown, C. M. L. (1988). *Human-Computer Interface Design Guidelines*. Norwood, NJ: Ablex.

Brown, J. S. (1991). Research that reinvents the corporation. *Harvard Business Review* (January–February), 102–111.

Brynjolfsson, E., and Hitt, L. (1993). *New Evidence on the Returns to Information Systems*. Cambridge, MA: MIT.

Brynjolfsson, E., Malone, T. W., Gurbaxani, V., and Kambil, A. (1994). Does information technology lead to smaller firms? *Management Science* (in press).

Bureau of Labor Statistics (1993). *Employment and Earnings 40,* no 12.

Burns, M. J., Warren, D. L., and Rudisill, M. (1986). Formatting space-related displays to optimize expert and nonexpert user performance. In *CHI'89 Human Factors in Computing Systems* (pp. 274–280). Boston: Association for Computing Machinery.

Bury, K. F., Boyle, J. M., Evey, R. J., and Neal, A. S. (1985). Windowing versus scrolling on a visual display terminal. *Human Factors, 24*(4), 385–394.

Card, S. K., Moran, T., and Newell, A. (1983). *The Psychology of Human Computer Interaction.* Hillsdale, NJ: Earlbaum.

Card, S. K., Robert, J. M., and Keenen, L. N. (1984). On-line composition of text. In *Proceedings of Interact '84* 1 (pp. 231–236). London: Elsevier.

Chapman, S. D. (1972). *The Cotton Industry in the Industrial Revolution.* London: Macmillan.

CIM success depends on people (1985). *Computer Graphics Today,* pp. 4, 14.

Clark, R. E. (1985). Evidence for confounding in computer-based instruction studies: Analyzing the meta-analysis. *Educational Communication and Technology, 33*(4), 249–262.

Cleverdon, C. (1979). Letter to the editor. *Information Science, 1*(4), 237–238.

Cron, W. L., and Sobel, M. G. (1983). The relationship between computerization and performance: A strategy for maximizing the economic benefits of computerization. *Information and Management, 6,* 171–181.

Cronbach, L. J., and Snow, R. E. (1977). *Aptitudes and Instructional Methods.* New York: Irington.

Cutler, K., and Rowe, C. (1990). Scanning in the supermarket: For better or worse? A case study in introducing electronic point of sale. *Behaviour and Information Technology, 9*(2), 157–169.

David, P. A. (1990). The dynamo and the computer: An historical perspective on the modern productivity paradox. *American Economic Review, 80*(2), 355–361.

David, P. A. (1991). Computer and dynamo: The modern productivity paradox in a not too distant mirror. In *Proceedings of OCED* (pp. 315–347). Paris:

Deming, W. E., (1982). Improvement of quality and productivity through action by management. *National Productivity Review* (Winter), 1991–2, 12–22.

Denison, E. F. (1989). *Estimates of Productivity Change by Industry.* Washington, DC: Brookings Institution.

Dertouzos, M. L. (1990). *Computers and Productivity.* Cambridge, MA: MIT Laboratory for Computer Science.

Dertouzos, M. L., Lester, R. K., and Solow, R. M. (1989). *Made in America: Regaining the Productivity Edge.* Cambridge, MA: MIT Press.

Doob, A. N., Carlsmith, J. M., Freedman, J. L., Landauer, T. K., and Tom, S. Jr. (1969). Effect of initial selling price on subsequent sales. *Journal of Personality and Social Psychology*, 345–350.

Drucker, P. (1988). Information is data endowed with relevance and purpose. *Harvard Business Review* (January–February), 45–53.

Drucker, P. F. (1991). The New productivity challenge. *Harvard Business Review* (November–December).

Drury, C. G. (1983). Task analysis methods in industry. *Applied Ergonomics*, *14*(1), 19–28.

Dumais, S. T., and Landauer, T. K. (1984). Describing categories of objects for menu retrieval systems. *Behavior Research Methods, Instruments and Computers*, *16*(2), 242–248.

Dumais, S. T., and Schmitt, D. G. (1991). Iterative searching in an online database. In *Proceedings of Human Factors Society* (pp. 396–402). Santa Monica, CA: Human Factors Society.

Dumais, S. T., and Wright, A. L. (1986). Reference by name vs. location in a computer filing system. In *Proceedings of Human Factors Society* (pp. 824–828). Santa Monica, CA: Human Factors Society.

East, H. (1980). Comparative costs of manual and on-line bibliographical searching: A review of the literature. *Journal of Information Science, 2*, 101–109.

Eberts, R. E., and Brock, J. F. (1988). Computer-based instruction. In M. Helander (ed.), *Handbook of Human-Computer Interaction* (pp. 599–627). New York: Elsevier Science Publishers.

Egan, D. E. (1988). Individual differences in human computer interaction. In M. Helander (ed.), *Handbook of Human Computer Interaction* (pp. 543–568). Amsterdam: North-Holland.

Egan, D. E., and Gomez, L. M. (1985). Assaying, isolating and accommodating individual differences in learning a complex skill. In R. Dillon (ed.), *Individual Differences in Cognition*. New York: Academic Press.

Egan, D. E., Remde, J. R., Gomez, L. M., Landauer, T. K., Eberhart, J., and Lochbaum, C. C. (1989). Formative design-evaluation of SuperBook. *ACM Transactions on Information Systems, 7*(1), 30–57.

Enslow, B. (1989). The payoff from expert systems. *Across the Board* (January–February 1989), 54–58.

Feigenbaum, E. A., McCorduck, P., and Nii, H. P. (1988). *The Rise of the Expert Company: How Visionary Companies Are Using Artificial Intelligence to Achieve Higher Productivity and Profits*. New York: Time Books.

Feldberg, R. L., and Glenn, E. N. (1987). Technology and the transformation of clerical work. In R. E. Kraut (ed.), *Technology and the Transformation of White Collar Work*. Hillsdale, NJ: Erlbaum.

Fitts, P. M. (1954). The information capacity of the human motor system in controlling the amplitude of movement. *Journal of Experimental Psychology, 47,* 301–391.

Fontaine, M. B. (1992). *L'Informatique de l'état: Evaluation du développement de l'informatique et de son impact sur l'efficacité de l'administration.* Paris: La Documentation Française.

Franke, R. H. (1987). Technological revolution and productivity decline: Computer introduction in the financial industry. *Technology Forecasting and Social Change, 31,* 143–154.

Furnas, G. W. (1985). Experience with an adaptive indexing scheme. In *Proceedings of CHI'85* (pp. 16–23). New York: ACM.

Furnas, G. W., Landauer, T. K., Gomez, L., M., and Dumais, S. T. (1987). The vocabulary problem in human system communication. *Communications of the ACM, 30*(11), 964–971.

Gabor, A. (1992). After the pay revolution, job titles won't matter. *New York Times,* May 17, Business Section, p. 5.

Gagne, R. M. (1974). *Principles of Instructional Design.* New York: Holt.

Gagne, R. M. (ed.). (1987). *Instructional Technology: Foundations.* Hillsdale, NJ: Erlbaum.

Gillain, N. (1992). L'Ordinateur est-il soluble dans l'administration publique? *Le Quotidien de Paris,* November 12, p. 13.

Goldsmith, J. (1994). CYC-O. *Wired* (April), 94.

Gollup, F. M. (1985). Analysis of the productivity slowdown: Evidence for a sector-biased or sector-neutral industrial strategy. In W. J. Baumol and K. McLennan (eds.), *Productivity Growth and U.S. Competitiveness* (pp. 160–186). New York: Oxford University Press.

Gomez, L. M., Egan, D. E., Wheeler, E. A., Sharma, D. K., and Gruchacz, A. M. (1983). How interface design determines who has difficulty learning to use a text editor. In *Proceedings of CHI'83 Human Factors in Computing Systems* (pp. 176–181). New York: Association for Computing Machinery.

Gomez, L. M., Lochbaum, C. C., and Landauer, T. K. (1990). All the right words: Finding what you want as a function of richness of indexing vocabulary. *Journal of the American Society for Information Science, 41,* 547–559.

Good, M. D., Whiteside, J. A., Wixon, D. R., and Jones, S. J. (1984). Building a user-derived interface. *Communications of the ACM, 27*(10), 1032–1043.

Gordon, J. A. (1989). Desktop publishing: Separating dreams from reality. *Public Relations Journal, 45*(11), 24–30.

Gould, J. D. (1981). Composing letters with computer-based text editors. *Human Factors, 23,* 593–606.

Gould, J. D. (1988). How to design usable systems. In M. Helander (ed.), *Handbook of Human Computer Interaction.* Amsterdam: North Holland.

Gould, J. D., Alfaro, L., Finn, R., Haupt, B., Minuto, A., and Salaun, J. (1987).

Why reading was slower from CRT displays than from paper. In *CHI + GI'87 Conference on Human Factors in Computing Systems,* (pp. 7–11). Toronto: ACM.

Gould, J. D., Boies, S. J., Levy, S., Richards, J. T., and Schoonard, J. (1987b). The 1984 Olympic message system: A test of behavioral principles of system design. *Communications of the ACM, 30*(9), 758–769.

Gould, J. D., Boies, S. J., and Lewis, C. (1991). Making usable, useful, productivity-enhancing computer applications. *Communications of the ACM, 34*(1), 75–85.

Gould, J. D., Conti, J., and Hovanyecz, T. (1983). Composing letters with a simulated typewriter. *Communications of the ACM, 26,* 295–308.

Gould, J. D., and Lewis, C. (1985). Designing for usability: Key principles and what designers think. *Communications of the ACM, 28*(3), 300–311.

Grady, R. B. (1992). *Practical Software Management and Process Improvement.* Englewood Cliffs, NJ: Prentice-Hall.

Grant, E. E., and Sackman, H. (1967). An exploratory investigation of programmer performance under on-line and off-line conditions. *IEEE Transactions on Human Factors in Electronics, HFE-8*(1), 33–51.

Gray, W. D., John, B. E., and Atwood, M. E. (1992). The precis of project Ernestine, or, an overview of a validation of GOMS. In *Proceedings CHI'92, Human Factors in Computing Systems.* Monterey: ACM.

Greene, S. L., Cannata, P. E., and Gomez, L. M. (1990). No IF's AND's or OR's: A study of database querying. *International Journal of Man Machine Systems, 32,* 303–326.

Greene, S. L., Gomez, L. M., and Devlin, S. J. (1986). A cognitive analysis of database query production. In *Proceedings of the Human Factors Society* (pp. 9–13). Santa Monica, CA: Human Factors Society.

Greenstein, J. S., and Arnaut, L. Y. (1988). Input devices. In M. Helander (eds.), *Handbook of Human Computer Interaction.* Amsterdam: Elsevier Science Publishers (North Holland).

Haynes, R. M. (1990). The ATM at age twenty: A productivity paradox. *National Productivity Review, 9*(3), 273–280.

House, C. H., and Price, R. L. (1991). The return map: Tracking product teams. *Harvard Business Review* (January–February).

Houwing, E. M., Withoff, M., and Arnold, A. G. (1993). Interface evaluation from users' point of view: Three complementary measures. In S. Ashlund Mullet, K., Henderson, A., Hollnagel, E. and White, T. (eds.), *Interchi'93, Conference on Human Factors in Computing Systems,* Adjunct Proceedings, 1993 (pp. 197–198). Amsterdam: ACM.

Hunt, H. A., and Hunt, T. L. (1986). *Clerical Employment and Technological Change.* Kalamazoo MI: W. E. Upjohn Institute.

Instone, K., Teasley, B. M., and Leventhal, L. M. (1993). Empirically-based redesign of a hypertext encyclopedia. In *INTERCHI'93 Conference on Human Factors in Computing Systems* (pp. 500–506). Amsterdam: ACM.

Jeffries, R. J., Miller, J. R., Wharton, C., and Uyeda, K. M. (1991). User interface evaluation in the real world: A comparison of four techniques. In *CHI'91 Human Factors in Computing Systems* (pp. 119–124). New Orleans: ACM.

Johnson, B. M., and Rice, R. E. (1987). *Managing Organizational Innovation: The Evolution from Word Processing to Office Information Systems*. New York: Columbia University Press.

Johnson, O. (ed.) (1989). *Information Please Almanac, Atlas and Yearbook*. Boston: Houghton Mifflin.

Jones, K. (1993). E.D.S. set to restore cash-machine network. *New York Times*, March 26, p. D3.

Jones, W. P., and Dumais, S. T. (1986). The spatial metaphor for user interfaces: Experimental tests of reference by name versus location. *ACM Transactions on Office Information Systems, 4*(1), 42–63.

Jorgenson, D., Gollop, F., and Fraumeni, B. (1987). *Productivity and U.S. Economic Growth*. Cambridge, MA: Harvard University Press.

Juran, J. M. (1989). *Juran on Leadership for Quality*. New York: Free Press.

Karat, C. M. (1990). Cost-benefit analysis of usability engineering techniques. In D. Diaper (ed.), *Human Computer Interaction—Interact 90* (pp. 351–356). Amsterdam: Elsevier.

Keister, R. S., and Gallaway, G. R. (1983). Making software user friendly: An assessment of data entry performance. In *Proceedings of the Human Factors Society* (pp. 1031–1034). Santa Monica, CA: Human Factors Society.

Kendrick, J. W. (1982). Interindustry difference in productivity growth. In W. Fellner (ed.), *A Study in Contemporary Economic Problems, 1982* (pp. 6–25). Washington, DC: American Enterprise Institute.

Kendrick, J. W. (1988). Technology and the services sector. In B. R. Guile and J. B. Quinn (eds.), *Technology in Services*. Washington, DC: National Academy Press.

Kieras, D., and Polson, P. (1985). An approach to the formal analysis of user complexity. *International Journal of Man-Machine Studies, 22*, 365–394.

Kling, R. (1991). Behind the terminal: The critical role of computing infrastructure in effective information system development and use. In W. Cotterman and J. Senn (eds.), *Challenges and Strategies for Research in Systems Development*. London: Wiley.

Kraut, R., Dumais, S., and Koch, S. (1989). Computerization, productivity, and quality of work-life. *Communications of the ACM, 32*(2), 220–238.

Kraut, R. E., and Streeter, L. A. (in press). Coordination in large scale software development. *Communications of the ACM*.

Kuhn, T. S. (1977). *The Essential Tension: Selected Studies in Scientific Tradition and Change.* Chicago, Il: University of Chicago Press.

Kulik, J. A., Kulik, C. C., and Cohen, P. A. (1980). Effectiveness of computer-based college teaching: A meta-analysis of findings. *Review of Educational Research, 50*(4), 525–544.

Kulik, C. C., Kulik, J. A., and Shwalb, B. J. (1986). The effectiveness of computer-based adult education: A meta-analysis. *Journal of Educational Computing Research, 2*(2).

Landauer, T. K. (1988a). Education in a world of omnipotent and omniscient technology. In R. S. Nickerson and P. P. Zodhiates (eds.), *Technology in Education: Looking toward 2020.* Hillsdale, NJ: Erlbaum.

Landauer, T. K. (1988b). Research methods in human-computer interaction. In M. Helander (ed.), *Handbook of Human Computer Interaction* (pp. 905–927). Amsterdam: North-Holland.

Landauer, T. K. (1992). Let's get real, a position paper on the role of cognitive psychology in the design of humanly useful and usable systems. In J. C. Carroll (ed.), *Designing Interaction* (pp. 60–73). Cambridge: Cambridge University Press.

Landauer, T. K., and Bjork, R. A. (1978). Optimal rehearsal patterns and name learning. In M. M. Gruneberg, Morris, P. E., and Sykes, R. N. (eds.), *Practical Aspects of Memory.* London: Academic Press.

Landauer, T. K., Egan, D. E., Remde, J. R., Lesk, M. E., Lochbaum, C. C., and Ketchum, D. (1993). Enhancing the usability of text through computer delivery and formative evaluation: The SuperBook project. In C. McKnight, A. Dillon, and J. Richardson (eds.), *Hypertext: A Psychological Perspective.* New York: Ellis Horwood.

Landauer, T. K., Galotti, K. M., and Hartwell, S. (1983). Natural command names and initial learning: A study of text editing terms. *Communications of the ACM, 26,* 495–503.

Landauer, T. K., and Nachbar, D. W. (1985). Selection from alphabetic and numeric menu trees using a touch screen: Breadth, depth and width. In *CHI'85 Human Factors in Computing Systems.* Gaithersburg, MD: Association for Computing Machinery.

Lee, E., MacGregor, J., Lam, N., and G., C. (1986). Keyword-menu retrieval: An effective alternative to menu indexes. *Ergonomics, 29,* 115–130.

Leontief, W., and Duchin, F. (1986). *The Future Impact of Automation on Workers.* New York: Oxford University Press.

Loveman, G. W. (1986). The productivity of information technology capital: An economic analysis. *MIT,* January 21.

Loveman, G. W. (1990). *An Assessment of the Productivity Impact of Information Technologies.* Cambridge, MA: MIT, Sloan School of Management.

Lucus, H. C. (1978). Unsuccessful implementation; the case of a computer-based order entry system. *Decision Sciences, 9,* 68–79.

McKinsey Global Institute (1992). *Service Sector Productivity*. NY: McKinsey and Co.

McKnight, C., Dillon, A., and Richardson, J. (1991). A comparison of linear and hypertext formats in information retrieval. In R. Macaleese and C. Green (eds.), *HYPERTEXT: State of the Art*. Oxford: Intellect.

McLeod, P. L. (1992). An assessment of the experimental literature on electronic support group work: Results of a meta-analysis. *Human Computer Interaction*, 7(3), 257.

Maddison, A. (1991). *Dynamic Forces in Capitalist Development*. New York: Oxford University Press.

Majchrzak, A. (1992). Management of technological and organizational change. In G. Salvendy (ed.), *Handbook of Industrial Engineering*. New York: Wiley.

Mandel, M. J., and Farrell, C. (1993). Jobs, jobs, jobs—eventually. *Business Week*, June 14, pp. 72–73.

Mantei, M. M., and Teory, T. J. (1988). Cost/benefit analysis for incorporating human factors in the software lifecycle. *Communications of the ACM*, 31(4), 428–439.

Marshall, C., Nelson, C., and Gardiner, M. M. (1987). Design guidelines. In M. M. Gardiner and B. Christie (eds.), *Applying Cognitive Psychology to User Interface Design* Chichester, UK: Wiley.

Martin, J., and McClure, C. (1983). *Software Maintenance: The Problem and Its Solution*. Englewood Cliffs, NJ: Prentice-Hall.

Mayhew, D. J. (1992). *Principles and Guidelines in Software User Interface Design*. Englewood Cliffs, NJ: Prentice-Hall.

Meyer, N. D., and Boone, M. E. (1987). *The Information Edge*. New York: McGraw-Hill.

Milsted, U., Varnild, A., and Jorgensen, A. H. (1989). Hvordan sikres kvaliteten af brugergraesnsefladen i systemudviklingen (Assuring the quality of user interfaces in system development.). In *NorDATA'89 Joint Scandinavian Computer Conference* (pp. 485–490). Copenhagen, as cited in Nielsen, J., and Molich, R. (1990). Heuristic Evaluation of User Interfaces. *Proceedings ACM CHI'90* (pp. 249–256). Seattle, WA: ACM.

Moad, J. (1991). Budget growth skids to 3.4%. *Datamation* (April), 44–47.

Mokyr, J. (1990). *The Lever of Riches: Technological Creativity and Economic Progress*. New York: Oxford University Press.

Morgan, C., Williams, G., and Lemmons, P. (1983). An interview with Wayne Rosing, Bruce Daniels and Larry Tesler. *Byte*, 8(2), 90–114.

Muller, M. J. (1992). Retrospective on a year of participatory design using the PICTIVE technique. In *CHI'92 Human Factors in Computing Systems* (pp. 455–462). Monterey, CA: ACM.

Muller, M. J., Dayton, T., and Root, R. (1993). Comparing studies that compare usability assessment methods: An unsuccessful search for stable criteria. In *IN-TERCHI'93 Human Factors in Computing Systems: Adjunct Proceedings*. Amsterdam: ACM.

Murphy, C. E. (1985). A comparison of manual and on-line searching of government document indexes. *Government Information Quarterly, 2*(2), 169–181.

Myers, B. A., and Rosson, M. B. (1992). Survey on user interface programming. In *CHI'92 Human Factors in Computing Systems* (pp. 195–202). Monterey, CA: ACM.

Nasar, S. (1993). 90's may be a decade of growth. *New York Times,* February 17, pp. D1, D18.

National Research Council (1994a). *Information Technology in the Service Society: a Twenty-First Century Lever.* Washington, DC: National Academy Press.

National Research Council (1994b). *Organizational Linkages: Understanding the Productivity Paradox.* Washington, DC: National Academy Press.

Nielsen, J. (1989). Usability engineering at a discount. In G. Salvendy and M. J. Smith (eds.), *Designing and Using Human-Computer Interfaces and Knowledge Based Systems* (pp. 394–401). Amsterdam: Elsevier Science Publishers.

Nielsen, J. (1992). *Applying Heuristic Evaluation to a Highly Domain-Specific User Interface.* Technical memorandum. Morristown, NJ: Bellcore.

Nielsen, J. (1993a). Iterative user interface design. *IEEE Computer,* in press

Nielsen, J. (1993b). *Usability Engineering.* Boston: Academic Press.

Nielsen, J., and Landauer, T. K. (1993). A mathematical model of the finding of usability problems. In *INTERCHI'93, ACM Conference on Human Factors in Computer Systems* (pp. 206–213). Amsterdam: ACM.

Nielsen, J., and Levy, J. (in press). Subjective user preferences versus objective interface performance measures. *Communications of the ACM.*

Nielsen, J., and Molich, R. (1990). Heuristic evaluation of user interfaces. In *Proceedings ACM CHI'90 Conference on Human Factors and Computing Systems* (pp. 249–256). Seattle WA: ACM.

Nielsen, J., and Phillips, V. E. (1993). Estimating the relative usability of two interfaces: Heuristic, formal and empirical methods compared. In *INTERCHI'93 Human Factors in Computer Systems.* Amsterdam: ACM.

Nilsen, E., Jong, H., Olson, J. S., and Polson, P. G. (1992). Method engineering: From data to model to practice. In *CHI'92* (pp. 313–320). Monterey, CA: ACM.

O'Neal, J. (1976). We increased typing productivity 340%. *Office* (February), 95–100.

Orlansky, J., and String, J. (1979). *Cost-effectiveness of computer based instruction in military training.* Washington, D.C. Institute for Defense Analysis.

Osterman, P. (1986). The impact of computers on the employment of clerks and managers. *Industrial Labor Review, 39* (January 1986), 175–186.

Paap, K. R., and Roske-Hofstrand, R. J. (1988). Design of menus. In M. Helander (ed.), *Handbook of Human Computer Interaction* (pp. 205–235). Amsterdam: Elsevier.

Perlman, G. (1988). Teaching user-interface development to software engineers. In Proceedings of the *Human Factors Society*. (pp. 391–394). Santa Monica, CA: Human Factors Society.

Petroski, H. (1982). *To Engineer Is Human*. New York: Random House.

Phillips, M. D., Bashinski, H. S., Ammerman, H. L., and Figg, C. M. J. (1988). A task analytic approach to dialogue design. In M. Helander (ed.), *Handbook of Human Computer Interaction*. Amsterdam: North-Holland.

Pinsky, D. (1991). $9 billion Minitel. *France Telecom dans L'actualité* (September).

Pressman, R. S. (1992). *Software Engineering: A Practitioner's Approach*. New York: McGraw-Hill.

Roach, S. S. (1985). *The New Technology Cycle*. New York, Morgan Stanley Economic Perspectives.

Roach, S. S. (1987). America's technology dilemma: A profile of the information economy. Memorandum. Morgan Stanley.

Roach, S. S. (1988). Technology and the services sector: The hidden competitive challenge. In *Technological Forecasting and Social Change*. New York: Elsevier.

Roach, S. S. (1991). Services under siege—The restructuring imperative. *Harvard Business Review*, 82–91.

Roach, S. S. (1992a). *Assessing the Impacts of a Productivity-Led Recovery*. New York, Morgan Stanley.

Roach, S. S. (1992b). *Inside the U.S. Economy*. New York, Morgan Stanley.

Roach, S. S. (1992c). *Technology Imperatives*. New York, Morgan Stanley.

Roberts, T. L., and Engelbeck, G. (1989). The effects of device technology on the usability of advanced telephone functions. *CHI'89 Proceedings*, 331–337. New York: ACM.

Roberts, T. L., and Moran, T. P. (1983). The evaluation of text editors: Methodology and empirical results. *Communications of the Association for Computing Machinery, 26,* 265–283.

Roose, T. (1985). Online or print: Comparing costs. *Library Journal*, September 15.

Solow, R. M. (1959). Investment and technical progress. In K. J. Arrow, S. Karlin, and P. Suppes, (eds.), *Mathematical Methods in the Social Sciences* Stanford, CA: Stanford University Press.

Srinivasan, A. (1992). Are there cost savings from bank mergers? *Federal Reserve Bank of Atlanta Economic Review, 77* (March), 17–28.

Strassmann, P. A. (1985). *Information Payoff: The Transformation of Work in the Electronic Age*. New Canaan, CT: The Information Economics Press.

Strassmann, P. A., Berger, P., Swanson, E. B., Kriebel, C. H., and Kauffman, R. J. (1988). *Measuring Business Value of Information Technology*. Washington, D.C.: ICIT Press.

Strassmann, P. (1990). *The Business Value of Computers: An Executive's Guide*. New Canaan, CT: Information Economics Press.

Streeter, L. A., Acroff, J. M., and Taylor, G. A. (1983). On abbreviating command names. *Bell System Technical Journal, 62*, 1807–1826.

Streeter, L. A., Kraut, R. E., Lucas, H. C., and Caby, L. (in press). The impact of national data networks on firm performance and market structure. *Communications of the Association for Computing Machinery*. New York: ACM.

Taylor, D. W., Berry, P. C., and Block, C. H. (1958). Does group participation when using brainstorming facilitate or inhibit creative thinking? *Administrative Science Quarterly, 3*, 23–47.

Temple, Barker, & Sloan (1990). *The Benefits of the Graphical User Interface*. Temple, Barker & Sloan. Unpublished report.

Tesler, L. (1983). Enlisting user help in software design. *SIGCHI Bulletin, 14*(1), 5–9.

Thor, C. G. (1990). Getting the most from productivity statistics. *National Productivity Review, 9*(4), 457–466.

Thor, C. G. (1994). *Perspectives '94*. American Productivity and Quality Center. Washington, D.C.

Thurow, L. C. (1981). Solving the productivity problem. In L. C. Thurow A. Packer, and H. J. Samuels (eds.), *Strengthening the Economy: Studies in Productivity* (pp. 9–19). Washington, DC: Center for Democratic Policy.

Tognazzini, B. (1992). *Tog on Interface*. Reading, MA: Addison-Wesley.

Trollip, S. R., and Sales, G. (1986). Readability of computer-generated fill-justified text. *Human Factors* (April), 159–163.

Tullis, T. S. (1981). An evaluation of alphanumeric, graphic and color information displays. *Human Factors, 25*, 541–550.

United States Department of Labor (1983). *Productivity Measures for Selected Industries, 1954–82*. Washington, DC: Government Printing Office.

Vacc, N. N. (1991). Word processing and handwriting: Writing samples produced by at-risk freshmen. *Journal of Educational Technology Systems, 19*(3), 233–250.

Virzi, R. A. (1992). Refining the test phase of usability evaluation. *Human Factors, 34*(4), 457–468.

Wasserman, A. S. (1991). Debate: Can research reinvent the corporation? *Harvard Business Review* (March–April), 175.

Weizenbaum, J. (1976). *Computer Power and Human Reason*. San Francisco: Freeman Publishing Co.

Whiteside, J., Bennett, J., and Holtzblatt, K. (1988). Usability engineering: Our experience and evolution. In M. Helander (ed.), *Handbook of Human Computer Interaction*. New York: North-Holland.

Whiteside, J., Jones, S., Levy, P. S., and Wixon, D. (1985). User performance with command, menu and iconic interfaces. In *CHI'85, Human Factors in Computing Systems* (pp. 185–191). New York: ACM.

Wixon, D., & Jones, S. W. (1991). Usability for fun and profit: A case study of the design of DEC RALLY Version 2. Internal report. Digital Equipment Corporation.

Wright, J. W. (ed.). (1992). *The Universal Almanac*. Kansas City: Andrews and McMeel.

Ziegler, J. E., and Fahnrich, K. P. (1988). Direct manipulation. In M. Helander (ed.), *Handbook of Human Computer Interaction*. New York: North-Holland.

Zuboff, S. (1988). *In the Age of the Smart Machine*. New York: Basic Books.

Zuboff, S. (1991). Debate: Can research reinvent the corporation? *Harvard Business Review* (March–April), 164–165.

Index